UNITED ARTISTS

T0308911

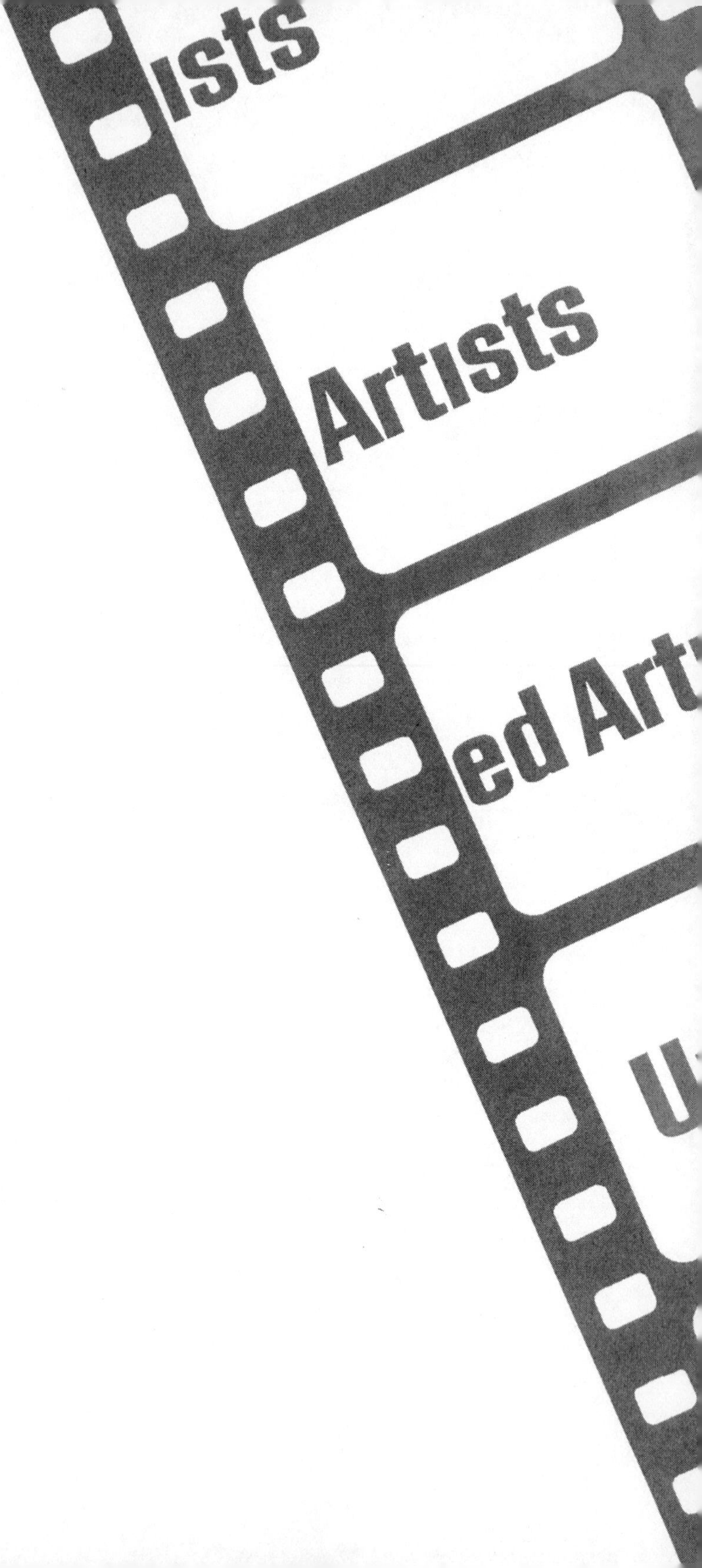
ists
Artists
ed Art
U

United Artists

The Company That Changed the Film Industry

Volume 2, 1951–1978

T I N O   B A L I O

The University of Wisconsin Press

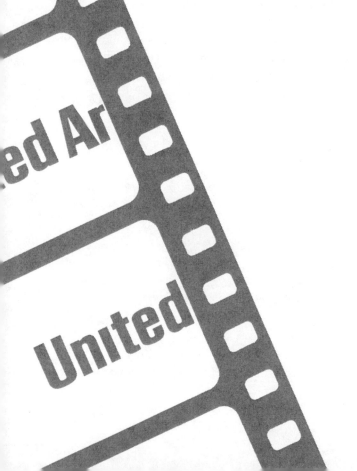

The University of Wisconsin Press
1930 Monroe Street, 3rd Floor
Madison, Wisconsin 53711-2059

www.wisc.edu/wisconsinpress/

3 Henrietta Street
London WC2E 8LU, England

5   4   3   2   1

Printed in the United States of America

Library of Congress Cataloging-in-Publication Data

Balio, Tino.
United Artists : the company built by the stars / Tino Balio.
   p. cm.
   Includes bibliographical references and index.
   ISBN 978-0-299-23004-3 (pbk. : alk. paper)
   ISBN 978-0-299-23003-6 (e-book)
1. United Artists Corporation—History. I Title.
PN1999.U5B3   2009
384'.80979494—dc22   2008046313

ISBN 978-0-299-23014-2 (volume 2)

C O N T E N T S

v

Contents

ILLUSTRATIONS

Illustrations

ACKNOWLEDGMENTS

I wish to thank Herbert Schottenfeld and Robert Schwartz, who in special ways have made this book possible.

I interviewed the following United Artists executives in addition to Schottenfeld: Arthur Krim, William Bernstein, Eric Pleskow, Leon Kamern, Joseph Adelman, Max E. Youngstein, Pedro Teitelbaum, Mike Medavoy, Alfred Sorg, John Dartigue, Vincent Giovinco, and Sidney Schemel. I also interviewed producers Walter Mirisch and Norman Jewison and his associates, Patrick Palmer and Larry DeWaay.

Graduate students in the Department of Communication Arts whose insights helped me interpret facets of UA's history are Kevin Hagopian, Kristine Karnick, Darrell Davis, Laura Thielen, and Ellen Tyler.

I am particularly grateful to Kevin Hagopian, to my colleague Professor David Bordwell, and to Professor David A. Cook and Professor Jack C. Ellis for reading the manuscript and providing many helpful suggestions.

In the production of the manuscript, I am grateful to Ronee Messina, Kriss Viney, Linda Henzl, Mary Zellmer, and especially Evelyn Miller.

For kind permission granted to reproduce photographs, I thank the Wisconsin Center for Film and Theater Research, the Museum of Modern Art/Film Stills Archive, Arthur B. Krim, and Walter Mirisch.

And I thank the University of Wisconsin–Madison Graduate School, which awarded me summer salary support in 1980 and 1983.

UNITED ARTISTS

INTRODUCTION

When Arthur Krim and Robert Benjamin took over United Artists in 1951, the company was hemorrhaging money, and receivers were almost at the door. United Artists had declined steadily after World War II and chances of a revival were slim. Mary Pickford and Charlie Chaplin, the two remaining owners of the company, hoped a buyer would save the day. Bids for millions came in, but it is doubtful they were made in good faith. Krim and Benjamin bid not a cent. Instead, they offered to take operating control of United Artists for a period of ten years on the condition that if the company turned a profit in any one of the first three years, they would be able to acquire half ownership of the company at a nominal cost. It took a lot of convincing by these two young lawyers to make Pickford and Chaplin realize their company was worthless as it stood. On February 7, 1951, they faced reality and signed the papers.

The new management revived a moribund UA by adopting a policy that had been anathema to the majors—the financing of independent productions. Within a year UA turned a profit, and the Krim-Benjamin team acquired half the company. By 1955 the team bought out Chaplin and Pickford's interests and owned the company outright. In 1957 they took United Artists public, and its stock was traded on the New York Stock Exchange. By 1966 United Artists had grown to become the largest producer-distributor of motion pictures in the world and ushered the industry into a new era.

This history analyzes the structure and operations of the company. My approach was suggested by Michael E. Porter's *Competitive Strategy: Techniques for Analyzing Industries and Competitors*.[1] Porter, a professor at the Harvard Business School, explains the behavior of American business as it shifted from sales growth to dominance over rivals. A blend of industrial organization and business administration, Porter's analytical techniques are well suited to making sense out of a period of film industry history that underwent radical transformation as a result of changing audience tastes, federal antitrust action, competition from television, and conglomerate takeovers. The twenty-seven-year management of Krim and Benjamin spanned all these changes. Moreover, the management survived three forms of corporate ownership—private company, publicly held corporation, and conglomerate subsidiary. Thus, UA makes an ideal example of a modern, that is, post-1950, motion picture company.

The story begins with Krim and Benjamin's apprenticeship at

Eagle-Lion Films, a company founded in 1946 as an alliance between the American railroad tycoon Robert R. Young and the British film magnate J. Arthur Rank. Young started out in the film business in 1943 by purchasing Producers Releasing Corporation (PRC), a Poverty Row studio that specialized mainly in cheap Westerns. But he had higher aspirations, and his alliance with Rank, who wanted access to U.S. theaters, offered a way to major status. The alliance called for Eagle-Lion to distribute Rank's pictures in the United States and for Rank to distribute Eagle-Lion's in Great Britain and other overseas markets. Organizing the company fell to Robert Benjamin, who had been working for Young as legal counsel handling his film business affairs. It was Benjamin who recommended his partner, Arthur Krim, to head the new company as president. Both Krim and Benjamin were partners in Louis Nizer's law firm in New York, which specialized in the film industry.

Chapter 1 vividly illustrates the barriers confronting newcomers to the business. Michael Porter identified these as emanating from economies of scale and product differentiation. Eagle-Lion was forced to produce a series of big-budget pictures that could compete with the best of Hollywood if it wanted to break into the majors. Young spent more than $12 million of his own money to upgrade PRC's studios and to produce the first season's roster. To run the studio, Krim hired Bryan Foy, who had formerly headed the "B" film units at Warner Bros. and Fox. Eagle-Lion's first season's roster found few takers among exhibitors. As a newcomer with roots in Poverty Row, Eagle-Lion could not borrow stars from the majors and had to make do with aging leading men on their way down and a few unknown young people working their way up. Moreover, Eagle-Lion's first films arrived on the market on the eve of an industry-wide recession that would last a decade.

Robert Young turned off the financial spigot after the first year. Beginning with the second season, Eagle-Lion shifted to a hybrid form of independent production by supplying a patchwork of secondary loans, studio credits, and completion money to attract producers. Krim's penny-pinching resulted in a form of product differentiation— a string of film noir pictures that put Eagle-Lion, albeit temporarily, in the limelight. Produced on low budgets, these pictures substituted action, color, natural locations, and authenticity for the usual combination of stars and pre-sold stories. The films included Anthony Mann's *T-Men* (1947), a semidocumentary based on Treasury Department cases; Crane Wilbur's *Canon City* (1948), a reenactment of a jailbreak at the state penitentiary in Canon City, Colorado, which was shot on site; and Alfred Werker's *He Walked by Night* (1948), a thriller depicting a brilliant psychotic killer. All made money and all received favorable press, but because Eagle-Lion did not supply the principal financing, it did not participate in the profits.

The postwar recession proved fatal to Eagle-Lion. With audiences becoming more selective, even class-A features found the going rough. The films J. Arthur Rank sent the company did nothing to improve Eagle-Lion's plight. With only one or two exceptions, Rank's pictures failed miserably at the box office. Krim resigned from the company in 1949, and Benjamin followed soon after. Robert Young lost a fortune on Eagle-Lion, but the experience of running the company enabled Krim and Benjamin to hone their analytical skills to discover opportunity in postwar conditions.

Chapter 2 describes how Krim and Benjamin captured the imagination and trust of talent and the banks. The conclusion of the *Paramount* antitrust case of 1948 is credited with being largely responsible for the rise of independent production after the war. By abolishing block booking and other unfair trade practices, the Supreme Court gave independents greater access to theaters, but if independents wanted access to the best houses, they had to have pictures that compared favorably with anything on the market. The antitrust action was no panacea for independents, but it *was* one of many factors in the transition to fewer and better quality pictures in the postwar period.

During the postwar recession studios pared producers, directors, and stars from the payrolls and disposed of their back lots. To attract talent to United Artists, Krim and Benjamin took the offensive. According to Michael Porter, such a strategy "is designed to do more than merely cope with the forces themselves [within an industry]; it is meant to alter their causes."[2] As the smallest company of the eight majors, UA's objective was to increase market share. It did so by differentiating itself from the its competitors; in return for distribution rights, UA offered independent producers complete production financing, creative control over their work, and a share of the profits. But these incentives in themselves did not account for the company's initial success. To gain the confidence of the filmmaking community, UA played the role of a maverick by starting trends, by challenging HUAC and the Production Code, and by investing in some offbeat pictures. The strategy worked, and by 1955 UA had signed many of Hollywood's top stars.

In deciding to finance UA's pictures, banks reversed a long-standing policy regarding independent production. Because motion picture attendance had markedly improved during the war, banks were willing to accommodate independent producers but only to the extent of providing partial financing—the so-called first money—and only if projects showed real box-office potential. With UA, the banks were willing to put up total financing for a film using only UA's guarantee of repayment. The box-office evaluation was left to the company.

Chapter 3 discusses UA's business structure and relationship with its producers. Unlike the old UA, which was designed to operate just above breakeven and funnel most of the distribution revenue back to the producer-owners, the new company was designed to generate two sources of profit—from distribution and from production. Distribution profits benefited the company and its stockholders; production profits benefited the company and the producer. In going public, United Artists demonstrated to potential investors that it could earn profits from distribution even though the films it financed lost money. The selling point was the distribution fee.

In handling a picture, UA charged the producer a schedule of fees ranging from 30 percent to 45 percent of the gross rentals, depending on the market. The fees were used to meet the company's fixed expenses of operating a worldwide sales network and to offset UA's risk as a financier. The distribution fee had the potential of generating profits because the marketing costs of a picture remained relatively fixed regardless of its box-office performance. A hit, therefore, could generate revenues well in excess of its distribution expenses. Distribution profits rewarded the company, to be sure, but they were also used to offset losses on production loans and to contribute to a pool for the financing of new projects.

For those pictures that earned back their investments, UA also enjoyed production profits. UA was generous with its production profits and typically divided them fifty-fifty with a producer. But UA as financier took the greater risk and had first call on the revenues. Of the hundred-plus pictures UA financed before going public, practically all failed to earn back their production costs in their initial runs. As a group, they generated only around $25,000 in profits. If UA's producers took it on the chin, the company went unscathed. Revenues increased from $20 million a year to more than $60 million during this period; correspondingly, UA's earnings jumped from $350,000 to more than $6 million.

For this scheme to work, UA had to do two things: (1) release a sizeable number of films each year just to break even, and (2) control production costs. Controlling production costs did not mean keeping costs low; it meant avoiding undue risks. Cost per se, then, was not the issue; it was cost against the potential return. That was the key. And that, in itself, was a management judgment. UA retained ultimate discretionary power before green-lighting a project by exercising approval rights over the basic ingredients of a production—story, cast, director, and budget—and by establishing tight fiscal controls. Approval rights permitted UA to judge the commercial potential of each creative component in a package; fiscal controls ensured that the producer lived up to his part of the bargain once shooting began.

To achieve volume distribution, UA contracted with creative producers, packagers, talent, and combinations thereof. Filling out its roster, UA adopted the "tonnage thesis." As defined by film industry analyst David Londoner, the thesis states that "distribution overhead is essentially fixed and that incremental product put through above break-even carries a disproportionately high profit contribution."[3]

Chapter 4 presents case studies of Burt Lancaster, Stanley Kramer, and Kirk Douglas as independent producers. Such producers were given multiple-picture contracts and special development incentives. The case studies describe how these units were set up and how they rationalized their production agendas. In addition to producing star vehicles for themselves, Lancaster and Douglas sponsored offbeat projects with social themes directed and written by newcomers. The most successful example was Hecht-Lancaster's production of Delbert Mann's *Marty*, the winner of UA's first Oscar for Best Picture in 1955 and other prestigious awards. Based on a teleplay by Paddy Chayefsky, *Marty* also started a "small film" vogue.

Chapter 5 presents a case study of the Mirisch Corporation, by far the most successful packager connected with United Artists. The brainchild of Harold Mirisch and his two brothers, Walter and Marvin, the Mirisch company operated as an "umbrella" organization that provided business and legal services to independents. The objective was to allow filmmakers to concentrate on production while the company managed the logistics of production, arranged the financing and distribution, and supervised the marketing.

The Mirisches decided from the start to concentrate on directors, on the assumption that directors would attract the stars. To produce its top-of-the-line product, Mirisch gave multiple-picture contracts to such ranking directors as Billy Wilder, John Sturges, Robert Wise, and George Roy Hill. These directors originated projects, worked with screenwriters to develop scripts, and regularly received the right of final cut. Mirisch gave promising younger directors like Blake Edwards and Norman Jewison freedom to develop, and when they proved themselves, they too were given long-term contracts with all the perquisites.

The Mirisches produced sixty-seven pictures for UA over fifteen years. They came in every size and style, and consistently took Hollywood's top honors. Three pictures won Oscars for Best Picture: Billy Wilder's *The Apartment* (1960), Robert Wise and Jerome Robbins's *West Side Story* (1961), and Norman Jewison's *In the Heat of the Night* (1967). Among the other acclaimed pictures were Wilder's *Some Like It Hot* (1959), John Sturges's *The Magnificent Seven* (1960), Blake Edwards's *Pink Panther* (1964), and Norman Jewison's *The Russians Are Coming, the Russians Are Coming* (1966).

Chapter 6 describes UA's marketing techniques. To differentiate itself from television fare, Hollywood adopted the big-budget philosophy of "make them big; show them big; and sell them big." UA's practices, which were representative of the industry, had two goals: to create a "must see" attitude and to upscale the value of its pictures in the minds of the public to justify higher ticket prices.

Blockbusters required a special form of release to recoup their heavy investments. Using a two-tier playoff, companies typically released a new film first in a few select theaters in metropolitan markets for extended runs and at high admission prices, and subsequently to large numbers of theaters in surrounding areas to capture the leavings. Companies also decided to release their big pictures during the peak seasons of Christmas, Easter, and summer, instead of at regular intervals throughout the year. When Hollywood focused on the youth audience during the 1970s, this two-tier playoff gave way to saturation booking, which is to say, a simultaneous release in many theaters in each market. Saturation booking, of course, was ideally designed to take full advantage of television advertising to reach large numbers of people over wide areas.

To further offset the risks of producing big-budget pictures, Hollywood found creative ways to generate additional revenue from book tie-ins, merchandising, and market research. Nonetheless, blockbusters remained as speculative as their box-office potential. The 1960s is replete with big expensive failures.

Chapter 7, 8, and 9 place UA's operations in a global context. During the 1950s, American companies had to rely on international distribution to compensate for the declining domestic market. In addition to marketing American films abroad, international distribution involved marketing foreign films in the United States and investing in production overseas. The two went hand in hand and had the goal of discovering and absorbing talented filmmakers wherever they could be found. The strategy manifested itself by bidding aggressively on imports, hiring foreign stars to give pictures some international appeal, and absorbing directors with production deals.

United Artists embraced all three strategies. From the start, UA made its pictures where they had to be made. Since UA had no studio to support, it had complete freedom and mobility to deal with independent producers all over the globe. An independent producer, in turn, could arrange to produce his or her films wherever to suit the needs of the story or the economics of the venture.

In chapter 7 we see how the art film market flourished after the war and catered to a small but influential audience that had become disaffected by regular Hollywood fare. The market was originally run by numerous independent distributors, who introduced successive waves of imports from national cinemas to the United States, beginning with Roberto Rossellini's *Open City* in 1946. By the 1960s, the art film market had been taken over by the Hollywood majors. Foreign films, especially those that depicted sex in ways forbidden by the Production Code, were attracting customers—and the majors wanted a part of the business. Columbia Pictures was the first major to enter the market in 1956 by acquiring Kingsley International, an independent, to handle its foreign films. United Artists followed suit in 1958 by acquiring Lopert Pictures, another independent. To acquire films, the majors eventually absorbed nearly the entire pantheon of European auteurs who showed commercial potential with deals that offered total production financing, directorial freedom, and entree into the lucrative U.S. market.

Chapter 7 also describes UA's investment in British pop culture, particularly the Swinging London scene, to reach the youth audience. The investment yielded Tony Richardson's *Tom Jones*, which won an Oscar for Best Picture in 1963, Richard Lester's *A Hard Day's Night* (1964) starring the Beatles, the James Bond series, and John Schlesinger's *Midnight Cowboy*, which won an Oscar for Best Picture in 1969.

Chapter 8 is a case study of the James Bond series and how these films were tailored for the international market, how UA's company's marketing sustained the series, and the way the company related to the producers.

Chapter 9 describes UA's alliances with French and Italian filmmakers, among them Louis Malle, François Truffaut, Federico Fellini, and Bernardo Bertolucci. This investment yielded the biggest foreign-film hit of the period, Bernardo Bertolucci's *Last Tango in Paris* in 1973.

United Artists' successful track record made it an object of a takeover. The American film industry entered the age of conglomerates during the 1960s as motion picture companies were acquired by huge multifaceted corporations. Gulf & Western's takeover of Paramount in 1966 started the trend, followed by Transamerica Corporation's buyout of United Artists in 1967. Chapter 10 describes Transamerica's acquisition strategy, the film industry recession of 1969, and the breakdown of the relationship between UA and its parent when Transamerica dropped its "hands off" policy and installed "new management techniques" to rein in the company.

United Artists turned itself around by 1974 and reestablished ties to the creative community. United then set an industry record by winning the Best Picture Oscar three years in a row, beginning with the Saul Zaentz–Michael Douglas production of *One Flew Over the Cuckoo's Nest* (Miloš Forman) in 1975, followed by the Robert Chartoff–Irwin Winkler production of *Rocky* (John G. Alvidsen) in 1976, and the Woody Allen production of *Annie Hall* in 1977. *Cuckoo's Nest*, moreover, achieved what no other picture in forty years had done—an Academy Awards sweep (*It Happened One Night* was the first, in 1934). Nominated for nine Oscars, *Cuckoo's Nest* won the top five—Best Picture, Best Director, Best Actor, Best Actress, and Best Screenplay Adaptation.

Despite this record, relations between UA and its parent continued to deteriorate. The Transamerica–United Artists merger was never a good fit for either company. Headquartered in San Francisco, Transamerica defined itself as a full-line financial service organization. Acquiring UA was part of its strategy to go into "leisuretime activities." But Transamerica had little understanding of the film business, and UA bristled at Transamerica's corporate culture. When UA experienced losses as a result of an industry-wide recession, TA did nothing to remedy the situation except express shock. Krim stemmed the losses and put the company solidly in the black by the mid-1970s, but Transamerica's stock was not sensitive to a single subsidiary's performance. In fact, Transamerica's stock had declined during this period, and Krim and his partners watched as their gains from the exchange of stock at the time of the merger were wiped out. In January 1978, UA chairman Arthur Krim, Arthur Pleskow, and other top UA executives resigned from the company and formed Orion Pictures, with aspirations of becoming another major studio.

After the walkout, UA's new management had the misfortune of falling into a blockbuster trap: A picture of enormous box-office potential immediately goes over budget. If the company pulls the plug, the entire investment is lost, and the company suffers the wrath of the creative community for not permitting the filmmaker to realize his masterpiece, so more money is pumped in with the hope that no more catastrophes occur. Such was the case of Michael Cimino's *Heaven's Gate*, the subject of chapter 11. Proposed at $7.5 million, budgeted at $11.5 million, and written off finally at $44 million, the fiasco led to at least temporary unemployment for almost everyone associated with the picture and ultimately to the demise of UA itself.

After suffering the humiliation of being associated with one of the most public motion picture failures of all time, Transamerica sold United Artists to Kirk Kerkorian, the Las Vegas developer and new owner of MGM, in 1981. In acquiring UA, Kerkorian merged it with MGM to create MGM/UA Entertainment. United Artists, the company founded by Mary Pickford, Charlie Chaplin, Douglas Fairbanks, and D. W. Griffith, disappeared as a separate corporate entity. Afterwards, Kerkorian treated the company more like an investment property than a film company by selling and buying all or parts of MGM/UA at least four times. Today, MGM/UA goes by the name Metro-Goldwyn-Mayer, Inc., and is a privately held company owned by a consortium of investors led by Sony Corporation of America and Comcast. Its largest asset is the United Artists Film Library. From time to time, MGM/UA attempted to resurrect United Artists in the hope of restoring its former glory. The United Artists brand name still conjures visions of quality films and creative freedom. The most recent attempt occurred in 2006, when MGM formed a partnership with Tom Cruise and Paula Wagner, his producer, to run the company. The company got off to a shaky start, and its future remains uncertain.

Looking back, Transamerica's multimarket structure, a product of the 1960s, was obsolete by the time it shed UA. Replacing it was the product-extension type of conglomerate. In the film industry, this structure was first typified by Warner Communications, which downsized its operations to focus exclusively on entertainment: (1) the production and distribution of film and television programming, (2) recorded music, and (3) publishing. The impetus for the restructuring was the growth of new distribution technologies such as cable, pay-TV, and home video. To survive as a viable motion picture company, UA would have had to restructure as well, but under the yoke of Transamerica, it is doubtful this could have happened. Nonetheless, UA's method of operation under the Krim management helped rescue the American film industry from the postwar doldrums and the decline of the studio system. It was an ideal setup that lasted for nearly three decades and attracted some of the best talent in the business. UA's brand of independent production moved production closer to the concept of one man–one film by granting filmmakers a fair amount of autonomy and creative freedom over the making of their pictures and rewarding them with a share of the profits. In the process, the policy gave UA a competitive edge over companies far richer and far healthier.

Forming Orion Pictures in 1978, Arthur Krim and his partners attempted to duplicate their success at United Artists by continuing the same policies to attract talent. Orion distributed through Warner Bros until 1982, when it acquired Filmways, a medium-sized distribution company, with backing from Warburg Pincus (a Wall Street investment firm) and HBO. Orion's goal was to produce around fifteen midsized pictures a year. To minimize risks, the company made presale arrangements for pay-TV, foreign home video, and foreign theatrical distribution. Four Orion pictures won Oscars for Best Picture—Miloš Forman's *Amadeus* (1985), Oliver Stone's *Platoon* (1987), Kevin Costner's *Dances with Wolves* (1991), and Jonathan Demme's *Silence of the Lambs* (1992)—and other awards. In 1987 Orion captured the largest share of the domestic theatrical market. Despite this record, Orion was always undercapitalized. Its hits were never big enough to offset the losses on its failures. The 1980s saw the majors trimming their sails to concentrate on distribution in all the emerging markets. Upping the ante, the majors also invested heavily in blockbusters, which dominated the theatrical and ancillary markets. Small films, or even midsized films like Orion's, had little chance of making it in the new environment. Orion Pictures declared bankruptcy in 1991; soon after, Krim and his partners left the company. In 1997, Kirk Kerkorian purchased the Orion film library as part of a buyout deal and included it with the United Artists films belonging to MGM/UA.

My research is based on corporate records of UA and on interviews with Arthur Krim and other company executives. Consisting of correspondence, letters of agreement, contracts, annual reports, legal files, and other materials, these corporate records constitute an addition to the original United Artists Collection that was donated to the Wisconsin Center for Film and Theater Research in 1969. The original collection covered the years 1919 to 1951 and formed the basis of my previous study of the company, *United Artists: The Company Built by the Stars*. For various reasons, including confidentiality, UA was not prepared to donate the vast amount of its post-1951 corporate records to the Center. However, for the purposes of this book, UA generously permitted me to make copies of whatever I needed. All the materials I selected are included in the addition and are open to researchers. An inventory of the addition is included as appendix 3 of this book.

Tino Balio

Madison, Wisconsin
May 1, 2008

Prelude at Eagle-Lion

When Arthur B. Krim and Robert S. Benjamin assumed operating control of United Artists (UA) in February 1951, Mary Pickford described the company as "sick unto death."[1] An apt evaluation, since UA, once considered the Tiffany's of the industry, had reached the brink of bankruptcy. Near despair, Mary Pickford and Charlie Chaplin, the two remaining stockholders of the company, accepted the Krim-Benjamin offer by handing over the management reins for ten years on the condition that if UA earned a profit in any one of the first three years, the Krim-Benjamin team would be allowed to purchase a 50 percent interest in the company for a nominal one dollar a share. A 50 percent interest in this major motion picture company amounted to 8,000 shares of common stock!

THE RISE OF UNITED ARTISTS

Founded in 1919 by Mary Pickford, Charlie Chaplin, Douglas Fairbanks, and D. W. Griffith, UA operated solely as a distributor of high-quality independent productions.[2] Unlike the other majors, UA never owned a studio nor had actors under contract. Pioneers in every sense of the term, UA's founders were strong-willed, temperamental, idiosyncratic, but eminently gifted artists who responded to the economic implications of stardom by becoming entrepreneurs. In forming UA, talent for the first time ever acquired complete autonomy over their work. Pickford, Chaplin, and their partners had risen from the ranks of contract players to reach the status of independent producers. As heads of their own production companies, they controlled all artistic aspects of their work—from the creation of the scenario, to the selection of the director, to the final cut. By organizing a distribution company, they could oversee, in addition, the crucial functions of sales, advertising, and publicity.

By forming UA, the founders had to supply their own production financing rather than rely on a studio, but they structured the company to reduce the hazards. UA was not expected to generate profits but to function as a service organization that operated at cost. UA could therefore charge a lower distribution fee than the competition and return to the producer a larger share of the film rentals. In other words, a UA producer could enjoy as production profits what otherwise would be distribution profits.

During UA's early years, its owners delivered some of the finest pictures of their careers. The premiere UA release was Douglas Fairbanks's *His Majesty, the American*, which was released on September 1, 1919. Fairbanks went on to produce such spectacular hits as *The Mark of Zorro* (1920), *The Three Musketeers* (1921), *Robin Hood* (1923), and *The Thief of Bagdad* (1924). Pickford's best-remembered pictures were *Pollyanna* (1920), *Little Lord Fauntleroy* (1921), *Tess of the Storm Country* (1922), and *Rosita* (1923). Griffith delivered *Broken Blossoms* (1919), *Way Down East* (1921), and *Orphans of the Storm* (1922), among others. Chaplin came through with the influential *A Woman of Paris* (1923), and his acknowledged masterpiece, *The Gold Rush* (1925).

Despite this record of excellence, UA by 1924 reached a precarious position. From the outset, the company faced a product shortage. Since UA did not finance motion pictures, it could not lure other stars to go the route of independent production. On the exhibition front, the battle for theaters was in full force. More and more of the country's most important houses were falling into the hands of big chains or were forming alliances to secure advantageous terms. In the early days, UA's pictures played in many second-rate theaters; in some parts of the country, the company was shut out completely. An early demise for UA seemed imminent until Joseph M. Schenck was brought in as a partner and named chairman of the board in 1924. An independent producer, Schenck had three stars under contract—his wife, Norma Talmadge; his sister-in-law, Constance Talmadge; and his brother-in-law, Buster Keaton.

To solve the product crisis, Schenck formed Art Cinema Corporation to finance and produce pictures for UA distribution. Schenck organized this company separate and apart from UA. Art Cinema took over the Hollywood studio belonging to Pickford and Fairbanks, named it United Artists Studio, and went into production, delivering over fifty pictures to UA. These included *The Son of the Sheik* (1926), starring Rudolph Valentino; *The Beloved Rogue* (1927), starring John Barrymore; *Evangeline* (1929), starring Dolores Del Rio; and *DuBarry, Woman of Passion* (1930), starring Norma Talmadge. In addition, Schenck personally produced three Buster Keaton masterpieces, *The General* (1927), *College* (1927), and *Steamboat Bill, Jr.* (1928).

To secure suitable exhibition outlets, Schenck formed the United Artists Theatre Circuit in June 1926. A publicly held company, separate from UA, the United Artists Theatre Circuit constructed and acquired first-run theaters in the major metropolitan areas. This move put pressure on the important theater chains, with the result that they accommodated UA's pictures. The United Artists Theatre Circuit is still in existence today, operating a nationwide chain of theaters.

Schenck's success in reorganizing UA was trifling compared with what he envisioned. Given the forces within the industry toward vertical integration, it was only natural for Schenck to propose combining the UA distribution company, theater circuit, Art Cinema, and production units into one consolidated organization. However, his UA partners, Chaplin in particular, vetoed the idea when it became obvious that as a result of the underwriting for the consolidation, control might pass to the banks, leaving the founders without a voice in the company they helped create. Schenck thereupon called off the negotiations and UA continued as before.

By the thirties, the motion picture industry had become, in economic terminology, a mature oligopoly. The merger movement had run its course, with the result that five companies dominated the screen in the U.S. Known as the Big Five, these companies were Warner Brothers, Loew's, Inc. (the theater chain that owned Metro-Goldwyn-Mayer), Paramount Pictures, Twentieth Century–Fox, and RKO (Radio-Keith-Orpheum). All were fully integrated: they produced motion pictures, operated worldwide distribution outlets, and owned large theater chains where their pictures were guaranteed a showing.

Operating in a sort of symbiotic relationship with the Big Five were the Little Three: Universal, Columbia, and UA. Universal and Columbia had their own studios and distribution facilities and were useful to the majors in supplying low-cost pictures to facilitate frequent program changes and double features. UA, the smallest of the eight, with headquarters at 729 Seventh Avenue in New York, had carved a niche for itself by functioning solely as a distributor for a small group of elite independent producers.

A different breed of independent producer soon filled UA's ranks—the "creative" producer. Epitomized by Joseph Schenck, the creative producer operated in much the same way as the head of a major studio, only on a much smaller scale. Schenck chose suitable properties for his stars, oversaw the development of their scripts, secured the financing, and supervised production. The pictures he made as "Joseph M. Schenck Productions" reflected his vision overall, rather than those of the stars, directors, and screenwriters in his employ. Schenck's stars may have participated in the profits, but they functioned at best as junior partners in the production process. Every prominent producer who joined UA from 1930 to 1950—Samuel Goldwyn, David O. Selznick, Alexander Korda, and Walter Wanger—was a "creative" producer.

The star system had come under the firm control of the major studios. The movement toward oligopoly control in the film industry had consolidated most of the power over creative matters into the hands of studio executives. To say that creative people were kept in a subservient position in the studio system is an understatement. Unlike the founders of UA, who used their leverage as stars to gain control of their work and to share fully in the profits of their pictures, studio personnel were little better than contract employees. Charlie Chaplin produced, directed, wrote, and starred in his pictures, oversaw their distribution and pocketed the profits. In contrast, Jimmy Cagney at the height of his career at Warner Brothers signed a contract in 1938 requiring him to perform in eleven pictures in four years at a straight salary. He received star billing and the right of approval over stories. Cagney received $150,000 per picture plus a percentage of the gross. Bette Davis, Warner's prima donna, earned less, $3,500 per week in 1938. Over the course of her career she won concessions on the number of pictures she was required to make, but not much else. She never did earn the right to choose roles or to have a say in how the studio handled her publicity.

During the thirties, UA sustained its reputation by adding several new producers to its roster. Howard Hughes delivered *Hell's Angels*

(1930), *The Front Page* (1931), and *Scarface* (1932). Reliance Pictures, the Edward Small–Harry Goetz company, delivered a string of pictures including *I Cover the Waterfront* (1933), *The Count of Monte Cristo* (1934), and *The Last of the Mohicans* (1936). Darryl Zanuck and Joseph Schenck, through Twentieth Century, produced eighteen moneymakers from 1933 to 1935, including *The House of Rothschild* (1934), *Moulin Rouge* (1934), and *Les Miserables* (1935). David O. Selznick delivered *A Star Is Born* (1937), *The Adventures of Tom Sawyer* (1938), and *Rebecca* (1940), among others. Alexander Korda, a British producer who gained international renown in 1933 by producing *The Private Life of Henry VIII* for UA, was made a partner in the company in 1935. Korda delivered over twenty pictures to UA over the next five years, including *The Scarlet Pimpernel* (1935), *Things to Come* (1936), and *Elephant Boy* (1937). And Walter Wanger turned in *Blockade* (1938), *Algiers* (1938), *Stagecoach* (1939), and *Foreign Correspondent* (1940), among others.

Samuel Goldwyn, who had been a UA partner since 1927, became the mainstay of the company by producing over thirty-five pictures in this period. Among them were *Whoopee* (1930), *Street Scene* (1931), *Arrowsmith* (1932), *Nana* (1934), *These Three* (1936), *Dodsworth* (1936), and *Wuthering Heights* (1939). Pickford and Fairbanks, in the meantime, retired from the screen, although they still held stock in the company. Griffith sold out his interest in UA in 1933. Chaplin produced only intermittently, but delivered two smash hits, *City Lights* (1931) and *Modern Times* (1936).

In a category of his own, Walt Disney released his phenomenally successful Mickey Mouse cartoons and Silly Symphonies through the company from 1932 to 1937. *Flowers and Trees, The Three Little Pigs, The Tortoise and the Hare, Three Orphan Kittens,* and *The Country Cousin* won an Academy Award for him each year he was at UA.

United Artists' Flaw

Despite the impressiveness of UA's output, the company was torn by dissension. As I have stated in my previous history of UA, *United Artists: The Company Built by the Stars,* UA's "flaw was that those traits of independence, flamboyance, and melodramatics that characterized the owners' work as artists could not be checked in the board room, severely handicapping the management of the company throughout much of its history."[3] The crux of the matter was that the founders held on to the reins of power long after they became inactive as producers.

They steadfastly refused to recognize the contributions of the active partners, Schenck and Goldwyn in particular, by vesting in them operating control of the company. Consequently, Schenck resigned from UA in 1935 and merged his Twentieth Century production unit with Fox. And Goldwyn, after unsuccessful attempts to take over UA, departed for RKO in 1940.

During World War II, UA's fortunes declined steadily. Korda's pictures had failed to generate much interest in the U.S., so Korda suspended production operations and sold back his stock in the company in 1944 for $950,000. UA opened its doors to many independent producers, some of them far below the company's previous standards. UA failed to attract the best of the field primarily because it did not supply production financing. The few pictures that perpetuated the UA reputation in this period were Korda's *Jungle Book* (1942), Noel Coward's *In Which We Serve* (1943), Sol Lesser's *Stage Door Canteen* (1943), James Cagney's *Johnny Come Lately* (1943), Lester Cowan's *The Story of G. I. Joe* (1945), and particularly Chaplin's *The Great Dictator* (1941).

The company had pinned its hopes on David O. Selznick, who was made a partner in 1941 to fill the production vacuum created by the loss of Goldwyn. To help Selznick expand his production schedule, UA took the unprecedented action of advancing him money to acquire properties. Selznick, however, did not deliver a picture until 1944. Although Selznick produced three hits, *Since You Went Away* (1944), *I'll Be Seeing You* (1945), and *Spellbound* (1945), UA expected more from him in the way of product.

Infuriated by Selznick's dilatory behavior, Chaplin instigated a lawsuit against Selznick for not living up to his contract. After Selznick filed a countersuit, the parties reached an out-of-court settlement in 1946 whereby UA repurchased his stock for $2 million. Because Chaplin and Pickford were on opposite sides of the case, they were irreconcilable afterward. By precipitating the fight to oust Selznick, UA not only lost its remaining name "producer," but also depleted its capital reserves. UA had reached a precarious financial state just as the industry entered a postwar recession, the result of dissatisfaction with typical Hollywood fare, the exodus to the suburbs, and problems of remitting earnings from foreign markets. As a result of the conditions, banks declared a holiday on the financing of independent films in 1948. This, in turn, led to a revolt among UA's producers, who either refused to deliver their pictures or struck deals with other companies. Thereafter, UA faced an insoluble product crisis; by 1949 the company had a deficit of $200,000 and was losing $65,000 a week.

To save the company, Pickford and Chaplin brought in a management team headed by Paul V. McNutt, former governor of Indiana and prominent Democratic politician, in July 1950. The McNutt group was given the right to operate the company for two years, during which time the group could exercise an option to purchase Pickford's and Chaplin's stock for $5.4 million. But after the deficit dipped to $871,000 at the end of 1950, McNutt looked for a graceful way out. McNutt was introduced to Krim and Benjamin in September 1950 by Matthew Fox, a mutual friend who discovered that McNutt was running into trouble. McNutt agreed to step aside and allow Krim to press his case.

THE KRIM-BENJAMIN TAKEOVER

Krim had a lot of explaining to do. Three years before, a syndicate headed by Si Fabian, president of Fabian Theaters, and Serge Semenenko, an officer of the First National Bank of Boston, had offered to purchase UA for $12.5 million. Pickford was willing to sell, but Chaplin was not and since the syndicate wanted to acquire total interest in the company, the deal was called off. McNutt had recently offered $5.4 million for the company. But now Krim offered not a penny. A realistic look at the company told why—UA was losing $100,000 a week by 1951. Moneys due to producers were being diverted to pay operating costs. A receiver would soon be at the company's door. Describing his negotiations with Pickford and Chaplin, Krim said,

> I wanted to convince them that unless they agreed on a solution
> quickly, theirs would be a bankrupt company. I spent a lot of
> time persuading them that . . . the McNutt option was not worth
> anything to them because McNutt had no intention of paying
> them the $5.4 million. Their only chance of salvaging anything
> was to bring in a management that would build the confidence
> of financing sources and the producers and turn this company
> around. Every day made that a much more difficult task because
> money was going into deficit operations that should really be
> going into building up the company. This was the whole process
> of negotiation. We were never talking about how much we would
> pay them. We wanted to convince them that they had nothing of
> value to offer and finally they got the message.[4]

After making their offer, Krim and Benjamin asked for a ten-day option to see what kind of working capital they could raise. In a day they succeeded in borrowing $500,000 from their good friend Spyros Skouras, the head of Twentieth Century–Fox. Although UA was his competitor, Skouras felt that a UA bankruptcy would be bad for the industry. The money came with strings attached, however; UA had to agree to give De Luxe Laboratories, a Fox subsidiary, its film processing work. Next, Krim and Benjamin secured a $3 million line of credit for production financing and operating funds from Walter E. Heller & Co. Heller was the largest factoring company in the country, with headquarters in Chicago. Heller's principal business was discounting of accounts receivable and commercial financing, including motion pictures. The Heller money came with strings attached as well. Although Krim's experience in the motion picture business made the loan a good risk, Heller required Krim and Benjamin to sign a personal guarantee of $250,000. "We told him we didn't have it," explained Krim, but Heller replied, "I want the guarantee because you will pay off the loan if anything happens."[5] With this money as a cushion, Krim and Benjamin exercised their option and took control of UA.

University educated, articulate, and members of a prominent law firm, Krim and Benjamin represented a new breed of showmen. Krim was born in 1910, the son of a successful businessman, and raised in comfortable suburban Mount Vernon, New York. In high school, Krim was captain of the cross-country team and president of his graduating class. Krim majored in history at Columbia University; he headed the debate team and earned Phi Beta Kappa honors. After entering Columbia Law School in 1930, he set a first-year scholastic record, served as editor in chief of the *Law Review,* and graduated first in his class. Turning down several offers from Wall Street law firms, Krim went to work for Phillips & Nizer, a law firm that specialized in the entertainment industry. Louis Phillips, a specialist in antitrust matters, was permanent house counsel for Paramount; his partner, Louis Nizer, was counsel and general secretary of the New York Film Board of Trade, which arbitrated disputes between distributors and exhibitors. When Krim joined the firm, it had only one other junior partner, Phillips's nephew, Robert Benjamin.

Benjamin, who was born in 1909, grew up in the Williamsburg section of Brooklyn. His family owned a kosher poultry market. After graduation from Boy's High School in Brooklyn at age fifteen, Benjamin put himself through the City College of New York and then through Fordham University Law School, where he graduated *summa cum laude* in 1931. Krim and Benjamin were made senior partners in the law firm in 1938. By then, Phillips, Nizer, Benjamin & Krim enjoyed a top reputation in the industry.

Benjamin entered the motion picture business in 1935, when he met Robert R. Young, the railroad tycoon and financier, and arranged Young's purchase of the Pathé Film Corporation, the third largest film processing lab in the country. The following year, Benjamin became general counsel and director of Pathé. Krim entered the business in 1940, when he became general counsel at National Screen Service, a producer of commercial "trailers." In taking these positions, Krim and Benjamin retained their partnerships in the law firm, which by arrangement performed outside legal services for the two companies. They maintained their identities as lawyers and their salaries went to the firm along with the retainer fees, a practice that continued even after the UA takeover.

During World War II, Krim served as special assistant to Army Under Secretary Robert S. Patterson, attaining the rank of lieutenant-colonel. Benjamin served as executive officer of the Signal Corps's Motion Picture Photographic Center in Astoria, Long Island, where many of the nation's leading filmmakers produced indoctrination and documentary films. After the war, Krim returned to his law practice; Benjamin expanded his movie connections by heading the J. Arthur Rank organization in America and by representing Rank on the board of Universal Pictures.

EAGLE-LION—THE ANGLO-AMERICAN ALLIANCE

Benjamin's association with Rank marked the formation of Eagle-Lion Films, Inc., a short-lived venture founded in September 1946 that linked American and British motion picture interests, respectively those of American railroad magnate Robert R. Young, and British industrialist J. Arthur Rank.[6] The two men reached a reciprocal agreement whereby Eagle-Lion would distribute Rank's pictures in the U.S. and other markets in the Western Hemisphere and, in return, Rank would handle Eagle-Lion's product in Britain, Europe, and other markets in the Eastern Hemisphere. As general counsel, Benjamin had the job of organizing the company from the ground up. One of his first moves was to recommend Krim as president.

The Eagle-Lion experience became a trial by fire for Krim and Benjamin, not to mention an expensive lesson in the motion picture business for Robert Young. Eagle-Lion attempted to do the impossible—break into the majors. It failed for two important reasons: the company could not gain access to stars or to first-run theaters. As the *Paramount* antitrust case demonstrated, the control of stars and first-run theaters by the majors had created formidable barriers to entry. Although the postwar years marked the end of an era for the movies,

Eagle-Lion lacked the resources to compete effectively. But the experience of operating the company proved invaluable to Krim and Benjamin and taught the two entrepreneurs survival tactics for the future.

Eagle-Lion figured into Rank's grand postwar strategy to establish parity for British films in the American market. Stated another way, Rank wanted playing time for his pictures and lots of it. Getting the majors to acquiesce would be a formidable task, since foreign films had been systematically shut out of the market for about a generation. But now Rank had considerable muscle. In Great Britain, the most important overseas market for American films, Rank dominated all branches of the film business. In exhibition, he owned over 500 theaters, comprising two of the three big theater circuits. In distribution, his General Film Distributors regulated the flow of pictures to the two circuits. In production, Rank owned most of the studio facilities in the country and financed a full roster of around twenty-five films a year through affiliated production companies. Outside Great Britain, Rank owned or controlled theaters in France, Canada, and Australia and had close ties with exhibitors throughout the British Commonwealth.[7]

Rank even had a foothold in the United States. In 1936, he purchased a quarter interest in Universal Pictures when a group of New York bankers headed by Cheever Cowdin forced motion picture pioneer Carl Laemmle to sell out. Afterward, Rank handled the Universal product in Great Britain, but because Universal no longer owned theaters or had much clout with exhibitors, Rank formed a brief alliance with UA during the war to distribute a package containing some of the best British pictures of the era, among them *Blithe Spirit* (1945), *Caesar and Cleopatra* (1946), and *Henry V* (1946).

Because the British market was not large enough to support indigenous production, Rank had to export to survive. To get playing time in the United States, he somehow had to convince the majors to make room for his pictures in theaters they owned and to allow his pictures to compete against those the majors produced.

On a goodwill tour of the U.S. during the summer of 1945, Rank told the industry that if American companies wanted special treatment in Great Britain, they had better reciprocate the favor here. But the majors would not budge, for several reasons. First, U.S. exhibitors generally disliked British pictures, for reasons that will be explained later. For another, the motion picture business was booming. During the war, dollars were plentiful, while commodities were not. Movies were the most readily available entertainment, which benefited Hollywood. Domestic film rentals for the eight majors jumped from $193 million in 1939 to $332 million in 1946. Every night was Saturday night at the movies. "B" pictures, low-grade pictures, pictures featuring unknown players—all commanded an audience. Weekly attendance by the end of the war reached 90 million, the highest ever.

Predictions for the postwar era looked even better. On the domestic scene, returning servicemen were expected to boost attendance. Indicators of rising wages, shorter working hours, and greater leisure also implied prosperity. On the foreign scene, American film companies had a huge backlog of pictures ready for the reopening of overseas markets.

Britain was the only important European market open to American films during the war and generated about half of Hollywood's foreign revenues. For many films, distribution in Great Britain meant the difference between profit and loss. Britain's status as an important market would remain unchanged, but Hollywood knew that Britain's screens absorbed 600 features a year, while British studios produced only about sixty pictures a year on the average. In short, Great Britain needed Hollywood rather than the other way around.

Rank therefore had to deal with the second tier of the American film industry if he wanted entree. A continuing link with UA was out of the question. Relations deteriorated during the war when Rank offered to invest in the company and received what he considered a humiliating rebuff. For the time being, Rank had to stick with Universal, another member of the Little Three. Universal had undergone reorganization in 1946 by merging with International Pictures, an independent production unit headed by William Goetz and Leo Spitz, to form Universal-International. The merger was an attempt by Universal to secure a stronger line of quality pictures to supplement the Deanna Durbin and Abbott and Costello pictures that had kept the studio in the black during the war. Because Universal had its hands full distributing its own product, the company could not take on the entire Rank line. Rank therefore needed an additional outlet for his pictures.

Forming an alliance with Robert Young was just the ticket. A self-made millionaire, promoter, and railroad tycoon, Young controlled an empire consisting of the C&O, Nickel Plate, Erie, and Missouri Pacific railroads, and interests in a dozen others, with combined assets of $2 billion, that included 23,000 miles of track, coal mines, trucking companies, and peach orchards. The properties were lumped together in a holding company called the Alleghany (*sic*) Corporation.[8]

Young made his fortune during the halcyon days of the pre-1929 crash. Deciding that the bullish market had flimsy underpinnings, he had the savvy to sell short. During the depths of the Depression, Young purchased a seat on the New York Stock Exchange at a rock-bottom price. Always on the lookout for bargains, he bought control of the bankrupt Alleghany Corporation in 1937 with the help of Allen P. Kirby, heir to the Woolworth dime-store fortune.

A financial nightmare, Alleghany made Young an easy target of the company's creditors, mostly large banking interests, who tried to unseat this forty-year-old upstart. Young waged a proxy fight and in the process sharpened many of the techniques he would later use to expand his empire. He used newspapers as one of his chief weapons and frequently published open letters to the small stockholder that hammered away at the role Wall Street bankers played in the downfall of the C&O. Young won the battle and became chairman of the C&O board and its finance committee. Afterward, he succeeded in placing his railroads on a firmer financial footing.

Anticipating a travel boom after the war, Young embarked on an expansion program. If the railroads slept, Young worried that the airlines would fill the void. Young envisioned a new era for railroading that included lightweight passenger cars, an efficient system of processing reservations, credit cards, and the elimination of tipping. He even wanted trains to be equipped with radios, libraries, and motion pictures.

Young made his first move by going after the Pullman Company, which owned and serviced almost every sleeping car in the country. He lost this battle, but in 1947, Young launched still another takeover of another railroad—the New York Central. His campaign for the stockholders' votes in 1947 rivaled a national election in scope, intensity, and public interest. Young was featured on the cover of *Time* magazine and was the subject of articles in *Fortune* and editorials in the financial press.

Why Young entered the motion picture business is a mystery. In 1943, he purchased Producers Releasing Corporation (PRC), a Poverty Row studio known mainly as a producer of low-budget Westerns. PRC produced mostly Western serials. Starring Buster Crabbe, George Houston, Tim McCoy, Bob Steele, and Al "Lash" LaRue among others, these pictures have been described by George N. Fenin and William K. Everson as "shoddy, cheap, carelessly made, badly photographed, and ineptly directed. Plot values were nonexistent, for the most part, and since casts were identical in almost every film . . . it was virtually impossible to tell one film from another."[9] But after the Young takeover, PRC's standards improved as the studio expanded its feature film production. Perhaps PRC somehow complemented Young's plans for railroading. In any event, Young became more deeply involved in motion pictures by going after the state's rights exchanges that had been handling PRC's product. By 1946, Young had created in PRC a vertically integrated company that owned a film processing lab, a studio in Hollywood, a production company, and a national distribution system.[10]

According to Krim, Young jumped at the opportunity to join forces with Rank. Born in Texas of humble origins, Young had turned into an "elitist," according to Krim.[11] After forming Eagle-Lion, for example, he tried to persuade the former King of England, the Duke of Windsor, to join the board of directors. Regardless, the Eagle-Lion venture looked promising to both Rank and Young. Rank found another outlet for his pictures, a company on the make, with the resources of a prominent industrialist. By collaborating with Rank, Young received the instant prestige he needed to build a reputation for his company. In addition, the alliance provided access to some of the best theaters overseas and saved Young the expense of establishing a foreign distribution network.

Publicity releases gave the impression that Universal and Eagle-Lion would divide the Rank product equally and thus be seen as coequals by the trade. But in actuality, Universal had first pick; Eagle-Lion had the privilege of distributing anything Universal rejected— the dregs, in other words.

The specific arrangements called for Rank and Eagle-Lion to distribute ten top pictures a year worldwide—five produced by each company. To comply with these requirements, Young through his holding company, Pathé Industries, formed Eagle-Lion Films, Inc., as a motion picture distribution subsidiary and Eagle-Lion Studios, Inc., as a motion picture production subsidiary. A spokesperson for Young made it quite clear that Eagle-Lion would produce films entirely apart from PRC, telling *Variety* that "if this one is our Chevrolet, you might say the other will be our Cadillac."[12]

Organizing the Company

Benjamin's first task as organizer was to scour the industry for manpower. As he explained to Young, "It is essential to engage production and distribution personnel whose past experience and industry-wide reputation will give the company a new flavor and respect in the industry. Such personnel are extremely difficult to obtain since they are presently employed by major motion picture companies who will offer any inducements in the way of compensation for their retention."[13]

To head the studio they hired Bryan Foy. Formerly the head of the "B" productions at Warner Brothers in the thirties and Twentieth Century–Fox during the war, Foy was known in the industry as the "Keeper of the B's." In recommending Foy to Young, Benjamin said, "Mr. Foy is an old showman, which in the motion picture industry is a highly complimentary characterization. It means that throughout his career he has developed an instinct for appreciating the public's desire, recognizing what stories would satisfy that desire and the ability to translate that story into a medium for a motion picture attraction." In Benjamin's opinion, Foy was "an expert producer of exploitation pictures in the middle class financial bracket, a producer who has specialized in making 'angle,' exploitable, and commercial product which despite the cost involved has substantial success at the boxoffice. At the same time it must be recognized that he is not a producer who makes double-A quality pictures."[14] Despite this caveat, Eagle-Lion asked Foy to do just that—make double-A product. To persuade Foy to sign, Young had to give Foy a stock option in the company and to top his salary at Fox, which amounted to a hefty $3,500 a week.

Next, they hired Krim to serve as president of the joint operations. As Krim explained it, "After I came back from the Army, I wasn't particularly anxious to go back to the full practice of the law. I was really looking around for something else in which to interest myself."[15] His responsibility, for which he was paid $1,000 a week, was to manage finances from company headquarters (located at 165 W. 46th Street in New York).

To produce its pictures, Eagle-Lion planned on using the PRC studio, which was located in Hollywood near the Goldwyn lot. But to produce quality pictures, they had to upgrade facilities at a cost of $1 million and hire new department heads.

Signing talent proved more difficult. Eagle-Lion's options were limited. The company could try to borrow important actors from the majors or develop stars of its own. Developing stars was a long and expensive process and was not a viable option. On the other hand, Eagle-Lion could not go begging. The majors protected themselves from such requests by restricting loans of personnel to major studios. Benjamin pointed out to Young that Republic, Monogram, and PRC had never been able to overcome that contractual barrier. Nor, with a few exceptions, could independent producers. The majors used this barrier to entry to relegate competition to a subordinate position. Eagle-Lion therefore had no choice but to sign up aging leading men—Louis Hayward and George Brent—and a dozen or so up-and-coming younger players such as Richard Basehart, June Lockhart, Lois Butler, and

Scott Brady. All would be given star billing in the hope that exhibitors and public alike would play along.

At the distribution end, the company rapidly expanded its sales force. It was a calculated risk, but Eagle-Lion wanted to be prepared to handle the quality pictures expected from Rank. To break into the big time, though, Eagle-Lion needed to do business with a higher grade of exhibitor, preferably the bigger chains with their first-run theaters. First-run theaters meant houses with large seating capacities located in the best commercial districts of important cities and high admission prices. Only by renting a picture to this class of theater on a percentage basis could a distributor collect the extraordinary rentals of a hit picture. PRC was forever consigned to Poverty Row because it could sell its product only on a flat rental basis to subsequent-run houses. Companies like PRC and Republic earned a fair return on "B" pictures. Demand for this type of product was steady. A company knew that if it kept production costs below a certain level, the pictures would bring in a nice profit. For example, PRC Westerns were made in eight days or less and cost about $135,000 each. Although the playoff was slow, they eventually grossed as high as $300,000, which was just enough over the break-even point to make the venture worthwhile.

The Studio System Production Policy

Young invested over $12 million of his own money to launch the Eagle-Lion ventures. In announcing the first season's roster, Krim stated that no film would cost less than $1 million. Eagle-Lion produced six pictures its first season. The leadoff was *It's a Joke, Son,* an inexpensive vehicle for Kenney Delmar, the Senator Claghorn of Fred Allen's radio show. According to *Variety,* it sagged "through most of its length under a mess of slapstick that's laid on with a heavy trowel." [16] Eagle-Lion's first stab at the big time was *Repeat Performance.* It starred Joan Leslie, who had just left Warner's over a contract dispute, and featured Richard Basehart, whom Eagle-Lion signed after he won the New York Drama Critics award for his performance in the Broadway production of *Hasty Heart.* The picture was a fantasy about an actress who murders her alcoholic husband on New Year's and gets her wish to live the year over again. It had the "proper ingredients to do good biz in most first-run situations," said *Variety.* [17] Eagle-Lion's other releases were *Out of the Blue,* a screwball comedy starring Virginia Mayo, George Brent, and Turhan Bey; *Adventures of Casanova,* a made-in-Mexico "horse opera yarn" starring Arthur de Cordova; *Love from a*

Stranger, starring Sylvia Sidney and John Hodiak; and *Red Stallion,* an outdoor action picture.

Released during the 1946–47 season, these big-budget pictures reached the market on the eve of an industry-wide recession. All the optimistic predictions about continued prosperity for the movies now began to ring hollow. The domestic boxoffice rose steadily to peak in 1946 and then late in 1947 began a steady decline that would last for ten years and result in a 50 percent drop in attendance. The decline began even before the commercial expansion of television, which took off in earnest in 1950.

When servicemen returned, the birthrate increased sharply; families with babies chose to listen to the radio at night rather than to go to the movies. Veterans swarmed into educational institutions and studies cut into their leisure time. And because the country was at peace, goods and services were diverted to civilian purposes. Purchases of houses, automobiles, appliances, and other commodities cut into disposable income.[18]

Although boxoffice receipts declined, movie production costs followed the inflationary spiral and increased by more than 60 percent for an average feature by 1948. As a result, the brunt of the boxoffice decline fell on production revenues, hurting independent producers and the production end of the integrated companies.[19] Overseas, the boxoffice for American films was booming, but the transfer of dollars back home was stymied by currency restrictions instituted by foreign governments. Profits of the Big Five declined 50 percent in the two years after the 1946 peak; the Little Three all suffered losses.

The sudden switch in audience tastes and viewing habits proved a disaster to Young's motion picture ventures, which posted losses of $2.2 million in 1947. Concerning Eagle-Lion, Krim said, "We made mistakes the first year by taking on players who added nothing to the boxoffice. As a result, we made films which were costlier than they had to be because we wanted names. Later, we learned these names meant little or nothing when the film reached the theaters."[20]

Independent Production

Eagle-Lion financed the first season's pictures with $8 million in loans from the Bank of America, which Young personally guaranteed. This brought Young's investment in Eagle-Lion to over $12 million and he decided to turn off the money spigot. Eagle-Lion adopted a new production policy. Beginning with the 1947–48 season, Eagle-Lion shifted from a studio system form of production to a hybrid type of independent production. As part of the reorganization, Bryan Foy resigned as head of production to become an independent producer for the company and Krim took over as studio chief, a position he assumed in addition to his other responsibilities. Eagle-Lion did not fully finance pictures the way UA planned to do under Krim and Benjamin; Eagle-Lion supplied a patchwork of financing consisting of second money, studio credits, and completion bonds to supplement conventional bank loans. In return, the producer was required to use Eagle-Lion's facilities. Partial financing meant that Eagle-Lion had to share the profits, but it also had the advantage of reducing fixed studio costs.

But before Krim could implement this new production policy, he first had to reduce the expense of operating two distribution concerns—Eagle-Lion Films and PRC—which amounted to about $4 million a year. PRC Pictures got the ax in August 1947. Product scheduled for PRC release was channeled into Eagle-Lion with the goal of keeping its distribution pipeline full, regardless of the quality of the pictures. At the same time, the producing activities of PRC Productions were gradually phased out in an attempt to erase completely any vestige of Poverty Row.

Krim then lined up independent producers, the most important of whom were Edward Small and Walter Wanger, in addition to Bryan Foy. Small was a Hollywood veteran responsible for a steady stream of solid box-office fare including *I Cover the Waterfront* (1933), *The Last of the Mohicans* (1936), *The Man in the Iron Mask* (1939), and *Brewster's Millions* (1945), all released through UA. Walter Wanger was the biggest catch, however. As Robert Benjamin said, "After twelve months of intense growing pains, during which the hierarchy of Hollywood was dented here and there, we finally broke through and arranged with Walter Wanger to produce exclusively for Eagle-Lion. Wanger had had top production executive positions with Paramount, Metro, United Artists, and Universal. His last ten pictures made for Universal made handsome profits. His record, therefore, stamped him as a person who would be of incalculable importance. This was even less important than the psychological benefit of attracting to our production program a man of respected ability and commercial worth of Walter Wanger."[21]

Keeping production costs to a minimum placed Eagle-Lion in a quandary. The company could not afford big stars or expensive properties, yet, at the same time, it had to secure "A" playing time and high rentals. As Krim explained it, "All the pictures have been planned on story ideas which can be brought in for costs ranging from $350,000 to $650,000—a cost range very few story ideas fit into. They are based on the best substitutes that we can think of for stars or pre-sold story values—action, color, natural locations, authenticity and similar ingredients. Yet even with these ideas, which are the least expensive pseudo A type pictures to make, the nerves and ingenuity of our production departments are being taxed to the extreme to have enough on the screen to get A playing time." [22]

What resulted from this penny-pinching was a form of product differentiation—a string of *film noir* pictures that put Eagle-Lion, albeit briefly, in the limelight. Don Miller analyzed these pictures and claimed that "Eagle-Lion set a standard; its influence was felt long after the organization had ceased to function." [23] The first entry, *T-Men* (1947) did for Treasury agents what *House on 92nd Street* did for the FBI. Produced by Edward Small and directed by Anthony Mann, *T-Men* took a case out of Treasury Department files and reenacted it in documentary fashion, à la Louis De Rochemont's *March of Time* newsreels. For marquee value, the picture had a medium name, Dennis O'Keefe. Shot on location in Detroit, Los Angeles, and several of its beach suburbs, the picture was produced for $424,000. By the end of 1949, *T-Men* had grossed a tidy $1.6 million, but because Small supplied his own financing, Eagle-Lion shared only 25 percent of the profits.

T-Men made stars out of director Anthony Mann and cameraman John Alton. Mann had earned his stripes on Poverty Row, working on assorted low-budget pictures, including PRC's *Railroaded*. After *T-Men*, Mann became one of the most-sought-after directors in Hollywood. Eagle-Lion signed him to a one-year contract at $750 a week, but "he could have commanded $2,500 a week and more at several other companies," said Krim. [24]

Cameraman John Alton also became a favorite of producers. Said Miller, "He was a—dare we say—genius at lighting, and notoriously fast at camera set-ups, one reason why he was assigned to so many low-budgeted, quicktime B-pictures . . . He could accomplish what Mann wanted, and so *T-Men* abounds in low-angle shots, deep-focus scenes with background and foreground crystal clear, and above all, skillful lighting." [25] Eagle-Lion tried to sign him to a term contract, but his demands were too onerous. However, he agreed to work for Eagle-Lion on a free-lance basis at $1,000 per week for a year, which was actually to Eagle-Lion's benefit since the company did not have to pay him between pictures.

Eagle-Lion's second hit was *Canon City* (1948), produced by Bryan Foy, directed by Crane Wilbur, with camerawork by John Alton. Shot almost entirely at the site of the Canon City, Colorado, state penitentiary in March 1948, the picture reenacted the jailbreak that took place the previous December. As Benjamin described it, "The events of the picture were shot as they actually happened. This was a true story, better than fiction, of twelve desperadoes on New Year's Eve, the capture of five of them, and the killing of seven. The story made national headlines."[26] Foy got Warden Best to play himself. Thousands of convicts performed as extras at no cost at all. Eagle-Lion used only five actors and introduced Scott Brady as one of the prison busters. Originally budgeted at $350,000, the picture came in at $424,000. However, it grossed $1.2 million and was cited by the press, including *Life* and *Look,* as one of the top pictures of the year.

Krim knew a good thing when he saw one and released a series of successful *film noir* pictures of a similar mold. Small produced *Raw Deal* (1948) as a follow-up to *T-Men,* using the same director, scriptwriter, star, and cameraman. Bryan Foy produced three pictures: *He Walked by Night* (1948), a straightforward thriller depicting a brilliant but psychotic killer, directed by Alfred Werker and starring Richard Basehart; *Trapped* (1949), a melodrama based on the Secret Service, directed by Richard Fleischer and starring Lloyd Bridges; and *Port of New York* (1949), a crime melodrama about narcotics and smuggling, directed by Laslo Benedek and starring Scott Brady.

Eagle-Lion kept production costs for these films to around $500,000 on the average. Cost cutting became something of an art. For Walter Wanger's *Reign of Terror,* a *film noir* picture set in the French Revolution, director Anthony Mann claimed that costs for the sets were held down to $40,000:

> I got William C. Menzies to do them after interesting him in something new—that is, finding out for how little not how much the entire job could be done . . . Costume films usually have mammoth sets, but we built completely with flats . . . Another thing, we used only Broadway actors—Richard Basehart, Arnold Moss, Norman Lloyd, Jesse Barker—because there is more authenticity in fresh faces . . . Ceilings were used and the lighting was arranged from the floor, skirting the need for rigging . . . "Imagination" was used to save costs in shooting the guillotine scene by placing the camera directly above the execution platform! We eliminated the necessity of shooting the back of the platform and most of both sides. By so doing, the mob scene was kept down to 90 people but gave the impression of many more.[27]

The *film noir* pictures demonstrated to Krim, "that Eagle-Lion could return substantial grosses for pictures without established star personalities by dint of sound exploitation . . . More and more exhibitors are beginning to consider us a permanent source of supply and are beginning to give us terms comparable to Universal and Columbia."[28] But breaking the barrier to first-run houses proved more difficult. Now

Eagle-Lion Crime Films

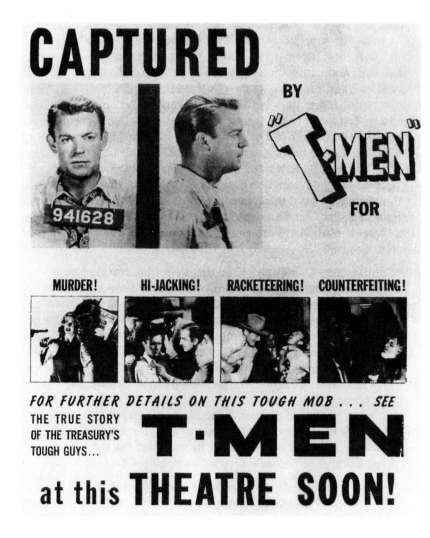

Containing no stars, *T-Men* (January 1948) had to be exploited on its merits. Produced by Edward Small and directed by Anthony Mann.

John Ireland and Dennis O'Keefe in *Raw Deal* (May 1948). A follow-up to the successful *T-Men* using the same director, scriptwriter, cameraman, and star, *Raw Deal* was ready for release within four months.

Canon City (July 1948). Twelve convicts broke out of the Colorado State Penitentiary at Canon City on December 30, 1947. Within a week, all were killed or captured; within six months, producer Bryan Foy had the story on the screen. Written and directed by Crane Wilber, the picture introduced Scott Brady.

Released four months after *Canon City*, *He Walked by Night* became the high point of Eagle-Lion's crime films. Richard Basehart's criminal was a crafty, lethal near genius, and quite mad.

Yul Brynner playing the arch villain made his film debut in *Port of New York* (December 1949), a semidocumentary involving a dope ring. Produced by Aubrey Schenck and directed by Laslo Benedek.

that Eagle-Lion had a few hits on its roster, it succeeded "by sheer dint of reasonably competent picture making" in securing favorable dates and terms. But in New York, the most important market in the country, the company had been completely boxed out of first run. Loew's and RKO controlled the first-run houses in the area and gave preferential treatment to the majors, leaving few if any dates for independents. In a letter to Joe Vogel, head of the Loew's chain, Krim called the situation "pathetic." Krim admitted that the first batch of pictures proved problematic and that "a new company could not expect to be bailed out the way in which older companies might be aided." However, now that Eagle-Lion had such pictures as *Canon City* and *Raw Deal* in release, Krim hoped for better treatment.[29] The situation did not improve.

Krim cautioned Young against adopting an adversarial policy, since it would likely make matters worse. But in 1950, after Krim resigned, Eagle-Lion filed a $15 million antitrust suit against Loew's and RKO charging that it was excluded from the New York market. In starting this action, Young might have been searching for ways to recoup his losses. Regardless, he lost the case and the appeal. The final verdict said:

> Plaintiff's argument would presuppose that any such merchandise, no matter what its grade, would do proportionately as well in New York as it does nationally. The fact that there are more Cadillacs per capita in New York, or more mink coats per capita in New York, than in the country as a whole does not establish that there is a conspiracy in New York against cheaper cars or cheaper furs.[30]

During the 1947–48 season, Eagle-Lion produced fourteen class-A independent productions at its studio. As of spring 1949, ten were in release, showing signs that Eagle-Lion might turn the corner; five earned a substantial profit—Small's *T-Men* and *Raw Deal,* Foy's *Canon City* and *He Walked by Night,* and Abbott and Costello's *The Noose Hangs High.* Two others broke even, and two showed substantial losses. These pictures from the 1947–48 production roster absorbed over $4 million in studio overhead. If Eagle-Lion had completely financed the roster and had enjoyed all the profits, the company would have made $1.2 million, but as it happened the company earned close to $200,000.

Krim reported that "this is the best production-distribution record that has been made in the industry in the past year and a half." To achieve this record, Krim ran an obstacle course: "We had little or no allowance for preproduction development; we had to beg at every turn for a bank loan; we could not select stories or producers or other talents on the basis of merit but rather had to select them on the basis of patchwork financing requirements. All this had to be done with limited management personnel and [while] we continued to make all sorts of deals to feed our mill with programme pictures and Westerns as well."[31]

Nonetheless, the financial prospects looked bleak because of the costly mistakes from the first season. Although the production loans had been reduced to $3 million as of 1948, Young could not be looked to for help except for a small investment in an occasional picture. Describing the crisis facing Eagle-Lion, Benjamin said:

> Our reputation is being impaired on several fronts from our delays in paying bills and defaults in forwarding reports. Although a herculean task is being performed, it is not wholly successful in preserving the prestige and reputation of the company. Rumors have emanated from producers and other creditors, who spread the word that we are months in arrears in payment of our debts, particularly to outside producers where the collections are in the nature of quasi-trust funds. It has been a miracle that through the cooperation and friendly business relations with the Bank of America, these rumors have not destroyed our credit lines.[32]

Because Young waffled, Eagle-Lion shuttered its studio in November 1948, right after completing the first batch of independent productions. In an attempt to camouflage the situation, Eagle-Lion announced a new production policy—"production in cycles to bring down the costs of operating a studio."[33]

The Rank Pictures

Rank's first pictures did nothing to alleviate Eagle-Lion's condition. In addition to experiencing the general apathy toward British pictures, they felt the full impact of the boxoffice slump. Rank's first picture, *Bedelia,* for example, grossed only $350,000. Rank had hoped to secure around 12,000 bookings for each of his pictures, but *Bedelia* had only 4,000. In the past, better-grade British pictures had averaged about 6,000 bookings.

Only a handful of British pictures had ever succeeded in the United States—Alexander Korda's *The Private Life of Henry VIII* (1933), Noel Coward's *In Which We Serve* (1943), and Laurence Olivier's *Henry V* (1946), plus a few others. Exhibitors claimed that audiences had problems with the British accent, the long-hair themes, and the unknown stars. The British, on the other hand, charged that the exhibition oligopoly in the United States had shut them out. *Variety*, in a famous article with the headline, "Stix Still Nix British Pix," sided with the exhibitors in stating that "pix from abroad . . . are still a very long way from achieving parity of interest with the home-grown product. Imports made boxoffice inroads only in such areas as New York, Los Angeles, San Francisco, and Boston which had cosmopolitan populations. The midwest and south continue to be as much citadels of isolationism in their picture tastes as in their politics."[34] Only an unusual and highly exploitable foreign film could break down this resistance.

British politics exacerbated the situation. To stem the dollar outflow in an attempt to stabilize the economy, the Labour government slapped a 75 percent import duty on American films on August 7, 1947. In retaliation, the major American film companies boycotted the country for over a year. But the Americans suffered little since they already had a substantial backlog of pictures in the country lined up for release. A compromise settlement, reached in March 1948, permitted Hollywood to withdraw a flat $17 million annually from the country for a period of two years; all other earnings were frozen. By instituting this form of protectionism, the Labour government hoped that American distributors would invest their frozen funds in British productions. Later that year, Parliament passed legislation that more than doubled the quota of British pictures that exhibitors had to present to 45 percent of their playing time.

During the boycott, Rank boosted production to fill the gaps. Afterward, he retaliated against the Americans for not promoting his product in the United States by boosting production still further with the goal of supplying his two circuits with all their quota requirements. The additional pictures, plus his regular feature production and reissues, just about filled the playing time of both circuits. Whatever open dates remained Rank allocated to the cream of American pictures and at terms that Rank dictated. Rank offered Paramount and RKO two booking dates for 1949; Fox, four; and UA, one. Eagle-Lion, which received two dates, told Rank, "You're putting us out of business." Rank replied that the "distribution of dates was made on the basis of quality pictures."[35] Eagle-Lion's first program continued to haunt the company again. Rank's Gaumont circuit, for example, had lost so much money that it balked at going through with all the bookings. Business was business and Eagle-Lion, just like any other American company, had to suffer the indignity of finding playing time in the small circuits and independent second-run houses.

But Rank won a Pyrrhic victory. Britain did not have enough movie-making talent to support the expanded production program and the result was a dreary parade of boxoffice flops. In 1949, Rank fired 1,800 production workers, sold off several of his studios, and cut back drastically on production. Stock prices of his theater chains hit eight-year lows.

Rank produced only two pictures of consequence in this period, the Michael Powell–Emeric Pressburger production of *The Red Shoes* (1948) and the Laurence Olivier *Hamlet* (1948). Although *Hamlet* did sensational business, Universal and not Eagle-Lion released it. Because of its special appeal, Universal distributed *Hamlet* as a road-show. Eagle-Lion thought *The Red Shoes* was also something special. Based on a Hans Christian Andersen fairy tale, *The Red Shoes* was in essence a backstage melodrama with temperamental ballerinas replacing the conventional showgirls. The picture was shot in Technicolor on location in London, Paris, and Monte Carlo and had a brilliant musical score played by the Royal Philharmonic Orchestra under the direction of Sir Thomas Beecham. For the New York premiere in August 1948, Eagle-Lion took over a shuttered legitimate theater and convinced the Theatre Guild to sponsor the production. After a warm critical reception, *The Red Shoes* settled in for a run of over eighteen months. Like *Hamlet* it played as a roadshow, but unlike *Hamlet,* which had received enormous publicity in *Time* and *Life, The Red Shoes* was not presold and had to be built almost from the ground up in each city.

The Red Shoes grossed close to $2 million, but Rank's other pictures were something else. Of the twenty-six Eagle-Lion had in release as of 1949, most grossed in the $15,000 to $50,000 range. Some grossed as little as $5,000 and one or two as high as $400,000. After deducting the distribution fees and print and advertising costs, Eagle-Lion remitted to the Rank organization less than $1 million on these twenty-six pictures, and most of this came from *The Red Shoes.* Eagle-Lion for its efforts collected about $1.4 million in distribution fees in comparison.

Trouble with Young

During the early days of Eagle-Lion, Young had been involved in a fight to merge the C&O with the New York Central and was content to stay on the sidelines of his motion picture operations. But after he lost the first round of the fight in early 1948, he jumped into the affairs of Eagle-Lion "with both feet." At first, he complained about such matters as the caliber of the sales staff. Young said, "PRC and Eagle-Lion have suffered badly through the custom of increasing personnel from strictly motion picture sources—largely an element which for one reason or another has not made good in the other companies . . . I base this feeling upon the very low caliber of help we have had in the top categories. I shudder to think what it has been in the lower strata." Young advocated recruiting personnel from the soap, automobile, and insurance industries.[36] Soon, though, Young became more than meddlesome. Benjamin discerned a personality change and said to Krim,

> He frightened me a little with his egomania. He made statements like—there isn't a single person in California whether he be writer, director, producer or actor, who wouldn't be tickled to work for Bob Young, instead of MGM, if we had the money . . . His emphasis on his own prestige and his emphasis on Bob Young as a personality was so marked as really to frighten me. It was as if the only basis for the new found prestige of Eagle-Lion in the industry is the personality of Bob Young. That in itself is not disturbing, but what an ignorance it shows of the struggle of Eagle-Lion to attain major status. What an unawareness he has of the lack of respect a Monogram or a Republic suffers from, which we too suffered from, and how difficult to overcome that atmosphere in attaining major company status. The only significance of the observations, Arthur, is that it makes me more convinced than ever that it is impossible for Bob Young to ever properly appraise the efforts of any of us, since, in the last analysis, successful accomplishment in gaining people of quality for our studio will be only the by-product of Bob Young's personality, prestige and dignity.[37]

Young's perception of himself obviously affected operations. To keep overhead expenses down, Eagle-Lion operated with a lean staff. Rank had been concerned about this, thinking the company penny wise and pound foolish. Krim, who functioned as head of the distribution office in New York as well as studio chief in Hollywood, needed help badly, especially on policy matters, and had hoped that Young would upgrade Benjamin's position to chairman of the board. Citing his rule that all executives must perform their duties on a full-time basis, Young refused—an odd decision since Benjamin had been devoting his time exclusively to Rank's and Young's interests. Benjamin believed that behind Young's decision lay a deep distrust of both his and Krim's integrity and objectivity. As he told Krim, "I don't care how he camouflages it—that's what he is saying. It is devastating to have your motives impugned at every turn."[38]

Under the guise of easing the management problem, Young appointed William C. MacMillan, Jr., a businessman from outside the film industry, to serve as vice president of Eagle-Lion in charge of operations. His job was to work under Krim to coordinate eastern and western operations "on a level just below policy." In actuality, Young foisted MacMillan on management and obviously he would be reporting directly to Young. But as Benjamin said, "We have bought a number of months of peace. In the last analysis, we have no position to lose because our relationship has substantially deteriorated. In getting Mac in, we are, of course, inviting our successor to the operation."[39]

Soon after, Young also appointed MacMillan vice president of Pathé Industries, Eagle-Lion's parent company. Krim first read about it in the *New York Times* and said to Young, "Since MacMillan is supposed to be working under me full time in Eagle-Lion, it seems to me that somebody should have consulted with me in advance—let alone given me a voice in the decision. In my opinion, an unworkable situation is now created in which an executive under me is also an executive in a higher echelon, which is, to say the least, confusing."[40]

To keep Eagle-Lion afloat, Krim suggested to the company's creditors that Pathé Industries be reorganized to create a new segregated Eagle-Lion under an experienced and enthusiastic management rather than to permit the current state of affairs to continue. To Young, Krim suggested that Pathé could build a firmer financial base by going public. Krim asked Young and his associates at the very least to form a financing corporation to supply Eagle-Lion with risk capital. Time was running out. The studio had been shuttered for six months; Eagle-Lion faced a severe product shortage; and the bills were piling up.

Krim reported to banker Serge Semenenko the toll on the company: "For some time now we have harassed our sales and advertising departments with so many special problems that they have not been able to pay attention to operations. This has reached a new peak in the last week—to such an extent that nobody has any time at all for selling. Coupled with this is the complete breakdown of morale. Under these circumstances it is entirely likely that we can fall short of our estimates by a very considerable amount."[41] Krim's predictions proved correct. A reassessment of the fourteen pictures Eagle-Lion financed for the 1948 season revealed that the company would have to write off about half the $4.5 million advanced as production loans.

For 1949, Eagle-Lion had scheduled for release the Rank pictures, described earlier, a package of David O. Selznick reissues, and a handful of independent productions. Only one picture amounted to much, Walter Wanger's *Tulsa,* which almost matched the performance of *The Red Shoes* at the box office. Wanger had produced only one other picture for Eagle-Lion—*Reign of Terror*. He planned others, but Eagle-Lion could not come up with the financing.

Realizing the impossibility of instituting a rational long-term policy for the company, Krim submitted his resignation to Young in May 1949. However, Krim agreed to stay on until principal photography on two upcoming Bryan Foy pictures had been completed. In a letter to Louis Nizer, his law partner, Krim said, "Naturally, Young and his cohorts are doing their best to make me the scapegoat, and I have been agreeably surprised by the fact that apparently the backlash has been stronger than their attacks."[42]

In reply, Nizer said, "Your resignation evoked renewed expression on all sides of appreciation for your achievements . . . Do not throw yourself away too easily in any new plan."[43] Krim's salary was sixty weeks in arrears. The retainer fee to the Phillips, Nizer firm was also in arrears and it took a considerable amount of effort to get Pathé to pay up.

Young appointed MacMillan president to fill Krim's spot. Eagle-Lion ceased production late in 1949 and functioned primarily as a conduit for independents. Eagle-Lion attempted to reverse its fortunes in 1950 by merging with Film Classics, a distribution company specializing in reissues. The deal fell through, but not before Eagle-Lion changed its name to Eagle-Lion Classics, which stayed with the company to the end.

Eagle-Lion threw in the towel in April 1951, when UA, now headed by Krim and Benjamin, took over the distribution of Eagle-Lion's current releases. As part of the deal, Eagle-Lion terminated the releasing pact with Rank and ceased distributing motion pictures. Soon after, Eagle-Lion Studios was placed on the auction block.

Why didn't Young understand the connection between stars and first-run theaters? According to Krim, "the answer is he should have."[44] Perhaps Young believed that his savvy in railroading as a promotional financier would work in motion pictures. Perhaps he believed that his wealth plus Rank's clout would give Eagle-Lion a fighting chance to become at least another Universal or Columbia. But the postwar recession in the motion picture business changed the odds. The recession forced the entrenched companies to compete more aggressively as the studio system and everything it implied began to crumble. Hollywood could no longer serve up anything and expect to satisfy audiences. Tastes and viewing habits had changed, although precisely how was unclear. The industry was out of kilter and a decade would pass before conditions stabilized.

THE LEGACY

Although Eagle-Lion ended up a costly mistake for Young, it proved an indispensable experience for Krim and Benjamin. Operating the company forced the pair into the trenches. They learned the hard way the world of independent production and the problems it had with financing. To keep going, Krim and Benjamin had to hone their analytical skills by evaluating the market value of all the creative ingredients that go into production. The success of UA under their management rested, in no small measure, on this ability.

Heading production in addition to distribution forced Krim to immerse himself in creative matters. The point needs underscoring, since this experience set him apart from the agents, television executives, and accountants who were later to head other major motion picture companies. It seems ironic therefore that UA, unlike its competitors, detached itself from production by giving independents complete autonomy over their work. It is fair to say that Krim learned to respect creative personnel and to understand that they sometimes do

United Artists' new management: (l. to r.) Robert S. Benjamin, Arnold M. Picker, Arthur B. Krim, Max E. Youngstein, and William J. Heineman

their best when left alone. Eagle-Lion also demonstrated to Krim and Benjamin the burdens of operating a studio. That UA did not own one, they never considered a liability; rather, they turned the situation to their advantage.

And finally, Eagle-Lion provided Krim and Benjamin with the nucleus of the new UA management team. Executive ranks of the old UA had been decimated; the personnel that remained were not particularly effective. Krim and Benjamin filled two top positions with former Eagle-Lion colleagues—William J. Heineman, as vice president in charge of domestic distribution, and Max E. Youngstein, as vice president in charge of advertising, publicity, and exploitation—the same positions they held at Eagle-Lion. To fill out the roster, Krim and Benjamin chose Seymour Peyser, a member of the Phillips, Nizer law firm, as general counsel; Arnold Picker, former head of the foreign department at Columbia, as vice president in charge of foreign distribution; and Charles Smadja, a veteran of the French film industry, as European sales manager. Heading the team, Krim served as president and Benjamin as chairman of the board. And as *Fortune* magazine pointed out, their responsibilities often overlapped and intertwined: "The two men chiefly responsible for the new look in Hollywood are rarely mentioned separately by anyone in the industry. No line separates their duties. One man picks up today where the other left off yesterday."[45] Typically, though, Krim handled negotiations with producers while Benjamin supervised company finances by acting as liaison with the banks and Wall Street.

Like the original company, the new UA was a cooperative venture, but this time for the benefit of management. Krim and Benjamin gave partnerships to the management team by cutting the members in on the deal with Chaplin and Pickford. Top members of the team received the same salary, $52,000 a year. As a gesture of fair play, Krim and Benjamin acted as one and drew $26,000 a year each. Like the arrangement with Eagle-Lion, Krim and Benjamin's salary was paid to the Phillips, Nizer law firm, which now served as outside legal counsel to the company. The compensation was modest by industry standards, but the reward would come through stock ownership by making a success out of UA.

C H A P T E R   T W O

Gambling on
Independent Production

Krim and Benjamin moved into UA headquarters located at 729 Seventh Ave., New York. The cracks in the studio system had deepened. The retrenchment programs that started in 1947 had accelerated as the majors pink slipped contract personnel, cut back on production, and reduced overhead wherever possible. But the majors fought fiercely to keep top talent. In this era of spiraling production costs, shrinking audiences, and industry fragmentation, the insurance value of stars became more important than ever. Many of the boxoffice favorites had lost their luster and were given their free-lance papers. Studios kept the big stars tethered by offering profit-participation deals. By 1949, the practice had become common. In one issue of *Variety* alone, the trade paper reported that Warner Brothers and Paramount had struck deals with John Garfield, Danny Kaye, Milton Berle, Bob Hope, and Bing Crosby that gave away profit shares as high as 33 percent. The most famous deal of the period was negotiated by Lew

Wasserman, MCA talent agency chief, who won 50 percent of the profits for his client, Jimmy Stewart, to star in *Winchester '73* (1950). Stewart pocketed $600,000 from this hugely successful Western and set talent champing at the bit.[1]

To keep top producers and directors in tow, the majors formed semi-autonomous production units that offered the lure of creative authority in addition to a share of the profits. Partially an economy measure, this shift in the method of studio operation to unit production reduced the need for front-office supervisory executives. In addition, the shift attempted to find a way to produce better-quality films that had some individuality and character. The amount of autonomy and profits a studio offered a producer or director depended on his track record. Nonetheless, the autonomy had "a mighty big string attached to it." Since the studio provided the financing for production and would naturally have the final say, said *Variety,* the success of the system rested on "how much the studio topper keeps out of a [filmmaker's] hair."[2]

For those filmmakers who ventured into independent production, conditions were still hazardous. During the postwar recession in the film industry, only a few independents came through with pictures that found acceptance at the boxoffice. Most producers barely got by and a not unconsiderable number lost money. As *Variety* pointed out, "Financial men are convinced that the cost structure of picture-making is out of line with today's market potential and thus that independent production is currently too risky for bank financing."[3]

Competition for talent and scarcity of bank financing were the principal barriers to entry facing Krim and Benjamin. But on the plus side, they had the UA name. The name was worth a fortune in recognition and acceptance. Said Krim, "Even though our pictures might be no better than Eagle-Lion's at first, we knew that a star wouldn't say I won't work with United Artists or that a theater circuit wouldn't say you don't belong here."[4]

The new management also benefited from the historic *Paramount* decision handed down by the Supreme Court in 1948. After ten years of litigation, the *Paramount* antitrust case had come to a conclusion. The court outlawed unfair distribution trade practices and mandated that the five vertically integrated film companies divorce their theater chains from their production and distribution branches. Thereafter, the Big Five could no longer give one another preferential treatment and usurp the playing time of the best theaters. Although every motion picture company could thereafter compete on an equal basis at the exhibition level, the *Paramount* case was no panacea. If UA expected access to first-run theaters, it had to have a product that could compete with anything the majors produced. For even though the divorced circuits were now required by the court to deal with their former studios at arm's length, which is to say the circuits could not give them preferential treatment, these circuits, as publicly held companies, had the fiduciary responsibility of maximizing profits by booking the best pictures available.

THE OFFENSIVE STRATEGY

In devising a plan of operation, Krim and Benjamin took the offensive. According to Michael Porter, such a strategy "is designed to do more than merely cope with the forces themselves [within an industry]; it is meant to alter their causes."[5] As the smallest company of the eight majors, UA's objective was to increase its market share. As Porter puts it, "slow industry growth turns competition into a market share game for firms seeking expansion."[6] As Hollywood retrenched in the face of television, UA turned the situation to its advantage by differentiating itself from the majors.

This was the plan: in return for distribution rights, UA would offer talent complete production financing, creative control over their work, and a share of the profits. In essence, UA would go into partnership with its producers. The company and a producer had to agree on the basic ingredients—story, cast, director, and budget—but in the making of the picture, UA would give the producer complete autonomy including the final cut. Talent would have to defer much of their salary until the picture broke even, but UA would help keep production costs down by not charging any administrative overhead, which at another company could boost budgets by as much as 40 percent. Since UA owned no studio, a producer could make his picture anywhere in the world to suit the needs of the story or the economics of the venture. Moreover, a UA producer could keep more of the money his pictures earned. UA's brand of independent production gave ownership of the picture to the producer, which enabled him to enjoy substantial income-tax advantages. Moreover, UA would not force talent into long-term contracts. Contracts with UA were to be nonexclusive, which meant that a producer would not have to go forward with a project until he was satisfied with the terms and circumstances of the venture.

Production Financing under the Old Regime

This decision to finance independent production marked a radical departure from the old UA. Formerly, UA producers had to secure production financing on their own. The rationale had been that UA's greatest strength resided in its policy of treating each of its producers equally. Should the company have a profit participation in any of its pictures, charges of favoritism would surely arise.

UA's producers, as a result, were left to their own devices. During the thirties, only the Bank of America and a few other institutions were willing to finance independent production. Even then, they limited their business to established producers like Sam Goldwyn or David O. Selznick and minimized risks by making residual loans. As preconditions for such a loan, the banks required a producer to have a distribution contract and completed pictures already in distribution. The former guaranteed that the proposed project would be marketed; the latter served as collateral to make good the loan. To secure the actual loan, the producer had to mortgage the proposed picture, plus one or two of the completed pictures, and to pledge the residual profits from the old ones and all the revenue from the new one. These conditions made it extremely difficult to break into the business and help explain why so few first-rank independents existed in this period.

The situation changed during World War II. The increase in demand for motion pictures convinced the banks that any feature distributed by a major company would always return around 60 percent of its production cost. This amount became the limit a bank would loan and was available to independents at regular interest rates. As Janet Wasko explains, "banks followed this policy of lending a percentage of a picture's negative cost without depending on past films to secure a loan. In other words, actual production loans rather than residual loans were arranged."[7] Bankers used a rule of thumb based on the expectancy that any "A" film would gross $1 million. Figuring the distribution fee at 25 percent and print and advertising costs at $150,000, the producer's share would amount to $600,000. Thus, banks typically would offer as "first money" 60 percent of the expected gross—up to $600,000—leaving the producer to come up with the "second money" and "end money" to complete the financing.

Although the war brought new entrants into independent production, most were speculators of various stripes. Out of desperation to secure quality product, UA helped finance Jimmy Cagney and Hunt Stromberg, a former MGM producer. UA had departed from its long-standing policy only twice before. In 1936, the company financed Walter Wanger Productions by setting up a $1 million revolving fund from the Bank of America. In 1941, UA borrowed $1.2 million to salvage Alexander Korda's *To Be or Not to Be*. But in all these ventures, the company lost money—a perpetual reminder of the hazards of production financing.

In lieu of financing, UA offered special distribution terms. UA's standard domestic distribution fee was 30 percent of the gross. Pickford and Chaplin, as owners, received the best terms—straight 10 percent distribution fees. To a select group of producers, UA gave sliding-scale terms beginning at 25 percent and decreasing to 10 percent. In other words, the more money a picture brought in, the less UA charged as a distribution fee. The theory was that a successful picture would pay the cost of distribution despite the lower fee. It sounded like a great idea, but in practice it didn't work. For example, UA's domestic gross in 1946 was the highest up to that time, but the company barely broke even. The vast amount of UA's business was being done at 10 percent rather than at the break-even point of 22 percent. Thus, although the rest of the industry earned extraordinary profits during the war, UA just barely limped along. After the banks declared a holiday on the financing of independent production in 1948, UA faced an insoluble product crisis that caused its near demise by 1950.

The Search for Product Begins

Starting out, Krim and Benjamin could not look to the banks for support. The new regime had to stabilize the company first and prove that its formula for independent production could work. Heller put up a $3 million line of credit, most of which could be used for production financing. Heller could be tapped for either first money, risk money, or a combination of the two. Loans were made at Krim's recommendation and in general could not exceed $200,000 for an average picture. In return, Heller took a profit participation of around 10 percent and charged interest on the loan.

The immediate task facing the new management was to keep the company afloat while it searched for product. To pay the fixed overhead of maintaining UA's worldwide operation, the company had to do $270,000 in business a week. When Krim and Benjamin stepped in, however, UA's billings had dropped to an all-time low of about $140,000 a week. This weekly shortfall of $130,000 could have sunk the company in a short time. The $500,000 loan from Spyros Skouras helped meet operating expenses and provided UA some breathing space.

UA had only a handful of pictures in release at the time of the take-over and prospects for lining up additional product looked grim. A few UA producers had pictures ready to go but were afraid to turn them over to a dying company. In the event of a UA receivership or bankruptcy, both of which looked imminent, they would lose everything. Krim assured them that there would be no receivership and no bankruptcy. He also had to remind them that their contracts were still in force. As a result, Krim could announce straight off the release of eight new pictures, among them Harry Popkin's *Second Woman,* I. G. Goldsmith's *The Scarf,* and two from Robert Stillman, *Sound of Fury* and *Queen for a Day.*

Saving the day for UA was Krim and Benjamin's friend, Matty Fox. Fox was starting a company called Motion Pictures for Television. He needed product and he knew that it would not come from the majors. But UA owned a small film library that included some old Walter Wanger pictures that had long been played out. These were what Matty Fox needed and he acquired them in a roundabout way: he proposed to Eagle-Lion that they should cut their losses by selling out to UA. UA would pay the company $500,000. Where could UA get the money? From Matty Fox. In return for the television distribution rights to the UA package, Fox agreed to pay UA $500,000 over two years, money UA could use to pay off Eagle-Lion over three years. Everyone was pleased with the deal, especially UA, which saw a competitor voluntarily go out of business. As a UA memorandum put it, "The great intangible of the value of the deal is that the only real competitor of the company is removed and that the position of United Artists is strengthened immeasurably both in making deals and in obtaining better deals."[8]

UA acquired over 200 pictures in the deal, which included the PRC library in addition to Eagle-Lion releases. A substantial number of pictures still showed some life, and from these, UA collected the tailings, that is, the residual rentals. UA placed the current pictures, which numbered around twenty, on its 1951 roster. These Eagle-Lion pictures consisted of programmers from Jack Schwarz, a half dozen British imports from J. Arthur Rank, which included Ronald Neame's *Oliver Twist* and Michael Balcon's *The Blue Lamp,* and independent productions from Sam Spiegel, Benedict Bogeaus, and Joseph Justman, among others. Despite their lackluster quality, the quantity of Eagle-Lion pictures grossed $200,000 a week and kept UA afloat. Their great tangible value enabled the new UA in the very first year to turn a respectable profit of $313,000. After the company commissioned Price Waterhouse & Co. to verify the results, Krim and Benjamin purchased 50 percent of UA for $8,000.

Two prestige pictures came UA's way rather unexpectedly the first year, which gave the fledgling company a much-needed boost. These pictures were Sam Spiegel's *The African Queen* (1951) and Stanley Kramer's *High Noon* (1952). A Polish-born promoter and independent producer, Spiegel had joined forces with John Huston in 1948 to form an independent production company called Horizon Pictures. UA distributed two of Horizon's first efforts in 1951, *The Prowler*, directed by Joseph Losey, a leftover from the previous regime, and *When I Grow Up*, which came as part of the Eagle-Lion package. Spiegel had started *The African Queen* project in 1949 by purchasing the rights to the C. S. Forester novel from Warner Brothers and by hiring acclaimed film critic James Agee to work with Huston on the screenplay. He secured financing from Romulus Films, Ltd., a British film distributor headed by James and John Woolf, which put up £250,000. In return, Romulus acquired the distribution rights to the picture in the Eastern Hemisphere.

Spiegel had contacted Krim early in 1950 when Krim was between motion picture jobs to inquire if any "financial types" might be interested in handling the picture in this country.[9] Now, as head of UA, Krim could answer in the affirmative. To acquire the picture, Krim went to Heller for a loan of $330,000 for advertising and publicity. After the release, UA kicked in an additional $200,000 to hype the ecstatic critical reception. Playing a gin-soaked skipper, Humphrey Bogart won an Academy Award, the first in the UA regime. "Never in the history of UA (and that history included the handling of such pictures as *Red River, Since You Went Away,* and *Spellbound*) have such terms been obtained from the big first-run circuits," Benjamin told Spiegel. UA originally predicted a gross of $3 million, but eventually *The African Queen* brought in $4.3 million. Results like this could not have been achieved at Eagle-Lion.

High Noon was another carryover from the old UA. Now ensconced at Columbia, Kramer still owed UA a picture on his five-picture contract. Losing Kramer to Columbia had been a blow to the company. Kramer had built a solid reputation as an independent who could keep costs low and bring in profitable pictures that earned critical respect. Forming a production company in 1948 called Screen Plays Corporation, Kramer started off with *Champion* (1949), based on a Ring Lardner short story, scripted by Carl Foreman, and directed by Mark

Robson. Shot in twenty days at a cost of $500,000, the picture made a star out of Kirk Douglas and earned a healthy profit. Kramer then produced *Home of the Brave* (1949), another Robson-Foreman combination. The picture was based on Arthur Laurents' Broadway play depicting the strains and tensions of a Jewish soldier during the war and his postbattle breakdown. Kramer changed the hero into a black soldier. Timely and profitable, *Home of the Brave* started a cycle of black problem pictures. *The Men* (1950) marked the entry into the company of a new director, Fred Zinnemann, and a new backer, Sam Katz, the veteran showman, founder of the Balaban & Katz theater chain, and former Paramount executive, who brought in $2 million of financing. The picture also marked the screen debut of Marlon Brando, who played a paralyzed ex-serviceman. *Cyrano de Bergerac* (1951) won critical acclaim, primarily because of José Ferrer who duplicated for the screen his successful Broadway role. He won an Oscar for his performance, but the picture, which cost $1.1 million, lost about $300,000. Kramer suffered a heavy loss on *Cyrano*. "The independent producer can't afford what department stores call a loss leader," he said. "One of these will put him out of business." [10]

The decision to give *High Noon* to UA actually rested with Columbia's studio chief, Harry Cohn. Looking over Kramer's list of properties, Cohn decided that Kramer should produce "the western without action" to fulfill his UA commitment. Kramer also had doubts about the picture—even with Gary Cooper in the lead. *High Noon*, of course, was a great hit and grossed $12 million. The New York Film Critics awarded *High Noon* best picture of 1952 and named Fred Zinnemann best director. In the Academy Award sweepstakes it was nominated for best picture; Gary Cooper won an Oscar as did the ballad "High Noon," composed by Dimitri Tiomkin with lyrics by Ned Washington. Grace Kelley, playing her first leading role in this picture, became a star.

The new UA was off to a brilliant start, but *The African Queen* and *High Noon* alone could not clear the company for financing from the banks. Krim and Benjamin realized that if UA was ever going to make it, they had to do something bold. Independent production had been hailed "as a kind of cure-all for what ails Hollywood, both artistically and commercially." It also had been praised "as a source of new freedom, new talent, and new ideas." [11] For example, when Frank Capra and partners William Wyler and George Stevens formed their independent production company, Liberty Films, in 1946, Capra announced that independent productions would be different—they would have individuality. Of his company, he said, "each one of these producers and directors has his own particular ideas on subject matter and material,

Humphrey Bogart and Katharine Hepburn in *The African Queen* (1951), produced by Sam Spiegel and directed by John Huston. Bogart won the Oscar for best actor.

Gary Cooper in *High Noon* (1952), produced by Stanley Kramer and directed by Fred Zinnemann. Cooper won the Oscar for best actor.

and the manner in which it should be treated. And each one, on his own and responsible only to himself, will as an independent producer have the freedom and liberty to carry out these ideas in the manner he feels they should be executed." [12]

Capra's idyllic description of independent production could not bear close scrutiny, but it illustrates the expectations talent had for independent production. UA could not succeed by offering money alone. Management had to devise a means of capturing the allegiance of talent as well. Under Krim and Benjamin's guidance, independent production gave the company flexibility. By selectively providing financing to a host of projects that were being submitted to it by agents, producers, and entrepreneurs of all kinds, UA played the role of a maverick by starting trends, by taking on the forces of repression in Hollywood, and by investing in some offbeat pictures.

PROMOTING 3-D

To stir up interest in the movies, the industry devised a number of strategies to help the boxoffice. Most of these strategies involved experiments with screen size and depth illusion. The revolution began in 1952 with the introduction of Cinerama and 3-D. Although both were comparatively short-lived, they provided business a shot in the arm and, if nothing else, proved that the public was not literally chained to the television set.

UA had the dubious distinction of promoting 3-D. On the heels of Cinerama, 3-D hit the market with the production of Arch Oboler's *Bwana Devil* in November 1952. The invention of Milton Gunzberg, the three-dimensional process (3-D), which he dubbed Natural Vision, required two projectors to exhibit and Polaroid glasses for the audience. This stereoscopic method, as opposed to the panoramic method of Cinerama, was regarded by the trade as the true third dimensional experience.

Arch Oboler, a former radio dramatist best known for a nighttime horror and suspense series called "Lights Out," introduced Natural Vision to the public. Using his savings and whatever he could borrow, Oboler scraped together $300,000 to produce the picture. At first, he even had to arrange his own distribution, since none of the big companies was willing to touch it. They might have been afraid of rendering their film libraries obsolete, but then again, they might have

Publicity poster for Arch Oboler's *Bwana Devil* (1952)

wanted someone else to take the financial risks of promoting an un-tested innovation. The entrenched firms had everything to gain and little to lose following such a strategy.

Bwana Devil opened in tandem at the Los Angeles Paramount and the Hollywood Paramount in November 1952. Although the picture was ineptly made with color mismatches and scenes out of focus, the public loved it. As *Variety* said, "for all its production quality short-comings, [*Bwana Devil*] may well prove to be as historic in its box office hypo as was Jolson's *Jazz Singer* and Foy's *Lights of New York*."[13] Oboler solicited bids for the distribution rights to the picture and the winner was UA. In acquiring worldwide rights to the picture in January 1953, UA paid Oboler $500,000 as a down payment and guaranteed him another $1,250,000 after the picture was placed in release.

In the wake of *Bwana Devil*, other studios jumped on the 3-D band-wagon, producing pictures in Naturescope, Paravision, Tri-Opticon, in addition to Natural Vision and other stereoscopic techniques. (Re-quirements for equipping a theater for 3-D were minimal: a high-intensity reflective screen—or the old one painted aluminum—and an interlocking system for the projectors.) A string of 3-D hits such as Warner's *House of Wax*, Paramount's *Sangaree,* and Universal's *It Came from Outer Space* silenced the skeptics for a while, but as Jack Warner said of 3-D, "It's a novelty, good for a fast dollar at the box office."[14]

It wasn't the Polaroid glasses that bothered audiences about 3-D—it was the puerile plots. Producers were unwilling to experiment with the truly creative potential of this innovation. By February 1954, *Variety* asked "What's happened to 3-D?" A check of the major studios re-vealed that not a single one was making a 3-D film, nor did any of them contemplate putting one in the works.[15] As for UA, which had such high hopes for *Bwana Devil* that it ordered 10 million Polaroid spec-tacles, it ended up with a loss on the picture of $200,000. Nonetheless, the venture enabled the fledgling company to become a player in the widescreen sweepstakes. The publicity value alone was worth the loss.

CHALLENGING THE AMERICAN LEGION

Chaplin and the Legacy of HUAC

UA anticipated publicity of an entirely different sort when it took on Chaplin's *Limelight* in 1952. Five years had passed since the company released Chaplin's previous picture, *Monsieur Verdoux,* but the con-

Charles Chaplin in *Limelight* (1952)

troversy it engendered was still vivid. The critical reception from the
daily press after the opening on April 11, 1947, had been hostile: "It
has little entertainment weight, either as somber symbolism or sheer
nonsense . . . It is also something of an affront to the intelligence"
(Howard Barnes in the *Herald Tribune*); "The film is staged like an
early talkie with fairly immobile camera, self-conscious dialogue, act-

ing that looks like the late twenties . . . an old-fashioned production, almost quaint in some of its moments" (Eileen Creelman in *The Sun*); "It is slow—tediously slow—in many stretches and thus monotonous" (Bosley Crowther in the *New York Times*).[16]

Chaplin's popularity had sunk to its all-time low as a result of the sensational lawsuits involving Joan Barry, the Mann Act, and the paternity of her child, and rising resentment over Chaplin's so-called pro-Communist stand during the war. Chaplin received a special dose of notoriety in 1947 when he learned from the newspapers that he was being called to testify before the House Un-American Activities Committee (HUAC), which was beginning a probe into the Communist infiltration of the motion picture industry. HUAC member John E. Rankin called for Chaplin's deportation: "He has refused to become an American citizen. His very life in Hollywood is detrimental to the moral fabric of America." By deporting him, said Rankin, "he can be kept off the American screen and his loathsome pictures can be kept from the eyes of American youth."[17]

In response to the news that he would be called to testify, Chaplin sent the following telegram to HUAC's chairman, J. Parnell Thomas:

> From your publicity I noted that I am to be "quizzed" by the House Un-American Activities Committee in Washington in September. I understood I am to be your "guest" at the expense of the taxpayers. Forgive me for this premature acceptance of your headlined newspaper invitation. You have been quoted as saying you wish to ask me if I am a Communist. You sojourned for ten days in Hollywood not long ago and could have asked me the question at that time, effecting something of an economy. Or you could telephone me now—collect. In order that you be completely up-to-date on my thinking I suggest that you view carefully my latest production "Monsieur Verdoux." It is against war and the futile slaughter of our youth. I trust you will not find its humane message distasteful. While you are preparing your engraved subpoena I will give you a hint on where I stand. I am not a Communist. I am a peace-monger.[18]

HUAC postponed Chaplin's appearance three times, then let the matter drop. But there followed a hate campaign of frightening proportions, led primarily by the Catholic War Veterans and the American Legion. These and other pressure groups succeeded in instituting boycotts against the picture. First the Independent Theatre Owners Organization in Columbus, Ohio, representing 325 theaters, called on theater owners "to give serious thought to the matter of withholding screen time" from *Monsieur Verdoux*.[19] Then Loew's and certain of the Paramount affiliates refused to supply play dates. *Monsieur Verdoux* had played only 2,075 dates and had grossed a mere $323,000 when Chaplin ordered it withdrawn from distribution two years later. Even though the picture grossed more than $1.5 million abroad, Chaplin felt that the UA sales force was responsible for its poor domestic showing, with the result that he lost confidence in his company.

The legacy of the HUAC investigation of Hollywood is well known. After the 1947 hearings, the leaders of the film industry found it in their economic best interests to capitulate to the Red Scare by instituting a blacklist that hung like a pall over Hollywood for ten years. HUAC investigated Hollywood a second time in 1951. These hearings continued sporadically until 1954, during which time prominent industry figures named names of people they knew as Communists. The blacklist grew. HUAC's hold on public opinion continued to grow in response to a series of national and international events: the fall of China to the Communists, the first successful atomic explosion by the Soviets, the outbreak of the Korean War, the rise of Joseph McCarthy, and the conviction of Alger Hiss. The combined forces of these events helped the committee achieve the goal of eradicating liberalism and radicalism in Hollywood.

The American Legion's role in dealing with the Red menace has been described by John Cogley in his *Report on Blacklisting*.[20] The Legion had long been concerned about Communism in Hollywood, but after the 1951 HUAC hearings, the organization stepped up the attack. The Legion published the names of over 300 industry personnel with alleged past Communist associations and circulated the list among the studios. Later, the Legion even functioned as a tribunal to provide clearances for those wanting to be rehabilitated. Hollywood acceded to the Legion and similar pressure groups in order to remove the threat, real and imagined, of pickets outside theaters.

The Krim-Benjamin management had its first brush with the American Legion when UA distributed *High Noon*. During the production of the picture, Carl Foreman, the writer and associate producer, appeared before HUAC during the 1951 mass hearings. When asked the inevitable question, "Are you now or have you ever been a member of the Communist Party?" Foreman invoked "the diminished fifth," a variation of the Fifth Amendment protecting self-incrimination. Foreman testified that he was not now a party member, but declined to answer if he had been in the past. Intimidated by the appearance, Kramer bought out Foreman's interest in the company and removed Foreman's name as associate producer from the credits. However, guild regulations left Kramer no choice but to leave Foreman's credit for the screenplay.

Protesting Foreman's association with the picture, Robert A. Bunch, District Commander of the American Legion in Washington, D.C., told UA: "We feel that the continued employment of communists and communist sympathizers in the production of motion pictures is totally indefensible. This situation is assuming the proportions of a national scandal, particularly in view of the fact that America's young men are dying on the battlefields of Korea at the hands of the ideological brothers of the Hollywood communists."[21] UA responded that it did not produce the picture and as distributor it had the legal obligation to market it.

The Limelight *Crusade*

The disastrous results of the *Monsieur Verdoux* publicity campaign convinced Krim and Benjamin that it would be counterproductive to attack political pressure groups head on. For *Limelight,* they wanted to keep the watchdogs at bay and allow the public to decide the picture's fate. UA faced an uphill fight. Canvassing the press, UA learned that big-name columnists such as Walter Winchell, Dorothy Kilgallen, Ed Sullivan, and others would not mention Chaplin except unfavorably. UA also learned that the Hearst papers would reject stories on Chaplin and favorable publicity of any kind. From other sources, UA heard that the *American Legion Magazine* planned on publicizing an article by Victor Lasky rapping Chaplin and that the Catholic War Veterans voted to picket the picture. UA therefore devised a distribution strategy to neutralize right-wing pressure groups by convincing exhibitors it was in their best economic interests to play the picture. Specifically, this meant concentrating "on building up the New York campaign and the New York business to such heights that no exhibitor can refuse, for selfish reasons, to play the picture once he knows that it is doing absolute top business."[22]

Although Chaplin was happy to turn the management of UA over to Krim and Benjamin, he did not automatically give *Limelight* to the company. For one thing, Chaplin financed the picture on his own and was under no obligation to UA. For another, Chaplin did not like the new distribution fees. Under his old contract, he had to pay only 10 percent domestic. Because these special terms had nearly ruined the company, Krim had insisted on canceling UA's distribution contracts with the owners as a condition of the takeover. He wanted to make the standard 30 percent fee prevail. But after Chaplin threatened to take *Limelight* to another distributor, Krim compromised by lowering the fee to 25 percent. Chaplin then balked over the foreign rights.

Claire Bloom and Charles Chaplin in *Limelight* (1952)

Since Pickford had handpicked UA's key personnel in foreign markets, Chaplin wanted nothing to do with them. Krim explained that the new regime had conducted a thorough housecleaning overseas and operations were now in capable hands. Chaplin acquiesced but only after Krim lowered the foreign distribution fees to 25 percent as well. Since UA's fees in foreign markets averaged around 40 percent, Chaplin won an even greater concession. But Chaplin was much more popular abroad than in the United States and Krim wanted the picture to bolster UA's relationships with foreign exhibitors.

Krim had to make additional concessions. Chaplin wanted absolute right of approval over exhibition contracts with theater circuits and with theaters in key cities. The new UA had innovated by permitting an independent producer to review proposed exhibition contracts on his picture as they came in. If the producer disliked a deal, he had the right to negotiate better terms within a specified period of time. Chaplin's experience with *Monsieur Verdoux* had made him leery of the big circuits and Krim was sensitive to this. As a final concession, UA agreed to subordinate the money it planned to advance for prints and advertising to the recoupment of *Limelight*'s production loan. In a typical deal, the producer footed the bill for prints and advertising. As rentals came in, UA deducted its distribution fee from the gross first. The remainder then paid off print and advertising costs. Afterward, the net producer's share, as it was called, was applied to the production loan. Since Chaplin put up $900,000 of his own money to finance *Limelight*, UA, in a spirit of fair play as Chaplin's partner, acquiesced.

Unlike *Monsieur Verdoux, Limelight* did not lend itself to a hostile critical reaction. *Verdoux* was a comedy of murders, a *film noir*, completely unrelated to the Little Tramp. Based on the real life story of Monsieur Landru who married and murdered a succession of women, *Verdoux* contained black humor, adult subject matter, and world-weary, unsympathetic characters. *Limelight* told the story of an aging comedian who has lost contact with his audience and who is regenerated by the power of innocent love for an aspiring ballerina. There were many autobiographical elements in the picture and Chaplin, for reasons of his own, wanted the picture to premiere in London, the city of his birth. Having completed the picture at his studio in Hollywood, Chaplin sailed with his family to England in September 1952 to arrange the premiere.

While Chaplin was en route, Attorney General James McGranery announced that he had ordered the Immigration and Naturalization Service to hold and question Chaplin on his return in order to "determine whether he is admissable under the laws of the United States."[23] Although Chaplin had been issued a Certificate of Re-entry before he left for Europe, the announcement failed to specify charges. Later, McGranery revealed his motives: "[Chaplin] has been publicly charged with being a member of the Communist Party, and with grave moral charges, and with making statements that would indicate a leering, sneering attitude toward a country that has enriched him."[24]

The *New York Times* criticized McGranery's action in an editorial which said, "Those who have followed him through the years cannot easily regard him as a dangerous person. No political situation, no international menace, can destroy the fact that he is a great artist who has given infinite pleasure to many millions, not in one country but in all countries. Unless there is far more evidence against him than is at the moment visible, the Department of State will not dignify itself or increase the national security if it sends him into exile."[25]

The American Legion, however, commended the Attorney General and adopted a resolution on October 12, 1952, four days before *Limelight*'s world premiere, urging exhibitors to reject the picture until the Department of Justice concluded its investigation. This resolution, along with the suggestion that Legionnaires might want to picket their local theaters exhibiting *Limelight,* was duly posted in the 18,000 American Legion posts throughout the country.

UA tried to pacify the Legion by falling back on legalities. Bob Benjamin told Lewis K. Gough, the Legion National Commander, that UA had agreed to distribute *Limelight* after Chaplin had received his Re-entry permit and before the Attorney General announced the investigation. Benjamin also pointed out that postponing the distribution of the picture would violate UA's exhibition contracts with theaters across the country and leave the company open to lawsuits.[26]

The implication was that if Chaplin had not gotten his Re-entry permit, UA might not have distributed the picture. Gough's reaction is not known, but clearly Benjamin's argument did not appease the Legion. Only a total ban on the picture would. Gough explained the Legion's hostility to Chaplin to a press conference in February 1953: "We fought for our country in three wars," said Gough, "and since we didn't achieve our objectives, we continue to fight for them now. We are continuing our collective efforts for Americanism and adequate national security." How Chaplin's picture affected national security, Gough did not say. Replying to published charges that the Legion had no right to intervene in the Chaplin case, Gough said, "If you carry this thinking to its logical conclusion, you will permit Communists to write books, to paint murals, to infiltrate every branch of educational and cultural life."[27] Gough implied that Chaplin was a Communist, although he did not risk saying so directly.

The world premiere of *Limelight* took place on schedule at the Odeon Theatre, Leicester Square, London, on October 16, 1952. Proceeds went to charity—the Royal London Society for Teaching and Training the Blind. The Royal Family was represented by Princess Margaret. Later that month, Chaplin presented a Royal Command Film Performance to Her Majesty, Queen Elizabeth. *Limelight* played the Odeon, Leicester Square, for twelve weeks and broke boxoffice records there.

Chaplin flew to Paris where *Limelight* was scheduled to open in four theaters on October 31. Thousands of fans greeted him at the airport. Following the opening, President Vincent Auriol conferred on Chaplin the French government's highest accolade, the Legion of Honor. As of March 1953, more than 500,000 people had attended the Paris showings. From Paris, Chaplin traveled to Amsterdam, Stockholm, Brussels, Rome, and Oslo to open his picture. (On this European tour to promote *Limelight,* Chaplin was accompanied by Arthur Krim.) Every country bestowed honors on the great actor and everywhere anti-American elements used the opportunity of greeting Chaplin to flay American illiberality. *Limelight* did spectacular business overseas, grossing about $7 million. It was UA's first big picture and "was the making of our foreign organization," said Krim.

The domestic run, however, failed to live up to expectations. *Limelight* premiered in New York on October 23, 1952. UA showcased the picture in two theaters—the Astor, a Broadway house that catered to the masses, and the Trans-Lux, an intimate-sized theater on the upper East Side, frequented by the intelligentsia. In playing the picture in these theaters only, UA adopted a tough-to-see distribution strategy. Such a strategy, coupled with a heavy advertising and publicity campaign, was designed to build up boxoffice grosses and erode exhibitor resistance prior to opening the picture around the country for its first-run release.

But *Limelight* did only so-so business in New York. The reviews were mostly favorable. There were no demonstrations of any kind, no attacks by the press, and only a few telephone calls to theater managers. After three weeks, UA decided to showcase *Limelight* in San Francisco, another city with a reputation for tolerance. UA expected that the picture would perform as well as *The African Queen* and *High Noon,* but the first week *Limelight* grossed about half as much as the former and somewhat less than the latter. The *San Francisco Chronicle* reported that "patrons reacted either enthusiastically or with apathy . . . Both in New York and San Francisco, *Limelight* evidently attracted confirmed Chaplin fans who would see this comedian in anything, any time. This public is not large enough to support any first-run Hollywood release, however."[28]

The American Legion's campaign to halt the playing of *Limelight,* meanwhile, had received the support of the Veterans of Foreign Wars, the Amvets, the Catholic War Veterans, the Jewish War Veterans, and all sorts of Americanism committees. Organized opposition included picketing, threats, press conferences, and citizens' rallies. The Legion acquired another powerful ally in Howard Hughes, Board Chairman of RKO Pictures and principal stockholder in the RKO theater circuit. Hughes wrote the Legion's Hollywood Post 43 that although he had no legal control over the theaters, he would do his best to persuade management to "take the necessary legal measures to cancel all bookings of *Limelight.*"[29]

By now, UA considered *Limelight* a crusade, not a distribution venture. And when Loew's Theaters reversed its position and accepted the picture, UA believed it had finally achieved a breakthrough. Joe Vogel, the president of Loew's, had originally refused to take the picture for the same reason he had rejected *Monsieur Verdoux*—he was afraid of public reaction. This refusal had been "the keystone of national reluctance" to the exhibition of the picture, said Benjamin, but UA's sensitive handling of *Limelight* demonstrated that it was safe to play the picture. Although the Loew's bookings "could be the greatest impetus for the national playoff and could thus avoid another *Verdoux* catastrophe," Chaplin vetoed the deal. Benjamin told Krim, who was with Chaplin on his European tour, that "I find it almost impossible to understand how Chaplin can so damage the picture . . . if that's the way Chaplin wants it, why should we keep fighting the inevitable. I don't know what instinct in us keeps us fighting; perhaps it is the reluctance to let his business unfamiliarity not only ruin the picture in this market, but stamp a great artist as a failure in the U.S. For surely a failure for *Limelight* in the U.S. following on *Verdoux* will lead to that national conclusion."[30]

Following the New York premiere, *Limelight* played in only about 150 theaters in the domestic market by February 1953, whereas a hit would have normally played 2,500 theaters in such a period. "The power of an ignorant and irresponsible censorship has been demonstrated," said William Murray in *The Nation* to explain *Limelight*'s performance.[31] Political pressure accounted for exhibitor resistance to playing the picture, but to what extent is unclear. Unlike the press's treatment of Chaplin during the *Verdoux* campaign, influential newspapers and magazines and even dissident veterans' groups during the *Limelight* release showed a tolerance remarkable in the era of the Red Scare. For example, the politically conservative *American Mercury* ran an article by William Huie which concluded:

> If Mr. McCarran and Mr. McGranery have any evidence that he has violated our laws, if they can prove beyond reasonable doubt that he is a member of the Communist conspiracy against this free government, then they should confront him down at Ellis Island. But if all they can prove is that Chaplin is a stinker, then they are only repeating what has been common knowledge for thirty years, and they should leave the man and his family alone.[32]

Perhaps because the right was divided over "the Chaplin case," the Legion had second thoughts over taking punitive action against a person who had not been proven guilty of violating any U.S. laws. In the greater New York area, *Limelight* played sixty-five neighborhood houses "without any significant disturbances," reported *Variety*. "Reps of a local American Legion post picketed the RKO Marble Hill and Fordham Theatres only briefly . . . but beyond this exhibition of the pic was normal."[33]

In Washington, D.C., the Legion picketed the two theaters playing

Limelight. Legionnaires carried signs reading "Does Chaplin's Pro-Communist Record Deserve Public Support?" and "American Legion Suggests That You Consider Chaplin's alleged pro-Communist Record" and passed out handbills listing Chaplin's alleged pro-Communist affiliations. Although attendance on opening day was not up to expectations, the manager of the two houses reported that attendance "has been building since."[34]

In New Orleans, the Legion succeeded in forcing the RKO Orpheum to withdraw the picture, but *The Item*, New Orleans' leading afternoon paper, took the Legion to task for its behavior, stating that "the Legion has been a valuable advocate of American ideals . . . but in its actions of this kind does the community and the nation a disservice."[35]

Limelight grossed a disappointing $1 million in the U.S. If causes need to be found for the performance, we would have to consider Benjamin's assessment of Chaplin's business acumen and also the picture itself. If one classifies *Limelight* as an art film—and it is fair to consider it such—the resistance of exhibitors and audience is more credible. From this perspective, *Limelight* did well, since Americans had generally shown an aversion to art films. Regardless, UA gave the distribution of *Limelight* a good shot and in the process called the bluff of powerful political pressure groups.

Chaplin, for his part, did not kowtow to the Attorney General. Rather than defend his politics, Chaplin took up residence in Vevey, Switzerland, and did not return to the U.S. until 1972, when on the eve of his eighty-third birthday, he was invited back to attend a screening in his honor at Lincoln Center and to receive a special Oscar from the Academy.

TAKING ON THE PRODUCTION CODE

UA took on another industry watchdog when it released Otto Preminger's *The Moon Is Blue* without a seal of approval from the Production Code Administration (PCA) in 1953.[36] The Production Code was a covenant between Hollywood and the guardians of public morality, most particularly the Roman Catholic Church. Coauthored by Robert A. Lord, a Jesuit priest, and Martin Quigley, a Catholic layman and publisher of the influential trade magazine *Motion Picture Herald,* the Production Code was foisted on the industry in 1930. When Hollywood departed from the moralistic precepts of the Production Code during the Depression, the Catholic Church formed the Legion of Decency in 1934 with the goal of boycotting offensive pictures until the industry created a mechanism of enforcement. Exerting irresistible economic pressure, the Legion of Decency at the height of its crusade had gathered more than 11 million pledges of support from church members. Ever since, the Legion of Decency had been the chief "gun behind the door" forcing Hollywood to direct its powers of persuasion to preserving traditional concepts of morality.

Critics of the industry accused Hollywood of hiding behind the Production Code to avoid any serious treatment of significant social, political, and moral issues that might stir up trouble from pressure groups. Hollywood's timidity was self-serving, without a doubt. Moreover, the enforcement mechanism behind the Code guaranteed that the screen would remain noncontroversial; for a picture to play in a theater owned by the majors, it had to have a PCA seal of approval. In essence, the majors exercised censorship over the entire industry. An independent producer who hoped to establish his name and business by treating such pressing social problems as race relations or extremist politics could find access to the important theaters blocked.

The PCA had been challenged only once in the era before the *Paramount* decrees. UA was involved in the challenge. In 1946, UA agreed to distribute Howard Hughes's *The Outlaw*, starring Jane Russell.[37] Hughes had first released the picture on his own in 1943 rather than cut it to win the Code seal. It played only in San Francisco for a short run. The Legion of Decency added to its notoriety by giving it a condemned classification.

For UA to accept *The Outlaw*, Hughes had to resubmit the picture as well as the advertising material to the PCA. Hughes made the required cuts and UA prepared acceptable advertising copy. After the release, Hughes bypassed UA to let loose a vulgar campaign that highlighted Jane Russell's large and considerably exposed breasts. The ads contained pictures with such captions as "How Would You Like to Tussle with Russell?" and "What Are Two Great Reasons for Jane Russell's Rise to Stardom?" After the PCA revoked its approval of the picture, Hughes took the Motion Picture Association of America (MPAA) to court charging the association with restraint of trade in violation of antitrust laws. Hughes lost the case and the major circuits refused to handle the picture. Nonetheless, the censorship battle, the unsavory advertising, and the denunciations by the Church proved irresistible to independent theaters and the picture grossed $3 million by 1948. After the picture played itself out, Hughes "with typical perversity," in Richard Corliss's words, "cut a few of Miss Russell's deep-breathing sequences and submitted *The Outlaw* to the Legion for reclassification."[38] The Legion changed the rating from "C" to "B"—morally objectionable in part.

Hughes's antics were in keeping with his behavior as an eccentric millionaire and perhaps were even an embarrassment to UA. In any event, they hardly dented either the PCA or the Legion of Decency. Strictures over movie content were loosened somewhat as a result of the *Paramount* case. The majors, having severed their theaters, lost their power to enforce the Code. But in this era of declining movie attendance, exhibitors—the most conservative group in the industry— were not about to alienate the likes of the Legion of Decency. Even the historic *Miracle* case of 1952 did not alter the situation much. The Supreme Court in a unanimous decision read motion pictures into the First Amendment. Although this ruling was a "giant step forward toward removing all the shackles of censorship of the screen," in the opinion of MPAA head Eric Johnston, "still to be captured and permanently razed are the censorship hurdles constantly being erected by pressure groups, large and small." Said *Boxoffice* magazine, "They regularly spring into existence under the tattered banners of religious, moral or patriotic interest in motion pictures, but all too often and all too transparently they stem from selfish machinations and desires of individuals or organizations for headlines, self-aggrandizement or personal financial gain."[39]

And although the *Miracle* case served the Legion of Decency "the first great defeat of Catholic motion picture pressure" in Richard Corliss's opinion, the tactics used by the Church in attempting to ban Roberto Rossellini's *The Miracle* were imprinted on the minds of exhibitors. Francis Cardinal Spellman, speaking from the pulpit, had urged every Roman Catholic to boycott the picture. Overstepping his authority as a church official, he said, "if the present law is so weak and inadequate to cope with this desperate situation then all rightthinking citizens should unite to change and strengthen the federal and state statutes to curb those who would profit financially by blasphemy, immorality and sacrilege."[40] Catholic War Veterans picketed the Paris Theater in New York, where the picture was playing, and the manager of the theater received bomb threats and was harassed by Fire Department inspectors.

Joseph Burstyn, the distributor, fought the case in the courts, but, as a foreign-film distributor, he was on the periphery of the industry. If such a controversy had been ignited by a Hollywood film, the backlash, coming on the heels of divorcement, the HUAC investigations, and television, presumably might have proved disastrous. But UA successfully defied the Production Code when it distributed two pictures produced by Otto Preminger—*The Moon Is Blue* and *The Man with the Golden Arm*. Both were released without the MPAA seal of approval and both were enormously successful at the boxoffice.

The Moon Is Blue *Campaign*

Signing Preminger was quite a coup. Preminger had built his movie career during the forties as a producer-director for Twentieth Century–Fox. Describing this experience, he said, "I was turning out a string of films following rules and obeying orders, not unlike a foreman in a sausage factory."[41] Some of these films were *Laura* (1944), *Fallen Angel* (1945), and *Forever Amber* (1947). Despite having one of the best contracts on the lot in 1950, Preminger had had his fill of the studio system. However, he had five years remaining on his contract. Somehow he persuaded Zanuck to put him on half time so he could devote six months of the year to other projects. After reading Hugh Herbert's new play, *The Moon Is Blue,* Preminger decided to produce and direct it himself before bidding on the motion picture rights. Producers Richard Aldrich and Richard Myers coproduced the play with Preminger. *The Moon Is Blue* opened in 1951 at the Henry Miller Theatre, starring Barbara Bel Geddes and Barry Nelson.

In taking on *The Moon Is Blue* in 1952, UA did not anticipate trouble with the Breen Office. The play had settled in for a long run; duplicate companies had played Chicago and San Francisco; and road companies had toured the country—all without incident. But the Breen Office denied the picture a seal, a decision that was upheld by the MPAA board of directors. Moreover, the Legion of Decency condemned the picture and Cardinal Spellman denounced it as an "occasion of sin."

Otto Preminger has taken most of the credit for fighting the censorship of *The Moon Is Blue.* In his autobiography, for example, he said, "I made an unprecedented contract with United Artists for *The Moon Is Blue.* I demanded and received autonomy and the right to the final cut of the film. Nobody could overrule my decisions. I had at last the freedom I had always wished for."[42] Not only is this remark self-serving, it also obscures the relationship between a distributor and an independent producer.

To produce *The Moon Is Blue,* Preminger formed a partnership with Hugh Herbert, the author of the play. UA put up the financing, but the company's precarious condition forced it to follow a prudent course. Essentially, UA required the principal participants in the production to share the risks by deferring their fees—Preminger and Herbert, their producers' fees; Preminger, his director's fee; and Herbert and his Broadway producers, their fee for the movie rights. As a further condition, UA insisted that Preminger sign William Holden, a proven box-office attraction, to play the lead. Moreover, Preminger had to persuade Holden to forgo most of his usual salary and take a profit participation

Otto Preminger

instead. Total deferments came to nearly $500,000 but in return UA gave the Preminger-Herbert production team 75 percent of the profits, 20 percent of which they divided with Holden. The cash outlay to produce the picture, which included a German language version, came to less than $400,000. Despite the censorship controversy, UA could afford to take the financial risk of distributing the picture.

In agreeing to finance a picture, UA retained the right of approval over the basic ingredients and protected itself from receiving a picture that could not get through the distribution pipeline because of censorship problems. The distribution contract required the producer to secure a seal of approval from the MPAA and an "A" or "B" certificate from the Legion of Decency. If the producer was unwilling or unable to conform, UA retained the right to cut the picture appropriately. If the picture encountered censorship problems during release, the producer had to cut any scene as required, to shoot additional scenes, or to do retakes—whatever was necessary to insure that the picture reached the market. Preminger's statement that he received the right of the final cut does not say much, since every UA producer received the right to visualize the picture as he saw best. But a producer could do so only after the script and dialogue had been approved by UA. In the case of *The Moon Is Blue*, UA knew from the beginning what it was getting and *chose* not to capitulate to censorship forces. Instead, the company orchestrated a plan of attack to exploit the picture fully.

In deciding to distribute *The Moon Is Blue*, UA had to resign from the Motion Picture Association of America (MPAA), the industry's principal trade organization, which consisted of the Hollywood majors. As a condition of membership in the MPAA, companies had to uphold the Production Code, which was administered by the arm of the MPAA called the Production Code Administration (PCA). Myth has it that the picture was rejected by the PCA because of "blue" language—lines such as "Lots of girls don't mind being seduced," "Men are usually so bored with virgins," and "He called me a professional virgin—what an awful thing to say." Preminger himself might have been the source, because as he reported to Gerald Pratley, he told the press and the media that Darryl Zanuck offered to help cut the picture to conform to the Code. "After all, it's only six lines," he quotes Zanuck as saying, to which Preminger replied, "I can't, I have made a public statement that I want to test my right as a citizen of the United States to show this picture to the American public as I have done it." Preminger explained to Pratley, "It is not on the pretense that this little comedy would suffer if I took out a few lines—that had nothing to do with it. I made it like this, and I want to show it like this."[43]

For the PCA, the issues were of greater consequence than a few risqué lines. Jack Vizzard, a PCA staff member, said *The Moon Is Blue* violated two important clauses in the Code: (1) "Pictures shall not infer that low forms of sex relations are the accepted thing"; and (2) "Seduction is never the proper subject of comedy."[44] Actually, the PCA found the entire plot offensive. In Vizzard's opinion, the plot implies that "free love" is acceptable and that Maggie McNamara, an aspiring television actress Holden picks up and takes back to his apartment, is eccentric for being clean, an oddball for clinging to her virtue. Preminger and defenders of the film said that, on the contrary, the plot was moral. Maggie wins her man, with her virginity intact. She wins because she is decent and thus virtue triumphs. Reviewers agreed with this assessment, basically, but as Vizzard says, "those who could not understand the objections raised against the film were looking at the story from the opposite end of the telescope."[45]

Maggie McNamara, David Niven, Dawn Addams, and William Holden in Otto Preminger's *The Moon is Blue* (1953)

UA previewed the picture in Los Angeles to test public reaction in
two parts of town—the Academy Theatre in conservative Pasadena
and the Village Theatre in the university community of Westwood. The
report from the Village preview said "the audience reaction was tremendous. They were with the picture from beginning to end, laughed

so much that at times the dialogue was drowned out and at the end of the picture broke into spontaneous applause. Their comments as they left the theatre were as enthusiastic as any I have ever heard." [46]

Although audience response was everything UA had hoped, the company adopted a cautious distribution strategy. The world premiere in June 1953 was set for Chicago, where Maggie McNamara played in a duplicate stage production for sixty-one weeks. Immediately afterward, the picture was scheduled to open in New York, Los Angeles, and San Francisco. No other bookings were planned until the picture proved itself—developed "legs," as they say—in these limited engagements. *The Moon Is Blue* stood the best chance in these key cities; theater fans who enjoyed the play could generate favorable word-of-mouth and movie audiences were likely to be relatively sophisticated.

In a show of support, the trade press backed UA's decision to release the picture. *Film Daily,* for example, called it a "grownup romantic comedy number. Sets up audience for 99 minutes of delightful adult fun and diversion, delivers every moment of the way." [47] The daily press focused on the PCA decision. Bosley Crowther of the *New York.Times* said: "The theme of this confection is as moral as a Sunday school book. It is that virtue triumphs. The good little girl gets the man." [48] Perpetuating the blue-language myth, Louis Sobol of the *New York Journal-American* said, "The few fragments of racy dialogue are certainly nothing that will stir forbidden impulses. I've read bawdier stuff in court trials reported in our daily newspapers. It's about time the movies—like the stage, grew up. The public did, years ago." [49]

Cardinal Spellman ignited the controversy over the picture when he issued a pastoral letter to his archdiocese warning Catholics that attending *The Moon Is Blue* was an "occasion of sin" because it had been condemned by the Legion of Decency. In his opinion, the picture "bears a serious potential influence for evil, especially endangering our youth, tempting them to entertain ideas of behavior conflicting with moral law, inciting to juvenile delinquency." More disturbing to the Cardinal was the effrontery of the producer and distributor in defying the Code: "The presentation of this picture is not only in defiance of Industry Code regulations," he said, "but it is also a challenge to prove, if possible, that these regulations, established by the industry itself, may be defied with impunity." [50]

Afterward, *The Moon Is Blue* ran into trouble in several cities with heavy Roman Catholic populations—Detroit; Poughkeepsie; Atlanta; Lawrence, Massachusetts; and Jersey City. [51] In Jersey City, the picture encountered what is euphemistically described as "extralegal action." A UA branch manager filed this report after police confiscated the print at the Stanley Theatre, the largest house in the city:

Local police seized the print early in the morning and we wisely sent two prints. They reopened with the second print and it, too, was seized. The theater manager was arrested and is out on $500 bail. When they attempted to use a third print, a bunch of recognized hoodlums were sent to the theater to chop down the projection room if need be, in order to take the third print. The management recognized the hoods and rather than have his theater wrecked, not only the theater but the screen and walls, decided to give it up as a bad job and substituted a Warner picture. The case was then brought to the local courts and the judge would have allowed the picture to play providing that both sides could agree on a compromise of an age limit, which would have been wise, but the opposition refused to compromise and the judge had no alternative but to uphold the actions of the local authorities. The case is being appealed. The story hit all of the newspapers and I received telephone calls from the Post, Times, Herald, etc., plus the daily trades. Jersey City is one of the most corrupt cities in the United States, where there must be dozens of houses of prostitution, gambling halls and what not. Additionally, while it is only across the river from New York City, they also have wide open burlesque houses, which are even banned here, so that a woman, or a man, or a teenager can frequent them, while they are prevented from enjoying a wholesome comedy.[52]

An editorial in the *New York Post* remarked, "The judge had to choose between humiliating the police officials or deciding that the innocuous movie comedy was a menace to public morals. In saving the police official's face [referring to Safety Commissioner Bernard Berry, who had recently lost a battle to ban the Kinsey report], he has certainly blackened his judicial eyes."[53] Elmer Rice, the playwright, speaking on behalf of the American Civil Liberties Union (ACLU), insisted that members of the public who wished to see the picture should be allowed to see it: "Under our Constitutional protection of free speech all groups have the right to propagandize for their point of view," but, he added, "where public officials conform to these pressures, resulting in a denial to the rest of the community of their right to see the film, we must register our firm opposition."[54] UA appealed the decision, but the picture did not play the area for a year—until the case was won.

Censorship on the state level represented a greater threat. Censorship boards existed in seven states, including New York, Pennsylvania, and Ohio, which represented a substantial proportion of the domestic market. Surprisingly, there was no unanimity of opinion—four states passed the picture. Only the censorship boards of Maryland, Ohio, and Kansas banned it. Spurred by the *Miracle* decision, UA fought each ban in the courts.

The decision of the Maryland State Board of Motion Picture Censors stated, "The suggestiveness in situation and the indecency of the dialogue are apparent throughout the picture. From beginning to end there is a concerted attention of the audience drawn to only one thing—sex and seduction. The fact that the picture is brilliantly acted can only add to the impact of the foulness upon the thinking of people, *especially young ones,* who, through the film's specious appeal to their sense of humor, are subtly offered a set of morally indecent standards."[55] Appealing the decision, UA argued that the standards of the Code may not be appropriately applied by a government censor. The Code was formulated to avoid offending any group on moral, political, or social grounds; to invoke its standards as law is objectionable for the reasons laid down in the *Miracle* decision that forbade censoring a film as "sacrilegious" if it offended any religious group. A full trial in the Baltimore City Court resulted in a reversal.[56]

UA appealed the Ohio case to the state supreme court. In reversing the decision, the Ohio court cited a recent U.S. Supreme Court case concerning the banning of *La Ronde* and *M* by the New York and Ohio boards of censors, respectively.[57] Justice William O. Douglas, speaking for a unanimous court, said, "The argument of Ohio and New York that the government may establish censorship over motion pictures is one I cannot accept," for reasons the *Miracle* decision made clear. The Supreme Court had not abolished censorship boards, but afterward, in the words of *Variety,* "There will be a little more carefully-worded law and a lot of less capriciously motivated personality at work in the practice of cutting and classifying."[58]

The Kansas action was carried first to the state supreme court, which upheld the state statute governing the review board, and then to the U.S. Supreme Court, which reversed the decision *per curiam,* that is, by merely citing the *Miracle* case.[59]

UA fought ten censorship actions on behalf of *The Moon Is Blue* and won every case. The wider distribution the picture received as a result accounted for an additional $500,000 in rentals, bringing the total gross by the end of 1954 to over $4 million—a hit by any standard in this period.

The publicity from the censorship controversies generated most of the interest in the picture. Although *The Moon Is Blue* was shut out of many theaters, where it did play it broke boxoffice records. In Indianapolis, for example, UA's branch manager reported that the picture had been playing at the Esquire for an incredibly long time—twenty-three weeks—and had grossed $85,000. "With complete honesty," he said, "I must report that I can't see the end of the engagement."[60]

In waging its battle against censorship, UA exposed the Code for what it was—a self-serving moralistic document that had no basis in law and that represented perhaps a minority view regarding acceptable content for motion pictures. More important, the picture exposed the limits of the Catholic Church's hegemony over the moviegoing public. Nonetheless, the MPAA dared not discard the Production Code which had served the industry so well for nearly twenty years. Conservative as always, the industry predictably adopted a wait-and-see attitude.

The Man with the Golden Arm *Campaign*

UA and Preminger attacked the Code a second time by releasing *The Man with the Golden Arm* in 1955. Based on Nelson Algren's novel, winner of the National Book Award, the film depicted a heroin addict's road to recovery. Since the Code specifically proscribed any portrayal of the use of illegal drugs, it was evident from the start that the PCA would reject the picture. Nonetheless, UA agreed to put up the financing, but postponed the decision to distribute it until the finished picture could be evaluated. This option can be seen as an escape hatch for the company, but since the cash outlay for the picture was more than twice that of *The Moon Is Blue*—around $1 million—UA must have had confidence in the project. The controversial subject aside, the film teamed up two rising stars—Frank Sinatra, who staged a dramatic turnaround in his career by winning an Academy Award for his role in *From Here to Eternity,* and Kim Novak, who became an overnight sensation in *Picnic.*

The rough cut of *Golden Arm* convinced UA it had a commercial vehicle that could be an effective deterrent against drug addiction. UA was reinstated as a MPAA member and expressed to MPAA president Eric Johnston that the picture deserved a seal. Robert Benjamin, UA's chairman, said, "Although we believe there is no comparison between the recent television shows on drug addiction and *The Man with the Golden Arm,* we feel it may serve a useful educational purpose if you would suggest to your New York assistants that they screen two or three of these television kinescopes, which we could make available. They would, in this way, inform themselves of what is currently being shown gratis over television, available as it is, to the entire family, including children, and thus recognize the substantial contrast with *Golden Arm.*"[61]

The appeals board of the MPAA once again upheld the PCA, but the MPAA stated it did not want to close the door to future amendment of the Code. It was implicit that the MPAA did not want to act on a matter of principle under pressure of special pleading, reported *Variety.*[62] Another reason may have been the news that Twentieth Century–Fox had purchased the rights to Michael Gazzo's controversial Broadway play, *Hatful of Rain,* which also dealt with drug addiction.

UA went ahead with distribution plans and duly dropped out of the MPAA for the duration. To its surprise, the Legion of Decency gave the picture a "B" ("morally objectionable in part for all") instead of the anticipated condemned rating. Now even the top circuits that had refused to play *Moon* decided to defy the Code by booking *The Man with the Golden Arm.*

As *The Man with the Golden Arm* went into general release, it was passed by the censors in the U.S. and in Europe with the exception of Maryland, which ordered a cut two minutes long showing Frankie Machine (Frank Sinatra) rolling up his sleeve, preparing to take an injection which his drug dealer is preparing. The actual injection is not depicted; the camera focuses on his face, and afterward we see the needle removed from his arm. The Maryland board cited a state law that prohibited advocating or teaching the use of or methods of use of narcotics and habit-forming drugs. The Baltimore City Court upheld the board, but on appeal, the Court of Appeals of Maryland reversed the decision, stating that the movie, if anything, deterred the use of narcotics.[63]

The Production Code Administration revised the Code significantly in 1956 by lifting the taboos on narcotic traffic, abortion, prostitution, and kidnapping. Ordinary profanity was allowed when dramatically valid and used with discretion, and the PCA was permitted to be more "liberal" in interpreting the other rules. Regarding the changes, one line of thought held that the new Code signified the industry's willingness to recognize that the document needed updating. Another argued that nothing significant had been done—the MPAA could have gone a lot further. A third reaction came from Elmer Rice who, speaking for the ACLU, said: "This is no revision. It's merely a gesture in the direction of those who think the Code is obsolete. The changes made are trivial."[64]

That the industry did not want to position itself on the forefront of social change should be obvious. It preferred a prudent course that allowed other forms of expression—plays and novels—and the more sophisticated foreign films to test the waters. Meanwhile, the liberal Warren Court could whittle away at the authority of the censors. Not until 1968 was self-regulation replaced by the more rational classification system. Nonetheless, UA's role should not be minimized. As Douglas Ayer and his colleagues have noted, it took courage and foresight to produce and release *The Moon Is Blue* and *The Man with the Golden Arm:* "In the early Fifties . . . no one had acted upon the perception, if indeed the perception had occurred, that the seal might no longer be a prerequisite for the exhibition of Hollywood films on a nation-wide basis. The success of the films made clear that such a situation existed."[65]

A VOTE OF CONFIDENCE FROM THE BANKS

Playing the maverick, UA continued showing profits and, by 1953, a number of important banks such as Bankers Trust, Chemical Corn Exchange Bank, Bank of America, and the First National City Bank of New York agreed to bankroll the company. That is, the banks decided to finance UA's independent producers, using as collateral not only the individual picture, but UA's guarantee of payment. The banks reached this decision despite the fact that UA earned relatively modest profits the first three years, amounting to $313,000 in 1951, $414,000 in 1952, and $621,000 in 1953.

The change of heart by the banks stabilized UA's operations and enabled the company to move from exclusively one-shot ventures to multiple-picture deals to attract important stars, directors, producers, and writers to the fold. Afterward, UA operated not only as distributor but also as an important financier of independent production. In the period 1953 to 1957, UA released fifty pictures a year, on the average. The number of pictures financed by the company rose from twenty a year to forty-seven.

The banks had reversed a long-standing policy. Banks had earlier been willing to only finance independent production by putting up first money and on the condition that the producer had a distribution contract and funds to complete his picture. George Yousling of the Security—First National Bank of Los Angeles, a leading motion picture financier, wrote in 1948 that in approving a production loan, his bank considered two basic risks: the completion of the picture and the repayment of the bank loan. Concerning the former, the bank examined the cost consciousness of the producer, his track record, the experience of the director, and the reputation of the cast and production staff. Concerning repayment, the bank evaluated the distribution contract and the boxoffice potential of the picture and reserved the right to approve the script, cast, and budget. Further, it asked such questions as: (1) Is it of an extremely controversial nature from the religious, racial, or ideological points of view? (2) Does it deal with immoral or other censorable matters? (3) Is it a story that has limited appeal and attraction in this country or abroad?[66] Why the bank adopted this attitude is understandable. After all, it was interested not as much in art as in protecting its investment.

Now, in dealing with UA, the banks turned over these approvals to management. Explaining the behavior of the banks, Krim said to Pickford: "The banks' confidence has been generated by the prudence and care we ourselves have manifested in our operation by reinvesting our profits and keeping our expenses down to the minimum consistent with efficient management."[67] But in retrospect, Krim understated the accomplishment. UA had built a reputation by defying conventional wisdom and industry practices. Financial institutions were saying in effect that UA represented the wave of the future.

SIGNING STARS

During the fifties, styles, genres, and even screen size changed, but a constant in the motion picture business was the insurance value of certain stars. Stars, in fact, became more important than ever. In this era of spiraling production costs, shrinking audiences, and industry fragmentation, financing a picture of any consequence without a name of proven boxoffice worth would have been unthinkable. Talent agents were quick to capitalize on the situation. Prior to the fifties, talent agents played a marginal role in the industry. At best, they succeeded in negotiating higher salaries for their clients during contract renewals. It was the studio that nurtured talent, selected properties to develop, and took the long view in building careers. But during retrenchment, the studios abrogated these functions, and in so doing, relinquished power to the talent brokers.

To capture its first big star, UA nearly had to give away the store. UA signed Burt Lancaster to a multiple-picture contract in June 1953 that provided full financing, 75 percent of the profits, an overhead allowance to develop properties, and, most notably, special distribution terms of 25 percent domestic. Since Krim had proclaimed to the industry that UA would never budge from the standard domestic fee of 30 percent (except for Chaplin), this concession was kept a secret and referred to inside the company as the "Lancaster terms."

Burt Lancaster in *Apache* (1954), presented by Hecht-Lancaster and directed by Robert Aldrich

The Rise of MCA

Negotiating the deal on behalf of Lancaster was Lew Wasserman, the president of the most powerful talent agency in the business, MCA. Known in the trade as the Octopus, MCA had more big-name clients than any other agency, with tentacles into nightclubs, Broadway, radio, motion pictures, and television.[68] Founded as The Music Corporation of America in 1924, MCA was the production of two men: Jules Stein, who built it from an insignificant booker of bands into the world's strongest talent agency; and Lew Wasserman, who in 1946, at the age of thirty-three, succeeded Stein as president. Bob Benjamin told *Fortune* that Wasserman was: "one of the two or three smartest men in the industry." *Fortune* magazine said, "he knows finance, he knows taxes, he knows the law" and quoted an industry executive as saying, "he knows more about your problems than you do yourself . . . He sits and reasons the whole thing out in dollars and tells you exactly how you can make it pay." Concluded *Fortune*, "This means of course, that he also knows precisely what the traffic will bear, which makes him a ruthless negotiator."[69]

In partnership with William Goodheart, Jules Stein organized the chaotic band business during the twenties and capitalized on the postwar entertainment boom. Starting out in Chicago as a booker collecting 10 percent commissions, Stein offered to bill bands under their leader's names in return for exclusive representation rights. Stein then convinced nightclub operators and hotel managers that rotating bands would draw larger crowds and new business. After the plan proved spectacularly successful, Stein introduced the exclusive deal whereby MCA, in a form of block booking, secured from operators of amusement places the sole right to book talent into their spots. By guaranteeing a continuous flow of product at the right prices, MCA assured itself a steady market for its clients and attracted new names to the fold. MCA represented around 65 percent of the major bands in the U.S. by the late thirties, including Harry James, the Dorseys, Guy Lombardo, Kay Kyser, and Benny Goodman.

Around 1938, Stein branched out into practically the whole gamut of marketable talent. This meant all-out war with all other agencies, particularly with the William Morris Agency. Stein had two protégés to assist him, David (Sonny) Werblin, who was in charge of the New York office, and Lew Wasserman, in charge of the Hollywood office. Both men were considered the greatest agents in the trade.

Control of the band business led quite naturally into representing singers, comedians, jugglers, and other performers. Soon MCA was packaging complete shows for both nightclubs and radio. Package deals were akin to exclusive-booking agreements, with the added advantage of enabling MCA to make much more profit than the standard 10 percent commission. In a radio-package deal, MCA offered an entire radio show—star, orchestra, announcer, writer, guest stars, and even a producer—all tied up in one neat package and ready to go on the air. Using this gambit, MCA abandoned the role of agent to become an employer of sorts. MCA hired its own clients for these shows and sold the packages for lump sums. The difference between what MCA paid for the ingredients of the shows and what it received from sponsors went into MCA's pockets. By the forties, MCA had a hand in more than ninety radio shows a week, ranging from the highest-rated coast-to-coast headliners down to soap operas. Among MCA's radio clients were Charlie McCarthy–Edgar Bergen, Frank Sinatra, Eddie Cantor, Jack Carson, Rudy Vallee, Abbott and Costello, and the Great Gildersleeve.

MCA's entry into the movie business was accomplished principally by buying out several other agencies. From agencies that wouldn't sell out or weren't worth buying, MCA bought individual contracts. The company's most important acquisition came in 1945, when it bought the Hayward-Deverich Agency in New York for about $4 million. Headed by Leland Hayward, this was the prestige company of the agency business, whose 200-odd clients included Fredric March, Ethel Merman, Barbara Bel Geddes, Henry Fonda, Jimmy Stewart, and Billy Wilder.

In acquiring the Hayward-Deverich Agency, MCA took Leland Hayward aboard as vice president. Since Hayward was also a Broadway producer, MCA encroached on the legitimate theater and devised ways of generating money that far exceeded the regular commissions from its clients. MCA first of all invested in its clients' plays. For instance, the agency backed Lindsay and Crouse's *State of the Union,* which was produced by Hayward and contained MCA performers. By virtue of its investment in the stage show, MCA shared in the profits from the Broadway run and the road version. Then MCA negotiated a deal with Paramount Pictures for the sale of the screen rights to the play. Paramount paid $300,000 up front plus 50 percent of the profits to playwrights Lindsay and Crouse and to producer Hayward. MCA collected its standard commission from the payment and, as a backer of the Broadway production, took a slice of the profit participation as well.

Agents had occasionally wrung profit participations from Hollywood studios when they negotiated the sale of motion picture rights to the best-selling novels and hit plays, but during the post–World War II recession in the industry, MCA seized the opportunity to extend the concept to its top stars. The first deal MCA negotiated reputedly won 50 percent of the profits for Jimmy Stewart's services in *Winchester '73.* Stewart earned more than $600,000 in the picture. In comparison, a star of the magnitude of Clark Gable in his heyday at MGM never earned more than $300,000 for an entire year's work.

The financial outlook for movie talent, and consequently for talent agencies, was far from heartening during the postwar recession. In a daring move to provide employment for a lot of actors, MCA formed a subsidiary called Revue Productions and produced a television program called "Stars over Hollywood" in 1949. After it became apparent that filmed shows, particularly series, would become a TV mainstay, MCA moved into television production in a big way by negotiating a blanket waiver from the Screen Actors Guild in 1952 that allowed the agency both to represent talent and to produce television shows in which talent appeared. The head of the Screen Actors Guild at the time was Ronald Reagan, an MCA client. Generally, the Guild had prohibited agents from producing programming because it would allow them to act as both the seller and the buyer. Since no other company won the same rights, the blanket waiver was a watershed for the company. MCA through its Revue subsidiary quickly became the un-challenged giant of television production.

The next question was whether or not MCA would try its hand at motion picture production. Not until 1962 did MCA do so; this was after the agency's growing power prompted the Justice Department to start a grand jury antitrust investigation. In 1962, MCA signed a consent decree in which it agreed to get out of the talent agency business. MCA also purchased Universal Pictures and its parent company, Decca Records, in 1962. Motion picture business had staged a turn-around by then, which made it much less risky to invest in production. During the interim, MCA preferred to collect a sure 10 percent commission on salaries, profit participations, and independent productions. Wasserman entrusted one of its biggest names, Burt Lancaster, to UA, signifying that this was where the action was.

Hecht-Lancaster

One of the few male stars to emerge in the postwar era, Lancaster made his screen debut in Mark Hellinger's underworld crime melo-drama, *The Killers,* in 1946. Lancaster appeared on loanout from Para-mount producer Hal Wallis, who had signed Lancaster to a seven-year contract after Lancaster received favorable notices in an unsuccessful Broadway play by Henry Brown, *A Sound of Hunting.* Representing Lancaster was Harold Hecht, a former dance choreographer and liter-ary agent who now handled actors. Under Robert Siodmak's direction, *The Killers* made Lancaster a star overnight and for the next several years he continued playing the role of social "primitives."

Lancaster commanded $200,000 per picture, but a good chunk of his salary went to Wallis on loanouts. Unlike most option contracts, Lancaster's had an escape clause of sorts. Hecht had negotiated a deal allowing Lancaster to produce one outside picture a year. In 1948, Lancaster formed an independent production company in partnership with Hecht, called Hecht-Norma (Norma in honor of Lancaster's wife) and produced *Kiss the Blood Off My Hands.* Since Lancaster was to star, they found financing on their own and arranged distribution through Universal-International.

In 1950, while Lancaster was still connected with Wallis, Hecht ne-gotiated an unusual deal with Warner Brothers permitting Warner to use Lancaster as a star in one of their pictures for each picture Hecht-Norma made with Warner as an independent producer.[70] The three pictures produced under this arrangement, *The Flame and the Arrow* (1950), *The Crimson Pirate* (1952), and *His Majesty O'Keefe* (1953) were swashbucklers and attempted to broaden Lancaster's screen persona by capitalizing on his experience as a circus stuntman. The biggest picture in Lancaster's career was on another Wallis loanout, this time to Columbia, for *From Here to Eternity* (1953). Lancaster's role playing the tough career soldier, Sergeant Warden, and his love scenes with Deborah Kerr showed a new side to the actor and solidified his status as a boxoffice attraction. *From Here to Eternity* was nominated for eight Academy Awards and won five, including best actor for Lancaster.

The concessions UA made to get Lancaster were worth it. On the first contract, Hecht-Lancaster, the new name of the production company, delivered five pictures. All save one starred Burt Lancaster. In *Apache* (1954) Lancaster played Massai, the legendary Apache who waged a one-man war against the U.S. Produced on a budget of $1 million, and directed by Robert Aldrich in widescreen and in Technicolor, the picture took in a quick $3 million the first year. *Vera Cruz* (1954), also directed by Aldrich, costarred Gary Cooper and was another rugged outdoor-action picture. The first release in the Superscope anamorphic process, *Vera Cruz* came in at $1.6 million and grossed more than $3.5 million in its first year. *The Kentuckian* (1955) marked Lancaster's debut as a director. Another action-adventure drama, this picture was in the "coonskin-capped" tradition started by Disney's Davy Crockett. Lancaster's title role as a widowed pioneer, *Variety* said, "seems a bit too self-conscious, as though the director and the actor couldn't agree."[71] *Trapeze* (1956), however, was right on the mark. Filmed by Carol Reed in the Cirque d'Hiver, Paris's famed one-ring circus, *Trapeze* costarred Tony Curtis and Gina Lollobrigida. Aerial footage and thrilling stunts gave the picture a ring of authenticity and provided much of the appeal.

The Hecht-Lancaster production best remembered today did not star Burt Lancaster but it did make a star out of a durable character actor, Ernest Borgnine. To audiences jaded with widescreen epics, *Marty* (1955), a simple love story of a lonely Bronx butcher and a plain schoolteacher, offered a refreshing change. Based on Paddy Chayefsky's teleplay for NBC's "Television Playhouse," *Marty* was adapted for the screen by Chayefsky and was produced at a cost of $330,000. Hecht chose Delbert Mann to direct and had the prescience to offcast Borgnine in the title part. Until then, Borgnine had played such roles as a sadistic sergeant in *From Here to Eternity* and a tough outlaw in *Vera Cruz*. Betsy Blair was another venturesome bit of casting since she possessed little boxoffice pull.

Contrary to Lancaster's later statements—for example, "who wants to see a picture about two ugly people?"—UA loved the script.[72] For

Academy Award for Best Picture / 1955

Marty

Walter Kelley, Robin Morse, and Ernest Borgnine

A Hecht-Lancaster presentation
Starring Ernest Borgnine and Betsy Blair
Directed by Delbert Mann
Produced by Harold Hecht

Other Academy Awards* and nominations
*Actor: Ernest Borgnine
Supporting actor: Joe Mantell
Supporting actress: Betsy Blair
*Direction: Delbert Mann
*Writing *screenplay*: Paddy Chayefsky
Cinematography: Joseph LaShelle
Art direction–Set decoration: Edward S. Haworth and Walter
    Simonds, Robert Priestley

Ernest Borgnine and Esther Manciotti

Ernest Borgnine and Betsy Blair

example, Bob Blumofe, UA's West Coast production representative, said the script "rings with truth and honesty. It is about real people with real names. I see tremendous opportunity for audience identification with what happens to these people."[73] Blumofe's only reservation was that the picture needed a star. Hecht and Lancaster considered Marlon Brando a possibility, but for reasons that are unclear, they decided to go without a name and probably had to keep the budget low to offset the risk.

UA originally handled *Marty* as an art picture. For the New York premiere, UA booked the Sutton, a 560-seat theater that usually played offbeat product and foreign films. UA gave the picture limited exposure and depended on word-of-mouth to build interest. Placing the picture in national release, UA booked medium-sized theaters that were willing to play the picture for extended runs. The strategy paid off: the first year, *Marty* grossed over $2 million and it ultimately grossed close to $4 million. *Marty* received the Cannes Grand Prix for 1955. At Academy Award time, *Marty* picked up Oscars for best picture, best actor, best directing, and best original screenplay.

The success of these Hecht-Lancaster pictures not only proved extremely profitable to the producers but also attracted other quality independents to UA. But Krim and Benjamin had no illusions that every star was suited to independent production. Benjamin said, "You need great drive, tremendous self-confidence, a need to be in business for yourself." Krim said, "We don't expect the stars to become full-fledged producers overnight. Some stars will have producers as partners in the venture; some will have business associates; others will have directors as partners; while still others will carry the business burdens themselves."[74] Despite the risks, stars took the plunge by going independent and, soon after 1955, UA's roster included Kirk Douglas, Frank Sinatra, John Wayne, Gregory Peck, Bob Hope, Yul Brynner, and Robert Mitchum in addition to Burt Lancaster.

THE CHAPLIN-PICKFORD BUYOUTS

In the midst of all this, Arthur Krim received a call from Charlie Chaplin in February 1955. "I want to sell my interest and I want to do it today or tomorrow. I don't want to do it three days from now or two days from now," Chaplin said. Krim recalls having once mentioned to Chaplin a figure of around $1.2 million for his quarter interest in the company. Chaplin said, "If you have a certified check in Vevey tomorrow, you have my stock." Krim got the money from Heller, and put Arnold

Picker on a plane to Vevey that night to deliver it. Krim and his management team could now have majority control of the company. But why had Chaplin acted so precipitously? A day after Chaplin received the certified check, the U.S. government put a stop order on all his possessions in this country because of outstanding tax claims. "He hadn't told us any of that, but we suspected something," said Krim. "His assets were later tied up for years, but he got that million-two out."[75] (The precise amount UA paid for Chaplin's 25 percent interest was $1,113,287.35). With that, Chaplin severed his relationship with UA, a company he helped found thirty-five years earlier.

On the heels of the Chaplin buyout, Mary Pickford requested a meeting with Krim and Benjamin in her suite at the Pierre Hotel in New York. Ever since the takeover, the relationship between Pickford and UA had been cordial and warm. Lavishing praise on the group for their zeal and dedication, Pickford once told them, "God will reward you for adding twenty years to my life."[76] The meeting at the Pierre was different. This was the first time another person was present at a meeting. Pickford brought along Richard Polimer and introduced him as the president of her investment company. Reflecting a changed mood, Pickford presented two demands: she wanted the company to declare dividends and to give her a blank check for production. Concerning the former, Krim and Benjamin explained that UA's financing program was predicated on an understanding with the banks that the company would plough back its earnings into production. How else could UA, with a meager earned surplus, sponsor $20 million in production loans for 1955? They also reminded Pickford that she had approved this policy in agreeing to the provisions of the Krim-Benjamin takeover contract.

UA agreed to provide financing subject to the regular rights of approval. UA would do so even though, to avoid conflicts of interest, they had vowed never to distribute a picture in which a stockholder or a member of management had a participation. UA tried to convince Pickford that no one in the company should compete with its producers. Management's rewards would come from building the worth of the company. Concluding the visit, Pickford said that they would rue the day.[77]

Krim and Benjamin now got a taste of the bitter intracompany wrangling of yore. As the first of a series of moves designed to harass UA, Pickford and Polimer visited UA's London and Paris offices in the summer of 1955 and conveyed the impression that they were suspicious of the Krim-Benjamin management. Upon her return, Pickford hired a lawyer, William A. Shea (of Shea Stadium fame) to press her charge that Krim and Benjamin had not lived up to the terms of the voting trust agreement and had fraudulently taken control of the company. She also demanded to examine the company's books. In response, Krim told Shea, "We wish to advise you that if Miss Pickford or anybody else jeopardizes this credit, or this standing, or that of this company's executives in the performance of their duties, by giving circulation to slanderous claims, or by engaging in any other improper conduct, she will have to answer for any and all damages thereby caused."[78]

A full audit had been conducted by Price Waterhouse & Co. in 1952 to verify the profit figures; nonetheless, in deference to Pickford who was, after all, a third owner in the company, Krim consented to another examination of the books. Krim insisted, though, that Pickford hire a CPA with a national reputation to conduct the audit. Instead, she brought in an accountant characterized by Krim as a "charlatan."[79] The examination covered production, distribution, and financing matters, most of which were confidential, but to what purpose UA was never told.

Six weeks into the audit, UA turned to the eminent jurist Simon Rifkind for advice. A former federal district judge, Rifkind advised putting an end to the examination until the courts directed otherwise or Pickford stated in writing what she wanted and why. On the counterattack, Pickford decided to take the company to court. Recognizing that Pickford had no case, Shea pressed for a settlement. By then Pickford's purpose was apparent; she was putting pressure on UA for a buyout. She wanted $5 million, but came down to a more realistic level—$3 million. UA paid her $2 million in cash and $1 million in the form of a debenture. Bankers Trust came through with a loan and in February 1956 the deal was closed. Krim and Benjamin and their associates now owned the company outright.

Pickford had the satisfaction of driving a hard bargain with UA and one-upping her former partner in her final deal with the company. She probably had a better grasp of UA's fortunes than Chaplin. The company's gross had jumped from $18 million in 1951 to $55 million in 1955. UA accomplished this feat "coincidental with and in inverse ratio to the television inroads." As *Variety* editorialized after the Pickford stock acquisition, "UA's enterprise has been daring, its operations vigorous, its . . . global coproductions are juicy with showmanship. Messrs. Krim, Benjamin, Heineman, Youngstein, Picker & Co. have proved that there is not a timetable or monopoly on know-how."[80]

The Company in Place

GOING PUBLIC

In an era of economic decline for the motion picture industry, UA achieved an outstanding record of growth. To meet the challenges of the future, UA expanded even further by going public in 1957. In so doing, UA became the last of the major motion picture companies to go the route of Wall Street financing. F. Eberstadt & Co., the investment firm that underwrote the stock offering, assessed UA's performance using a variety of measurements. I have argued that Krim and Benjamin's strategy at the outset was to go for market share. Eberstadt's analysis provides the documentation. One measurement pertained to dues paid to the Motion Picture Association of America (MPAA). A film company's annual dues were based on its share of the total gross revenues of all members. In the period 1950–55, UA's contribution more than doubled. Other measurements, more technical in nature, compared UA's performance to the majors in three ways: (1) revenues; (2) profit margins; and (3) net income to net worth. In every case, the industry average remained relatively flat, whereas UA's performance rose dramatically.

The stock issue raised $14 million and consisted of common stock and debentures. Management still controlled the company after the public sale and Krim and Benjamin still ran the show. In recapitalizing the company, the syndicate received 750,000 shares of class B stock, a substantial majority of the outstanding stock. Krim and Benjamin owned nearly half, a group of senior executives consisting of Heineman, Youngstein, Picker, and Smadja each owned 11.8 percent; and two others, about 3 percent each. The syndicate agreed to empower Krim and Benjamin to serve as "parents" for ten years with full power to vote their stock for all corporate purposes and to sell or dispose the stock on behalf of the syndicate. Krim and Benjamin now started drawing the same salary as their partners—$52,000 a year.

The class B stock owned by management was similar to class A, straight common, in that holders of both were entitled to one vote per share. They differed in that dividends could be declared only for the straight common, meaning that management had to convert their holdings to become eligible for dividends. In other words, the board of directors could declare dividends for public stockholders and not necessarily for the benefit of management exclusively. However, at no time during the Krim-Benjamin regime did management take any dividends or emoluments.

Within weeks of the public sale in July 1957, UA's common stock, which sold over-the-counter at first, was admitted to trading on the New York Stock Exchange. In the opinion of Herbert Schottenfeld, who had been a senior member of UA's legal department since 1951, and who had succeeded Seymour Peyser as general counsel in 1962, "very little changed after going public. Although the law required formal meetings, the same people operated the company. The number of outside directors was small and represented the financial community which had underwritten the stock sale. They felt that they should have an insider position on the board to know what was happening. They had a vital interest in having a voice if that voice was required. But they never exercised that voice because conditions never warranted it. I don't think in any sense did the change act as any real restraint on the management of the company."[1]

UA made a second stock offering in 1958 and arranged other methods of financing to diversify into related entertainment fields. Financing independent production remained the crux of UA's operations (the formula is described in the next section of this chapter). Although enormously successful in motion pictures, UA's formula failed when applied to television production and records. Television and recorded music, like motion pictures, were dominated by a few large firms that controlled distribution. As just one of the many suppliers, UA had to play an unaccustomed role.

THE SHIFT TO INDEPENDENT PRODUCTION

By the time UA went public, all the majors had opened their doors to independents.[2] Michael Conant has charted this trend; he estimates that in 1949, independents produced around 20 percent of the 234 pictures released by the eight majors. UA released twenty-one, or about half of the independent productions. In 1957, the majors released 291 productions, of which 170 (58 percent) were produced by independents. In 1957, UA released 50; the other 120 were produced by independents for the other seven companies. Stated another way, independent production outside of UA accounted for 10 to 12 percent of the releases of the majors in 1949 and 50 percent in 1957.[3]

The *Paramount* decrees, television, runaway production, and the blockbuster trend all contributed to the transition. The studio system went by the boards, as actors, writers, directors, and other contract personnel were pared from the payrolls. Actors were particularly affected: in 1947, 742 were under contract; in 1956, only 229. The labor force shrank as well. Employment fell off from the postwar peak of 24,000 in 1946 to around 13,000 ten years later.[4] The huge physical plants that served the companies so well in the era of the studio system now became white elephants. Companies attempted all kinds of cost-cutting measures, although none could achieve UA's streamlined operations. Economic facts now favored the growth of unit production. According to Conant, "the minimal optimal scale of operations is the production unit organized to produce a single motion picture. Since the production inputs and processes of each picture are unique, the optimal technical unit and the optimal managerial unit both appear to be the production of a single picture."[5] By 1970, the transition, with the notable exception of Universal Pictures, had become complete. The majors functioned essentially as bankers supplying financing and landlords renting studio space. Distribution now became the name of the game.

The power of the majors did not diminish in the transition. First of all, the gains from the *Paramount* decrees did not materialize as anticipated. The courts prescribed divorcement and divestiture as the cure for the industry's monopolistic ills. On the production level, divorcement certainly contributed to the boom in independent production. On the distribution level, divorcement and the prohibition against block booking enabled minor distributors, especially the Little Three (Universal, Columbia, UA), to capture a larger share of the market. And on the exhibition level, divestiture weakened the buying power of the former affiliated circuits and the block-booking ban enabled the independent exhibitor to gain more control of his operations.[6]

Nonetheless, the *Paramount* defendants continued to dominate business during the sixties and do so even to this day.[7] Changing audience tastes and the expansion of commercial television were major factors; simply stated, decreasing demand for motion picture entertainment foreclosed the distribution market to newcomers. Distribution presents high barriers to entry. To operate efficiently, a distributor requires a worldwide system of exchanges and enough cash to finance about thirty pictures a year. During the fifties, overhead ran anywhere from $25 to $30 million a year and financing a full roster of pictures cost twice that much. Since the market absorbed less and less product during this period, it could support only a limited number of distributors—about the same as existed at the time of the *Paramount* case. Without new competition, the distribution gross collected by the majors amounted to a market share of 90 percent in 1972, the same share they collected during the halcyon days of the thirties and forties.[8]

Ironically, the *Paramount* case actually enabled the majors to increase their bargaining power vis-à-vis exhibitors. Excess capacity in the form of empty theater seats could have driven down film rentals, but distributors countered this possibility by a straightforward means—they reduced the number of releases by about 50 percent, forcing exhibitors to compete harder to acquire product. Thus, in the face of shrinking admissions, the majors actually increased their share of the boxoffice take—from 30 percent in 1948 to over 45 percent by 1963.[9] In other words, the bargaining power of the majors forced the exhibitors to bear the brunt of the onslaught from television.

Moviegoing trends also militated against change. The industry lured people back to the theaters with widescreens, 3-D, color, location shooting, and all the ingredients that went into the "big picture." But audiences did not resume their old ways; they became selective. As *Variety* quipped in 1959, people "no longer consider every film exciting because it moves on the screen." Motion pictures became a special event which had the effect of widening the gap between commercial winners and losers. Where second-rate product may have barely scraped along before, it now did dismal business. On the other hand, pictures striking the public's fancy acted like magnets for the consumer dollar. Hollywood, as a result, concentrated its production efforts on fewer and more expensive pictures in its quest for profits. But because production financing became riskier than ever, the majors were not about to venture far afield from the tried and true, or to place the values of art over those of commerce, or as I will explain later, to relinquish important controls over production to independents.

Conditions at home forced the majors to fortify their positions overseas. Pictures could no longer break even in the domestic market as a matter of course. Forced to export to stay alive, Hollywood had to think internationally by backing pictures that would find acceptance in the important world markets. Acting in concert under the aegis of the MPAA, the majors succeeded in breaking down all kinds of protective barriers erected by foreign governments after World War II to protect their national film industries and thereby succeeded in keeping the channels of distribution open for American pictures. By the sixties, the majors could boast that their pictures earned half of their revenues abroad, on the average.[10] Such being the case, independent producers needed the majors with their worldwide distribution networks more than ever.

Finally, the majors retained their power by learning to accommodate to television. Hollywood found that it could profitably coexist with the broadcasting industry by producing programming for the networks and by utilizing television as a lucrative secondary market for motion pictures—releasing vintage films at first, but then newer product at rental levels starting at $200,000 in 1960 and approaching $1 million per picture by the end of the decade.[11]

The industry rebounded from the devastating effects of divorcement, changing audience tastes, and competition from television. But how did these factors affect the relationship between the majors and the independent producer? By analyzing UA's method of operation, we can discover how the prototype of today's motion picture company set the pattern.

But at the outset, we should reiterate just what made UA distinctive. Although the other majors shifted to unit production and shared the profits with independents, UA's brand of independent production gave it an edge over its competitors. *Fortune* published an article on UA in 1958 entitled "The Derring-Doers of the Movie Business" that spotlighted Krim and Benjamin's achievements in revolutionizing the industry.[12] The article contained the pitch UA had been making to independent producers all along and to Wall Street when the company went public. No longer skeptical, talent, the business community, and the press had taken notice of this upstart company.

The first point was that, unlike the other majors, UA was strictly a motion picture *distribution* company. UA neither owned a studio nor produced motion pictures under its own name. UA financed motion pictures simply to guarantee a steady supply of product. Much of what was distinctive about UA followed from this different operation.

Second, UA offered independent producers autonomy, once the basic ingredients (story, cast, director, and budget) had been approved by all parties. As Otto Preminger said, "Only United Artists has a system of true independent production. They recognized that the independent has his own personality. After they agree on the basic property and are consulted on the cast, they leave everything to the producer's discrimination. Most of the time, when the others make an independent contract, they want to be able to approve the shooting and the final cut." [13] Preminger exaggerated somewhat, but the point is that UA gave a producer complete autonomy over the making of his picture, including the final cut. As UA liked to say, a producer had the right "to visualize the picture as he saw fit." Company executives never asked to see rushes or asked a director to justify creative decisions. Working at another company, an independent operated under the eye of the studio head whose staff viewed rushes every day whether the producer liked it or not simply because the rushes would be screened in the studio's theater. A prominent director under contract with UA was quoted as saying, "When I was at --- they looked at my rushes every day. That's like a novelist having to send in his daily few pages to his publisher as he writes them. What kind of talent can work that way?" [14] Krim and Benjamin realized they might die by the sword granting autonomy to filmmakers, but they decided to adopt the policy from the start.

Third, UA gave an independent producer ownership in his picture, which offered tax savings in addition to profit participation. Moreover, the producer made his picture under his own name. Concerning screen credits, the director quoted above said, "Don't let anyone kid you that they're not important. If you're an independent with other major studios, you won't get top credit on the opening title. With UA I get top credit and somewhere down at the bottom there'll be a modest line, 'Released by United Artists.' Benjamin and Krim stick to their roles; they don't make believe they're producers and they don't compete with us for kudos." [15]

Fourth, UA allowed a producer to set up his production any place in the world to suit the needs of the story or the economics of the venture. UA's producers regularly took advantage of foreign subsidies, frozen funds—i.e., funds that could not be removed from foreign jurisdiction—and tax benefits from incorporating abroad. But the other majors could not give independents this leeway. These companies had large amounts of money tied up in their studios and naturally wanted to rent their facilities to the filmmakers they were backing. But the day of the big studio was over. There no longer was a need for a company-owned studio—pictures could be made anywhere. *Variety* said, "It is generally believed that the entire theatrical output of Hollywood can now [1958] be made in one studio, such as Metro's or Warner's." [16] Nonetheless, until the majors dismantled or sold off some of their studios, they would continue to tack on a standard overhead fee to the budgets of independent productions that inflated costs by as much as 40 percent. Steven Bach has said that the overhead charge was viewed by producers as "at best an override and at worst legalized larceny." [17] UA, by contrast, owned no studio and charged no overhead fee. Working for UA, a producer rented only what he needed and when he needed it. This situation lowered production costs and made the venture potentially more profitable.

Fifth, UA permitted independents to appoint their own sales representatives to collaborate in the distribution of their films. UA adopted this policy to dispel any feeling a producer might have that the company was not using its best efforts to sell his picture. The sales rep had the authority to review every exhibition contract on the picture in the domestic market. If the rep did not like the terms, he could try negotiating a better deal within a specified period of time. In checking the results on his picture overseas, UA tried to give the producer red carpet treatment there as well.

In short, UA tried to create what Krim called "the psychological climate" to nurture long-term relationships with independent producers. Since the other majors had produced and distributed pictures under their own logos from the start, they found it difficult to provide the same treatment to independents. But as the years went on, said Krim, "the other majors came closer and closer to UA's way of doing things. They did so because they had no alternative." [18]

UA'S METHOD OF OPERATION

UA's operations generated two sources of profits—one from distribution and another from production. The former were generated by the distribution fee for the benefit of the company; the latter for the benefit of both the company and the producer. In handling a picture, UA charged the producer a schedule of fees ranging from 30 to 45 percent of the gross receipts, depending on the market. These fees went to meet the company's fixed expenses on a worldwide network of ninety sales offices that employed over 2,000 people and cost $15 million a year to maintain. Thus, the company had to do a sizable volume of business each year just to break even. But the distribution fee not only paid for housekeeping bills, it also generated profits. Since the marketing costs of a picture remained relatively fixed regardless of its boxoffice performance, a hit could generate revenues well in excess of distribution expenses. Distribution profits rewarded the company, to be sure, but they were also used to offset losses on production loans and to contribute to a pool for the financing of new projects.

For those pictures that earned back their investments, UA also enjoyed production profits. Since the distribution fee offset UA's risk as financier, the company could afford to be generous with the production profits. UA typically divided the profits with a producer fifty-fifty, but in special cases, such as for Preminger and Lancaster, UA gave away 75 percent. These were the rewards for a producer's efforts. But UA as financier took the greater risk and earned first call on the revenues.

Table 3.1 illustrates the risks of production financing. It appeared in a report prepared by the investment house of F. Eberstadt & Co. that was designed to acquaint stockbrokers with the motion picture distribution business.

The 100-plus pictures UA financed in this period generated a paltry $24,145 in production profits by 1957. However, the distribution fees from these pictures present a different situation. In this period, UA's gross—i.e., revenue from film rentals—increased from $20 million to more than $60 million; correspondingly, earnings before taxes jumped from $350,000 to over $6 million. The obvious conclusion is that UA could have operated profitably even if it earned nothing from its par-

Table 3.1. United Artists Corporation Results of Production Financing, 1951–1956

Year	Profits on Pictures	Producer Advances Written Off	Net Profits (or Losses) Less Write-Offs	Films Financed by the Company
51	0	$ 57,528	$ (57,528)	0
52	0	21,489	(21,489)	7
53	$ 44,600	477,378	(432,778)	20
54	313,737	730,227	(416,490)	20
55	961,765	447,759	514,006	27
56	1,686,253	1,247,829	438,424	39
Totals	$3,006,355	$2,982,210	$ 24,145	113

Source: United Artists Corporation Underwriters Report prepared by F. Eberstadt & Co. March 19, 1957

ticipation in production profits. What this comparison does not show, but as a further indication of the importance of the distribution fee, is that only in a few instances did UA fail to recover, through its distributor's share of the gross revenues, an amount equal to the loans it advanced for production costs.

Production financing took several forms, but the ones most often used were either institutional financing from within—that is, the use of internally generated funds from production and distribution—or guarantees by UA of bank loans for individual pictures. In dealing with UA, a bank did not judge the boxoffice potential of a project, but looked to the company's net worth and overall earnings record in making its financing decision.

Although UA's brand of independent production accorded talent more freedom than it ever enjoyed during the days of the studio system, the company retained ultimate discretionary power by exercising approval rights over the basic ingredients of a production and by establishing tight fiscal controls. Approval rights permitted UA to judge the commercial potential of each creative component in a package; fiscal controls insured that the producer lived up to his part of the bargain once shooting began.

Not owning a studio and all that entailed gave the company some latitude in the selection of pictures. As Herb Schottenfeld explained it, "I think that UA understood at all times that it didn't have to have a blockbuster or even a successful picture every time out of the gate. UA guaranteed a separate production loan for each picture, but its relationship with the banks was such that all loans with an individual institution were usually cross-collateralized. Based on the company's track record, the banks had sufficient confidence in UA's ability to pick balanced programs. No financier ever felt called upon to foreclose on any of the loans. A single bomb or even a series of moderately unsuccessful pictures could not sink the company." [19]

In evaluating a project, UA did not measure the potential profits, but, rather, the potential loss. The company might lose some big ones in the process, but that was worth the risk. As Krim put it, "We are determined to avoid disaster in individual pictures. That means we must constantly weigh and gauge how many pictures we can profitably handle, and we must make sure that we don't take undue risks. Our policy here is to consider every picture a failure from the start. That's the way we figure it. Then, if it's a success, well that means the hard work has paid off and we're agreeably surprised." Some pictures are a safer investment at $12 million than others are at $3 million. The classic example was the James Bond series. "For *Dr. No,* we allowed a budget of a million-two and we wouldn't let them go over one dollar," said Krim. "*Dr. No* grossed six million and was a mild success. We then allowed *From Russia with Love* to go to two million. *Russia* did better so we let *Goldfinger* go to three. By the end we were permitting budgets to go to sixteen million, but still the investment was safe."[20]

Cost *per se,* then, was not the issue; it was cost against the potential return. That was the key. And that was a management judgment. In reaching a decision on a project, Krim said, "we do not have a hard and fast rule that all of us must agree. We may go forward even if only one of us is in favor if the others are persuaded by his reasoning that the risk is worth taking."[21] Ultimately, though, Krim had veto power. But there was a big difference between a one-man decision and a one-man veto, as the attempt at consensus implies.

UA prided itself on reaching production decisions quickly. One independent producer was quoted as saying, "There's an absence of procrastination at UA. When you submit a deal to them you get a quicker yes or no than from the other companies. The reason for this—and it's important to the movie business—is that the people who run UA, the operating heads, also control the company. They don't have to submit the proposal to the board of directors or an executive committee."[22]

The ranks of independent producers had swelled considerably during the fifties and UA's roster contained a mix of creative producers, packagers, talent, and combinations thereof. The creative producer, such as Stanley Kramer, Otto Preminger, Joseph L. Mankiewicz, and Anatole Litvak, typically had experience in most phases of the production process and had earned his stripes in the studio system. In going independent, this type of producer acquired material, oversaw the development of the screenplay, hired the talent, controlled the budget and directed the picture. In other words, he was involved in all facets of production and the picture bore his stamp.

A packager also assembled the ingredients, but unlike the creative producer, a packager typically took a secondary position in the production. Producers more often than not were talent agents. During the breakdown of the studio system, agencies such as William Morris and MCA took over the traditional Hollywood production function of scientifically putting together a team of talent, from script to star, from author to director, from casting to actual physical shooting. After the Department of Justice forced MCA to choose between agenting and producing in 1962, MCA chose the latter and its former employees established their own agencies, joined others, or went into independent production.[23]

In turning independent, the star or director typically surrounded him/herself with a support staff consisting of an associate producer, production manager, story editor, accountant, legal representation, and, of course, an agent. Theoretically, the staff concerned itself with business affairs and the logistics of production, whereas the independent pondered creative matters. In turning independent, artists still required the services of agents. A good agent did not just see how good a deal he could make, he also tried to take the long view to nurture and sustain his client's career. However, deal making in this new setup became more complex.

Before the Krim-Benjamin era at UA, the producing function was handled mainly by the nominal producer of the picture, but as a result of the new entrants into the independent ranks, the producing function became subdivided. Different credits were invented to reflect the reorganized division of labor. The term "executive producer" might designate the packager; "producer" the creative producer; and "associate producer" the line producer. Regardless of the terminology, certain important administrative tasks had to be performed to organize the production, to hire the cast and crew, and to keep the production on budget.

Anatomy of the Deal

Projects typically took the form of a "package" consisting of a story, property, director, and/or star. Nearly all projects emanated from outside the company. As Benjamin said, UA strove "to have as many minds working for us as possible. After all, there is a limit to one man's ingenuity. It's better to have fifty men looking for the unusual, and striving to achieve it, than to have two or three. The trick is to attract the right people."[24] The package was the seed of the motion picture deal. If it interested UA, the company drew up a production-financing agreement and a distribution contract setting forth the conditions of the deal. The project progressed in steps. The first, which the industry called research and development, involved writing and/or revising the screenplay, preparing the budget and production schedule, and securing the director and cast. These are the basic ingredients of a project, designated as the "above-the-line" costs in a budget. UA had the right of approval over these ingredients.

In this era of blockbusters, launching a big-budget project was sometimes a long, drawn-out process. An example is Kirk Douglas's

The Vikings. The production history of this picture "would make an ordinary businessman blanch," said *Fortune,* which focused on *The Vikings* in a feature story on UA. The following excerpt illustrates Douglas's step deal:

- February 1955: After a couple of months spent by U.A. and Bryna [Douglas's production company] executives searching for and reading material about the Vikings, Douglas found a book he liked. It was *The Viking,* by Edison Marshall. Douglas sent it to Krim. Krim thought it would take too much money to turn the book into a good screenplay. But he sent it on anyway to U.A. Vice President Max E. Youngstein, who was vacationing in Haiti. Youngstein recommended that it be bought "if the price is reasonable." The asking price was about $75,000, plus a large percentage of the movie's net profits, which Krim didn't think was "reasonable."
- October 1955: Continued reading of plays, books, stories, and even juveniles having failed to turn up a better vehicle, U.A. bought movie and TV rights to Marshall's book for $30,000 plus 6 per cent of the net and transferred ownership to Bryna.
- May 1956: Douglas got an OK from Krim and Robert Benjamin, U.A.'s board chairman, to hire Richard Fleischer to direct *The Vikings.* Fleischer was to get $50,000 cash, a deferred payment of an additional $50,000, and 5 per cent of the net.
- June 1956: Bryna hired Noel Langley to write the screenplay. Another $50,000 was thus committed by U.A., making a total of $180,000 so far; and 11 percent of the movie's take had been surrendered. There was still no formal agreement between Bryna and U.A. on *The Vikings.*
- Summer 1956: Bryna representatives in Europe went looking for a location in Norway, studio space in Germany, a castle in France, and a shipwright who could build tenth-century longboats.
- October 1956: U.A. had by now advanced Bryna $75,000 in pre-production costs, was committed for $105,000 more. Douglas estimated he would need another $100,000 for pre-production costs in the next few months. Benjamin and Krim told him to go ahead.
- January 1957: The screenplay was completed and read at U.A. Max Youngstein's verdict: "I think this can now be a very big money picture." Three longboats were under construction ($16,000).
- Febuary 1957: U.A.'s total advance on *The Vikings* was up to

$250,000. (U.A. had also, meanwhile, loaned Bryna $108,000 for three other movies in the planning stage.) U.A. had security for its money—Bryna's interest in *The Indian Fighter,* then being shown, plus *The Vikings* script—but there was still no final Bryna-U.A. contract on *The Vikings.*

• March 1957: Douglas and Krim got together in Hollywood to draw up a contract. U.A. agreed to loan $2,500,000 for *The Vikings* if Douglas were the sole star, $3,250,000 if he enlisted a co-star (which he subsequently did). If costs went above these figures, U.A. would provide the additional money but would receive additional "protection"; i.e., for each $250,000 in excess, Douglas agreed to make another picture for U.A. and himself assume a quarter of a million in initial costs. U.A. was to get 25 per cent of *The Vikings'* net profit plus its standard distribution fee: 30 per cent of the gross in the U.S., Canada, and England, 40 per cent elsewhere. (As Kirk Douglas said recently, "They make tough deals, but they talk my language.")

Krim sent his partner Benjamin—both of them are lawyers—a memo that reflected neither the devotion a lawyer is supposed to have for hard and fast agreements, nor the distrust that is traditional in Hollywood. "I realize," Krim wrote, "there are many loopholes, but Kirk said we could rely on the kind of people we are dealing with. We are therefore going forward in large measure based on moral considerations as well as the legal document." [25]

Everything in the budget was negotiable, theoretically, but in general UA required the principal creative participants of an independent production to function in varying degrees as coventurers with the company by deferring most of their salaries until the cash costs of the picture had been recouped. UA paid a producer's fee up front to the producer for multiple-picture deals. The company also paid the producer an overhead fee to maintain continuity of his administrative staff. Creative personnel receiving profit shares, such as the screenwriter, star, and director, were known collectively as "third party participants." Profits paid to them came from the producer's share or, on occasion, from UA's and the producer's on a formula basis—e.g., if a star was to receive 10 percent of the profits, UA might contribute 40 percent and the producer 60 percent. Top stars might demand, in addition to their fees, a percentage of the gross in lieu of profit participation, in which case the cost would be borne equally by the producer and the company. The first time UA agreed to a percentage deal was to get Gary Cooper to costar with Burt Lancaster in *Vera Cruz* in 1954. At the time, this type of deal was rare, but by the seventies, percentage deals became "almost the starting point for negotiation with important talent." [26] Participation could begin after break-even, or at a negotiated dollar point, or "off the top"—that is, from the very start of distribution, among other variations.

If UA and the producer could not agree on any of the basic ingredients, the producer had the right of "turnaround"—that is, to set up the project elsewhere to get the picture made. In picking up a project, a company had to reimburse UA for its research and development (R & D) expenses. The turnaround provision was particularly important in multiple-picture deals. In attempting to establish long-term relationships with talent, UA emphasized its policy of nonexclusivity. UA wanted first approval rights from its producers, but if mutually satisfactory terms could not be worked out, the producer was free to take his project elsewhere. If the project found no takers it was abandoned and the development costs either written off or charged to the producer's next picture.

When UA gave the go-ahead, the project entered the preproduction period, during which a start date was set and the department heads and other "below-the-line" personnel were hired for the production and postproduction periods to make the picture. At this point, UA arranged for the complete financing, usually by guaranteeing a bank loan—and, when the picture was to be produced abroad, by securing frozen funds and/or foreign subsidies. To finance Kirk Douglas's *The Vikings* (1958), for example, UA guaranteed a $1.5 million loan from New York's Chemical Corn Exchange Bank. French and German banks agreed to lend $500,000 each in francs and marks. A loan of $263,000 in kroner came from Norway; $393,000 in sterling was borrowed in England. Foreign loans, which financed the location shooting, were guaranteed in part from UA funds in blocked accounts. Banks did not evaluate the commercial value of the picture; their primary consideration in making the loan was UA's financial situation. As a UA executive said, "Banks naturally want to know about the picture and they like to see a script, but the loan commitment is probably already made by the time they receive one. They like to know—maybe it would impress their loan committee to know who's in it or who's directing it. But I don't think they really are concerned [about the financial possibilities of the picture] because they are looking to the credit of UA and not to the picture for repayment." [27]

Although a producer had creative control while shooting a picture,

UA kept tabs on its investment. As the person responsible for watching the money, the line producer had to submit to UA daily call sheets, production reports, and a running account of the cash flow. On location, UA assigned a disbursing agent to cosign the checks. UA, in other words, did not just turn over the money to the producer outright.

UA assumed a producer would be frugal since an escalation of the budget would jeopardize his profits. Nonetheless, UA built into the financing agreements safeguards to keep the picture on track. Natural disasters and other catastrophes such as the death of the star were covered by insurance. But even in the best of circumstances, many unforeseen things could delay shooting. Since these were also unavoidable, the company might build in a 10 percent contingency to the budget. Delays caused by producer negligence or by an excessively slow director were more serious, so UA did one of several things. A first-time producer might be required to furnish a completion bond guaranteeing that extra money would be forthcoming to finish the picture no matter what. The producer had to secure completion money on his own, typically from a bonding company, which asked for a share of his profits and sometimes a fee as conditions for the loan.

UA placed different constraints on an established producer. Once he exceeded the 10 percent cushion, he might begin losing profit points—that is, a portion of his percentage of the profits—or his profit participation might be delayed until the company recouped the overage plus a penalty. Penalizing the producer involved only a finite amount of money; if the production got out of hand, UA protected itself by retaining the right of takeover. This was the ultimate remedy, but also the most radical and perilous course to take. The company preferred to apply pressure. As one UA producer said, "All of a sudden we would start getting phone calls when we hadn't got phone calls before. We would feel pressure, the director would feel pressure."[28] Too much pressure or renegotiating the contract might cause the director to rebel and lose even more time. But closing down the production while a replacement director was found could be even more costly for a whole different set of reasons.

In reality, there wasn't much UA could do to keep producers within budget except to deal with the right people. In giving the green light to a producer, William Bernstein said, "You're taking the risk that you've made the right choice. What ultimately it always comes down to is have we bet on the right people? They are the ones who are executing the film and if you guess wrong, if you're dealing with a fiscally irresponsible producer or director, they can hurt you terribly."[29]

In return for financing the picture, UA received worldwide distribution rights in all media, film gauges, and languages. The company also received worldwide soundtrack album rights and music-publishing rights. Concerning remakes and sequels and ancillary rights to the underlying literary material, UA might share joint control with the producer.

The term of UA's distribution contracts was only five years at the time of the Krim-Benjamin takeover, but after the company started the financing program it was able to increase the term first to ten years and then to perpetuity. Obviously, the longer UA could distribute a picture, the more revenue it could collect from ancillary markets. UA's library of current feature films therefore consisted of pictures for which UA had limited-term distribution rights, pictures for which it had perpetual rights, and pictures which the company owned outright as a result of a buyout. A producer normally did not sell his interest in a picture, since the point of going into independent production was to benefit from the annuity provided by long-term distribution. But, at times, producers wanted out for tax purposes or simply because they needed cash. The price UA offered was negotiable like everything else in the relationship and was based on the residual value of the picture. In a buyout, UA purchased a producer's participation in the picture. Partnership with a producer required a range of distribution matters to be handled by mutual consent; a buyout gave UA more flexibility over marketing. In confronting new technologies UA wanted all the freedom of movement it could muster.

To make certain the picture got through the distribution pipeline, UA demanded that the finished picture conform to a designated theatrical running time and receive a seal of approval from the PCA and an "A" or "B" certificate from the Legion of Decency. If not, UA retained the right to ask for the appropriate cuts. If the picture encountered censorship problems during release, UA could require the producer to cut any scene, to shoot additional scenes, or to do retakes—whatever was necessary to insure that the picture reached the market.

In devising distribution strategies and promotion campaigns, UA sometimes granted the producer consultation rights, but only for the domestic market. UA did not tell a producer how to shoot his picture and in return did not want to be told how to handle the marketing— even though the costs of prints and advertising were ultimately billed to the producer. Distribution, after all, was UA's stock-in-trade. Each year, the company released a minimum of twenty to thirty pictures in all budget levels and popular genres—westerns, mythological and biblical epics, teenage exploitation pictures, and even French New Wave art films. A producer might know something about the U.S. market, but not necessarily much about Italy, Japan, Australia, or South Africa.

After the picture was released, revenues were allocated to the participants in accordance with the degree of risk they'd taken. Rentals from theatrical exhibition are known in total as the "distribution gross." From every dollar collected, UA deducted its distribution fee; the remainder, called the "producer's share," went first to reimburse UA for print and advertising costs; second, to pay off the production loan and completion money; and third, to pay the deferred salaries. Thereafter, the revenues (with the distribution fee still being deducted) constituted profits and were divided among the participants in the agreed-upon proportions.

In multiple-picture deals, profits were typically cross-collateralized. Essentially, cross-collateralization treated the pictures of a producer as a group with the profits and losses averaged. Producers considered the provision onerous, but UA wanted protection against a situation whereby a producer enjoyed windfall profits on one film, while the company absorbed substantial losses on his other pictures. UA sometimes refined the condition by crossing pictures in groups of two or three or limiting the producer's liability to 25 to 100 percent of his profits, depending on his track record. Stanley Kramer, for example, produced five pictures for UA from 1955 to 1960. The pictures were crossed in groups of two and three. In the first group, *Not as a Stranger* (1955) and *The Pride and the Passion* (1957) were produced at negative costs of $1.5 and $3.7 million, respectively. *Stranger* had a worldwide distribution gross of over $8 million and earned a profit of $1.8 million, a substantial amount based on the investment. *Passion*, however, grossed only $6.7 million worldwide and lost $2.5 million, also a substantial amount. UA's total exposure came to over $5 million. Because the two pictures were cross-collateralized, UA lost $700,000 ($2.5 million minus $1.8 million) instead of the total loss on *Passion* of $2.5 million. Correspondingly, Kramer earned no profits instead of $1.8 million for *Stranger*. The pictures in the second group all lost money, which UA had to absorb on its own.

This analysis is a simplified version of a complex process, but it typifies the relationship between an independent producer and UA. It would be simplistic to think of this relationship simply as a struggle between the creative artist on the one hand and business people on the other. Both parties were interested in profit maximization by creating commercially successful motion pictures.

Negotiations between the distributor-financier and independent producer focused mainly on two questions: can the picture earn back

Some Calculated Risks

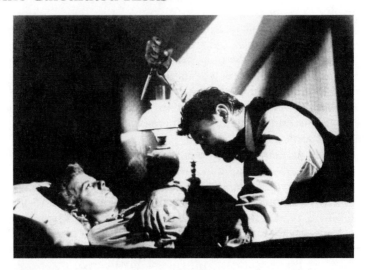

The Night of the Hunter (1955): Shelley Winters and Robert Mitchum. Paul Gregory produced this adaptation by James Agee of Davis Grubb's novel about a murderous, hymn-singing psychopath in pursuit of two children who hold the key to a fortune. Directed by Charles Laughton, his one and only direction effort, the picture is now regarded as a classic.

Twelve Angry Men (1957). Produced by Henry Fonda and Reginald Rose, based on Rose's teleplay. Sidney Lumet, the director of the teleplay, also directed the film. Shot in twenty days, the picture was Lumet's first feature.

Paths of Glory (1958): Wayne Morris, Kirk Douglas, and Ralph Meeker. This antiwar picture, which was banned in parts of Europe and in U.S. military movie theaters for some years, established Kubrick as one of America's top directors.

Lilies of the Field (1963). Produced and directed by Ralph Nelson, this low-budget comedy about a black who helps a group of East European nuns build a chapel in the Arizona desert held instant appeal to audiences. Lilia Skala was nominated for an Oscar for best supporting actress. Sidney Poitier won the Oscar for best actor.

its costs? and, to what degree is each party to share the risks? The former involved mainly a marketing decision. Given a company's limited financial resources, it had to select projects to attract the largest audiences. However, the company could not always play it safe; its share of the market would most likely decrease if it regularly followed trends. Taking the calculated risk with a controversial or offbeat picture—with *The Moon Is Blue* (1953), *Marty* (1955), or *Paths of Glory* (1958)— was necessary to revitalize and attract audience interest. UA never risked its money foolishly for art's sake. As a condition for backing an experimental venture, the company insisted that production costs be cut to the bare bones to minimize risks. The cash outlay for *Marty* and *The Moon Is Blue*, for example, amounted to less then $400,000 each, making them small-budget pictures compared to the blockbusters being turned out by the industry.

Which brings up the second issue. Although UA competed for talent and fresh ideas, the company put up the money and established the parameters—the rules—if you will, of the game. An independent producer might have the clout to negotiate a hefty salary and producer's fee up front in addition to a healthy share of the profits, but for UA and, most likely for other majors, one thing was not negotiable—the distribution fee. The distributor, as a result, had first call on the rentals and the producer the leavings. To place this ranking in perspective, we can look to the apportionment of boxoffice receipts. For every dollar taken in by theaters in 1960, the distributor collected as rental about forty cents on the average. After deducting the distribution fee and print and advertising costs, less than twenty cents remained to cover negative costs.[30] Spiraling print and advertising expenses after 1960, the result of saturation booking and an increased use of television advertising, left even a smaller share for production. But given the uncertainties of the market, UA and the other majors would have it no other way.

DIVERSIFYING

Going public enabled UA to diversify. In 1957, the company formed three subsidiaries—United Artists Television, United Artists Records, and United Artists Music—with the goal of becoming an integrated entertainment organization. UA had distributed feature films to television all along, but now the company extended the concept of independent production to television and music. The hope was that the diversified operations would cross-fertilize one another, to generate synergy, in other words. A successful motion picture, for example, might provide the idea for a television dramatic series. Or it might contain an exploitable soundtrack or title song, like *High Noon, Moulin Rouge,* or *Limelight.* Cross-fertilization could work the other way, too. A hit single or album could plug the movie. A star in a TV series could be exploited in a movie. And a pop singer could be linked to a package involving recordings and motion pictures.

Distribution of Features to Syndicated Television

From the start, Krim and Benjamin believed motion pictures and television could live together without the threat of mutual extinction. The size of the pie had decreased as a result of television, but a substantial audience for the movies still existed. As Krim noted, "Hollywood is producing bigger films in terms of gross sales and is enjoying patronage of greater and more selective audiences for these blockbusters."[31] Nonetheless, during the early fifties, UA followed the general trade policy of the majors and withheld its films from television. This policy was adopted out of deference to exhibitors who feared that movies on TV would put them out of business. According to *Variety,* 1952 marked the first year when exhibitors learned "that theaters and TV could live side-by-side and survive—quite comfortably—in the resultant battle for the audience . . . exhibs now hue [*sic*] to the line that their screens and those of video sets have little more in common than the fact that moving images are presented on them . . . And from this attitude springs their more tolerant approach to studio production activities in the TV field. However, they still roar in defiance of the distributor who lets his films go on the air, and they distrust all experiments with subscription television, the effects of which they can not yet gauge."[32]

Rapprochement with television began in 1955, when RKO, with Howard Hughes at the helm, withdrew from motion-picture production and sold its pre-1948 film library to General Teleradio for $15 million. Two months later, Warner Brothers sold its library of pre-1948 features and shorts to Associated Artists Productions. Other companies followed suit, and by 1958, an estimated 3,700 features, mostly of pre-1948 vintage, had been sold or leased to TV for an estimated $220 million.[33] Believing that these older features did not have sufficient entertainment value to compete with the new product, theater owners stayed calm.

UA became the first major company to break the post-1948 barrier. Krim and company had been acquiring television rights to its pictures from the beginning and by 1957 had leased over 100 to TV. UA charged its producers the same distribution fee for television as it did for the theatrical market. If the picture had yet to break even, the producer's share of the TV sale was applied to the loan. If UA had a profit participation in the film and the production costs had been recovered, the company divided the rentals with the producer and the other participants—after deducting its distribution fee, of course.

The post-1948 features UA released to television consisted mainly of British product, including Eagle-Lion's. UA held back its hits until it could get a better fix on the market. Nonetheless, the competition took advantage of this opportunity to undercut UA's relations with exhibitors. In response, UA pointed out that the year 1948 was artificial since it had nothing to do with quality or ratings. (The Screen Actors Guild was attempting to negotiate an industry-wide contract requiring the payment of residual compensation to its members who appeared in features made after 1948 that were leased to television.) UA owned no pre-1948 pictures; the majors, however, had released literally thousands of pictures to TV, sometimes flooding the market with as many as 750 films at one time. The majors had yet to release post-1948 product to TV only because they were contractually unable to do so, having failed to negotiate a deal with talent guilds over residuals.

In 1957, UA consolidated its position in the syndicated television field by acquiring Associated Artists Productions, the television distributor that owned the pre-1948 Warner Brothers film library. UA paid $27 million for the package, which contained 800 sound and 200 silent features, 1,400 shorts, and two cartoon series—"Looney Tunes" and "Merrie Melodies." In addition, the package contained 200 Monogram features and Paramount's Popeye cartoons.

Financing the AAP acquisition, said Krim, was like "paying for the cow with its own milk." AAP had outstanding unbilled contracts on the film libraries amounting to the $27 million purchase price. These contracts were for first-run showings on syndicated television. AAP's owners needed cash in a hurry, so UA went to Manufacturer's Trust for the entire amount. As security, UA put up the pictures. Within no time, the pictures paid for themselves. Said Krim, "that library was worth many many millions of dollars to us over the years. In 1978, we could have gotten the same $27 million for what was still left in the library. In the interim twenty years, I guess the Warner pictures must have grossed $150 million."[34]

In 1959, UA acquired the film library of yet another Hollywood major—RKO. General Teleradio wanted the RKO film library primarily for its five independent television stations in New York, Los Angeles, San Francisco, Boston, and Memphis. Shortly after the purchase, the company sold the television distribution rights to these pictures outside the five markets to Matty Fox for $15 million. Fox, in turn, sold the domestic residual rights to UA for $3.7 million. By 1960, UA had the most valuable film vault in the industry.

Television Production

UA got a late start in television production. The majors had caught on to the potential of television and began producing regular filmed programs for the networks early in the fifties. A decline in theatrical production had left studios idle and majors now saw the value of collaboration. By the end of the decade, when UA entered the market, most prime-time shows emanated from Hollywood. The working relationship between the film industry and commercial broadcasting had become Hollywood the supplier and New York the exhibitor. For the networks, filmed programming served as a form of quality control in which acting and directing errors could be edited out and poorly rendered scenes reshot. For producers of television, film production offered the possibility of residuals. Programming could be preserved for future syndication as broadcasting times of stations increased to include afternoon and morning hours and as commercial television systems developed worldwide.

Putting the independent producer concept to work, UA Television in its first year financed five series, each consisting of thirty-nine half-hour episodes. Two reached the networks during the 1959–60 season. "The Troubleshooters," a Meridian Pictures production starring Keenan Wynn and Olympic star Bob Mathias, was bought by Phillip Morris for Marlboro cigarettes and slotted on NBC Friday nights, and "The Dennis O'Keefe Show," a Cypress production, was picked up by Oldsmobile and aired on CBS Tuesday nights. The hoped-for synergy with UA's motion picture producers materialized in two series—"Tales of the Vikings," a spinoff from Kirk Douglas's *The Vikings,* and "Miami Undercover," a Schenck-Koch production, starring Lee Bowman and Rocky Graziano. These two series made it only on syndicated TV. The fifth venture, "Hudson's Bay," a Northstar Pictures production starring Barry Nelson, was never telecast anywhere.

Pursuing a different tack in 1960, UA acquired Ziv Television Programs, a company that had a long history in the television syndication

Broderick Crawford in "Highway Patrol." Produced by Ziv Television (1955–59), this action series proved to be one of the highest-rated syndicated shows.

field. Founded by Frederick W. Ziv, Ziv-TV was the largest syndication company in the history of television and the leading programming force outside the networks during the 1950s. Starting out in 1937 as a Cincinnati-based producer and distributor of radio programming, Ziv went into TV at the very beginning, when the networks had yet to fill all of prime time in every market. To take advantage of this opportunity, Ziv produced half-hour programs that could be easily slotted in and around network option time. Ziv produced every conceivable type—adventure, science fiction, mystery, comedy, documentary, and so forth. His best-sellers, some of which were spin-offs from radio, included "Mr. District Attorney," "I Led Three Lives," "Boston Blackie," "Sea Hunt," and "Highway Patrol." Produced for $30,000 to $40,000 an episode, these programs brought in $80,000 to $100,000 from network affiliates and independent stations.

When UA purchased Ziv for around $7 million in 1960, it also assumed $10 million of debt. In taking over this property, UA changed the name of its television subsidiary to Ziv–United Artists. The timing of the acquisition could not have been worse. As Krim said, "We acquired this company at the very moment when syndication began to decline and network control of the marketplace increased. We walked into a buzz saw. I mean we were chopped down quickly by the change in the market."[35] Actually, the first-run syndication market had been declining since 1956 in inverse proportion to the growth of the three networks. Commercial television had been growing by leaps each year until by 1959 almost every family, at least in metropolitan areas, owned a TV set. As the market became saturated, the networks competed for affiliates to increase the number of viewing homes covered by a network show. The impetus for this is obvious; the more potential viewers for a program, the higher the advertising rate. An average network show was carried by around 100 stations in 1955; by 1960, the number of broadcast outlets averaged 150. Because the networks preempted the best hours of the broadcast day of its affiliates, it helped foreclose outlets for first-run syndication, which by 1964 had become virtually extinct.[36]

After seeing what was happening to the syndication market, UA attempted to become a program supplier to the networks and, according to Krim, "that's when we made another big mistake."[37] The market for network television programming resembled that for motion pictures in that there were a few buyers (the networks) and a large number of sellers (the producers). In the early days of television, prime-time programming emanated from advertising agencies, which either purchased product outright from Hollywood or produced it to suit their needs. The networks, in turn, functioned as distributors by selling time on the networks. Soon, though, the networks decided to exercise their monopsony power by taking control of programming. Economics, as always, played a part in the decision. As a result of rising production costs and the trend toward longer programming, fewer advertisers could afford to bankroll a show on a weekly or even an alternate-weekly basis. To get the most for their money, sponsors began to spread their commercial messages over a number of programs—spot buying—rather than concentrate them in one program or a few. ABC innovated the multishow buy in 1957, and as the practice of shared sponsorship proliferated, the historic network time-buying formats went out. Once cost factors forced a program into the participation fold, control swung from the hands of a particular advertiser to the network.

Rather than producing programming for prime time on their own, the networks preferred to deal with program packagers. In so doing, the networks shifted the risks to suppliers. Program packagers filled around a third of prime time in 1957, but by 1964, they accounted for nearly three quarters.[38] During this eight-year period, a total of over 200 packagers came and went; in any given year, about 70 were active. Not surprisingly, MCA and other major film companies ranked among the top suppliers, but close behind were any number of independent TV producers—Bing Crosby, Desilu, Four Star, Filmways, and QM, to name a few.

Ziv-UA produced twelve pilots, principally for James Aubrey at CBS. "We were constantly told that we were going to get three or four hours on the air, but they didn't select a single pilot," said Krim.[39] UA phased out Ziv's production operations in 1962 and changed the name of the subsidiary back to United Artists Television (UA-TV). Rather than producing programming, UA-TV returned to financing independent television production.

Getting off to a slow start, UA-TV placed only one program in the 1962–63 network sweepstakes—"Stoney Burke," an hour-long Western produced by Daystar Productions for ABC. At the end of the season, the show was canceled. For the 1963–64 season, UA-TV achieved a remarkable turnaround, placing six programs on prime time. Three were one-hour programs—"East Side, West Side," "The Outer Limits," and "The Fugitive." Modeled somewhat after "The Defenders," "East Side, West Side" was shot in New York and depicted the problems faced by a Manhattan social worker. Produced by David Susskind's Talent Associates, and starring George C. Scott and Cicely Tyson, the show was too serious and too depressing for TV tastes and was dropped after one season. Daystar's second entry, "The Outer Limits," was a science-fiction anthology series with guest stars and scary plot twists. ABC picked up the option for a second season, but placed it opposite "The Jackie Gleason Show" and the show bombed. "The Fugitive," however, produced by Quinn Martin for ABC, proved to be one of the most successful dramatic shows of the season. Starring David Janssen, who played a man on the run, the series lasted four years, maintaining strong ratings and a loyal audience. Two half-hour shows, "The New

Phil Silvers Show" and "The Patty Duke Show" were also winners. "The Patty Duke Show," produced by Peter Lawford's Chrislaw Productions, ran for three seasons, both on ABC and in Great Britain on the BBC. (Lawford parlayed the popularity of the program into a feature film for UA called *Billie,* in which Miss Duke repeated the tomboy role she played on TV.)

For the 1964–65 season, UA-TV came up with the popular "Gilligan's Island," produced by Sherwood Schwartz for Phil Silvers' production company, Gladasya Inc. The mindlessness of "Gilligan's Island" fit in well with James Aubrey's successful programming strategy, represented by the likes of "Beverly Hillbillies," "Petticoat Junction," and "Mr. Ed." "Gilligan's Island" lasted three seasons on prime time, followed by a long life in syndication.

After the 1964–65 season, UA-TV hit the doldrums. Network control over programming was complete and competition among suppliers more ferocious than ever. During the 1960–64 period, UA's television sales for new and continued series came to around $37 million, a 2.6 percent share that ranked UA 8 out of 20.[40] UA, as a result, phased out this aspect of its operations and concentrated on the distribution of feature films to television.

Distribution of Features to the Networks

By 1960, post-1948 features finally hit the television market with force and television thereafter became an integral part of the motion picture business. Before, conventional theatrical exhibition had been considered the primary source of revenue, with anything from TV just "gravy." But as relations between the two industries stabilized, television income became expected and planned for. Few new film projects were put into production without assessing their potential on TV. Television distribution typically began eighteen months after the end of the theatrical run, first to the networks and then to local stations.

Run-of-the-mill features leased to the networks fetched $150,000 for two showings in 1960, compared to an average sales price of $10,000 per film for the RKO library in 1955. Prices rose steadily, nudging the $800,000 mark by 1968, as the networks scheduled movies every night of the week. This figure was the average price for a regular feature in a package deal that allowed a network to air each picture twice. Hits and blockbusters commanded much higher prices.

UA began to sell packages of recent hits to CBS and ABC in 1964. The group for ABC, which included features like *Exodus, Judgment at*

Nuremberg, The Misfits, and *Some Like It Hot,* was "widely acknowledged [at the time] as the best package of features ever to play television.[41] But after these first deals, UA held back its product, "for the simple reason that the networks were playing one company against the other," said Krim.[42] In addition, UA anticipated a major move by NBC.

To counter the upward spiral of prices for feature films, NBC in 1965 had commissioned Universal to produce more than sixty low-cost made-for-television movies (MFT) over a five-year period. The network introduced the new hybrid in 1966 with "Fame Is the Name of the Game" on a series entitled "World Premiere." Although the MFT would eventually become a prime-time staple, the form initially lacked the prestige value and presold attraction of a hit movie.

For this reason, perhaps, NBC devised another scheme to protect its ratings; it also involved UA. Early in 1966, Arthur Krim received a call from Julian Goodman, president of NBC, saying the network had decided to go into motion pictures in a big way. NBC wanted UA's entire film library and suggested a complete buyout of the company. Upon reflection, however, NBC's legal counsel determined that a merger with UA would violate antitrust laws. The negotiation then shifted to NBC's buying just the film library. "They couldn't do that either, but they could acquire rights," said Krim. "Everything fell nicely into place and we made a deal, by far the biggest ever made to that time." Signed early in 1967, the deal was for $125 million and involved around seventy pictures produced after 1960. This averaged $1.2 million per film and represented the highest price ever paid until then for a package of major films.[43] Four of these pictures—*West Side Story, It's a Mad, Mad, Mad, Mad World, The Greatest Story Ever Told,* and *Tom Jones*—were sold for the unprecedented amount of $5 million each. As *Variety* described it, UA had "grabbed the lead in the home bijou market." Through its distribution fees and profit participation in these pictures, UA was able to pocket about half the money from the sale. UA's success in leasing feature films to television not only offset theatrical losses but also created a separate source of profits. Eventually, that made UA a prime candidate for conglomerate takeover.

Music Recording and Publishing

Like its entry into television production, UA started late and with little experience in music recording and publishing. The recording industry took off during the fifties as a result of the LP revolution, which began in 1948, as well as the growth of leisure-time spending and the bur-

The Beatles in *A Hard Day's Night* (1964), produced by Walter Shenson and directed by Richard Lester

geoning teen market. Record sales rose from around $80 million annually at the end of World War II to some $350 million in 1958.[44] There were approximately 15 million phonographs in the home of 1946; by 1969, the figure was estimated at 60 million. The remarkable boom in phonograph manufacturing "almost exactly paralleled that of the television industry," said *Variety's* Herm Schoenfeld.[45]

When UA formed United Artists Records in 1957, the recording industry was dominated by Columbia Records, RCA Victor, Capitol, and Decca. All the Hollywood majors either had diversified into the record business or were about to do so. Hundreds of record labels competed hotly for the consumer's dollar.

To break into this market, UA used its subsidiary to cross-promote UA's pictures through the sale of soundtracks and singles based on motion picture music. As a secondary and long-term function, the subsidiary set out to build a catalog of popular and classical records to fill the gaps in the market. To accomplish this, UA transferred its brand of independent production to the music field. As a UA promotional piece put it, "In its musical counterpart, independent record producers submit their album ideas. The best of the proposals, as selected by the company, are actually produced by the originator." The function of

United Artists Music was to license music from UA's pictures for performances on radio, television, records, and tapes.

Starting out inauspiciously in 1958 with the soundtrack of *Paris Holiday,* which starred Bob Hope, Fernandel, and Anita Ekberg, United Artists Records went on to release best-selling soundtrack albums and singles of *The Magnificent Seven, Exodus, Never on Sunday, The Pink Panther,* and *Goldfinger,* among others. UA's greatest hit was The Beatles' *A Hard Day's Night,* which sold 2 million copies after its release in 1964 and set an all-time record for soundtrack sales up to that time. By 1964, UA Records could describe itself as "the foremost record company in the film music field."

The results of UA Records' other operations were less than gratifying, however. UA discovered that synergy between motion pictures and records existed only with soundtracks. The few recording stars attracted to UA consisted of Vaughn Monroe, Steve Lawrence, Diahanne Carroll, and duo pianists Ferrante and Teicher, plus a few others. The popular music market changed drastically during the sixties. Herm Schoenfeld of *Variety* reported that 1966 "was the very end of the trail for the 'moon-june-spoon' school of pop songwriters and the beginning of a new epoch when hipsterism, nihilism and the rebellion of youth against their elders became the indispensible passwords to the best-selling charts."[46]

UA's catalog of releases, which included light classic, popular, folk, jazz, showtunes, and even speeches, had become dated. And the company was not prepared to invest the millions needed to discover and promote new talent. Nonetheless, the revenues of UA's music subsidiaries amounted to about 25 percent of the company's total revenues by 1966. The UA music companies obviously did not change the nature of UA's operations, but they did help stabilize its motion picture business.

After the takeover of UA by Transamerica Corporation (TA) in 1967, UA was forced to make another assault on the record business. Against UA's advice, TA acquired Liberty Records in 1968 for $22 million and merged the company with United Artists Records to form Liberty/ United Artists Records. A conglomerate with enormous financial resources, TA was moving aggressively from insurance and financial services to the leisure-time field. UA had been its first plum; Liberty was the next, or so TA hoped.

TA's purchase of Liberty was part of the trend toward mergers and acquisitions in the music business. As Herm Schoenfeld put it, "the music biz has become caught in the conglomerate whirlpool. Big business, which previously didn't know the difference between a copyright and an upright has begun swinging into the publishing and disk fields and wrapping up every firm in sight."[47] The year TA acquired Liberty, Warner Bros.–Seven Arts bought Atlantic Records for $17 million, which moved Warner up to number four in the recording industry; Gulf & Western absorbed Paramount and its Dot Records subsidiary; MCA added Kapp Records to its Decca, Uni, and Revue labels; and Twentieth Century–Fox acquired the venerable ASCAP music publishing firm, Bregman, Vocco & Conn.

The attraction for big business was that the recording industry had expanded immensely. In fact, it would soon surpass the motion picture industry in annual revenues and rank just behind broadcasting. A sign of the times was that an increasing number of hit records sold over 1 million copies each. By the middle sixties, about twenty-five disks and albums had entered the so-called golden circle (denoting 1 million sales); by 1969, the number was expected to reach the one hundred mark.[48]

Liberty's reputation as a "comer" in this business was a prime attraction for TA. Headquartered in Hollywood, Liberty started out in 1955 on a shoestring. Under the leadership of Alvin S. Bennett, Liberty signed unknown but promising artists to build a catalog of 2,000 LPs representing every segment of the popular-music field. Its top recording artists were Johnny Rivers, Cher, Gary Lewis, the Ventures, and the Fifth Dimension. Unlike United Artists Records, which distributed its product through independent jobbers, Liberty had established a strong, worldwide distribution system that handled 80 percent of the company's volume. Also unlike UA Records, Liberty owned recording studios, pressing plants, and warehousing. By combining UA Records and Liberty, TA created an operation that ranked sixth in the industry.

Liberty/UA showed profits the first two years, but in 1970 and 1971, the subsidiary lost $5.1 million and $3.8 million, respectively. This downturn occurred at the same time that UA experienced its first serious setback in twenty years. In 1970, UA racked up a pretax loss of $85 million. The loss resulted from problems that were besetting the entire film industry—problems such as mounting production costs, changing markets, and unpredictable tastes, which were shared by the record business as well.

The seventies began an era of "profitless prosperity" for many record companies, said *Variety*.[49] If sales moved ahead, so did costs. During the middle sixties, scores of independent producers and labels ground out hits, but rising costs thereafter made it progressively more expensive to produce and promote enough records to cover the entire spectrum of pop music. And only by producing a large number of records could a company develop talent and stand a chance to score a hit.

Since no market existed for the mediocre release, the record business was feast or famine. Market conditions therefore dictated the consolidation of the industry as record companies either fell by the wayside, or, like Liberty, were absorbed by conglomerates.

TA had anticipated that Liberty's association with UA would help the record company attract talent, but the two companies really didn't cross-fertilize one another to any appreciable extent. Nor could the mighty resources of the conglomerate insulate the record company from the ferocious competition that characterized the business. Keeping a superstar, for example, proved just as difficult as developing one. *Variety* reported that Clive J. Davis, president of Columbia Records, the largest record company in the business, had regularly spent spectacular sums of money to capture talent. It was understood in the industry, said *Variety*, that Davis had given a guarantee of over $3 million to Neil Diamond as an inducement to come over from MCA Records. Competition at the distribution level was equally cutthroat. Following Davis's firing from CBS for "misusing" $90,000 of corporate funds, a Federal grand jury investigated allegations that record companies regularly used payola, which now consisted of sex and drugs in addition to cash, to guarantee that their releases would be promoted on the air.[50]

After UA reorganized its record subsidiary (changing its name back to United Artists Records), replaced top management, and sharply reduced overhead, Liberty staged a turnaround in 1972. Reorganizing further, TA unloaded Liberty's record-distribution company in 1973 and then Liberty's production arm in 1975.

UA, meanwhile, bolstered its music publishing subsidiary by purchasing Robbins-Feist-Miller from MGM in 1973. Robbins had one of the most important catalogs in the music business and included many old standards and rights to most of the music from the MGM musicals. In the retrenchment that resulted from the 1969–72 recession in the motion picture industry, MGM and other film companies sold off assets, which included record subsidiaries, music publishing companies, studios, and backlots. Although the MGM music publishing companies were a good buy for UA and more than paid for themselves in a few years, the combined revenue from UA's music and records sales accounted for around 25 percent of the company's total in 1976, the same percentage as ten years before. UA, in spite of TA, remained primarily a motion picture distribution company throughout its history.

EXODUS

CHAPTER FOUR

Making Them Big

After going public, UA was off and running. In 1957, UA's worldwide theatrical gross came to $63 million; ten years later, when the company merged with TA, the gross hit $150 million. UA lost money once and that was only $800,000 in 1963, the first such loss in the thirteen-year Krim-Benjamin regime. UA rebounded afterward on the strength of James Bond, the Beatles, and Peter Sellers to set a new high for itself in 1965. In comparison with UA's achievement, the gross of the eleven other national distributors in this same period rose just 15 percent—from $610 million to $700 million.[1]

Industry recognition in the form of Academy Awards also set records. UA won Oscars for best picture five times during the sixties—for *The Apartment* (1960), *West Side Story* (1961), *Tom Jones* (1963), *In the Heat of the Night* (1967), and *Midnight Cowboy* (1969). Best actor awards went to David Niven (*Separate Tables*, 1958), Burt Lancaster (*Elmer Gantry*, 1960), Maximilian Schell (*Judgment at Nuremberg*, 1961), Sidney Poitier (*Lilies of the Field*, 1963), and Rod Steiger (*In the Heat of the Night*, 1967). In 1959, UA set a record by winning a total of twelve Oscars out of nineteen categories. In addition, the Academy presented honorary awards to UA producer Stanley Kramer and to Jerome Robbins, the director-choreographer of *West Side Story*.

Describing UA's financing policy after going public, Krim said, "We developed a volume business so that our basic distribution fee could create a profit margin to offset any writeoffs on unsuccessful pictures. When we did $150 million worldwide, our commission amounted to $50 million. Our distribution overhead ran between $30 to $35 million a year. With a $150 million distribution gross, we had a $15 or $20 million spread. With $200 million, we had a $30 or $40 million spread."[2]

UA adopted the "tonnage thesis." As defined by market analyst David Londoner, the thesis is that "distribution overhead is essentially fixed and that incremental product put through above break-even carries a disproportionately high profit contribution." Londoner warned, however, that "any practice that says 'go for the market share and earnings will take care of themselves' is a fine one until the competition emulates it. Obviously, if every one of the majors adopts it, there will be too much product, audiences will be spread too thin, and losses on the production side may be so great as to offset the profit contribution from distribution."[3] But the majors cut back on production; they released an average of 448 films a year from 1948 to 1952; an average of 366 from 1953 to 1957; and 240 from 1958 to 1964.[4] The mid- and low-budget pictures were the casualties as the industry swung away from the routine film and toward the blockbuster.

UA released forty films a year, on the average, from 1957 to 1962, servicing three markets—the class-A, the class-B, and the art-film market. In terms of quantity, about eight to ten fell in the first category each year; as many as twenty-five fell in the second, and three to five in the third. Beginning in 1963, UA reduced its volume of releases by half and thereafter distributed mostly "A" product that fit the comedy and/or action bill.

There would always be a place for pickup deals and one-shot arrangements, but to operate efficiently UA had to be assured of a steady flow of pictures. The company therefore rationalized its acquisition policy by developing long-term relationships with experienced producers who were willing and capable of sustaining a production operation. Such producers were difficult to find. UA had fifty independents under contract in this period. Many of them delivered nothing, a few delivered one or two pictures, and only a half dozen or so came through as hoped.

In the remainder of this chapter and others that follow, I have presented case studies of UA's principal suppliers. The case studies are grouped by markets, beginning with the "B" market, the "A" market, and finally the art-film market. Separate chapters are devoted to the Mirisch Corporation, which delivered an incredible sixty-seven pictures in eighteen years, and the Albert R. Broccoli–Harry Saltzman team, the producers of the equally incredible James Bond films.

Since the art film played an integral role in UA's foreign production activities, the related case studies are presented in two chapters devoted to UA's international operations. To tap the art-film market in the United States, UA acquired Lopert Films, an independent art-film distributor, and created a foreign-film distribution subsidiary called Lopert Pictures Corporation in 1958. Over the next ten years, Lopert released films of Jules Dassin, Tony Richardson, Ingmar Bergman, and François Truffaut, among other European filmmakers.

The case studies are presented primarily from the point of view of the producer, unlike the previous chapter which discussed the financing of independent production from UA's perspective. The goal now is to analyze how UA's suppliers differentiated their product to create a niche in the market. Every major category of independent is represented—the producer-director, the star as producer, and the packager.

THE "B" FILM MARKET

Demand for low-budget product remained strong throughout the fifties. As Freeman Lincoln explained, "The little picture is almost a necessity to the exhibitor in a small town where most of the available audience has seen a picture after a three-day run. The little westerns and other simple action pictures are important in many areas where the people generally prefer them to extravaganzas or to highbrow problem films. They are in heavy demand by the hundreds of exhibitors whose audiences insist on a long evening's entertainment, and so must have a 'second feature'."[5]

Even metropolitan areas required low-budget product. Subsequent-run theaters—the "nabes" in trade jargon—drew from a limited audience and, to attract the same moviegoers week after week required a steady supply of product for frequent program changes. These theaters also needed medium-budget films to fill the gap between releases of "A" features. As Thomas Doherty described it, "With the wait between 'A' features growing and the supply of alternative fare declining, many exhibitors faced a serious product shortage."[6]

Drive-ins faced a similar problem as their numbers increased almost tenfold during the fifties to nearly 5,000. Although distribution patterns changed to grant some of these theaters first-run status, drive-ins catered more and more to teenagers who thrived on the low-budget teenpic.

UA's principal suppliers of programmers were: Edward Small; Bel-Air Pictures, the production unit of Aubrey Schenck and Howard W. Koch; and Security Pictures, the production unit of Sidney Harmon and Philip Yordan. Edward Small was by far the most important. A specialist in low-budget fare, Small had become an enormously successful producer. *Variety* described him as a "one-man film industry." In one eighteen-month period around 1948, for example, he had sixteen pictures in release with Columbia, Fox, Eagle-Lion, and UA.[7] Joining up with Krim and Benjamin in 1952, he produced seventy-five "programmers" over the next ten years. In addition, he found time to produce several "A" pictures, including Billy Wilder's *Witness for the Prosecution* (1958) and King Vidor's *Solomon and Sheba* (1959).

Since only a limited demand existed for "B" product, producers had to pay strict attention to costs. Budgets on Small's pictures ranged from $100,000 to $300,000. UA sold this product on a flat-rental basis to a predetermined number of accounts, and as a result, could predict the gross to within 5 to 10 percent. By carefully monitoring costs, a producer could earn back the investment and then some. But Small only expected to break even in the theatrical market. For Small, profits resided in the ancillary value of his pictures; a picture released to syndicated television, for example, could fetch $70,000 on the average.

Programmers added nothing to UA's image; they were fodder for the distribution mill and required little effort or money to sell. Grossing between $300,000 and $500,000, a single picture did not generate much of a distribution fee. But UA made up for that with volume by releasing about twenty-five programmers a year. The strategy had the effect of reducing company overhead. Consider, for example, Edward Small's pictures. By 1954, he had delivered eighteen pictures. "If we spread the distribution earnings from these pictures over a two-year period," said Krim, "they take care of better than 25 percent of our expenses worldwide."[8] From 1957 to 1962, Small delivered nearly sixty pictures, which threw off more in fees and provided an even thicker cushion.

Like his counterparts on Poverty Row, Small followed trends and stuck to Westerns, crime melodramas, and exploitation films at first, and later teenpix. Shot within seven to nine days, Small's programmers had a running time of around seventy minutes. His seasoned production staff knew how to cut corners and keep the assembly line moving. The "stars" were lowercase names who received in the neighborhood of $25,000 per picture.

The most durable genre of the period was the Western. UA released from six to twelve a year until the genre died out after 1960. By then, the reviews went like this: "Even incurable western buffs would find nothing novel in the way of plot or character" (*Five Guns to Tombstone*). Or like this: "With the output of theatrical westerns down considerably since television went sagebrush-happy, this unpretentious item should be welcomed in situations where people gather to witness westerns on a big screen. There's absolutely nothing to *Noose for a Gunman* that's new or different in the western genre."

Another staple was the crime melodrama. Often shot in documentary style, this type of picture exploited sensational subject matter from the current scene. Small's *Pier 5, Havana* (1959), for example, depicted the aftermath of the Cuban revolution. And Small's *Kansas City Confidential* (1952), *Chicago Confidential* (1957), and *Hong Kong Confidential* (1958) cashed in, respectively, on a million-dollar Brinks holdup, a Senate probe of union racketeering, and British and American espionage activity. This genre was also killed off by television. A review of *Three Came to Kill* (1960) said, "The picture is little more than graduate school 'Dragnet,' the sort of fare that no longer has any real business being in the theatre."

As more and more young people entered the market, the teenpic came into vogue. The "teen" market had the potential for a great attendance revival. As *Variety* noted, these people represented the "restless" element of the population, the ones who didn't want to stay at home to watch TV and who were "still immune to any sophisticated disdain of run-of-the-mill screen offerings."[9]

The teenpic cycle was triggered by three hits—*The Creature from the Black Lagoon* (Universal-International, 1954); *The Blackboard Jungle* (MGM, 1955); and *Rebel Without a Cause* (Warner, 1955). Afterward, Hollywood went on a kick producing science fiction, horror, rock 'n' roll, and drag-racing films all aimed at teenagers. American International Pictures (AIP) rode the crest of this wave into the front ranks of independent film companies. Said Thomas Doherty, "For over twenty years, AIP gauged the tastes of successive generations of American teenagers, accumulating a filmography that documents the shifting trends, values, and lingo of its audience of the moment."[10]

For the teenpic market, UA had no hits on the order of AIP's *I Was a Teenage Werewolf* (1957) or Allied Artists' *The Invasion of the Body Snatchers* (1956) or pictures that developed the cult following of *Rebel Without a Cause*. Following industry practice, UA occasionally released its "B" product in pairs to form complete exhibition packages. A package might contain one "chiller" and one "spacer," as *Variety* called

Low Budget Productions for Nabes and Drive-Ins

Edward Small's *Kansas City Confidential* (1952)

Edward Small's *Pier 5, Havana* (1959): Cameron Mitchell and
Allison Hayes

Mat ad for a B-feature double bill

horror and science-fiction films respectively, or two of the same genre. As an example of the former, UA paired these two 1958 Edward Small productions: *Curse of the Faceless Man* and *It! The Terror from beyond Space*. As an example of the latter, UA paired these two 1959 crime melodramas by Small: *Vice Raid,* starring sex starlet Mamie Van Doren as a Detroit call girl, and *Inside the Mafia,* an exposé combining two incidents, the murder of kingpin Albert Anastasia in a Gotham barber's chair and a convention of Mafia leaders at a mountain lodge in Apalachin, New York.

This double-bill strategy appealed to drive-ins in particular. Each feature a shade longer than an hour TV show, these combinations lasted about the same time as one conventional "A" feature and had the advantage of appealing to two different (or, just as frequently, overlapping) teenage markets. They also provided a convenient intermission for the concession stand.

The market for "B" pictures dried up by the early sixties. Television killed off the Westerns and the crime melodramas, and the majors appropriated the teenpic by producing clean versions. But new distribution strategies also took their toll. In the fifties, a new picture typically opened simultaneously in one or two first-run theaters in thirty-five markets. When day-and-date distribution came along to take advantage of the geographical coverage of television advertising, a picture might play 800 to 1,500 theaters the same day. When this happened, former subsequent-run houses, drive-ins included, began to play new releases the same time as first-run theaters.

THE "A" FILM MARKET

To rekindle interest in the movies, Hollywood not only had to contend with television but also with other leisure-time activities. As the economy expanded, more and more Americans moved to the suburbs. People had more discretionary income than before and more options to spend it on. Moreover, workers enjoyed a shorter workweek and more paid vacation.[11] Leisure-time activities thrived. But money spent on bowling, boating, amateur photography, golf, hi-fis, recreational vehicles, and resorts drew disposable income away from the movies. Hollywood sought a piece of the leisure-time action with determination and with imagination.

Movies made a comeback by 1955, but audiences had changed. Moviegoing became a special event for most people, creating the phenomenon of the big picture. Where the middling picture may have barely scraped along before, it now did dismal business. On the other hand, pictures striking the public's fancy acted like magnets for the consumer dollar.

The trend had started by 1952 as pictures such as UA's *The African Queen,* MGM's *Quo Vadis?* and Paramount's *The Greatest Show on Earth* smashed boxoffice records. Cinerama and 3-D boosted business in 1953 and, following the introduction of CinemaScope, a turnaround was in the making. The innovation of Twentieth Century–Fox, CinemaScope debuted in *The Robe,* at the Roxy in New York on September 16, 1953. After a week of sensational business, the picture opened in a hundred other cities with the same results. Partly because of CinemaScope and partly because of its theme, *The Robe* set an industry record, grossing over $15 million (domestic) and $5 million (foreign).[12] Up to then, only about 100 pictures had grossed more than $5 million; in just eighteen months after *The Robe,* over thirty had done so.[13]

Abel Green, editor of *Variety,* stated on the first anniversary of CinemaScope that "the picture business—an industry founded on the very shoals of high adventure—has done it again . . . Here was a carefully charted course which called for steel and nerve. It was no penny-ante gamble. The stakes were high and the loss could have been greater."[14]

In adopting the big-budget philosophy, the industry differentiated its product from the entertainment fare on television. Roughly, the formula became "make them big; show them big; and sell them big."[15] Making them big meant investing in properties that were pretested and presold, such as best-selling novels, Broadway hits, and even successful television dramas. It also meant shooting on location. Demand for authentic locales sent Hollywood's production crews all over the free world and created what became known as "runaway production." Showing them big meant presenting pictures in a spectacular fashion using widescreen and wide film processes such as CinemaScope, Todd-AO, and Panavision. These processes projected bright and sharp images on giant curved screens and utilized stereophonic sound to approximate an illusion of depth. Selling them big meant long runs in roadshow situations backed by custom-made exploitation and promotion campaigns.

In short, Hollywood upscaled its top product in the face of waning consumer demand and raised the price of admission. Between 1946 and 1962, the total number of moviegoers dropped 73.4 percent, but boxoffice gross declined by only 48.3 percent. Without ticket price inflation (45.7 percent), the drop in boxoffice would have amounted to 70.4 percent.[16]

The overall financial health of the industry improved markedly after 1964. The blockbuster trend accelerated. Going into the sixties, only twenty pictures had grossed over $10 million in the domestic market; by the end of the decade, nearly eighty had topped that figure. In *Variety's* list of all-time boxoffice champions as of 1969, (see table 4.1), eight of the top ten pictures were products of the sixties. (I include *Ben-Hur* since it was released at the end of 1959.)

With the glaring exception of *The Graduate*, which, along with *Easy Rider, Midnight Cowboy, Bonnie and Clyde*, and others, marked a radical shift in audience tastes beginning in 1967, the money winners were almost exclusively family pictures—biblical epics, spectaculars, musicals, comedies, and action pictures. The company most closely associated with the family trade was Walt Disney Productions, which struggled for survival after the war to become a broadly based entertainment-recreation company during the sixties. (Disney's growth as an entertainment conglomerate is described in chapter 10.) Although motion picture revenues represented only about half of Disney's total intake, they represented a substantial 9 percent share of the domestic gross captured by the ten national distributors in 1970.

Disney achieved the status of a motion picture major by shifting from animation to live-action documentaries and features and by forming a national distribution outlet called Buena Vista, in 1953. In the face of unreliable motion picture business, Disney kept production small, to around a half dozen pictures a year. The formula for the live-action features crystallized in such early productions as *Treasure Is-*

Table 4.1. Variety's Top Ten Boxoffice Champs, 1969

Title (Distributor and Date)	Domestic Distribution Gross (in thousands)
1. *The Sound of Music* (20th; 1965)	$72,000
2. *Gone with the Wind* (MGM; 1939)	71,105
3. *The Graduate* (Avco Embassy; 1967)	43,100
4. *The Ten Commandments* (Par.; 1956)	40,000
5. *Ben-Hur* (MGM; 1959)	39,105
6. *Doctor Zhivago* (MGM; 1965)	38,243
7. *Mary Poppins* (Disney; 1964)	31,000
8. *My Fair Lady* (WB; 1964)	30,000
9. *Thunderball* (UA; 1965)	27,000
10. *Cleopatra* (20th; 1963)	26,000

Source: *Variety*, January 7, 1970, p. 25

land, The Story of Robin Hood, and *The Sword and the Rose* and it was with this type of picture that Disney made it big. During the sixties, Disney's hits included *Swiss Family Robinson* (1960), *101 Dalmations* (1961), *The Absent-Minded Professor* (1961), *The Jungle Book* (1967), and *Mary Poppins* (1964). Produced at a cost of $5.2 million, *Mary Poppins* became the boxoffice winner of 1965 and eventually grossed $45 million worldwide. On the strength of this picture, the revenues of Walt Disney Productions in 1965 were up more than 800 percent over 1954 to $110 million, and profits were up over 1,400 percent to $11 million.[17]

Disney's diversification into television and leisure time cross-promoted his pictures and carved a special niche for the company in the theatrical market. For the other majors, the market remained volatile. This unpredictability of audiences led *Variety* to evaluate a typical year's business at the boxoffice as follows: "It was a strange year at the nation's boxoffices with some very big, very expensive releases failing to make it; some medium-weights turning out to be heavyweights; and most pleasant of all, some admittedly 'little' pictures really catching the public's fancy."[18] Other than Disney's releases, precious few "little" pictures captured big boxoffice dollars. In 1960, the year *Ben-Hur* racked up a $17 million domestic gross, Paramount released Alfred Hitchcock's *Psycho,* which was produced at a cost of $1 million and grossed $8.5 million to earn the number-three spot on *Variety's* annual list of winners. In 1962, the year UA's *West Side Story* won top honors, UA also released the Greek-made *Never on Sunday,* directed by Jules Dassin, which cost a paltry $150,000 and grossed a hefty $4 million. More often than not, the offbeat film died in the stix, such as Stanley Kubrick's *Lolita.* Said *Variety,* "A big study lamp is warranted for *Lolita.* Here's a case of a picture getting off to raves, very strong money at the start (in the first runs), strong word of mouth and a genuinely provocative campaign. It had all the earmarks of klondikesville. The estimated gross of $4,500,000 is respectable. But so much more was looked for. Seems that the little girl with the sun glasses and lollipop didn't go over so well in the neighborhoods as she did in the showcases."[19]

Although the majors relied mostly on blockbusters to drum up business, the risks of producing these pictures were as great as their boxoffice potential. Blockbusters not only cost more to produce; they also required more time for recoupment. A medium- or low-budget film could be produced and placed in general release in a few months; but a big-budget picture took a year or more to produce and required a time-consuming method of distribution. Blockbusters were typically released first in limited engagements, such as roadshows, and then placed in general release. Foreign distribution further prolonged the payoff. Nearly every major studio, including UA, was brought to the brink of disaster by one or two of these extravaganzas that turned out to be financial disappointments. The decade is replete with big expensive pictures that failed to make it. After releasing the enormously successful remake of *Ben-Hur* in 1959, which grossed $75 million worldwide in two years, MGM squandered its profits on the remake of *Mutiny on the Bounty,* which cost $30 million to produce and which was largely responsible for MGM's loss of over $17 million in 1963. Twentieth Century–Fox's *Cleopatra*, originally budgeted at $2 million, escalated to $44 million and forced Fox president Spyros Skouras to relinquish his position to Darryl Zanuck in 1962 (a year before *Cleopatra's* premiere) and was largely responsible for Fox's loss of nearly $40 million in 1962.

It took more than three years for *Cleopatra* to earn back its investment, but this did not dissuade Zanuck from adopting a "key picture" philosophy to keep Fox afloat. Zanuck turned the company around in 1963 when *The Longest Day,* which he had previously made as an independent producer, became an instant success. Afterward, he placed into production a series of blockbusters beginning with *The Sound of Music* (1965), *The Agony and the Ecstasy* (1965), and *The Bible* (1966). Robert Wise's production of *The Sound of Music,* starring Julie Andrews, became Fox's biggest money-maker. Produced at a cost of $20 million, the picture played more than twenty months on a reserved-seat basis in as many as 266 roadshow engagements and outgrossed *Gone with the Wind* (1939), which had been released six times over twenty-seven years. Although in keeping with Hollywood's strategy of producing biblical epics, Carol Reed's *The Agony and the Ecstacy* and Dino DeLaurentiis' *The Bible* did not generate the revenue predicted by Fox. Nonetheless, the record-setting pace of *The Sound of Music* propelled Fox to the top of the Hollywood pecking order by 1966.[20]

Then Zanuck's luck ran out. Fox lost $37 million in 1967 and in 1970, dragged down by such turkeys as *Dr. Doolittle, Hello Dolly!, Star,* and *Tora! Tora! Tora!,* it posted a staggering $77.4 million loss. Fox's fortunes were symptomatic of the industry's. Beginning in 1969 and lasting until 1972, Hollywood experienced one of the worst recessions in its history. Going into the sixties, Hollywood regarded the sale of feature films to the networks as frosting on the cake—as a source of profits. But as the big-budget philosophy caught on and budgets soared, the majors regarded television as a means of covering the downside— that is, as a means of amortizing production costs. *Cleopatra* offers a good example of television's new role. After three years in release, which included a massive worldwide publicity and exploitation campaign, a tough money policy for the roadshow that required huge, non-returnable advance payments from exhibitors and top-dollar, reserved-seats-only tickets from viewers, and finally, a playoff that involved a total of 8,500 theaters, *Cleopatra* had still not recovered its costs. It took an extraordinary television deal to push the picture into the black. In 1966, Fox consummated a deal with ABC for two showings of *Cleopatra*—price, $5 million, which *Variety* said at the time represented "the largest amount ever given for a single picture to be shown on TV." [21]

Cleopatra was just one picture in a seventeen-picture package. Three other pictures—*The Longest Day, The Agony and the Ecstasy,* and *Those Magnificent Men in Their Flying Machines*—fetched $7.2 million as a group. This sale led a Fox executive to remark, "We know that if we upgrade the value of the film for the theater, it upgrades the value on television." [22] Such a policy had disastrous consequences at the end of the decade, when the networks, fully positioned with product, stopped bidding on features. For a while, at least, the majors stopped making blockbusters.

UNITED ARTISTS' BLOCKBUSTERS

UA released only a few blockbusters before going public: *The African Queen* (1952); *Vera Cruz* (1954); *Barefoot Contessa* (1954), an Italian-American coproduction filmed in Italy under the direction of Joseph L. Mankiewicz and starring Humphrey Bogart and Ava Gardner; *Alexander the Great* (1956), a spear-and-sandal epic shot in Spain and Italy, written, produced, and directed by Robert Rossen and starring Richard Burton; and Michael Todd's *Around the World in 80 Days* (1956).

Around the World set the boxoffice record in the widescreen sweepstakes. The public loved just about everything in the picture—the action-packed plot starring David Niven, Cantinflas, Robert Newton, and Shirley MacLaine, the fifty cameo appearances of such stars as Robert Morley, Red Skelton, Marlene Dietrich, and Noel Coward; the subtle satire; the theme song by Victor Young; and especially the magnificent locales shot in Eastman Color and in stunning Todd-AO. At Academy Award time, *Around the World* picked up Oscars for best picture, color cinematography, film editing, music score, and original screenplay.

A former Broadway impresario and founding partner of Cinerama, Todd had joined forces with American Optical Company in 1953 to innovate a 65mm panoramic system developed by American Optical

Academy Award for Best Picture / 1956

Around the World in 80 Days

Cantinflas and David Niven

A Michael Todd Co. presentation
Starring David Niven, Cantinflas, Robert Newton, and Shirley
  MacLaine
Directed by Michael Anderson
Produced by Michael Todd

Other Academy Awards* and nominations
Direction: Michael Anderson
*Writing *screenplay*: James Poe, John Farrow, and S. J. Perelman
*Cinematography *color*: Lionel Lindon
Art direction–Set decoration *color*: James W. Sullivan and Ken Adam,
  Ross J. Dowd
Costume design *color*: Miles White
*Film editing: Gene Ruggiero and Paul Weatherwax
*Music *score*: Victor Young

Charles Boyer and Cantinflas

Robert Newton, David Niven, and Shirley MacLaine

which they dubbed Todd-AO. For his first venture, Todd scored a coup by securing the rights to Rogers and Hammerstein's Broadway hit *Oklahoma!* Rogers and Hammerstein had turned down all previous offers for their hit musical, but they were so taken with the visual quality and sound of the Todd-AO system they finally acquiesced. Rogers and Hammerstein, moreover, helped finance the picture by going into partnership with United Artists Theatre Corporation (no relation to UA, the distribution company) to form a venture called Magna Theatre Corporation.[23] Released in 1955 by Magna, *Oklahoma!* became a smash hit. *Oklahoma!* opened first in key cities in theaters specially equipped for Todd-AO. Later, in smaller situations, the picture was shown in a CinemaScope version and at regular prices.

As *Variety* said of Mike Todd in its review of *Around the World,* "If anyone bet against him on this one, they might as well start paying up right now." Based on Jules Verne's novel *Around the World in 80 Days,* the picture was originally budgeted at $2.5 million. But Todd miscalculated; shooting on location all over the world with a cast of thousands cost more than anticipated. The final cost came to $6 million. In need of additional financing, Todd made the rounds at the studios. UA put up $2 million, but only on the condition that the repayment of this loan would take first position and that UA would take over the distribution of the picture.

Like *Oklahoma!, Around the World* was roadshowed the first time around in select theaters on a two-a-day basis. After the premiere in New York's Rivoli on October 17, 1956, it opened in all the key cities in Todd-AO for the year-end holidays. And also like *Oklahoma!,* it played wide in a CinemaScope version. By the end of 1958, *Around the World* grossed $23 million. UA's profit participation in the picture was only 10 percent, but nobody at the company complained.

Public financing eased UA's entry into the big-picture era, but unlike Twentieth Century–Fox, UA avoided disaster by hedging its bets. In addition to exercising the usual rights of approval, UA also kept production costs generally low. As pointed out by Robert W. Crandall, the average cost of a film during the heyday of the blockbuster rose from $2 million in 1965 to $3 million in 1968.[24] The average cost of a UA release during this period was $2.3 million. Even UA's blockbusters cost less. UA released from one to three big pictures a year from 1957 to 1969. Production costs ranged from $3.5 million for Kirk Douglas' *The Vikings* (1958) to $21 million for George Stevens' *The Greatest Story Ever Told.* The Stevens picture was an anomaly since the average cost for UA's blockbusters came to a sensible $8.8 million.

But budgets by themselves do not reveal the extent of risk. UA also hedged its bets by cross-collateralizing profits in multiple-picture deals.

Because Stanley Kramer's *Not as a Stranger* was crossed with *The Pride and the Passion,* UA lost $700,000 on the two pictures instead of $2.5 million. The first blockbuster UA released after going public, *The Pride and the Passion* demonstrated the inherent risks of the blockbuster because even the star power of Cary Grant and Frank Sinatra could not turn a profit.

Another typical form of protection was the presold property, such as a Broadway musical or a best-selling novel. After agreeing to finance Otto Preminger's *Exodus* (1960), for example, UA cross-promoted Leon Uris' novel, which Preminger read in manuscript, to help keep it on the best-seller list for 79 weeks, during which time the novel sold 400,000 copies in hardcover and 3,000,000 copies in paperback. Preminger's film, the first American picture shot entirely on location in Israel and Cyprus, cost $4.1 million to produce and grossed close to $20 million worldwide.

And finally, UA evaluated the track record of the producer. For example, UA would not permit Saltzman and Broccoli to venture into non–James Bond pictures until the series had generated a substantial cushion. Broccoli individually produced *Chitty, Chitty, Bang, Bang* in 1969, a virtual imitation of the Disney classic, *Mary Poppins.* Based on a collection of children's stories by Ian Fleming, the author of the James Bond novels, *Chitty* cost $12 million to produce and lost $11 million in its theatrical run. Saltzman individually produced *The Battle of Britain* in 1969, an imitation of *The Longest Day.* On *Battle of Britain* and four other Saltzman productions, UA lost a total of $19 million. But as great as these losses were, they were more than offset by the distribution fees and production profits UA enjoyed from the Bond pictures.

Despite such protections, UA got stung by a blockbuster. The picture was George Stevens' *The Greatest Story Ever Told,* which had the distinction of becoming the most ambitious and expensive film ever to be shot in the United States. (Other blockbusters squandered their money overseas.) Stevens had originally spent three years and $2.3 million to develop Fulton Oursler's best-seller, *The Greatest Story Ever Told,* for Twentieth Century–Fox. However, after Fox lost close to $16 million on its film operations in 1960, the board decided to jettison the project. Explaining the decision, a board member said, "Fox had an inventory of nearly $100 million in scenarios and unreleased films. . . . and cannot commit itself to a project whose final cost it doesn't know."[25]

In acquiring the rights to the property, UA paid no money out-of-pocket; instead, the company agreed to reimburse Fox its development cost—$1 million of which had gone to Stevens as salary—from profits of the picture. UA's deal with Stevens called for a producer fee of $300,000 and a division of profits 25 percent to UA and 75 percent to

Max Von Sydow in George Stevens' *The Greatest Story Ever Told* (1965)

Stevens. More unusual, the deal gave UA no overbudget protection. Normally when a producer went overbudget, he gave up profit points, but not Stevens; for *The Greatest Story Ever Told*, UA had unlimited completion responsibility.

UA probably made this concession for several reasons. First, the picture was originally budgeted at a modest $7.4 million based on a twenty-three-week shooting schedule in the United States. In other words, Stevens did not present *The Greatest Story* as a spectacular like *The Ten Commandments* and *Ben-Hur,* but as a drama of the life of Christ. Second, biblical pictures had been spectacularly successful. *The Greatest Story* in the hands of a man of Stevens' stature, Fox president Skouras often said, had the potential of grossing $100 million and of becoming the most successful picture ever made. Third, UA bet on the man: Stevens had a reputation for integrity and ability— Stevens had been president of the Screen Directors' Guild and the Academy of Motion Picture Arts and Sciences; he had won Academy Awards as producer-director for *A Place in the Sun* (1951) and *Giant* (1956); and he was the recipient of the Academy's Irving G. Thalberg Memorial Award (1953). On the basis of the two pictures just mentioned and others ranging from *Swing Time* in 1936 to *Shane* in 1953 to *The Diary of Anne Frank* in 1959, *Time* described Stevens as "beyond question the most respected and probably the most able director in the American film industry."[26] And last, Stevens had been linked to *The Greatest Story* for so long that even before production began, *The Greatest Story,* along with *The Diary of Anne Frank,* prompted the Jewish National Fund to present Stevens with its Humanitarian Award. The award was presented to Stevens at a banquet in Beverly Hills a month before the start date of the picture.

Stevens' achievements and the promise of the picture, therefore, must have been all the protection that UA required. Unfortunately, the picture ran into problems from the start. Principal photography, scheduled to begin in September 1962, had to be delayed for over a month because the Panavision 70 camera and equipment were not ready. Then the housing contractor was late in providing accommodations at the remote location sites located in Glen Canyon, Utah, and Pyramid Lake, Nevada. Once shooting started, bitterly cold weather at Glen Canyon forced the company back to the studio, with several weeks of work remaining to be completed at that location. Shooting at Pyramid Lake had to be extended by half again as a result of the most severe snowstorm in over fifty years. These delays added $2.6 million to the budget.

But the trouble may also have resided in Stevens. When shooting started, William Trombley reported Stevens as lacking any sense of urgency. "We will take as much time as we need, and the picture will cost what it will cost," said Stevens. Whatever its original conception, *The Greatest Story* blossomed into a financial extravaganza. As Trombley described it, the picture had "117 speaking parts, employed 30 Academy Award winners before and behind the cameras and provided 5,000 man-days of work for principal actors and 30,000 for extras. A half dozen writers, among them poet Carl Sandburg, worked on the script. Forty-seven major sets were built, including nine that cost more than $100,000 each. Complete villages of tents, trailers, and prefab bungalows were erected at location sites in Nevada and Utah. Aides of Stevens recruited enough animals to make up a Who's Zoo. The search for four white donkeys—one for Christ to ride and three stand-ins—alone took six months."[27]

UA had fallen into the blockbuster trap. A picture of enormous box-office potential goes overbudget immediately into production. What to do? If the company pulls the plug, the entire investment is lost and the company suffers the wrath of the creative community for not permitting the filmmaker to realize his masterpiece. So more money is pumped in with the hope that no more catastrophes occur.

UA had revised the budget upward to $12 million for *The Greatest Story* by the summer of 1963 and the picture completed principal photography seventeen weeks behind schedule. The rationale to pump more money into the production was easy. For one thing, the religious press had been waxing enthusiastic over the picture. After visiting the set, one religious reporter said, "One can hardly evaluate all the signs without sensing that *The Greatest Story Ever Told* may be—at long last—the motion picture about the life and influence of Christ for which millions have been waiting." For another, the new Cinerama process which UA planned to use for the roadshow had proven to be an attraction in itself. The new Cinerama process eliminated the three-panel division of the original process by screening the full image through one specially equipped projector. After observing the results of the process on *How the West Was Won,* which was then in current release, UA said "This picture would be just another big western if it were released in an ordinary process, and it would be likely to gross $15,000,000 worldwide. As a result of it being in Cinerama . . . a reasonable estimate of the ultimate gross of the picture is that it will be approximately $40 million world-wide. *The Greatest Story Ever Told* is so far superior to *How the West Was Won* that it is highly unlikely that it would not exceed the gross of *How the West Was Won.*"[28]

Out of such stuff are blockbuster dreams made. UA released *The Greatest Story* in February 1965, in time for the Easter Holiday season. Although UA attempted to keep the production cost secret, to focus attention on the merits of the picture, word soon got out that the price tag had come to $21 million.

The Greatest Story premiered at the Warner Cinerama Theater in New York on February 15, 1965. Two days later, the picture had its West Coast premiere in Los Angeles at Pacific's Cinerama Theater. The critical reception was about as acerbic as any on record. Brendan Gill of *The New Yorker* said, "If the subject matter weren't sacred in origin, we would be responding to the picture in the most charitable way possible by laughing at it from start to finish; this Christian mercy being denied us, we can only sit and sullenly marvel at the energy with which, for nearly four hours, the note of serene vulgarity is triumphantly sustained."[29]

"Three hours and 41 minutes worth of impeccable boredom," said *Time:* "Its sole distinction lies in its contrast to those rambunctiously zealous camp meetings that Cecil B. DeMille used to patch together out of breastplates, flexed muscles and Persian rugs."[30] Bosley Crowther of the *New York Times* said, "By staging the story of Jesus against the vast topography of the American Southwest and mingling the mystical countenance of Max von Sydow, the Swedish actor, with a sea of familiar faces of Hollywood stars, the producer-director George Stevens has made what surely is the world's most conglomerate Biblical picture."[31]

Critics found just about everything offensive—Stevens' literal and orthodox interpretations, the excessive running time, the sets "by Hallmark," the music, and particularly the cameos. As *Time* put it, George Stevens "summoned unto him so many actors great and small that Galilee often seems but a stone's throw from Desilu."[32] Shana Alexander said in *Life*, "I resented the tricky insurance of 'cameo' casting which gave us brief, jarring glimpses of Shelley Winters as a leper, Carroll Baker as the woman who wipes the blood from Christ's brow, John Wayne as a centurion at the Crucifixion. I disliked the cheap, Sunday-School symbolism of making Sidney Poitier play the one man who helps Christ carry the cross."[33] *Variety*, which gave the picture a relatively favorable review, nonetheless coldly appraised the situation stating that "it should attain global payoff with all deliberate slow speed, with particular expectations from Catholic countries."[34]

Responding to the reviews, Robert Benjamin told a UA stockholder, "We do not feel that the adverse reviews . . . will have any substantial effect on the picture's success." UA planned a slow and deliberate campaign that was designed to build the picture's prestige. For example, the Washington, D.C., premiere on March 10, 1965, was sponsored by the United Nations Association and the Eleanor Roosevelt Memorial Foundation under the "patronage of the President of the United States and Mrs. Johnson" as a benefit for the International Cooperation Year.

Krim told UA stockholders that *The Greatest Story* would be "seen over a longer period of time by more people and over a longer period of time than has been true of any other motion picture in the history of motion pictures."[35] The prediction was based on advance sales. De-

Making Them Big

Table 4.2. United Artists' Boxoffice Champs, 1957–1969

Title (Producer and Date)	Domestic Distribution Gross (in thousands)
Thunderball (Saltzman-Broccoli, 1965)	$27,000
West Side Story (Mirisch-Seven Arts, 1961)	25,000
Goldfinger (Saltzman-Broccoli, 1964)	22,500
It's a Mad, Mad, Mad, Mad World (Kramer, 1963)	19,300
You Only Live Twice (Saltzman-Broccoli, 1967)	18,000
Tom Jones (Woodfall, 1963)	17,200
Hawaii (Mirisch, 1966)	16,000
Irma La Douce (Mirisch, 1963)	12,100
In the Heat of the Night (Mirisch, 1967)	11,000
Midnight Cowboy (Hellman-Schlesinger, 1969)	11,000
The Russians Are Coming, the Russians Are Coming (Mirisch, 1966)	10,000
The Apartment (Mirisch, 1960)	9,300
From Russia, with Love (Saltzman-Broccoli, 1964)	9,200
Exodus (Preminger, 1960)	8,700
What's New, Pussycat? (Feldman, 1965)	8,700
Some Like It Hot (Mirisch, 1959)	8,300
The Alamo (Wayne, 1960)	8,000
Chitty, Chitty, Bang, Bang (Broccoli, 1968)	7,500
The Greatest Story Ever Told (Stevens, 1965)	7,000
A Shot in the Dark (Mirisch, 1964)	6,700
The Thomas Crown Affair (Mirisch, 1968)	6,100
The Vikings (Douglas, 1958)	6,049
The Pink Panther (Mirisch, 1964)	6,000
A Hard Day's Night (Shenson, 1964)	6,000
Help! (Shenson, 1965)	6,000
Hang 'Em High (Eastwood, 1968)	6,000
Solomon and Sheba (Small, 1959)	5,500
Dr. No (Saltzman-Broccoli, 1962)	5,500
The Great Escape (Mirisch, 1963)	5,500
Elmer Gantry (Brooks, 1960)	5,200
On the Beach (Kramer, 1959)	5,000
Judgment at Nuremberg (Kramer, 1961)	5,000
The Good, the Bad, and the Ugly (Grimaldi, 1967)	5,000
The Pride and the Passion (Kramer, 1957)	4,500
McLintock! (Wayne, 1963)	4,500
Boy, Did I Get a Wrong Number (Small, 1966)	4,400
Sergeants 3 (Sinatra, 1962)	4,300
The Devil's Brigade (Wolper, 1968)	4,200
The Misfits (Seven Arts, 1961)	4,100
The Horse Soldiers (Mirisch, 1959)	4,000
Never on Sunday (Dassin, 1960)	4,000
Topkapi (Filmways–Dassin, 1964)	4,000

Source: *Variety*, January 7, 1970, pp. 25, 27, 32.

spite the reviews, the advance sales in such keys as New York, Los Angeles, and Chicago had more than offset the number of tickets being used up for each week's performance—the criterion by which distributors projected the potential length of a hard-ticket run. One year after its release, *The Greatest Story* had grossed $12.1 million, almost equally divided between domestic and foreign. Although UA remained confident that the picture would eventually recoup its full cost over a five- to ten-year period, well beyond the normal recoupment period, the company decided to adopt a "conservative accounting procedure" by writing off 60 percent of *Greatest Story* in 1965. Much of the write-off was recaptured in 1967 by leasing the picture to NBC for $5 million. Television marketing thereafter made the film an Easter and Christmas perennial, ultimately reducing the loss even more.

UA became involved in another uncontrollable picture after Krim and Benjamin left the company. The picture, Michael Cimino's *Heaven's Gate*, helped to destroy UA. That *The Greatest Story Ever Told* did not do significant damage was the result of the large number of hits the company had in release during this period. UA's boxoffice champs are listed in table 4.2, along with their domestic distribution grosses. (As *Variety* points out when it publishes its annual compilation, a picture can be presumed to gross an equal amount in the foreign market.) Most of the pictures listed in table 4.2 are described in the following analyses of UA's principal suppliers.

Stanley Kramer

UA's assessment of Stanley Kramer is probably best expressed by Bosley Crowther, film critic for the *New York Times*, who described Kramer as "one of a slowly diminishing breed [of American producers] not particularly noted for its contentiousness and audacity [who] has run up an excellent record of forceful films on vital themes."[36] Crowther spoke on the eve of the world premiere of Kramer's *Judgment at Nuremberg*, which was held in West Berlin in December 1961. Crowther had championed Kramer for more than a decade, perhaps because the themes of Kramer's pictures seemed to reflect the liberal sentiments of his paper. In a piece he wrote for the *New York Times Magazine* in 1950, Crowther described him as a "new Hollywood genius" who had the knack of producing pictures of high artistic merit on low budgets. Looking over his output during the fifties, Crowther said, "by surreptitiously producing the first all-out film about race prejudice" (*Home of the Brave*), by arousing the ire of civil defense and military authorities by producing *On the Beach,* a strong film based upon the premise that everyone in the world would be killed by fall-out from an atomic war,"

Stanley Kramer

and by charging the American Legion with being "un-American" by trying to dictate employment policies to the movie industry, Kramer had been labeled a "character" by conservatives in Hollywood, "the foremost of the very few willful independents."[37]

Kramer characterized himself as a creative producer pitted against the system. "The entrenched managements of the large film companies," said Kramer, are "more critical and obstructive toward me (and toward the forward progress of motion pictures) than all the others," he said. "They are the ones who are toughest, most reactionary and adamant about what sort of pictures should be made and what sort of people should make them."[38]

Presumably, Kramer was referring to his experience at Columbia where he produced eleven pictures, among them *Death of a Salesman* (1951), *The Four-Poster* (1952), *The Member of the Wedding* (1952), *The Wild One* (1954), and *The Caine Mutiny* (1954). Signing Kramer to a multiple-picture contract in 1951 was part of Columbia's attempt to expand its class-A production and move into the big time. Kramer functioned as head of a semiautonomous production unit that had the right to choose stories and cast. Kramer's staff had been with him from the start, and included production designer Rudy Sternad, composer-conductor Dimitri Tiomkin (whose place would later be taken by Ernest Gold), editor Harry Gerstad, and production manager Clem Beauchamp. Harry Cohn wanted Kramer to use Columbia's personnel to reduce studio overhead. Kramer prevailed, but at a price; Cohn tacked on the regular 25 percent overhead charge for the use of Columbia's studio and facilities. Columbia supplied the financing up to $900,000 per picture. Kramer could go as high as he wished, but had to provide the overage himself. Since Kramer had built his reputation producing low-budget pictures, it seemed unlikely that he would require any outside financing.[39]

Midway through the second year of his contract, Columbia tightened the reins. Kramer had six pictures in release, none of which showed signs of earning a profit. (*High Noon* was given to UA for distribution to fulfill Kramer's old pact with the company.) The pictures had been "artistic successes," but Columbia wanted something more commercial. As one Columbia stockholder put it, "We're interested in dividends, not awards."[40] Thereafter, Columbia reappropriated the approval rights and insisted that Kramer cut back on production.

Kramer completed his commitments to Columbia in 1955 and began a new phase of his career as a producer-director. Concerning this decision Kramer said: "One of the things I regret about my life is all those years I had to be a money raiser, a producer. Some people say I should have stayed a producer, that I was better at it than directing. But to tell the truth, I was ill equipped to be a producer. I always wanted to be a director. I had been training for it since my early days as an editor and a writer. And as soon as I could break away from producing and move on to directing, I did so."[41]

But being a creative producer meant more than taking on the directing assignment; it meant knowing the rules by which "the big boys" who still controlled the "all important machinery of distribution" conducted their enterprise. Of these rules, he said, "I have to know which ones I must abide by in order to safely break other ones." A creative producer need not compromise nor invalidate his integrity and the "purity" of his art. Said Kramer, "The trick is to be creative in how one abides by the rules." To clarify what he meant, Kramer said, "My object with *Nuremberg* . . . was to make it as 'purely' as I could; in so far as writing, casting, directing and all artistry were concerned. But within that purity I was conscious of the demands on me. It had to be pure so it could take along with it the elements that are supposed to be crass." As an example of a crass element, Kramer cited the necessity of casting name stars for the picture.[42]

With UA, Kramer started off with a two-picture deal that provided total financing, an overhead allowance to keep his production staff intact, a producer's fee of $100,000 per picture ($50,000 of which was deferred) and 60 percent of the profits. He then proceeded to make two "oversized potboilers."

Kramer described the initial effort, *Not as a Stranger* (1955), as "the first open and respectable assault on the unsavory aspect of the modern medical profession."[43] Based on the best-selling novel by Morton Thompson, the rights to which Kramer acquired when the book was in galleys, the picture starred Robert Mitchum as the arrogant doctor "who practiced medicine but didn't know how to treat people."[44] Produced at a cost of $1.5 million, *Not as a Stranger* earned a profit of $1.8 million.

Kramer required three years to prepare *The Pride and the Passion* (1957), his first go at a blockbuster. As a UA publicity release announced, "As an independent producer who has always dared to compete with the mightiest, most expansive and most expensive projects of the major film companies, Kramer became convinced that his next production must, perforce, contain all the technical elements that have brought a new era of dramatic excitement, and, consequently, new prosperity to the screen."

Based on another best-seller, *The Gun* by C. S. Forester, *The Pride and the Passion* told the story of a band of dedicated guerrilla fighters who drag a huge cannon across Spain to defeat Napoleon's forces occupying Avila. *Passion* contained all the elements of the epic film—"matching, if not surpassing, the dimensions of *Gone with the Wind* and *The Ten Commandments*." It had an international cast, consisting of Cary Grant, Frank Sinatra, and Sophia Loren, colorful backgrounds (shot on location in Spain in "the three-dimensional pictorial beauty of Vista Vision") and spectacle—the *raison d'être* for the picture was a cannon, described in the script as "the most extraordinary machine of destruction in its time . . . with a barrel over forty feet long, wheels eighteen feet high; its weight, six thousand pounds; its power, awesome and deadly at great range."

Produced for $3.7 million, a modest amount even by fifties' standards, *The Pride and the Passion* "was more than a bomb—it was a bust!" said Kramer.[45] Commented Peter Cowie, the picture was "scarcely distinguishable from other historical spectacles (*War and Peace* and *Raintree Country* were two typical examples of the period), and generally speaking its characters were lost in the very vastness of the production."[46] Grossing only $6.7 million worldwide, *The Pride and the Passion* lost $2.5 million; since it was cross-collateralized with *Not as a Stranger*, Kramer ended up with no profits on the two ventures and UA was stuck with a $700,000 production loss.

However, in negotiating a new six-picture deal with Kramer in December 1957, UA bought out all of Kramer's interest in *Not as a Stranger* and *The Pride and the Passion* for $550,000. Kramer still showed promise, and for his next contract UA gave him even better terms. Kramer agreed to produce personally and direct three pictures and to produce three "non-Kramer" pictures. UA paid him a producer fee of $75,000 each for the first group and $50,000 each for the latter. UA also provided him an overhead allowance of $600,000 payable at the rate of $100,000 per year. As an extra incentive, UA upped the profit participation from 60 to 70 percent.

Kramer's next picture, *The Defiant Ones* (1958), is generally regarded as one of his best works. The picture won the New York Film Critics Best Picture Award. (Although Kramer's films never won an Oscar for best picture, the Academy honored him with the Irving Thalberg Award in 1961.) *The Defiant Ones* dealt with race relations, like Kramer's *Home of the Brave* and *Pressure Point* that came before and *Guess Who's Coming to Dinner* that came after. In *The Defiant Ones,* two convicts, "an arrogant white man" (Tony Curtis) and "an intelligent Negro" (Sidney Poitier), both chained together, make their break for freedom from a Southern chain gang. As the posse hunts them down, they learn respect for one another. *Variety* described Kramer's direction as "sensitive and skilled," surprising, since this was "only his third try at calling the scenes." Produced on a modest budget of $778,000, the picture earned a profit of $1 million. Screenwriters Nathan E. Douglas and Harold Jacob Smith won the Oscar for best original screenplay.

Discovering that Nathan E. Douglas was actually the pseudonym for the blacklisted writer Nedrick Young, an official of the American Legion publicly issued a protest. It was no doubt prompted by an editorial in the *Los Angeles Herald Express*, a Hearst newspaper, which proclaimed "the Commies are back." The paper took Otto Preminger to task for hiring Dalton Trumbo, a member of the Hollywood Ten, stating, "it was clear that the gates were wide open and that whoever took a plea of the 'Fifth Amendment' could get a job." The editorial concluded with the reminder that in 1951 the motion picture industry "was voluntarily and spontaneously boycotted by the American people." Kramer replied to the American Legion via a nationwide television hookup that he would hire whomever he pleased regardless of the writer's "past affiliations or suspected affiliations."[47]

On the Beach (1959) was based on Nevil Shute's best-seller about the last months of southern Australia, the last safe spot on earth, whose inhabitants await the poisonous fallout from a nuclear war. Shot in Australia on a budget of $2.9 million and starring Gregory Peck and Ava Gardner, *On the Beach* lost $700,000. *Variety* complained that the impact of the picture was as heavy "as a leaden shroud . . . the spectator is left with the sick feeling that he's had a preview of Armageddon, in which the contestants lost."[48] UA promoted the picture as a "status symbol"—meaning as something to be seen despite its grim nature—and released it simultaneously in eighteen cities worldwide, including Moscow and Tokyo. Senator Wallace F. Bennett of Utah accused Kramer of being a pacifist, of distorting the facts, and of playing the Soviet's game by alarming the public with unjustifiable fears. The film was misleading, said Bennett, because "it has been clearly demonstrated there would be many survivors of an atomic attack."[49]

Inherit the Wind (1960) tackled evolution. Based on the successful Broadway play by Jerome Lawrence and Robert E. Lee that dramatized the Scopes trial of 1925, Kramer's production paired Spencer Tracy and Fredric March to play the characters modeled after Clarence Darrow and William Jennings Bryan, respectively. The picture had its world premiere at the Berlin Film Festival, the official American industry entry nominated by the Motion Picture Export Association (MPEA). During the screening, the standing-room-only audience broke into applause twenty-two times, after which Kramer received a ten-minute ovation, according to a UA press release. "The film got extravagant reviews," said Kramer, "but it died at the box office."[50] Produced at a cost of $2 million, *Inherit the Wind* grossed only $2 million worldwide and lost $1.7 million.

Judgment at Nuremberg (1961) probed Germany's war guilt. Abby Mann adapted the screenplay from his teleplay, originally presented on CBS's "Playhouse 90" in 1959. Set in Nuremberg in 1948, the time of the Nazi war-crimes trials, the drama did not deal with well-known Nazi leaders, but with members of the German judiciary who went along with the infamous legal mandates of the Nazis that resulted in the deaths of 6 million innocent people. Kramer's picture was produced at a timely moment and was perhaps even suggested by the publication of William L. Shirer's tremendously popular book, *The Rise and Fall of the Third Reich* (1960), and the impending trial of Adolph Eichmann in Israel.

To focus attention on the picture, UA chose Berlin for the premiere. The event was sponsored by Willy Brandt, mayor of West Berlin, who introduced the picture. "We may like or dislike or disagree with many things," said Brandt, "but here it is."[51] "The film was totally rejected," said Kramer. "It never did three cents' business in Germany. It played so many empty houses it just stopped. People asked how could I, an America, try to rekindle German guilt? Well, I said that it would indeed have been better if the Germans had made it, but the fact is they didn't. So I did."[52]

A star-studded cast headed by Spencer Tracy, who played the presiding American judge, and Burt Lancaster, the principal defendant, failed to drum up much interest, but the picture's three-hour length probably also helped do it in. *Judgment at Nuremberg* grossed only $6 million and lost $1.5 million on its $3 million investment.

Kramer spent three years on his next project, a change-of-pace comedy entitled *It's a Mad, Mad, Mad, Mad World* (1963). In the meantime, he produced three pictures that were directed by others. Kramer had accused Hollywood of scorning the French New Wave, Italian Neorealism, and Britain's Angry Young Men. These filmmakers, he said, "are not even dreamed of much less understood, by the heads of our big companies. Our people simply will not meet the foreign challenge. Even the young creative people who did appear and burst forth with stimulating ideas in the first rush of original television plays . . . have not been allowed to continue and expand into more exciting stuff as they have been taken over by Hollywood. They have been forced to conform to conventional formulas or go home."[53]

UA permitted him to try his hand at three so-called unconventional projects. *Pressure Point* (1962), directed by Hubert Cornfield, who collaborated on the screenplay with S. Lee Pogostin, was based on a composite of case histories from Dr. Robert Lindner's book, *The Fifty-Minute Hour: A Collection of True Psychoanalytic Tales* (1954). Sidney Poitier played a psychiatrist and Bobby Darin an American-German Bundist imprisoned for sedition. The picture attacked bigotry. Produced for less than $1 million, *Pressure Point* grossed only $665,000 worldwide and lost $991,000. *A Child Is Waiting* (1963), directed by John Cassavetes and based on an Abby Mann teleplay, dramatized the problems of retarded children. Burt Lancaster and Judy Garland starred. Produced at a cost of $2 million, the picture grossed $925,000 and lost

$2 million. *Invitation to a Gunfighter* (1964) was directed by Richard Wilson who wrote the screenplay with Elizabeth Wilson. Kramer described it as a psychological western "different in scope but . . . exactly like *High Noon* in techniques and approach."[54] Other than the marquee value of Yul Brynner, this confused picture had little going for it. Produced for $1.8 million, it lost $900,000 on a world gross of $3.1 million.

To say that Kramer had high expectations for *Mad World* would be an understatement. Describing the project to Arthur Krim, he said, "Bill Rose [the screenwriter] has collected the routines and plotted out an outline with me for a four-hour comedy spectacle which will be the biggest film of all time."[55] Not quite, but as *Variety* prophesied, "It's a mad, mad, mad, mad picture and it's going to make a lot of money." In essence, the picture was a series of chase scenes—à la Mack Sennett—containing an enormous star-studded cast—à la Mike Todd's *Around the World in 80 Days*—headed by Spencer Tracy and featuring Sid Caesar, Phil Silvers, Jonathan Winters, Terry-Thomas, and dozens of others. *Mad World* grossed $26 million, but because production costs also reached blockbuster proportions—$9 million—profits amounted to only $1.25 million.

UA had earlier extended Kramer's contract by three pictures, which he would direct as well as produce. To fulfill his commitment, Kramer proposed *Ship of Fools*, based on Katherine Anne Porter's novel. UA, however, gave Kramer its blessing to take the project elsewhere, which he did—to Columbia, which also produced Kramer's *Guess Who's Coming to Dinner*. *The Secret of Santa Vittoria* (1969), based on the best-selling novel of Robert Crichton, was Kramer's final project for UA. He had the prescience to acquire the rights to the book just as it came out in August 1966. The price was $300,000. Crichton's book stayed on the best-seller list for forty-nine weeks and went from hardcover to paperback, selling millions in nearly every country around the world. Kramer chose Anthony Quinn to play Italo Bombolini and Anna Magnani to play his wife Rosa. Shot on location in the Italian village of Anticoli Corrado during the summer of 1968, the picture was brought in at a cost of $6.3 million. Although UA thought it had a winner, the picture did disappointing business—$6.5 million worldwide.

Hecht-Hill-Lancaster

A remarkable string of hits had catapulted Hecht-Lancaster into the forefront of the independent ranks in Hollywood. The company's reputation rested on a group of solid commercial action pictures, but *Marty*

(1955) added an extra dimension. Hecht-Lancaster had demonstrated to the trade not only the durability of Lancaster's appeal as a star but also an uncanny knack for starting trends. No one could have predicted the phenomenal success of *Marty*. Made at a negative cost of $350,000, when the industry trend was toward the big-budget picture, the returns against the original outlay for *Marty* established a record at the time. After winning the Academy Award for best picture, UA boosted the gross by another $1 million during the rerelease. No longer treating *Marty* as an art film, UA saturated the market with 500 prints.

In negotiating a new deal with UA, Hecht-Lancaster had the leverage to extract major concessions. Two issues were of prime concern to UA—the reduced distribution fee and the Hecht-Lancaster overhead payments. Word that UA had lowered its distribution fee to 25 percent domestic to close the deal had leaked out and, according to Krim, UA was being "pounded from every direction."[56] Krim explained to Lew Wasserman, Hecht-Lancaster's agent, why the distribution fees had to be changed: As a starter, Krim said, "It is the nature of the business that great success breeds irritations and divorce rather than amicability. UA, though, would try to disprove this rule." Wasserman countered with data "prepared by somebody in the Hecht organization, showing the millions of dollars that UA was going to make in distribution fees." Krim told him that "this again was the inevitable result of success—that we had an overhead load of $13,000,000 a year to carry around the world and that if we could not get it out of successful pictures, where could we get it? It was a fallacy to consider the distribution fee solely as profits. By clipping us, they would be reducing the very strength which has given them a home."[57] Wasserman agreed to drop the special distribution terms after Krim came up with a bonus plan that achieved the same results.

Concerning the overhead payments, Krim had earlier reported, "I have the completely helpless feeling of not knowing enough about the internal operations of Hecht-Lancaster . . . I feel that we are at a great disadvantage in this relationship. We must find out such things as what money they are spending for purchase and development of other properties; what money they are spending on personal withdrawals for themselves; what money they are spending unnecessarily on overhead."[58]

Hecht-Lancaster decided to stay with UA and turned down "many offers from other directions even though, as Lew [Wasserman] put it, in some of these offers they might have improved the distribution percentages which apply under our contract."[59] Hecht-Lancaster, however, won important concessions. In signing a new five-picture contract in 1956, UA made Hecht-Lancaster the beneficiary of a bonus

Burt Lancaster in *Birdman of Alcatraz* (1962)

plan based on volume in lieu of a reduced distribution fee. For the purpose of a bonus, UA treated the five future pictures and the old ones in
release as a group. Should the group gross at least $45 million in the
following three years, UA agreed to pay Hecht-Lanchaster $50,000 for
every additional million dollars the pictures brought in. Before the
bonus plan could go into effect, however, each picture had to break

even. UA made other concessions also. UA agreed to contribute a portion of its profits from the pictures to a profit-sharing plan for key Hecht-Lancaster executives and to provide other incentives to help the company attract talent.

UA also agreed to relieve Hecht and Lancaster of any obligation to repay preproduction advances and overhead payments on future pictures. Instead, UA would look to the pictures for recoupment. In essence, UA subsidized Hecht-Lancaster's operations to the extent of $5,000 a week and indemnified the two partners against losses on their productions. In the original deal, UA expected the team to share the risks of running their business. Preproduction expenses, for example, were added to their production budgets. UA wanted the pictures to bear the burden. Should the pictures as a group lose money, Hecht and Lancaster as individuals had to forego a substantial portion of their producer fees. But for the new five-picture deal, UA removed this provision for all practical purposes.

However, UA protected itself at the other end by holding Hecht-Lancaster liable should a picture go over budget. Krim no doubt insisted on the clause as a result of *Trapeze* (1956). Describing UA's experience with the picture, Krim said, "I feel that we will be put to an unusual test in respect to *Trapeze*. I told Lew that if anybody else were to make [the picture], it would cost $1 million less, but he said, and I had to agree, that we had to take this operation as it was and either go ahead or drop the picture but not expect to change them."[60] Typically, a producer was penalized for going over budget by losing profit points, but UA had made an exception in Hecht-Lancaster's case and had even agreed not to cross-collateralize *Trapeze* with *The Kentuckian* (1955), which lost money.

New contract in hand, Hecht-Lancaster expanded its horizons and announced a production schedule of six pictures a year. With offices in Beverly Hills and New York—the former acting as a production headquarters and the latter as a story department—and a permanent staff of thirty-eight employees, Hecht-Lancaster now had the look of a Hollywood major, *sans* studio. Overhead to maintain this operation came to $300,000 a year. Hecht-Lancaster hoped to bring in outside filmmakers with fresh ideas, especially those on the fringes of Hollywood, by assisting in story development, casting, and all phases of production. To help oversee operations, Hecht-Lancaster promoted James Hill, the head of its story department, to partner and changed the name to Hecht-Hill-Lancaster.

Expanding further, the organization established its own publicity offices in Europe and the Far East, making it the first independent production company to take that step.[61] UA acquiesced to the plan, although Max Youngstein had reservations. As he told Arthur Krim, "The appointment by Hecht-Hill-Lancaster (H-H-L) of foreign publicity representatives . . . is going to set up another precedent which every top producer is going to follow, and once again, we will have additional costs . . . It may be the price we have to pay for our operation. On the other hand, I think it is absolutely unnecessary in 99 percent of the cases, without any benefit to Hecht-Hill-Lancaster, or to United Artists."[62]

Starting out, H-H-L organized a two-pronged production program— one designed for Burt Lancaster and the other for outside filmmakers. The strategy that guided both was inspired by *Marty*. *Marty*, a picture "that dealt with the world of the mundane, the ordinary, and the untheatrical," in Paddy Chayefsky's words, had seemingly demonstrated that an audience existed for nonmainstream entertainment, for an American art film based on social realism. H-H-L, as well as other independents, therefore turned to the breeding ground of this movement, the television anthology drama. During the early days of television, anthology series consistently ranked among the most popular forms of programming. At the height of their popularity, from 1953 to 1956, the networks broadcast twenty such programs a week. Produced live from New York and utilizing unknown Broadway talent, these programs started out adapting popular plays. As the need for more material developed, producers turned to literary classics, short stories, well-known novels, and finally original teleplays. Influenced by Italian Neorealism, these teleplays often told stories about ordinary people in ordinary situations—slices of life—but, unlike their Italian counterparts, they had upbeat endings.

Influenced by *Marty*, the "small film" came into vogue. Such films typically used the talents of TV writers and directors and were low-budget items shot on location in black and white. UA may have been the principal distributor of these pictures. In addition to the Hecht-Hill-Lancaster product, the company released two small films produced by Stanley Kramer—*Pressure Point* and *A Child Is Waiting* (starring Burt Lancaster). In 1956, UA released Michael Myerberg's production of *Patterns*, based on Rod Serling's *Patterns of Power*, a drama of corporate politics in the boardroom. In 1957, UA released *Twelve Angry Men*, a Henry Fonda–Reginald Rose production based on Rose's teleplay and directed by former television producer-director Sidney Lumet. And in 1962, UA released Fred Coe's production of *The Miracle Worker*, based on William Gibson's teleplay. Coe had been the producer of the most prominent anthology series of them all, "NBC Television Playhouse," which presented *Marty*.

Hecht-Hill-Lancaster's initial release on its new contract was *The Bachelor Party* (1957), a sequel of sorts to *Marty*. It did not star Ernest Borgnine, but, like *Marty*, the picture was written by Paddy Chayefsky and directed by Delbert Mann. The cast also consisted of unknowns or unprovens from television and stage. Shot on location and containing characters which *Variety* described as from the same "upper lowers" of New York, *Bachelor Party* went over budget and cost three times as much as *Marty*. It received good critical reviews and Carolyn Jones, playing "a sexpot Greenwich Village character," received an Academy Award nomination. But, unlike *Marty*, the picture failed to generate much interest.

Producing a sequel like *Bachelor Party* is an obvious and predictable commercial strategy; the influence of *Marty* on Lancaster's pictures, though less apparent, nonetheless exists. Lancaster starred in four vehicles, *Sweet Smell of Success* (1957), *Run Silent, Run Deep* (1958), *Separate Tables* (1958), and *The Devil's Disciple* (1959). With the exception of *Run Silent, Run Deep*, the pictures were low-budget productions based on offbeat properties that permitted Lancaster to play roles running counter to type. And they clearly were designed to appeal to a more mature audience.

Sweet Smell of Success, directed by Alexander Mackendrick from a screenplay by Clifford Odets and Ernest Lehman, depicted the seamy side of Broadway. Lancaster teamed up with Tony Curtis for the second time, but unlike *Trapeze,* the two stars were offcast—Lancaster played a powerful and unscrupulous syndicated columnist, "bespectacled and quiet but smoldering with malice and menace" and Curtis, an obsequious and corrupt press agent. The picture went considerably over budget. It was the "greatest failure our company ever made . . . We lost a fortune on it," said Lancaster.[63]

Lancaster reverted to type in *Run Silent, Run Deep*, playing opposite Clark Gable in an action picture of submarine warfare in the Pacific during World War II. Robert Wise directed. Although moderately successful, this picture failed to reverse the fortunes of the Hecht-Hill-Lancaster organization.

Of *Separate Tables, Variety* said "the Hecht-Hill-Lancaster organization deserves credit for undertaking a story that does not meet the conception of what is generally considered sure-fire material in today's market. More importantly, it has the ingredients to interest and draw the more discriminating filmgoer."[64] Based on Terence Rattigan's hit play, *Separate Tables* was a character study of a group of lonely and desperate residents of a small British seaside hotel. For the movie version, Rattigan and screenwriter John Gay adapted the play to include parts for two Americans, played by Lancaster and Rita Hayworth—"a writer hurt by life and living a don't-care existence" and his former wife "whose narcissism and desire to dominate men leads to Lancaster's downfall," as *Variety* put it. (In real life, Rita Hayworth was married to Lancaster's partner, James Hill.) The picture contained a galaxy of other stars, including David Niven, Wendy Hiller, and Deborah Kerr. Directed by Delbert Mann (his third assignment for the company), *Separate Tables* received considerable critical acclaim; David Niven and Wendy Hiller won Oscars for best actor and best supporting actress and the picture, its screenplay, and David Raskin's score received Oscar nominations. Although the picture is today remembered as an interesting experiment of the fifties, it was not a commercial success.

Lancaster experimented one more time before UA pulled the plug. *The Devil's Disciple* (1959), based on George Bernard Shaw's comedy of how the British, bumbling and fumbling, lost the American colonies, was originally planned as a big-budget picture in color costing around $1.5 million. *The Devil's Disciple* was shelved when a satisfactory script could not be developed. Montgomery Clift was considered as a possibility to play the peace-spouting minister, Anthony Anderson, opposite Lancaster's cowardly scoundrel, Dick Dudgeon. However, the project was reactivated when Kirk Douglas expressed interest in the project. Douglas's Bryna Company coproduced a scaled-down version in black and white. Now, Douglas played Dudgeon and Lancaster played the minister. To play British Commander General "Gentleman Johnny" Burgoyne, they signed Laurence Olivier. Filmed in England to take advantage of subsidy money, *The Devil's Disciple* was directed by Alexander Mackendrick. Midway into production, he was replaced by Guy Hamilton. The finished picture, as a result, had two styles. *Variety* assessed the picture as "fumbling and unsatisfactory . . . that all is not lost may be credited almost entirely to Laurence Olivier."[65]

The pictures produced by outside filmmakers fared no better. A total of four were produced beginning in 1959; all were "small films." *The Rabbit Trap* (1959) and *Cry Tough* (1959) were produced by Harry Kleiner, a screenwriter who had worked with Preminger on *Carmen Jones*. Written by J. P. Miller, based on his original teleplay, *The Rabbit Trap* brought back Ernest Borgnine to play a "simple story about Mr. Average rebelling against a system that keeps him so."[66] Philip Leacock, a British filmmaker, directed. *Cry Tough* was written by Kleiner, based on an Irving Shulman novel. It dealt with problems of second-generation Puerto Ricans living in squalid Spanish Harlem. John Saxon, playing the role of an ex-convict, delivered his best performance to date, said *Variety*.[67] Paul Stanley directed. The third picture, *Take a Giant Step* (1959) was produced by Julius J. Epstein, a screenwriter who worked as a team with his brother at Warner's and who won an Academy Award for *Casablanca*. The script to *Take a Giant Step* was written by Louis S. Peterson, based on his Broadway play about a black youth growing up in an all-white middle-class town in New England. *The Summer of the Seventeenth Doll* (1960) was produced as another vehicle for Ernest Borgnine. An adaptation of an Australian play by Ray Lawler and shot on location in Australia under the direction of Leslie Norman, the film contained variations of character relationships and incidents from *Marty* and *Bachelor Party*. These four pictures as a group went over budget $500,000 and they all lost money, demonstrating once again that there was no market for this kind of picture. *Marty* had been a fluke.

UA forced H-H-L to retrench at the end of 1959, and reduced the weekly overhead payments from $5,000 to $1,500. H-H-L closed its London and New York offices and made plans to unload its plush Beverly Hills headquarters. Thereafter, the company carried only a minimum staff. H-H-L owed UA nearly $3 million in over-budget guarantees for *The Bachelor Party* and *Sweet Smell of Success;* $1.7 million in unabsorbed overhead charges; $700,000 on abandoned stories; and $500,000 on commitments to writers. In addition, there were losses and overages on the low-budget pictures amounting to about $1 million.

As a means of reducing the indebtedness, H-H-L agreed to produce two additional pictures. They would star Burt Lancaster and, for a change, be of the blockbuster/action variety. UA, in addition, signed separate deals with each of the three partners, since there were strong indications that H-H-L would soon fold. *Variety* had reported that "The boys have been drifting apart for some time."

H-H-L abandoned the two blockbusters when scripting difficulties proved insuperable. As a substitute, the company produced *The Unforgiven* (1960), an adult Western about the unbending hatred between white settlers and local Kiowa Indians in the Texas Panhandle. John Huston, the director, described his participation in the project "as a mistake." "Some of my pictures I don't care for," he said, "but *The Unforgiven* is the only one I actually dislike."[68] Huston saw in Ben Maddow's script a story of racial intolerance in the frontier town, but H-H-L wanted him to make a swashbuckler about a larger-than-life frontiersman.

H-H-L initiated its own dissolution in February 1960, but a settlement with UA was not reached until 1966. Meanwhile, Lancaster, on his own, played the title role in Richard Brooks' production *Elmer*

Gantry (1960), for which he won an Academy Award for best actor. "Some parts you fall into like an old glove," said Lancaster. "Elmer Gantry really wasn't acting. It was me."[69] Lancaster then starred in two Stanley Kramer productions, *Judgment at Nuremberg* (1961) and *A Child Is Waiting* (1963).

Harold Hecht personally produced four pictures for UA. They were made not only in an attempt to pay off H-H-L debts, but also to meet H-H-L's unfulfilled commitments to talent. The first two pictures starred Burt Lancaster and were directed by former television director John Frankenheimer. *The Young Savages* (1961) was a kind of "nonmusical east side variation on *West Side Story*," said *Variety*. "It is a sociological crossword puzzle, a twisted riddle aimed at detection of the true motivation for juvenile crime as set against the backdrop of New York's teeming East Harlem district."[70] Lancaster played the role of an assistant district attorney who proves that a young Puerto Rican is not guilty of murder.

In *Birdman of Alcatraz* (1962), Lancaster played Robert Stroud, a convicted murderer who had spent a staggering total of forty-three years in solitary confinement and who had become regenerated accomplishing remarkable feats of scientific research on bird diseases. Lancaster won the New York Film Critics Award as best actor and was nominated for an Oscar. Frankenheimer established a new reputation for himself.

The final two Hecht productions reverted to the action formula. Both starred Yul Brynner and were based on screenplays coscripted by Waldo Salt. And both were disasters. Shot in Argentina under the direction of J. Lee Thompson, *Taras Bulba* (1962) teamed Brynner and Tony Curtis. A picture depicting the clashes between cossacks and Polish cavalry in the sixteenth century was, in the words of Bosley Crowther, "a mishmash of blood-and-thunder fable that would look wild in a comic book, let alone in a clearly costly picture on the huge colored Panavision screen."[71] *Flight from Ashiya* (1964) was shot in Japan under the direction of Michael Anderson as a coproduction of Daiei Films and Harold Hecht. This time Brynner was teamed with Richard Widmark in a melodrama involving three men of the U.S. Army's Rescue Corps. Howard Thompson's assessment in the *New York Times* said, "Occasionally it's diverting to see just how consistently bad a picture can be. Anyone interested should catch *Flight from Ashiya*."[72]

James Hill produced only one picture on his own for UA—*The Happy Thieves* (1962), a vehicle for his wife, Rita Hayworth, costarring Rex Harrison and directed by George Marshall. The picture belonged "to that popular genus of film comedy depicting the zany misadventures of a band of lovably darling crooks who attempt to execute a bold, ingenious heist . . . Should generate a mildly comfortable response," concluded *Variety*.[73]

UA settled with Burt Lancaster in 1964 by buying out his interest in the earlier Hecht-Lancaster pictures. The amount came to $920,000. During the negotiations, Krim wrote to Lancaster: "I just want you to know that whether it be as producer, director, or star or a combination of any two or more of the capacities, we would like to keep doing pictures with you for many years to come."[74]

The settlement with Hecht dragged on until 1966, the result in part of a $2.2 million fraud claim UA filed against Hecht pertaining to *Taras Bulba*. UA had agreed to finance the picture based on a budget of $3.8 million. However, the picture went way over budget—to the tune of $2.2 million. UA had not been able adequately to monitor production work in Argentina, and by the time the company had returned to California to shoot interiors, the damage had been done. UA discovered that the script had been changed, more extras had been hired than stipulated, and other expenses had been added to the budget. In Hollywood, Hecht had authorized unbudgeted set construction, excessive dubbing, editing, and other postphotography processing. UA paid the bills to make sure the picture was completed and to minimize its losses. Nonetheless, UA was left with a loss of $4.5 million.

UA claimed that Hecht had intended from the start to change and alter the budget once production began and filed a breach-of-contract suit against Hecht. This was the only time UA actually sued a producer for a breach of contract after the picture was completed and delivered. The case did not go to trial, but it ultimately played a part in the buyout of Hecht's interest in all the Hecht-Hill-Lancaster pictures. As Herb Schottenfeld, UA's general counsel, remarked, "We created a larger ball of wax and as a result we were satisfied. Nobody ever wins everything in a lawsuit or a settlement. But we thought our position well justified and that the price we paid for Hecht's interest in the pictures was appropriately reduced. Hecht came back to us once or twice after that but I don't think we ever came close to making a deal."[75]

Kirk Douglas

UA had such high hopes for Kirk Douglas that it spotlighted Douglas's blockbuster, *The Vikings,* in a feature story that *Fortune* magazine did on the company in 1958.[76] Produced at a cost of $3.5 million and more

Kirk Douglas in *The Vikings* (1958)

than two years in the making, *The Vikings* (1958) showed Douglas off at his popular best. However, launching him as an independent had been a problem. For his debut, Douglas produced and starred in *The Indian Fighter* (1955), a conventional but successful frontier actioner in CinemaScope and Technicolor. Like his good friend Burt Lancaster, Douglas wanted to experiment in offbeat properties, but Krim cautioned him to be patient:

> I would like to say, Kirk, that Bob [Benjamin] and I were greatly impressed with the spirit of our conversations in California and we think of Bryna [Douglas's company] as being one of the important and developing units in our operation. I am sorry that because of your penchant for selecting offbeat properties, we seem to be having child birth difficulties. Once we have profits, both yours and ours, to work with, these difficulties will naturally tend to diminish, if not disappear, because then we would be more relaxed about gambling with you on some of these experimental areas. For the present, we would like to stick to safe ventures. *Indian Fighter* is a good example of the protection in the commercial area. I don't say, by a long shot, that we should be making only action westerns, but I do feel that in your own interests in building up the kind of reserves which will give you greater latitude later, this is the time to ride to the hilt some of the tried and true values.[77]

Since *The Vikings* was having such a long gestation, UA relented and financed an odd assortment of low-budget items; *Ride Out for Revenge,* an adult Western starring Rory Calhoun and Lloyd Bridges; *Spring Reunion,* a comedy that brought back Betty Hutton to the screen after a four-year absence; *The Careless Years,* a vehicle for teenage idol Dean Stockwell. All were produced in 1957 and all three lost money. Meanwhile, as Douglas searched for other suitable properties for himself, he starred in three pictures for outside studios: *Lust for Life* (1956), *Top Secret Affair* (1957), and *Gunfight at the OK Corral* (1957). And for Stanley Kubrick, another UA producer, Douglas starred in *Paths of Glory* (1957).

UA established a relationship with Kubrick in 1955 when it picked up *Kiss Me Kill Me,* which was written, produced, directed, and photographed by Kubrick, who was then twenty-seven. UA paid $100,000 for the picture and released it as *Killer's Kiss.* As part of the deal, UA agreed to give Kubrick another $100,000 for a second picture. Teaming up with producer James B. Harris, Kubrick directed *The Killing* (1956), starring Sterling Hayden. Despite UA's warning that Hayden could not support a picture over $100,000, Harris and Kubrick drew up a budget over twice that amount. Although *The Killing* won plaudits, UA's prediction proved true—the picture lost $130,000.

UA's initial reaction to *Paths of Glory* was negative. Max Youngstein told Harris, "I tell you that unless the script is substantially changed or unless a really top, top star is obtained, you have to count us out on this one." [78] After the script was substantially rewritten by Calder Willingham, a young screenwriter who worked with David Lean on *The Bridge on the River Kwai* (1957), UA rejected the project again because the picture probably would be banned in France (which it subsequently was). But after Douglas became "wildly enthusiastic" about the script, UA agreed to finance it up to a cash cost of $850,000. Working on a straight acting contract, Douglas was paid a salary of $350,000. To get their picture financed, Kubrick and Harris had to forego director and producer fees. Their reward could come only from profits, which were to be divided 60 percent to Harris-Kubrick and 40 percent to UA. Explaining to Krim his decision to star in *Paths of Glory*, Douglas said, "I hope you understand my attitude. Frankly, no one would like to build up new creative talent more than I. Besides the remuneration, I find it very gratifying. Also I think I can be a tremendous help. Ask Kubrick and Harris. If they're honest they'll tell you the chaotic state of the script when I first arrived here in Munich. You never knew that I was almost on the return plane back to the States. But I think *Paths of Glory* is turning out very well, and Kubrick needs a lot of assistance, much more than he cares to admit. He is still a very talented boy." [79]

Although Douglas described *Paths of Glory* as "a worthwhile class picture for me as well as UA," the picture just barely broke even. Douglas did not come up with another bankable project after *The Vikings*. He submitted *Spartacus* to UA but it was rejected "because of a prior inconsistent commitment," in Krim's words. Douglas thereupon signed on with Universal, which was more than willing to finance *Spartacus* since Douglas had agreed to star in three other pictures for the company. Krim believed that Douglas would have made the switch regardless. Lew Wasserman, Douglas's agent and head of MCA, had recently acquired the studio facilities of ailing Universal-International and, as part of the deal, agreed "to give Universal a fair share of their top stars." [80]

But Douglas's explanation was that he found independent production unprofitable. Three years after *The Vikings*, he said, "I have not seen one nickel from this project. I have not even obtained enough to fully cover all of the overhead costs that my own company incurred in regard to this picture . . . Obviously, at this point, I am a little bitter and ashamed to even admit to people that I haven't seen a nickel on *The Vikings.*" In contrast, as a free-lance star, he said, "A few years ago I sneaked in a little picture for Universal-International called *Man Without a Star.* I shot it in four-and-a-half weeks. Did a great deal of work on the script myself. So far I have earned over $600,000 on this teensy-weensy picture."[81]

Krim responded, "Our door is wide open and we are ready, anxious, able and willing to do business with you again and often. As far as an attractive deal is concerned, you know that except for certain general principles on which our whole company has been built, we are very flexible and I am sure that we can work out details which will be advantageous to you and under which we can live." Krim then reminded Douglas of "certain compensations and other financial obligations taken over by us which will establish that our relationship has been very much a two way street."[82] These included a $190,000 obligation on an unsuccessful TV series based on *The Vikings;* an investment of $200,000 in properties that had been abandoned; and compensation in the amount of $600,000 that UA paid Douglas for his services in *Indian Fighter, Paths in Glory,* and other pictures. As a final reminder, Krim pointed out that UA was willing to buy out his residual interest in *The Vikings* for $1.2 million.

Sticking to company principles also lost Stanley Kubrick. UA was willing to finance the development of a screenplay for *Lolita,* but because Harris and Kubrick made what a UA executive described as "one of the most presumptuous and arrogant demands for a deal that we have ever had, particularly when it comes from a couple of youngsters like these," UA decided to back off.[83]

These case studies reveal, first of all, that independent producers wanted to break free of commercial restraints by sponsoring new talent and by producing pictures dealing with social issues. In the realm of art, these producers were liberals. They were stimulated by lofty ideals, to be sure, and also by the profit motive. More interesting, they wanted to experiment with the unconventional using UA's money. UA had nothing against such motives, but wanted its producers to stick to the tried and true first to build up a kitty. UA's rationale was easy to understand since the vast majority of pictures produced by its principal suppliers lost money in the theatrical market.

To judge the commercial success of creative talent solely on box-office performance would, of course, be misleading. Independent producers earned their livelihood primarily from fees for producing, directing, and acting, and from buyouts based on the residual value of their pictures in ancillary markets, such as network and syndicated television. UA earned its livelihood primarily from distribution fees. Factoring in this source of revenue explains the business consideration in sticking with a producer longer than prudence might warrant. In Stanley Kramer's case, for example, his pictures did not generate much in the way of theatrical profits, but UA came out ahead in the relationship primarily as a result of *It's a Mad . . . World*.

But UA stayed with its suppliers over the long haul also out of loyalty. UA understood that a producer might hit a dry spell or have a run of bad luck; they would not summarily cut him off. These producers had the experience and know-how to make things happen. This might seem simplistic, but in Hollywood, not every director or star had the organization skills, business sense, or drive not only to make a motion picture but to produce one that achieved an acceptable commercial standard. Besides, in sticking with its producers, UA could and did protect itself by exercising approval rights over the basic ingredients and by collecting the distribution fee. In so doing, UA kept the distribution pipeline full with reasonably good pictures.

These independent production units exhibited many weaknesses as businesses, but the most significant had to do with product differentiation. Kramer and Hecht-Hill-Lancaster in particular placed their eggs in single baskets—each produced essentially one kind of picture. Since these types only had limited appeal, the producers placed themselves at a disadvantage from the start by not diversifying. The Mirisch brothers understood these drawbacks and, as the discussion in the following chapter reveals, they devised a special brand of independent production.

CHAPTER FIVE

The Studio without Walls

The stated objective of the Mirisch organization was to "find the best filmmakers and provide them with the very best story material and the most talented associates—enable the filmmaker to do the thing he most wants to do—concentrate completely on the films, on what appears on the screen and let a small, effective organization handle all the other complex matters that are part of making a movie, ranging from negotiating contracts and financing, to persuading actors to work under the Mirisch banner, to arranging pre-production logistics, and, perhaps most important, taking the completed film and supervising its merchandising on a coordinated, world-wide basis."[1]

The Mirisches organized essentially an "umbrella" company. If a director wanted to make a picture, he didn't have to put together all the pieces—the Mirisches provided a ready-made format. The Mirisches entered into joint ventures with talent and in return received a management fee and a share of the profits. As *Business Week* noted, "They are, in fact, managers in the sense that the old major studios were managers, which leaves the creative producers time to create. Unlike the majors, the Mirisches don't burden themselves with bricks and mortar. They rent office space by the week and sound stages by the day. The overhead stays low."[2]

Since the organization attracted talent that might otherwise not have become aligned with UA, Krim considered the organization a second West Coast production office. As Krim said, "there was nobody better than Harold Mirisch at building relationships with talent who were aspiring to have a certain amount of creative freedom and to have a share of the fruits of their own labor, and who were not lusting to be the owners or in control of their pictures. They were happy to have the administrative support, the in-house support of the Mirisches."[3]

The Mirisches produced sixty-seven pictures for UA in about a decade and a half. They were in every size and style and consistently won Hollywood's top honors including three Oscars for best picture—*The Apartment, West Side Story,* and *In the Heat of the Night.* Pictures from the Mirisches kept UA's pipeline full with quality product. The other majors hit dry spells in terms of numbers and quality, the result, in part of changes in management, financial difficulties, and infighting. The Mirisches alleviated this problem for UA. As Herb Schottenfeld said, "UA was able to assure the exhibitor that the company was in there for the long run and could supply a steady diet of top films— films that regularly captured Academy Award honors."[4]

PRELUDE AT ALLIED ARTISTS

"I remember Harold Mirisch coming over to my office at the Goldwyn studio and opening up a whole new relationship," said Krim. "The association with Allied Artists was not working out. He knew our objectives and thought we could have a good marriage together. He wanted to build a company that would provide a stake for himself and his brothers. He wanted a home, a multiple-picture home for big directors whom he could attract by working out deals similar to those he had for them at Allied Artists. As so often happened in those years at UA, I didn't let him out of the office until we had shaken hands on a deal."[5]

Harold Mirisch, the *pater familias* of the company, was the half brother of Walter and Marvin Mirisch. Starting out as an office boy for Warner Brothers, Harold managed Warner's Midwest theater circuit, based in Milwaukee. In 1942, he joined RKO and returned to New York to become chief film buyer for the entire chain. In 1948, he went to work for Steve Broidy's Monogram Pictures as vice president in charge of distribution and played an integral role in upgrading the studio.

Tony Curtis, Marilyn Monroe, and the Mirisch brothers: Marvin, Walter, and Harold

Walter Mirisch went to work for Monogram in 1945 after graduating from the University of Wisconsin and the Harvard Business School. Beginning as Broidy's assistant, Walter moved into production and introduced a new series to Monogram's lineup called *Bomba the Jungle Boy,* starring Johnny Sheffield, who played Johnny Weissmuller's son, Boy, in the Tarzan series. Walter produced two Bomba pictures a year for six years, during which time he branched out to produce other pictures, which were, he said, "progressively improving in quality." In 1951, Walter Mirisch, age twenty-nine, was made executive producer of Monogram, which soon had a roster of producers that included Walter Wagner, Maurice and Frank King, Roy Del Ruth, and Lindsley Parsons.

Marvin Mirisch, the third member of the triumvirate, linked up with his brothers in 1952, when he was appointed assistant secretary of Allied Artists, the new name of Monogram Pictures. Marvin was eventually made vice president of the studio. Marvin started out as an office boy at Grand National, another Poverty Row studio. After graduating from CCNY in 1940, he started the Theatres Candy Company (with the eldest Mirisch brother, Irving) a concession business that grew to encompass 800 theaters throughout the Midwest.

Allied Artists provided an ideal training ground for the Mirisch brothers, just as Eagle-Lion had for Krim and Benjamin. The studio produced a relatively large program of pictures each year and fought hard to find theaters for them. Budgets were tight and economy was the byword.

As the market for "B" pictures dried up after the war, Monogram was forced to produce pictures of a generally higher quality—pictures containing production values that could conceivably play at the top of the bill in regular theaters. Steve Broidy formed Allied Artists as a wholly owned subsidiary of Monogram in 1946 to produce and distribute this higher grade. Although the parent and subsidiary companies used the same personnel, Broidy hoped the Allied Artists name would create the image of creative personnel united to produce and distribute quality films.

Not having the financial resources to attract big names and important properties, Allied Artists, like Eagle-Lion before it, specialized in "nervous A's." Produced for around $200,000, this type of picture contained lower-echelon stars and was based on original material or material in the public domain. Containing no "presold" elements, the "nervous A" required exceptional effort to promote and distribute. These limitations forced Allied Artists at first to produce pictures based on material that could be easily exploited—such as *The Phenix City Story* (1955), directed by Phil Karlson, and a group directed by Don Siegel consisting of *Riot in Cell Block 11* (1954), *Invasion of the Body Snatchers* (1956), and *Crime in the Streets* (1956).

Allied Artists attempted to break into the big time by signing John Huston, William Wyler, and Billy Wilder. According to Walter Mirisch, Harold was instrumental in this effort, which essentially granted the three directors liberal stock options in the company. John Huston was scheduled to lead off with *The Man Who Would Be King,* based on the Rudyard Kipling work, but changed his mind. Meanwhile, William Wyler made *Friendly Persuasion* (1956) starring Gary Cooper and featuring Dorothy McGuire. Based on the novel by Jessamyn West and produced at a cost of over $3 million, *Friendly Persuasion* earned a showcase booking at Radio City Music Hall and won the Golden Palm at Cannes. It was nominated for six Academy Awards, but won none. Billy Wilder's first entry, *Love in the Afternoon* (1957) teamed Gary Cooper with Audrey Hepburn. Based on the novel *Ariane* by Claude Anet and coscripted by Wilder and I. A. L. Diamond in the first of their many collaborations, *Love in the Afternoon* cost $2.1 million to produce. Allied Artists lost money on both pictures, but not as a result of unfavorable reviews or audience rejection. *Friendly Persuasion* and *Love in the Afternoon* lost money because to finance each picture, Allied sold off the foreign distribution rights. "As a result of the disappointing failure of the two films to do as well as we had hoped, said Walter Mirisch, "Allied Artists, still seriously underfinanced, pulled back its wings and decided that it really couldn't continue to produce expensive films."[6]

GETTING ORGANIZED

Krim's handshake with Harold Mirisch created a new opportunity for the brothers. The original terms of the relationship were typical of most multiple-picture deals. UA agreed to finance a minimum of four pictures a year for three years beginning September 1, 1957. The pictures were to be cross-collateralized, with the profits split fifty-fifty. The regular distribution fees prevailed. To maintain continuity of operation, UA paid the brothers a substantial weekly producer fee and funded the overhead costs of the organization. UA, however, was not about to subsidize another Hecht-Lancaster operation. The Mirisch office was located at the Goldwyn studio and was comfortable but not lavish, in the fashion of old Hollywood. Their physical circumstances were a far cry from the grandeur of Beverly Hills, the headquarters of Hecht-Lancaster. As reported by *Variety,* the company will concentrate on low overhead while maintaining as high quality as possible . . . Approximately 98% of all costs of a picture will be on the screen."[7]

The unusual aspect of the deal involved a bonus plan. Harold Mirisch had envisioned building a company that UA would buy out in cash or in stock. And when the Mirisches demonstrated that they could live up to their potential, UA provided them the option. On September 1, 1959, the second anniversary of their "marriage," UA extended the contract from twelve pictures to twenty. After they produced the twenty pictures, UA gave the Mirisches a choice of taking profits from their pictures on a cross-collateralized basis or of selling their interest in the pictures under the following provisions: for pictures that broke even, the Mirisches were entitled to a bonus equal to 2½ percent of the distribution gross earned within two years after general release in the United States. Breakeven was set at two and one-half times negative cost. On pictures that lost money, UA agreed to pay a bonus of 1 percent of the gross. At UA's option, payment could be made in stock in lieu of cash.

As gross deals go, 2½ percent of the gross may not seem like much, but a package of twenty pictures had the potential of providing rewards far exceeding UA's regular deals where profits were cross-collateralized. (This will be demonstrated later when the results of the first twenty pictures are tallied.) UA gave the Mirisches an opportunity of converting a net-profit deal into a form of a gross deal—at the time an unusual, if not unique, arrangement in the industry. This bonus was payable in addition to the producer fees, which by sixties' standards were substantial—$3,000 a week for the brothers for the term of the contract.

In aligning themselves with UA, the Mirisches incorporated under the name Mirisch Company, Inc., which was owned 96 percent by the brothers and 4 percent by key employees. Harold Mirisch was president, Marvin, vice president and secretary-treasurer, and Walter, executive in charge of production. Unlike the star-centered production units, Mirisch had only know-how, zeal, and relationships going for it. The brothers were experienced in all facets of production. Harold Mirisch described himself as a "businessman, not a creator . . . When I read a script I can smell what it might do and I have a pretty good sense for who would be best to work on it. But I've no desire to get into production myself. That's why we hire top people, even producers to do that work for us."[8] Walter said that Harold "played mother hen over the making of the pictures. Also, he had marvelous relationships. People loved him and he was able to conceive and work out financial arrangements and deals that were extraordinary. I think he was one of the best loved men who operated in that area of our business."[9]

Walter, in addition to producing pictures in his own right for the company, oversaw property development either directly by personally working with writers or indirectly by assigning projects to producer-directors to develop. Marvin coordinated the production requirements, negotiated most of the business deals with talent, and oversaw the legal and accounting operations. In the postproduction phase, Harold conferred with UA on distribution and publicity. This is a schematic version of their duties, but the point is that Mirisch operated under strict controls, like all UA's producers. As Krim stated, "They could not spend anything without our approval. As far as we were concerned, they were like our west coast office or subsidiary. They gave autonomy to a lot of their people, but always with our blessing. Everything with the Mirisches was done with the closest of contact and we had great respect for what they were doing and therefore there was a minimum of controversy."[10]

As the phrase "studio without walls" implies, the Mirisches had no crushing overhead to burden them. The Mirisches rented office space at the Goldwyn studio just thirty feet from UA's production office and utilized the studio facilities on an *ad hoc* basis. The staff consisted merely of a production manager, a lawyer, and a publicist. To keep operating costs to a minimum, Mirisch expanded and contracted its staff as needed.

In their urge to support and nurture talent, Mirisch kept a low profile. As far as the outside world was concerned, the brothers lived in relative obscurity. As *Time* quipped, "the mighty name symbolizing the new Age of the Independent Producer is roughly as well known as the incumbent ruler of Bhutan." Nonetheless, to the creative community, the reputation was potent. As UA executive David Picker remarked, "the current Hollywood shop talk is that in order to make a UA deal you have to go with the Mirisches."[11]

The Mirisches decided from the start to concentrate on directors, on the assumption that directors would attract actors. As Walter Mirisch explained, "We felt one couldn't attract the stars without either outstanding material or directors with whom they were anxious to work. We obviously tried to develop material, but at the same time we continued to develop the relationships with the directors. The actor works on a picture for twelve or fourteen weeks and then he wants to start work again. As a rule, he's not a person who wants to sit in an office and work with a writer and develop a screenplay."[12]

To produce its top-of-the-line product, Mirisch signed multiple-picture contracts with such ranking directors as Billy Wilder, John Sturges, Robert Wise, and George Roy Hill. These contracts were nonexclusive, which meant that a director could take a project to another studio if UA and the Mirisches turned it down or simply take a directing assignment elsewhere for whatever reason. The Mirisches gave promising younger directors like Blake Edwards and Norman Jewison freedom to develop and, when they proved themselves, they too were given multiple-picture contracts with all the perquisites. To produce the remainder of the Mirisch output, the company hired directors who can best be described as workmanlike. As experienced craftsmen, directors such as Joseph Newman, Michael Curtiz, Daniel M. Petrie, Walter Grauman, Gordon Douglas, and a host of others could get the job done. They worked at a straight salary and typically were assigned to projects after the scripts had been prepared.

Deals with first-rank directors were typically joint production ventures. The terms depended on the director and circumstances, but in joint production ventures the Mirisches essentially went into partnership with a director and shared the profits. Billy Wilder had by far the sweetest deal with the Mirisches. His first contract called for two pictures. He was paid a director's fee of $200,000 per picture plus 17½ percent of the gross after each picture reached breakeven (artificially set at about twice the negative cost). When a picture grossed $1 million after breakeven, Wilder's participation rose to 20 percent of the gross. Concerning production controls, Wilder once said, "All the Mirisch Company asks me is the name of the picture, a vague outline of the story and who's going to be in it. The rest is up to me. You can't get any more freedom than that." [13] This is an exaggeration, obviously; nonetheless, Wilder could pretty much write his own ticket.

Norman Jewison is a good example of a promising second-tier director. In signing him to a two-picture deal in 1964, Mirisch paid him a director's fee of $125,000 per picture plus 25 percent of the profits. He was to function as producer-director, which gave him a chance to assist in script development, to select the cast, and to participate in various postproduction duties. Mirisch retained the right of the final cut. However, after Jewison's first effort, *The Russians Are Coming, the Russians Are Coming,* he was given a new five-picture deal with much more liberal terms.

Directorial freedom is relative, to be sure. As a contract director at Universal, Jewison "was allowed a certain number of weeks of preparation, a certain number of weeks for shooting, and the right to make the first cut. After that it was goodbye. It became the studio's picture afterwards," said Patrick Palmer, Jewison's long-time associate producer. "The studio did all the post-production work, graded the final answer print and the soundtrack. The studio also did the titles. The studio earlier had examined the script to determine if a scene were to be shot on location, on the back lot, or if a process shot were to be used instead. The studio did all the casting. During shooting, the studio looked at the dailies before the director did. Department heads were very powerful." [14]

In contrast, "those who worked for the Mirisches," said Palmer, "were able to negotiate greater preparation time, at least mutual approval rights of cast, cameraman, editor, etc. Mirisch would not just arbitrarily assign someone to a film. Personnel would be introduced to one another. If they felt comfortable with one another, great, they would team up." [15] Directors typically expected to work with writers and their involvement in this phase of production obviously benefited the picture, but it also insured loyalty to the company. Directors had nonexclusive contracts and could be lured away by the competition. In nurturing John Sturges, for example, the Mirisches apparently had to urge him to take on the responsibility of working with a writer full time. The objective was to get a screenplay tailor-made to Sturges' tastes. As Marvin Mirisch told Krim, Sturges had rejected five projects: "Had we not insisted that he work with the writer on this script, the screenplay would never come out as he sees it and he would then try to wheedle out of making the picture."[16]

On an administrative level, Mirisch provided its directors a full line of financial services in addition to secretarial and production help. As Krim explained, "the Mirisches received reports from us and they in turn passed on the information where appropriate. We allowed the Mirisch company to give important directors the right to look at our books directly. But over the years, most relied on Mirisch to do that for them even though they had the right to it directly."[17] Mirisch charged a service fee, but the fee was hardly exorbitant; Mirisch charged 5 percent of the first million of the below-the-line costs and 2½ percent of the remainder for each picture. This was significantly less than what the majors were charging.

THE FIRST TWENTY-PICTURE DEAL

As Mirisch started out, the oldest and most powerful of the major studios were experiencing enormous difficulties doing exactly what this fledgling outfit wanted to do—make quality pictures. The first Mirisch entry was *Fort Massacre* (1958), a program Western starring Joel McCrea, directed by Joseph Newman, and produced by Walter Mirisch. McCrea had starred in a popular Western series at Allied Artists. The second entry, *Man of the West* (1958) starred Gary Cooper, another carryover from Allied Artists. This Western, also produced by Walter Mirisch, had the substantial price tag of $1.5 million and was directed by Anthony Mann from a screenplay by Reginald Rose.

The Mirisches' third entry, *Some Like It Hot* (1959) hit pay dirt. Produced and directed by Billy Wilder for around $3 million, it was a huge hit, grossing $13 million during its first release. *Fort Massacre* barely broke even and *Man of the West* withered at the box office, so this was definitely a shot in the arm for the Mirisches. Wilder and his collaborator, I. A. L. Diamond, fashioned a comic masterpiece, brilliantly performed by Marilyn Monroe, Tony Curtis, and Jack Lemmon. *Some Like It Hot* was hailed as UA's most successful non-roadshow attraction to date. According to *Variety*, the picture played in some 18,000 situations out of a total of 20,000 domestic, which included 14,000 hardtops and 6,000 drive-ins.[18] The picture brought Marilyn Monroe the first serious critical acclaim of her career, helped make

Jack Lemmon one of the most sought-after stars of the sixties, and was the first of a long string of Mirisch entries to receive Academy Award honors.

Living up to his billing, Billy Wilder had catapulted the Mirisch company into the forefront of the independent producer ranks by giving the company a sense of credibility. The company had lived up to its own publicity. However, in their eagerness to sign Wilder, the Mirisches had given away too large a slice of the profits. Marilyn Monroe worked for 10 percent of the gross in excess of $4 million; Tony Curtis 5 percent of the gross over $2 million; and Billy Wilder 17½ percent of the first million after breakeven and 20 percent thereafter. A disgruntled Bob Benjamin noted that when UA's standard distribution fee of 30 percent was added to this 32½ percent participation, less than a third of the gross was available to recoup the negative cost. *Some Like It Hot* generated only about $500,000 in profits from its first theatrical release. Wilder, on the other hand, pocketed $1.2 million; Monroe, $800,000, and Curtis, around $500,000.

No one disputed Wilder's value after his next picture. *The Apartment* (1960) was nominated for ten Academy Awards and won five Oscars, including best picture, best screenplay, and best director. Handcrafted by Wilder and I. A. L. Diamond, who wrote the original screenplay to fit the talents of Jack Lemmon (who was beaten out of the best actor Oscar by Burt Lancaster for his performance in *Elmer Gantry*), this picture presented a quintessential portrait of the fifties Organization Man. The critical reception was somewhat icy. Stanley Kauffmann called it a "tasteless gimmick"; Hollis Alpert termed it a "dirty fairy tale"; and Dwight Macdonald found it "immoral," "dishonest," and "without style or taste." [19] Audience response differed. As a result of word of mouth, the boxoffice picked up, eventually tallying a gross of over $9 million, well short of *Some Like It Hot,* but more profitable. Both pictures cost about the same to produce, but because Jack Lemmon and Shirley MacLaine were paid straight salaries of $175,000 each, *The Apartment* earned over $1 million in profits from its theatrical run. These two stars would never come as cheap again.

Wilder's third production for the Mirisches was *One, Two, Three* (1961), a Cold War comedy shot in Germany that starred James Cagney, Horst Buchholtz, and Pamela Tiffen. Produced at a cost of $3 million, the picture grossed a disappointing $4 million, and lost $1.6 million. For his next effort Wilder produced *Irma La Douce* (1963). To play the parts of a Parisian streetwalker and the young gendarme, Wilder insisted on hiring MacLaine and Lemmon. MacLaine now commanded a salary of $350,000 against a percentage of the gross escalating from

5 to 7½ percent; Jack Lemmon received a salary up front, a profit participation of 15 percent, plus a deferred salary of $100,000. Despite the mixed reviews, *Irma La Douce* grossed $15 million and became Wilder's biggest grosser. But because of the special terms for MacLaine and Lemmon, UA and Mirisch were left with only $440,000 in profits. However, production profits were not the only measure of Wilder's importance to the Mirisches.

The remainder of the Mirisch output in this twenty-picture deal was drawn from all creative sources, including original screenplays, adaptations of hit plays, and best-selling novels. The range of material extended from Westerns to musicals and from comedies to drama. In other words, the Mirisches attempted to reach as many important segments of the market as possible.

In signing William Wyler to produce and direct *The Children's Hour* (1962), the Mirisches had hoped to establish a long-term relationship with another director of stature to produce serious pictures for the adult market. Based on Lillian Hellman's controversial Broadway hit, *The Children's Hour* was Wyler's second go at the play. He directed the first version for Sam Goldwyn in 1936 under the title *These Three*. For the remake, which starred Audrey Hepburn, Shirley MacLaine, and James Garner, Wyler remained faithful to the play by not blunting the implication of lesbianism. The picture received a Code Seal, but had to bear the tag "not recommended for children." The marquee value of the stars, the adult theme, and Wyler's direction could not save the picture. Produced at a cost of $3.6 million, *The Children's Hour* lost $2.8 million on a gross of $3 million. *Variety* provided one explanation for the poor performance: "If there is a fault to be found with the new version, it is that the sophistication of modern society makes the events . . . slightly less plausible in the 1961 setting into which it has been framed." [20]

The Mirisches tapped another Lillian Hellman play, *Toys in the Attic* (1963) in another attempt to reach the adult market and also to establish a relationship with a new young director, George Roy Hill. Produced by Walter Mirisch and starring Dean Martin, Geraldine Page, Yvette Mimieux, and Wendy Heller, this picture also lost a bundle— $1.2 million on a $2.1 investment. *Variety's* prognosis was that "the public is tiring, plausibly, of Southern-fried neurosis operas." [21]

The Mirisches had better luck with action pictures. Following *Fort Massacre* and *Man of the West*, the Mirisches produced *The Gunfight at Dodge City* (1959), starring Joel McCrea, *The Horse Soldiers* (1959), starring John Wayne, and *The Magnificent Seven* (1960), starring a galaxy of talent.

Academy Award for Best Picture / 1960

The Apartment

Jack Lemmon

A Mirisch Company presentation
Starring Jack Lemon, Shirley MacLaine, and Fred MacMurray
Directed and produced by Billy Wilder

Other Academy Awards* and nominations
Actor: Jack Lemmon
Actress: Shirley MacLaine
Supporting actor: Jack Kruschen
*Direction: Billy Wilder
*Writing *story and screenplay*: Billy Wilder and I. A. L. Diamond
Cinematography: Joseph Lashelle
*Art direction–Set decoration: Alexander Trauner, Edward G. Boyle
Sound: Samuel Goldwyn Studio Sound Dept., Gordon E. Sawyer,
     sound director
*Film editing: Daniel Mandell

Shirley MacLaine and Jack Lemmon

John Sturges, the producer-director of *The Magnificent Seven,* specialized in the action genre. In signing him to a multiple-picture contract in 1958, Walter Mirisch reported that "with Sturges we have a definite asset in attracting top male stars. He has worked with most of them and, as a director, he has been getting magnificent notices." [22] Sturges' credits included *Bad Day at Black Rock* (1955), *Gunfight at the OK Corral* (1957), and *The Old Man and the Sea* (1958). Based on Akira Kurosawa's *The Seven Samurai, The Magnificent Seven* linked the talents of Charles Bronson, Yul Brynner, James Coburn, Steve McQueen, and Eli Wallach and became a huge popular success.

Sturges' second picture, *The Great Escape* (1963) teamed up another group of macho types—Steve McQueen, James Garner, Richard Attenborough, Charles Bronson, Donald Pleasance, and James Coburn—in an account of a massive breakout of 250 prisoners from a German prison camp in 1942. Produced at $3.8 million, *The Great Escape* ranked among the Mirisches' most expensive projects, but it had Steve McQueen going for it and an audience that had become enamored of blockbusters in the same mold, particularly *The Bridge on the River Kwai* and *The Guns of Navarone. The Great Escape* grossed considerably more than *The Magnificent Seven*, but because of *Escape's* higher production cost, the two pictures earned approximately the same amount of profits—around $300,000.

Kings of the Sun (1963), another spinoff of *The Magnificent Seven*, provided a vehicle for Yul Brynner. A kind of Western set in the Mayan past, this big-budget picture produced at close to $4 million was shot entirely in Mexico under the direction of J. Lee Thompson. It was described by *Variety* as "exploitable merchandise and an acceptable avenue of escape for audiences that prefer their adventure spectacle pictorially extravagant, historically simplified and melodramatically passionate."[23]

Following a different tack, the Mirisches produced two Elvis Presley vehicles—*Follow That Dream* (1962) and *Kid Galahad* (1962). These pictures "were not part of any major scheme. They were just rather two good commercial ventures," said Walter Mirisch.[24] Presley, the biggest name in rock 'n' roll, had previously starred in over thirty pictures beginning with *Love Me Tender,* produced by Twentieth Century–Fox in 1956. The Mirisch pictures were made following Presley's discharge from the Army and coasted on a new Presley craze. Both were produced by David Weisbart, a former executive at Fox who produced one of Presley's first pictures. A light romantic comedy with songs, *Follow That Dream* was, in *Variety's* opinion, "an especially large ozone item." *Kid Galahad* cast Elvis as a boxer in a familiar prizefight story with songs.

Comedy, though, remained the most successful genre, thanks to the fortuitous linking of Blake Edwards with Peter Sellers. In signing a multiple-picture contract in 1962, Edwards became Mirisch's first golden boy. He received a multiple-picture contract that gave him a producer fee of $50,000, a director fee that escalated from $137,000 to $200,000; and one-third of the net profits plus 2½ percent of the gross after break-even. Starting out as a writer-producer at Monogram, Edwards worked his way up to television, and, with the assistance of Dick Powell, directed for "Four Star Playhouse." In 1958, Edwards created the popular television series, "Peter Gunn," which ran for three seasons. His directing career in the movies began in 1955, making "B" features for Columbia and Universal-International. The big break occurred in 1959 when Edwards directed and coscripted *Operation Petticoat,* starring Cary Grant and Tony Curtis. This Universal release opened at the prestigious Radio City Music Hall and was enormously successful at the boxoffice, quickly becoming one of the largest-grossing films in the studio's history up to that time. Now in the big leagues, Edwards went on to direct a string of commercial and critical hits that included *Breakfast at Tiffany's* (1961) for Paramount and *Days of Wine and Roses* (1962) for Warner Brothers before joining the Mirisches.

The Mirisches originally hired Peter Ustinov to play Inspector Clousseau in *The Pink Panther.* "Some three or four weeks before we were to start production," said Walter Mirisch, "Mr. Ustinov decided he didn't want to be in the picture. We were furious. I think we even sued him. But we scurried around and tried to find someone else and came up

Peter Sellers in *A Shot in the Dark* (1964), directed by Blake Edwards

with Peter Sellers. As the picture was being shot, the Clouseau character really took over and it became the center of the film." [25]

The Pink Panther (1964) opened in the Radio City Music Hall, a first for the Mirisches and the Krim-Benjamin regime. Sellers had just starred in Stanley Kubrick's *Dr. Strangelove* and attracted all the attention in *The Pink Panther,* leading the Mirisches to produce a follow-up immediately, *A Shot in the Dark* (1964), also directed by Edwards. In addition to starting an enormously successful comedy series, *The Pink Panther* spun off an immensely profitable children's industry "ranging from Saturday morning cartoons, to huge stuffed toys and federal government wall stickers reminding children to turn out the lights before leaving their rooms." [26]

Separate and apart from this twenty-picture deal, the Mirisches took on a special assignment to produce three properties that UA had taken over from Seven Arts Productions. Originally a distributor of telefilms, Seven Arts had branched out to become an entertainment conglomerate involved in the promotion, packaging, production, and distribution of properties to the stage, television, or motion pictures. Seven Arts' motion picture activities were headed by former agent Ray Stark. For its first UA project, Seven Arts produced John Huston's *The Misfits* (1961), which was based on Arthur Miller's original screen drama and starred Marilyn Monroe and Clark Gable.

UA terminated its relationship with Seven Arts after *The Misfits* when it determined that Seven Arts' diversification plans included distributing feature films in the theatrical market. Continuing the relationship would have created a conflict of interests. As part of the settlement, UA arranged for the Mirisches to develop three properties originally purchased for Seven Arts—two Broadway hits, William Gibson's *Two for the Seesaw* and the Laurents-Bernstein *West Side Story,* and the best-selling novel by James Gould Couzzens, *By Love Possessed.*

Although *By Love Possessed* and *Two for the Seesaw* bombed, *West Side Story* made boxoffice history. In translating the Arthur Laurents– Leonard Bernstein Broadway musical from stage to screen, Robert Wise and codirector Jerome Robbins "reconstructed its fine material into nothing short of a cinema masterpiece." Bosley Crowther's assessment was shared by just about everyone. [27]

West Side Story premiered at the Rivoli Theatre in New York on October 18, 1961. It played there on a roadshow basis for 68 weeks, meanwhile fanning out to become the boxoffice champion of 1962. Its domestic gross of $19 million placed the picture fifth on *Variety's* 1963 list of all-time boxoffice winners, following *Gone with the Wind, Ben-*

Hur, The Ten Commandments, and *Around the World in 80 Days,* in that order.[28] Worldwide, *West Side Story* grossed $30 million. And it won just about every award a film could—ten Academy Awards, including best picture, best direction, and best supporting actor (George Chakiris) and actress (Rita Moreno), the Directors Guild Award, the Producers Guild Award, and the New York Film Critics Award, among others.

Despite the awards and spectacular boxoffice results, *West Side Story* did not earn as much profit as might be expected—only a moderate $2.5 million. Acquiring the rights to the musical were expensive—10 percent of the gross. Moreover, Jerome Robbins and Leonard Bernstein, members of the Broadway team who worked on the film, had percentage deals. Robert Wise, the director, was given a contract for 25 percent of the profits, although he sacrificed most of his share in penalties when he allowed the production to go $2.5 million over budget. Since the losses on the three Seven Arts pictures offset the profits by $1.4 million, none of the participants—that is, Seven Arts, Mirisch, and UA—earned profits. However, as a result of the enormous success of *West Side Story,* which probably generated around $12 million in distribution fees for UA, the Mirisches were awarded a flat $1 million payment.

At the conclusion of the twenty-picture deal, the Mirisches decided to take the bonus instead of profits. Only five pictures earned a profit—three Billy Wilder hits, *The Magnificent Seven,* and *The Great Escape.* The twenty-picture group lost $8.7 million as of 1963 on a total theatrical gross of $92 million. Despite the loss on production, the deal proved tremendously lucrative for UA. These twenty pictures generated around $32 million in distribution fees by 1963. After deducting the losses of $8.7 million, over $23 million remained. Stated another way, UA kept around 25 percent of the gross as fees after deducting the production losses. Actual distribution expenses are not available, but it is fair to presume that UA made a bundle.

The buyout took the form of a tax-free exchange of stock. For their efforts, the Mirisches received 62,069 shares of UA class-B common stock. (Class-B stock was held by Krim and Benjamin as joint tenants, which meant they voted the shares, and was convertible one-to-one into class-A common.) The stock was worth $1.8 million at the time of the transaction in March 1963. Stock had growth potential, which gave the Mirisches an incentive to do even better.

The buyout neither constricted UA's cash flow nor diluted the value of the outstanding shares because the twenty-picture package had an enormous residual value. For one thing, most if not all of these pictures

West Side Story

Natalie Wood and Richard Beymer

A Mirisch Pictures presentation in association with Seven Arts
  Productions
Starring Natalie Wood, Richard Beymer, Russ Tamblyn, Rita Moreno,
  and George Chakiris
Directed by Robert Wise and Jerome Robbins
Produced by Robert Wise

Other Academy Awards* and nominations
*Supporting actor: George Chakiris
*Supporting actress: Rita Moreno
*Direction: Robert Wise and Jerome Robbins
Writing *screenplay*: Ernest Lehman
*Cinematography *color*: Daniel L. Fapp
*Art direction—Set decoration *color*: Boris Leven, Victor A. Gangelin
*Costume design *color*: Irene Sharaff
*Sound: Todd-AO Sound Dept., Fred Hynes, sound director and
  Samuel Goldwyn Studio Sound Dept., Gordon E. Sawyer, sound
  director
*Film editing: Thomas Stanford
*Music *score*: Saul Chaplin, Johnny Green, Sid Ramin, and Irwin
  Kostal
*Honorary award: Jerome Robbins for his brilliant achievements in
  the art of choreography on film.

George Chakiris and the Sharks

Rita Moreno and the Jets

had yet to be released to network and/or syndicated television. And for another, there were remake rights and ancillary rights still to exploit. UA had perpetual distribution rights to the pictures, but now that the company owned the pictures outright, it would not have to share in any of the future proceeds with the Mirisches. On the other hand, the Mirisches could enjoy the rewards of their labor now rather than later. Thus, a *quid pro quo* was effected.

Fortunately, documentation in the collection is available to measure the residual value of the package. An analysis by UA in 1968 revealed that the theatrical and television gross on the twenty pictures had jumped from $92 million in 1963 to $125 million. The production losses on the pictures had dropped from $8.7 million to $5.3 million. The net distribution fee (distribution gross minus production losses) reached $33.7 million, up from $23 million five years earlier.

THE SECOND TWENTY-PICTURE DEAL

The Mirisches signed on for another twenty pictures on December 1, 1963. As would be expected, they received better terms. Shortly afterward, however, the trades reported that the Mirisches were talking to Paramount and speculated that they might be looking for a new home after fulfilling their UA commitments.[29] Whatever their grievances, which were not made public, UA renegotiated the deal and gave the Mirisches a new contract that kept them tied to the company until 1974. This new deal, effective September 1, 1964, called for a total of forty-eight pictures to be produced in three separate groups, one of twenty and two of fourteen.

UA no longer bothered to offer a profit participation; instead the company agreed to pay the Mirisches a minimum bonus of $6 million in cash or $3 million in stock for the second group of twenty pictures. (The amounts would be worth almost the same, since the $6 million was taxable as ordinary income, whereas the $3 million counted as tax-free exchange of stock.) That was the minimum; the maximum was to be figured at 5 percent of the gross for profit pictures and 2 percent of the gross for loss pictures. Both these percentages were double those of the original deal. In addition, the Mirisches were to be paid $1,014,000 in producer fees for a three-year period.

Production costs of the Mirisch pictures for both twenty-picture packages ranged between $1.5 to $3.5 million, on the average. Pictures in this range were considered safe investments since they contained sufficient production values to meet audience requirements in this age of blockbusters and had the potential of breaking away from the pack to earn substantial profits. But compared to the extravaganzas being turned out by the industry, these production costs were relatively low.

The Mirisches' first venture into the realm of the megapicture was *Hawaii*. Although it was released in 1966, the picture had been in the works almost from the start. Mirisch purchased the movie rights to the James A. Michener novel shortly before its publication, at the blockbuster cost of $600,000 against 10 percent of the gross after breakeven. *Variety* said the acquisition set an industry record.[30] Published by Random House, *Hawaii* immediately hit the best-seller list and stayed there for over a year. Read by an estimated 100 million people, this saga became one of the most widely read novels of the time.

Mirisch hired Fred Zinnemann to produce and direct. Daniel Taradash, who had written *From Here to Eternity* for Zinnemann, was signed to do the screenplay. Beginning work in 1960, the team set out to develop a script encompassing the major thread of this 1,000-page book, from the colonization of the islands to sometime just prior to statehood. It was a herculean task. After working more than a year without developing a satisfactory structure for the story, Taradash was replaced by Dalton Trumbo. After two more years' labor, Zinnemann proposed producing a four-hour film that would be shown in two parts, rather than compressing the action into a picture of normal length. After UA vetoed the idea, Zinnemann bowed out.

He was replaced by George Roy Hill, the director of *Toys in the Attic*. To resolve the story problem, Mirisch decided to concentrate on the first half, which described the period 1820 to 1841, when the islands became commercialized, corrupted, and converted to Western ways. Filmed on location in Norway, New England, and Tahiti, in addition to the islands, *Hawaii* starred Julie Andrews, Max von Sydow, and Richard Harris. The picture was originally budgeted at $10 million, but it went over by $4 million. "It was a very troubled picture in its production," said Walter Mirisch by way of an understatement. Actually, most of the slippage was the result of the slowness of Hill's directing, as well as the problems of working in difficult locations. A distraught Marvin Mirisch in a progress report to Krim said, for example, that Hill took twelve nights to shoot one night sequence consisting of six and a half pages of script, a sequence that Hill had scheduled for six nights.[31]

Hawaii grossed close to $19 million, the most of any picture in the group. Walter Mirisch described the results as "not unsuccessful."[32]

The picture opened on a hard-ticket basis in ten markets, including Honolulu, and for awhile outpaced other UA roadshow champs, such as *West Side Story* and *Around the World in 80 Days*, during similar runs. Mirisch produced a sequel to *Hawaii*, called *The Hawaiians*, in 1970, also based on the Michener novel. Scripted by James R. Webb and directed by Tom Gries, this film concentrated on the growth of Hawaii in the present century as huge numbers of Chinese and Japanese flooded into the islands as cheap labor. Charlton Heston starred.

Krim's evaluation of the Mirisch track record at midpoint pretty much summarizes the relative performance of the two groups of pictures: "The theatrical loss on the first twelve pictures, including abandonment, will come to something between $24 million and $27 million. Eight of the first ten of these pictures show losses, several of them very substantial losses; the jury is out on the next two, but the chances are that both of them will also show losses from theatrical release." [33]

The theatrical market was unstable during the sixties, the result of racial tensions, demographic changes, social unrest, and backlash to the Vietnam War. Mirisch again presented a diversified program top-heavy in comedy, but also Westerns, romance, musicals, comedies, and science fiction, among others. Most of the pictures in the group were flops, but because UA and the Mirisches minimized risks by closely evaluating each project, no major catastrophes occurred—with perhaps one notable exception—so that what was lost in the profit column was made up by volume distribution.

Without a doubt, the greatest disappointment for both UA and Mirisch was the decline of Billy Wilder. Wilder had been instrumental in creating the Mirisch success story and, in return, the brothers made him a partner in their company by giving him 10 percent interest. For the second group of pictures, Mirisch signed Wilder to a three-picture contract that paid him handsomely. Rather than being cross-collateralized, the pictures were accounted for separately and for each picture Wilder was to be paid $400,000 against 10 percent of the gross until breakeven, after which he would receive an incredible 75 percent of the profits.

Despite the disappointing results of *One, Two, Three*, which could be rationalized in part by deteriorating Soviet-American relations, which dampened much of the comic impact of the plot, Wilder was still looked upon as a mainstay, a pantheon director who had the touch. Unfortunately, Wilder's next production, *Kiss Me, Stupid* (1964), starring Dean Martin and Kim Novak, was an outright failure. Although the picture received a Production Code seal, it was condemned by the Legion of Decency, which stated that Wilder "has regrettably produced a thoroughly sordid piece of realism which is esthetically as well as

Billy Wilder directing Kim Novak in *Kiss Me, Stupid* (1964)

morally repulsive. Crude and suggestive dialogue, a leering treatment of marital and extramarital sex, prurient preoccupation with lechery compound the film's condonation of immorality." [34]

Based on the reception of the previews, UA decided to remove its corporate label and release the picture in the U.S. through Lopert Films, its art-film subsidiary. *Variety* had stated, "Wilder, usually a director of considerable flair and inventiveness (if not always impeccable taste), has not been able this time out to rise above a basically vulgar, as well as creatively delinquent, screenplay." [35] *Time* was more vitriolic: "The careers of producer-director Billy Wilder and his favorite collaborator writer I. A. L. Diamond can be traced in a curve that peaked in such frantic, funny, wickedly knowing comedies as *Some Like It Hot* and *The Apartment,* plunged downward in *Irma La Douce,* and now lands in the murk of *Kiss Me, Stupid,* a jape that seems to have scraped its blue-black humor off the floor of a honky-tonk nightclub." [36] *Kiss Me, Stupid* played big a few weeks in Los Angeles, Chicago, and New York, but after the curiosity was exhausted, the picture died.

UA assured the trade it still had faith in Wilder by announcing, just five months after the opening of *Kiss Me, Stupid*, that the company had extended his contract by three additional pictures. But, in fact, UA and the Mirisches had their apprehensions. The records indicate that UA passed on one Wilder submission based on a play called *The Count of Luxemborg*. Although Wilder's next production, *The Fortune Cookie* (1966), featured Jack Lemmon and won an Oscar for Walter Matthau as best supporting actor, it, too, lost money.

Blake Edwards did not live up to his billing, either. Mirisch publicity had touted him as having "carved a very special niche for himself as a top comedy producer-director in the tradition of Preston Sturges and Frank Capra." Even before *The Pink Panther* was released, Mirisch had a sequel in the works. The previews had convinced them that Inspector Clouseau was destined to be the "darling of the cash customers." The sequel was based on a Broadway play entitled *A Shot in the Dark*, which in turn was an adaptation of the French hit, *L'Idiote* by Marcel Achard. Julie Harris and Walter Matthau starred in the Broadway version. Mirisch acquired the movie rights originally for Anatole Litvak who was to produce and direct it as a coventure. Sophia Loren had been signed to play the starring role of a Parisian housemaid who is accused of killing her Spanish lover, the chauffeur of the household. However, Loren changed her mind about the production and breached her contract. The venture with Litvak was terminated and, as Mirisch attempted to sort out matters, the project was turned over to Blake Edwards and screenwriter William Blatty to develop as a vehicle for Peter Sellers. Edwards and Blatty had been working on a project called *What Did You Do in the War, Daddy?*, which they temporarily shelved.

To play the female lead, Mirisch signed Elke Sommer, who was hyped as a "very curvaceous blonde from Germany who has made an impact both as a pin-up queen and a blossoming sex-symbol." Peter Sellers, who always thought his pictures bad when he first saw them, according to Walter Mirisch, told UA that "*Shot in the Dark* has turned out to be a very bad film and that comes from the one who instigated it." UA replied that "it is one of the funniest pictures ever made."[37] But this didn't prevent the picture from losing money, the result of cost overruns and Sellers' uncooperative behavior on the set.

Edwards directed his next picture, *The Great Race* (1965), for Warner. Although the picture failed, Mirisch brought Edwards back to the fold with a six-picture contract that gave him $375,000 per picture as producer-director plus 20 percent of the gross after breakeven. In addition, Mirisch agreed to pay him $150,000 as a writer's fee when appropriate. For his next picture they reactivated *What Did You Do in the War, Daddy?* (1966). It was a disaster. Produced at a cost of almost

$7 million, the picture grossed only $4 million. In an interview for *Millimeter* magazine, Edwards blamed Walter Mirisch for foisting the project on him: "I told him that I didn't think it was a good time to do a war comedy—it was right in the middle of the Vietnam War, there were a lot of Gold Star mothers and the perspective on war was not what it should be for this kind of satire." Later in this interview, though, Edwards described it as "a black comedy way ahead of its time."[38]

As Edwards admitted, he was having serious domestic and personal problems and these no doubt affected his work. In any event, Edwards' career went into decline. He made only one other picture for Mirisch, *The Party* (1968), which teamed Edwards and Sellers for a third time. The picture had "all the charm of two-reel comedy, as well as the resulting tedium when the concept is distended to 10 reels . . . one joke script, told in laudable, if unsuccessful, attempt to emulate silent pix technique."[39] After this boxoffice failure, Edwards and the Mirisches could not find another project that was mutually agreeable.

However, the Mirisches attempted to revitalize the Clouseau character by producing *Inspector Clouseau* (1968) with Alan Arkin in the title role. Arkin had burst into the comedy limelight in *The Russians Are Coming, the Russians Are Coming* (1966), Norman Jewison's first project for the Mirisches. Tom and Frank Waldman, who collaborated with Edwards on the screenplay for *The Party,* wrote the screenplay and Bud Yorkin, who scored a hit with *Divorce, American Style,* directed. But the chemistry did not work.

Interest in Westerns declined during the sixties and with it the career of John Sturges. After *The Great Escape,* he made *The Hallelujah Trail* (1965), a Western spoof starring Burt Lancaster and Lee Remick. A big-budget item packaged in Ultra Panavision and released in Cinerama's single-lens process, the picture fell far short of earning back its negative cost of $7.2 million. Sturges' *The Satan Bug,* also released in 1965, was a change of pace. Based on a novel by Ian Stuart (*nom de plume* for Alistair MacLean), the picture was a suspenseful melodrama about bacteriological warfare starring George Maharis and Richard Basehart. Produced at a modest $1.8 million, the picture did not break even. With *Hour of the Gun* (1967), Sturges returned to the Western, by continuing the story of Wyatt Earp after *Gunfight at the OK Corral,* which he directed for Hal Wallis at Paramount in 1957. A talky follow-up starring James Garner, Jason Robards, and Robert Ryan, the picture died at the box office.

This period saw the rise of the last big Mirisch producer-director, Norman Jewison. Born in Toronto, Canada, Jewison, like many new-generation Hollywood directors, apprenticed in television, starting as a writer for the BBC and then as the producer-director of a top-rated variety show for the Canadian Broadcasting Company. In 1958, CBS hired Jewison to inject life into the ailing "Hit Parade." Jewison soon won other assignments on such specials as "The Broadway of Lerner and Loewe," "The Judy Garland Show," and "The Harry Belafonte Hour." Jewison moved to Hollywood at the request of producer Stan Margulies at Universal who wanted someone with a fresh approach to direct *40 Pounds of Trouble* (1963), starring Tony Curtis. Afterward, Jewison directed two other pictures at Universal, *The Thrill of It All* (1963) and *Send Me No Flowers* (1964).

Jewison's first assignment at Mirisch was *The Russians Are Coming, the Russians Are Coming* (1966). Based on a book by Nathaniel Benchley called *The Off Islanders,* it had been around for a some time, but it was Jewison's choice. William Rose was hired to write the screenplay, but he worked so slowly that Jewison had time to make two pictures elsewhere, *The Cincinnati Kid* (1965) and *The Art of Love* (1965). When Rose finally turned in the script, "it was a revelation," said Walter Mirisch.[40] Under Jewison's direction, this Cold War comedy with a cast of screen newcomers (Alan Arkin and Tessie O'Shea) and old pros (Paul Ford and Theodore Bikel) became the sleeper of the year. *The Russians Are Coming* narrowly missed out in the Oscar balloting for best picture to *A Man for All Seasons*. Nonetheless, it became the first moneymaker out of nine in this Mirisch group, grossing $12 million the first time around on an investment of $3.9 million.

For his next project, Jewison accepted the Mirisch offer to direct *In the Heat of the Night* (1967). Developed by Walter Mirisch and adapted by Stirling Silliphant from a novel by John Ball, *Heat* told the story of Virgil Tibbs, a black homicide detective from Philadelphia who is forced to work on a murder case with a small-town chief of police in Mississippi. Seen against the backdrop of the civil-rights movement, *Heat* can be considered another attempt by the Mirisches to produce a socially relevant film. Linking Jewison to the picture was no doubt prompted by his handling of the Cold War sensibilities in *The Russians Are Coming.*

Virgil Tibbs was Sidney Poitier's third starring role in 1967 after *To Sir, With Love* and *Guess Who's Coming to Dinner.* As *Variety* pointed out, "Poitier increasingly is offered [by Hollywood] as a symbol of the thoughtful, efficient Negro whose technological know-how (no dropout, he) enables him to help, compete with and, when necessary, show up whites."[41] Poitier had earlier appeared in *Lilies of the Field* (1963), a UA release directed by Ralph Nelson, which won Poitier an Oscar for his performance as a jovial handyman who builds a nice new chapel for a group of white refugee nuns. Playing the role of the bigoted sher-iff in *Heat* opposite Poitier was Rod Steiger. The combination was irre-sistible. *In the Heat of the Night* won the Academy Award for best pic-ture, the third such honor for the Mirisches in eight years, a record that has not been surpassed by any other producer, major or minor. Rod Steiger picked up the Oscar for best actor and Sterling Silliphant the Oscar for best screenplay. Made for a relatively modest $2 million, *Heat* initially grossed $16 million.

Jewison's direction of *In the Heat of the Night* won him a new five-picture contract that might be considered the best deal any UA producer had received to that time. It was tailored to keep Jewison happy for a long time. Functioning now as producer-director, Jewison's compensation increased incrementally. On the first two pictures he was to receive a total of $300,000 as fees (broken down $250,000 for producing and $50,000 for directing) plus 20 percent of the gross after breakeven. On the last three, his fees escalated to $550,000 with bonuses along the way that at the end would make his fees average out to $550,000 per picture. After completing the fifth picture, he was to receive another bonus consisting of 2½ percent of the gross on any picture that grossed $500,000 over breakeven. Should Jewison decide not to produce and/or direct any three pictures, he had the option of acting as executive producer, which paid a producer fee plus one-third of the profits.

In producing and directing *The Thomas Crown Affair* (1968), Jew-ison turned in his third moneymaker in a row. Steve McQueen, now at the height of his popularity, played the part of a wealthy industrialist who masterminds a Boston bank robbery. Faye Dunaway, fresh from *Bonnie and Clyde,* played the insurance investigator sent to expose him. Written by Alan R. Trustman, a prominent Boston lawyer, the pic-ture is best remembered today for the most sexually symbolic chess game ever played and the longest, deepest kiss ever filmed. What dis-tinguished it at the time were some special effects and a patina of *haute couture.* The former consisted mainly of split and multiple-screen images inspired by Montreal's Expo '67 and the latter by Faye Dunaway's thirty-one smashing costume changes. "If style could be purchased," said *Time,* "Norman Jewison . . . would surely have in-cluded it. Unable to do so, he has turned out a glimmering, empty film reminiscent of an *haute couture* model: stunning on the surface, con-cave and undernourished beneath."[42] Regardless, the picture grossed a healthy $11 million on an investment of $4.3 million.

This second batch of twenty pictures grossed $165 million by 1968 compared to $125 million for the first group. Although the gross,

Academy Award for Best Picture / 1967

In the Heat of the Night

Sidney Poitier and Rod Steiger

A Mirisch Corporation presentation
Starring Sidney Poitier and Rod Steiger
Directed by Norman Jewison
Produced by Walter Mirisch

Other Academy Awards* and nominations
*Actor: Rod Steiger
Direction: Norman Jewison
*Writing *screenplay*: Stirling Silliphant
*Sound: Samuel Goldwyn Studio Sound Dept., Gordon E. Sawyer,
    sound director
*Film editing: Hal Ashby
Sound effects: James A. Richard

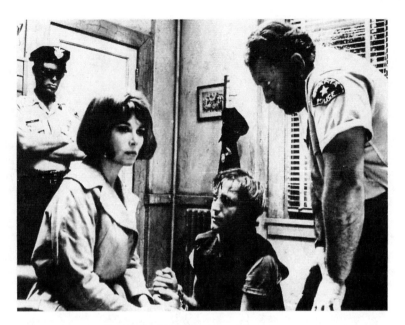

Lee Grant, Scott Wilson, and Rod Steiger

Sidney Poitier

Stirling Silliphant, Norman Jewison, and Walter Mirisch on the set of *In the Heat of the Night*

which included fees from television, had increased by $40 million, so had the losses—$31 million compared to $5.3 million. Distribution fees from the second group came to $52 million; after deducting the $31 million loss, UA was left with $21 million compared to $35 million from the first. Another way of comparing the relative performance of the two groups is that on the first, UA netted in distribution fees 28 percent of the gross, whereas on the second, UA netted 14 percent.

The Mirisches qualified for the bonus nonetheless and received $3 million in stock. UA reassessed its relations with the Mirisches afterward. The theatrical market had become more volatile than ever. By the end of the sixties, the Civil Rights movement, the Vietnam War protests, and the cultural upheaval they created had radically altered not only moviegoing habits but also the very constituency of the motion picture audience. This upheaval, from 1969 to 1972, caused a recession in Hollywood that brought several studios, including UA, to the brink of disaster. The industry rebounded, but not until the majors streamlined operations, reduced operating costs, and cut back on production.

In reassessing its relations with producers, UA's foremost concern was whether the deal with the Mirisches could and should be continued, particularly after Harold Mirisch's death. In Krim's opinion, Harold Mirisch had been the real moving force behind the independent production company. After Harold Mirisch died in 1968, discussions about future relationships ensued. According to Herb Schottenfeld, "Walter and Marvin convinced UA that while they didn't have the background that Harold brought into the deal, they had participated with Harold during all the years of the UA relationship and were more than expert in their respective fields. And since the perception of Hollywood was that the Mirisches were inordinately prolific and successful, they could still have access to the types of people attracted to Harold."[43]

THE LAST PICTURES

The Mirisches still had twenty-eight pictures to go on their contract. The deal progressed in two stages of fourteen pictures each, the terms for which were pretty much the same. The Mirisches continued their policy of producing sequels in an attempt to reduce the uncertainties of the market. *The Magnificent Seven* had spawned *Return of the*

Seven (1966), *Guns of the Magnificent Seven* (1969), and *The Magnificent Seven Ride* (1972). All were low-budget entries produced in Spain with different groups of actors, mostly second tier. So were the directors—Burt Kennedy, Paul Windkos, and George McCowan, respectively. The sequels received uniformly unfavorable reviews, but all did good business, particularly in foreign markets.

Exploiting the blackpix trend and the Academy Award honors won by *In the Heat of the Night*, The Mirisches produced two sequels starring Sidney Poitier—*They Call Me Mister Tibbs* (1970), directed by Gordon Douglas, and *The Organization* (1971), directed by Don Medford. In *Heat* Tibbs played a homicide detective from Philadelphia; in the sequels he has the rank of homicide lieutenant and the setting is now San Francisco, the latter change presumably influenced by *Bullitt*. At best, the two pictures just about broke even.

The attempt to tap the youth audience proved a disaster. John Huston directed a period piece called *Sinful Davey* (1969), a comedy about a nineteenth-century teenage highwayman, starring John Hurt. The picture was shot in Ireland where John Huston resided to save on U.S. taxes. *Variety* described his direction as "club-footed."[44] Produced at more than $3 million, *Sinful Davey* grossed $550,000. *The First Time* (1969), the first production of Roger Smith and Allan Carr, starred Jacqueline Bisset and a cast of unknowns in a comedy of three teenagers awakening to sex. Shot entirely at Niagara Falls and Toronto, the picture received favorable reviews, but got lost in the mix. *Halls of Anger* (1969), produced by Herbert Hirschman and directed by Paul Bogart, was a topical picture about a group of middle-class white kids being bused to an all-black high school in the ghetto. *The First Time* and *Halls of Anger* were low-budget pictures, produced for $900,000 and $1.6 million, respectively.

Norman Jewison's youth entry, *Gaily, Gaily* (1969), attempted to have it both ways: "It is a film that may capture the attention of both those among the older film attendees, yearning backwards for a more innocent time, and the youth audience who may find empathy with the young man striving to break away from his roots and to live a free life in the big city."[45] *Gaily, Gaily* was a comedy loosely adapted from Ben Hecht's autobiography, *A Child of the Century,* set in Chicago *circa* 1910. Beau Bridges starred. Jewison's previous pictures had been moderately priced, but *Gaily, Gaily* cost over $8 million. Much of the budget went to recreating pre–World War I Chicago on the backlot of the Goldwyn studio. The picture did not even gross $2 million.

Jewison produced but did not direct a second picture for the youth market, *The Landlord* (1970). The picture marked the directorial debut of Hal Ashby, a film editor and long-time Jewison associate. Again starring Beau Bridges, *The Landlord* was a comedy about a bored rich youth who buys an apartment building in a black ghetto. Many stylistic flashes including fantasy tableaux and other tricks imitating Richard Lester could not save this picture.

Jewison more than acquitted himself with his next production, *Fiddler on the Roof* (1971). This picture, which Jewison directed and coproduced with Mirisch, was the most profitable UA release up to that time, grossing more than $50 million. In an unusual move, UA had bid on the movie rights to this property with the idea of securing the services of the creative team that produced the play on Broadway—particularly producer Harold Prince, director and choreographer Jerome Robbins, and playwright Joseph Stein. UA acquired the rights to the musical in December 1966 for $2 million down and 25 percent of the world gross after breakeven.

The fact that UA acted on its own to purchase the musical created problems with its producers, since any number of them had expressed an interest in the property. Harold Mirisch said, "This establishes United Artists in the producing business and makes you a competitor of ours and of all your other producing entities. It is obviously impossible for us to operate in the market, subject always of course to your approvals, if we are to be in direct competition with you for talent and properties."[46]

A proviso in the deal to acquire *Fiddler* stipulated that the picture could not be released before 1971 on the presumption that the legit theater versions would be playing until then. In the interim, UA decided to offer the project to the Mirisches, who in turn looked to Jewison to do the actual producing. To oversee the production, Mirisch was assigned 15 percent of the profits; to direct and produce, Jewison received 20 percent in addition to $550,000 cash; and Hal Prince 2½ percent. UA kept 62½ percent of the profits for itself.

By the time the film version of *Fiddler* opened in November 1971, the play had become the longest-running musical in theatrical history, surpassing the previous record of 2,844 performances set by *Hello Dolly!* Three touring companies took the production on the road. In London, the play ran for more than 2,000 performances at His Majesty's Theater. Overseas, more than 30 successful productions had been mounted in Japan, Mexico, Turkey, Brazil, Iceland, and even behind the Iron Curtain. It was reckoned that over 35 million people had seen the show. Over 20 million records of the complete score had been sold. If there ever was a presold picture, this was it.

Critics were not kind. Jay Cocks of *Time,* for example, said "*Fiddler on the Roof* now joins the company of *Star, Hello Dolly!, Paint Your Wagon,* and *Dr. Doolittle*—the last, lumbering dinosaurs from the era of big-budget musicals."[47] Vincent Canby of the *New York Times* said the picture was "typical of what's wrong . . . with almost every other movie adaptation of a Broadway show . . . they've not just opened up the play, they've let most of the life out of it."[48] Stanley Kauffmann titled his review, "Mogen David Superstar."[49]

Regardless, the picture was a smash hit and earned healthy profits for everyone involved—Jewison, $1.95 million; Mirisch, $1.5 million; Harold Prince, $245,000; and UA, $6.1 million. UA, in addition, earned distribution profits of $8 million from its fees of $16 million. The authors of the play earned $4.5 million from their percentage of the gross.

Without *Fiddler,* the fourteen-picture deal with the Mirisches would have proven disastrous. This group grossed a total of $102 million as of 1973 including fees from television distribution. UA's share amounted to $33 million; production losses came to $32 million, leaving a surplus of $1 million. But UA lost money on the deal; actual distribution expenses far exceeded the surplus. Without *Fiddler,* the excess of production losses over distribution fees would have come to $23 million in addition to the actual distribution expenses.

The fourteen pictures, all losses except *Fiddler* and *The Magnificent Seven* sequels, yielded the Mirisches a bonus of $2,386,000. This time UA opted to pay cash. UA again reassessed its relations with the Mirisches. As Krim explained, "things were not the same as they used to be. With Harold away the social relationship and general atmosphere of the company which had attracted big directors no longer was there. The mainstay of the team, Billy Wilder, had gone into decline. For the Mirisches, the deal made no sense for them any more because there were no profits, only the bonus for loss pictures. It was very modest. Their individual salaries were below what they wanted for themselves. The presentation Marvin and Walter made to us of a renewal proposal was out of line with what was appropriate. We did not just say we wanted to terminate the arrangement; on the contrary, we said in view of our long relationship we would like to continue if we can do it on a basis that is viable for us. Because they felt they needed more than we were able to give, we dissolved the relationship."[50]

Walter Mirisch gave this explanation: "These had been very bad years for UA and they wanted us to cut all of our overhead. [UA cut the Mirisches' operating overhead and production overhead by about one-half in 1970.] The order was to get rid of people. So we had to break our relationship with the directors we had brought in, and we got rid of our permanent staff. Then, with our overhead down to the bone, we made fewer pictures."[51]

In renegotiating the deal, UA relieved the Mirisches of the obligation to produce the final fourteen pictures on their contract. They could produce nothing if they wished and UA, in turn, stipulated that it would finance only what it wanted and on a very selective basis. The bonus deal was eliminated. Pictures would be cross-collateralized in groups of two and profits would be split fifty-fifty. Although the Mirisches were tied to UA on an exclusive basis until August 31, 1974, UA guaranteed the Mirisches around $800,000 in producer fees. Mirisch produced four more pictures before the relationship was finally terminated in 1974—Billy Wilder's *Avanti* (1972), Michael Winner's *Scorpio* (1973), and two Richard Fleischer pictures, *The Spikes Gang* (1974) and *Mr. Majestyk* (1974).

During the sixties, the Mirisch operation had been an ideal structure for independent production. As Walter Mirisch said, "Picture making is still largely a function of relationships. The idea that people can come together, complement one another's efforts and resolve that they want to work together is still fundamental to motion picture making."[52] (In recognition of Walter Mirisch's achievements as a producer, the Academy presented him the Irving G. Thalberg Memorial Award for 1977.) The Mirisches' umbrella structure was designed to attract and nurture talent. They were able to attract first-rank directors such as Billy Wilder, John Sturges, Norman Jewison, Blake Edwards, and Robert Wise, as well as many a lesser name.

The motion picture market expanded during the sixties to encompass a broad constituency and the Mirisches diversified their production output to tap all segments of the market. In the process, the Mirisch pictures consistently won Hollywood's top honors. Many of the great Hollywood films of the sixties are Mirisch pictures, including *The Apartment, Some Like It Hot, West Side Story, The Magnificent Seven, In the Heat of the Night,* and the Pink Panther pictures. The many Mirisch pictures enhanced UA's film library and went on to fill UA's coffers as they were reissued to exploit television and other ancillary markets.

The changed motion picture market of the seventies more than any other cause led the breakup of UA's relationship with the Mirisches. The recession in Hollywood that began in 1969 caused UA and the other majors to cut back on production—and for good reason. Audiences had become more fickle than ever, transforming motion picture production from a risky business into what some considered a crap shoot. A Mirisch-type of operation began to seem a burden and no longer made economic sense to UA. Instead of subsidizing a satellite production operation like Mirisch, UA adopted the policy of dealing with all its producers directly. UA also began to pare down the number of picture commitments it made.

THE BIGGEST STORY OF OUR TIME!

GREGORY PECK · AVA GARDNER
FRED ASTAIRE · ANTHONY PERKINS
ON THE BEACH

Selling Them Big

When television replaced the movies as the main source of entertainment for Americans, the function of motion picture promotion
changed. During the days of the studio system, promotion served to
sustain the moviegoing habit and to funnel people to first-run theaters.
Although Hollywood publicized pictures individually, stars received
the lion's share of attention. It is fair to say that the public was interested in stars first and story second. Stars obviously never lost their
drawing power, but during the widescreen era, the big picture acquired an appeal of its own. Although average audience attendance declined by 50 percent from 1948 to 1956, high-quality pictures in color,
widescreens, and stereophonic sound had demonstrated that a fascina-
tion with the movies still existed. Since production costs for these pictures increased tremendously, promotion took on two goals: to create a
"must see" attitude and to upscale the product in the minds of the public to justify higher ticket prices.

Simultaneously, Hollywood devised new ways to offset the risks of
increased production financing. First, Hollywood added a new wrinkle
to the practice of basing big-budget pictures on presold properties

such as best-selling novels and hit Broadway plays—the tie-in. In a tie-in, a film company would, as an example, cross-promote a best-selling novel to presell the movie. Preselling became institutionalized during the sixties as motion picture companies diversified into recorded music, book publishing, merchandizing, and television.

Second, the industry realized that motion pictures no longer had universal appeal and began targeting audience segments. Before television, pictures moved through the distribution channels like clockwork, regulated by runs, clearances, and zoning. Over a course of time, a picture played every area of the country from metropolis to village. After television, Hollywood used various patterns of playoff—exclusive, day-and-date, multiple, saturation, and variations of the same—to match the picture to its intended audience.

Third, the majors reduced risks by capturing the lion's share of the boxoffice. Bargaining with exhibitors, they added sliding scales, guarantees, advances, extended playing time, and floors and ceilings to the customary percentage terms, which permitted distributors to enjoy extraordinary rentals when a picture hit it big but in return protected the exhibitor from excessive losses when the picture bombed.

In this chapter, I analyze the techniques UA used after going public to market its important pictures. UA did not break new ground distributing and promoting motion pictures as it did in the area of production financing. For the most part, the company adopted conventional industry practices. However, it was the application of these practices that set UA apart.

To get a feel for this aspect of UA's business, consider a piece that Max E. Youngstein wrote for *Variety* entitled, "Return to Showmanship."[1] Youngstein lamented the demise of the showman, whom he described "as the backbone of show business." "With his racy enthusiasm and inventiveness," said Youngstein, "he generated an excitement and glitter that dressed up his wares and took a real hold on the attentions of his public." "The showman isn't dead today," he continued, "but he's hard to find, and the moods and men who dominate the motion picture medium are edging him towards extinction." In place of showmanship we have merchandising: "Merchandising is very respectable. You can't even say it unless your jacket is on. It involves high fashion rituals like programmed planning in depth, market surveys and motivational research. Along Madison Avenue, it's credited with hopping up sales of deodorants, vinyl plastics and other ornaments of our culture. But it can't sell movie tickets and never will." "The new god is Taste," explained Youngstein, "and lurking off-stage to support his authority are the censors, the bluenoses and the pressure groups. With so many people sniffing from the wings for delicacy, the press agent has discarded the old handbook by Barnum and now gets his cues from Elsie Dinsmore and Stover at Yale." Concluding, Youngstein said, "Now that we're delivering the best product in the history of the business, it's virtually suicidal to settle for timid, tired showmanship."

THE PROMOTION BUDGET

Promoting the big picture fell into two phases, the preproduction/production phase and the prerelease/release phase. For convenience, I will refer to them as the production and release phases, respectively. The producer pretty much handled the first and UA's Advertising, Publicity, and Exploitation Department the latter.

Promotion was a catchall term for advertising, publicity, and exploitation. The term "marketing" later replaced it, as the industry began to experiment with audience research. Advertising is a paid announcement appearing in communications media such as newspapers, radio or television broadcasts, or outdoor posters. Publicity is an announcement *that has not been purchased* that appears in communications media. Exploitation consists of such things as the gala premiere, the hoopla of the internationally renowned film festival, or the visit of a film star to a distant city to open a new shopping center. UA budgeted virtually all promotion expenses, including the costs for prints, with the approval of the producer. And for good reason, since his picture had to recoup the outlay. Promotion expenses during production mainly covered publicity and were tacked on to the production budget. Most of the promotion expenses, however, were incurred in distribution. Since UA paid these expenses as a form of cash advance, the amount became another form of indebtedness and took first place after the distribution fee. Thus, after UA deducted its distribution fee from the rentals, the money went first to recoup the costs of prints, advertising, and promotion and afterward to pay off the bank loan and so forth.

As a rule of thumb, UA based the promotion budget largely on the anticipated income; the higher the estimate, the higher the budget in proportion. For a $1 million grosser, UA budgeted between $100,000 to $150,000; for a $3 million grosser, $400,000 to $600,000; for a $4 million grosser and over, $750,000 to $1 million. However, to launch blockbusters, UA spent $2.5 million, on the average.

Promotion costs during the production phase ranged from a low of

$61,000 for *Fiddler* to $265,000 for *It's a . . . Mad World* and typically consisted of salaries for a unit publicist, unit photographer, and special writers; press junkets; and trade-paper advertising. UA spent money judiciously. Vetoing some expensive preproduction ideas relating to *West Side Story,* Max Youngstein said, "I want not one penny spent that isn't absolutely necessary." Responding to one of Stanley Kramer's plans, he said, "It looks like we are off again on a really runaway situation, and Stanley, there is no use kidding ourselves about it. Today these runaway expenses for pre-production and launching which are actually expended or committed for before one really has thinking time with respect to the picture itself, don't just hurt you, they kill you in our market."[2]

Launching a picture, UA spent whatever it took to do the job right. During the run of a picture, UA constantly monitored and adjusted the promotion budget. On *Fiddler,* for example, UA doubled the budget four months after the premiere—from $1.4 million to $2.8 million—when it became apparent that the picture would become a big, long-running hit.

In placing a picture into release, UA negotiated a cooperative advertising campaign with exhibitors. The respective shares depended on the basic rental agreement—a flat amount for a flat rental and a percentage in a percentage deal. In the case of a percentage deal where UA and the exhibitor negotiated a 90-10 split, for example, the parties each paid the same percentage of the advertising costs.

THE PREPRODUCTION/PRODUCTION PHASE

Publicizing the big picture typically began with a news release announcing the acquisition of the movie rights to the property. UA played up the purchase price to reflect the property's commercial value. Signing the screenwriter, director, and principal cast provided additional opportunities for publicity. Of interest mostly to the trade, these matters could generate a great deal of coverage when handled by a master showman. To cast the title role of *Saint Joan,* based on the play by George Bernard Shaw, Otto Preminger conducted a thirty-seven-day talent search throughout the United States, Canada, and Western Europe. In addition to auditioning 3,000 contestants personally, Preminger appeared on TV and radio and spoke to college groups and literary societies. The $100,000 campaign culminated on the "Ed Sullivan Show" when Preminger introduced his discovery, Jean Seberg, a seventeen-year-old girl from Marshalltown, Iowa, to an audience estimated at 32 million. As Max Youngstein told Krim, the talent search paid off: "A cover story in *This Week Magazine*, plus the *Life* break, plus the *Look* break, plus the many TV and local newspaper breaks, adds up to value received. I think it also gives us a theme for selling the picture which might bring in young people to a George Bernard Shaw play, and that is to keep hammering home the Cinderella theme of Jean Seberg."[3]

In another preproduction stunt, Preminger held a news conference to announce that Dalton Trumbo, a member of the Hollywood Ten, had written the screenplay to *Exodus*. As *Variety* noted, "this was the first acknowledgment by a producer, prior to the filming of a property, that one of the 'unemployables' had actually worked on a script." The American Legion, at a convention in Minneapolis, passed a resolution condemning independent producers who employed Communists. The story naturally was picked up by the press. Although many people in the film community lauded Preminger for flouting the blacklist, others regarded his action as "an opportunistic publicity gimmick," said *Variety*, on the level of his fight with the Legion of Decency over *The Moon Is Blue*, his battle with the Production Code on *The Man with the Golden Arm*, and his casting of attorney Joseph Welch, who represented the Army in the McCarthy hearings, for the judge in *Anatomy of a Murder*.[4]

UA's Publicity, Advertising, and Exploitation Department developed the campaign in consultation with the producer. Although it covered all phases, the campaign could be modified after the picture was "in the can," after the premiere, and even during release. In the preliminary idea sessions they explored a whole range of possibilities (for example, "Sinatra as a gypsy flamenco would get us some great pictures"). Many more ideas were proposed in the early stages than ever made their way into an action plan (for example, that El-Al name one of its planes "Exodus").

The campaign had the goal of delineating and controlling how the picture should be perceived and interpreted. By developing appropriate language and image, UA hoped that the media would "read" the picture in a predetermined way. In other words, UA wanted a picture to be judged on terms that it would establish. Beginning with prepublication exploitation of the novel, the campaign for *Exodus* was "to keep foremost the idea that this is not a book specifically for Jewish interest, but rather that its contents are exciting universally." It also tried to establish that "*Exodus* is not a book about ancient Israel, but rather one of events that took place in contemporary history."[5]

The campaign for *West Side Story* stated:

the Miracle Worker a mighty motion picture experience...touch it ...sense it...feel it... you can't forget it!

STARRING ANNE BANCROFT / INTRODUCING PATTY DUKE

Mat ad for *The Miracle Worker* (1962)

We must avoid the characterization of the film as a story of juvenile delinquency. Our general aim will be to project the image of a modern film which expresses the vitality, strength, color, joys, fears, hopes and conflicts of young people against a contemporary setting. We will stress the love story, the Romeo and Juliet theme, played out on the pavements of New York.

The campaign for *Fiddler on the Roof* stated:

> It is about love. It is about a man and his relationship with his family, his people, the world who are not his people and his god. It is about oppression. It is about pride and dignity. It is a small village in the Ukraine called Anatevka which is located just south of anywhere. It is about all these things, and all these things have pertinence to people everywhere.

Inherit the Wind had twin objectives:

> • *Inherit the Wind* is to be treated as a film of enormous importance and excitement—a film that re-creates the full impact of an event that rocked both this nation and the world at large. As such, the film itself must become a great event.
> • Although much emphasis will be placed on the Scopes trial itself, every effort will be made to break out of the "academic" area of the evolution discussion into the excitement and impact of the courtroom duel, the stars themselves and the tremendous dramatic excitement generated by the film.

These campaigns succeeded, for the most part. A sampling of the breaks and reviews pertaining to *West Side Story* reveal that journalists bought the youth theme and downplayed the gang warfare. However, in the case of *Fiddler,* Richard Schickel, for one, proved recalcitrant:

> The souvenir booklet they sell in the lobby explains heavily that *Fiddler* is all about "human values," about "breaking down of traditions," about "love . . . pride and dignity, sorrow and oppression." All the things that Really Matter, in short. But these are empty generalizations. Almost any putative work of art is about one or more of them. But when they are the work of honest artists we hardly notice, so absorbed are we in the fates of specific and highly individualized people. In this movie "meaning" is present in every gesture.[6]

Inherit the Wind proved that a campaign could not have it both ways. That is, the picture could not be perceived both as a "great event" appealing to intellectuals and a "courtroom duel" appealing to the masses. Reacting to the world premiere of the picture in London, a rather frantic Stanley Kramer told Max Youngstein,

> I think London has been a huge mistake . . . In my own career, there has never been a series of reviews to match our London reviews. It is all "masterpiece"—"never such a battle of Giants,"

etc., etc., etc. Our ads were just high-class ads—as okayed by me—and, I think, a mistake. And I think they will be a mistake at home. We know by now we have a top-quality film—if we can't sell it—or *administer* it—it will be our own fault in tactics . . . I think the answer is obvious. Dayton—Scopes—Darrow and Bryan—it's all a circus—provocative on Bible and prejudice and monkeys—and we're proceeding on a professional intellectual piss-pot level of two heads of two elderly gentlemen with a vague copy-line inferring *quality of performance*. *I think it's a circus*— and I think it ought to be ballyhooed.[7]

In line with manipulating the perception of a picture, UA attempted to target a specific audience. UA never conducted "audience research" to test tastes, preferences, viewing habits, etc. These would become the goals of market research later in the seventies. UA's method was simple and straightforward. Executives viewed a film and on the basis of their experience in the business determined a likely audience to go after. At the same time, they made certain that the campaign stressed the picture's universal appeal.

In promoting *West Side Story*, UA knew that the picture would appeal to adults. The goal was to tap the teenage market. They did so by convincing *Seventeen* to devote an entire issue to the picture and by mailing promotional materials to scores of youth groups. Similarly, for *Fiddler on the Roof*, UA knew that it had the Jewish audience. The campaign, and it was a massive effort, targeted churchgoers of all beliefs.

After UA and the producer formulated the campaign, the unit publicist and staff implemented and supervised promotion during the production. Consisting of feature writers, photographers, and perhaps an art editor, the staff prepared a press information kit containing the "official" information about the film. These materials consisted of news releases, background information, production notes, biographies of the stars and crew, and feature stories written in three languages, in addition to a packet of stills in color and black and white.

The information played up the supposedly unique features of a production. Subtlety played no role in these endeavors. For example, *Solomon and Sheba* was touted as "one of the monumental pictures of all time." In addition to the great battle scenes, the picture presented

the most daring and realistic pagan orgy every filmed. While the sound track reverberates to the pulse-quickening rhythms of Prokofieff's [*sic*] "Scythian Suite," more than 150 scantily clad dancers undulate through their rites of supplication to the pagan god of love and fertility. The central figure in the dance is Gina Lollobrigida, wearing below the midriff a low-slung crescent-shaped belt from which sways a diaphanous and transparent jeweled skirt. In her navel is a crescent-shaped ruby, which gleams and glitters while she performs the orgiastic dance which ends in her seduction of Solomon.

By emphasizing uniqueness, publicity could differentiate a picture from its predecessors in the genre: "Although *Fiddler* is called a musical, many of the stars have never sung professionally before. Jewison himself had never before made a musical. This is a dramatic, personal story heightened by musical song, not the other way around. People will not stop suddenly, stride to center stage and sing; they will be moved by the drama of the moment to express their feelings in song." Unlike *The Ten Commandments* and other biblical epics set in the ancient world, *Exodus* juxtaposed "colorful backgrounds" such as the "brooding towers of the crusader fortress at Acre," "the picturesque ruins at Caesare where Roman emperors once held court," and "Kafr Kana, the Arab village where Christ performed his first miracle 2,000 years ago" with events from modern history—the establishment of a Jewish State in Palestine.

Another facet of publicity might stress a picture's authenticity. For example, we are told that the temple in *Solomon and Sheba* "was built according to the description in the sixth chapter of First Kings in the Bible." Before producing *Fiddler,* "Jewison and key members of his team visited Israel and talked with Hassidic Jews, studied their various sects, shared with them the Sabbath meal. Everyone immersed themselves in the literature of Shalom Aleichem and researched the life of the *shtetl* as outlined in the book, *Life Is with People*." Publicity for *The Greatest Story Ever Told* pointed out that George Stevens, the director, had conferred privately with Pope John XXIII and Ben-Gurion; had engaged Carl Sandburg to help write the script; and had further insured both reverence and authenticity by never working without a specially made reference book containing seven translations of the Gospels.

At this stage, UA might also hire "distinguished" writers, photographers, or artists to create special publicity materials. For *West Side Story,* UA retained Hollis Alpert, the movie critic for the *Saturday Review,* and photographer Richard Avedon to create features with unusual angles. For *Solomon and Sheba,* UA commissioned the American artist, Symeon Shimin, to create a mural dramatizing the "scope and excitement" of the picture. Measuring forty by eleven feet, the mural

Promoting Super Technirama 70 in *Solomon and Sheba* (1959) using a mural created by Symeon Shimin

depicted scenes from the movie and provided the basis for a full-scale national advertising campaign. The reputation of these free-lancers supposedly increased the likelihood that the material would be picked up by prominent publications or appear as exhibits in big cities.

When a picture was produced overseas, UA frequently invited entertainment-page editors, feature-story writers, TV personalities, and other journalists from the major international markets to visit the set. Upon arrival they were handed the press kits. For members of the print media, the publicity staff staged press conferences and arranged individual interviews with the stars and director. For television people, the staff set up a TV studio and shot the interviews on tape for use back home. UA paid all expenses for these junkets; journalists flew first class and were put up in the best hotels. The purpose of these junkets was to make journalists feel indebted and under a moral obligation to do a story or series of stories upon their return.

Stories about new pictures and stars were fodder for the entertainment sections of newspapers and women's magazines. Articles in such publications might contain "Pygmalion stories," such as how Carlo Ponti transformed Sophia Loren from "a skinny, dirty-faced kid living in the slums of Naples into a star" playing opposite Frank Sinatra and Cary Grant in *The Pride and the Passion*. After visiting Norman Jewison on location for *Fiddler on the Roof*, reporters typically filed "Here I am in Zagreb" stories that talked about the Balkan weather, which was uncooperative, and the Yugoslavian peasants—"See those wrinkled faces," a typical story read, "They've been battered and burnt by the sun and the wind for sixty years. You can't reproduce that in a film studio."

A major break constituted a story with artwork in *Life, Look, Time, Newsweek,* or other magazines with large national circulations. Developing these leads, however, took considerable time, effort, and money. These magazines wanted out-of-the-ordinary news and information—that is, the "biggest," "first," "best," and/or "worst." In addition, each wanted an unusual story angle that would appeal to the specialized tastes of its readers.

METHODS OF RELEASE

Prior to television, the release pattern in the U.S. followed a rigid pattern known as the run-clearance-zone system. The industry had divided the country into thirty markets, with each market subdivided into zones and within each zone theaters classified as to run. First-run theaters were located in the downtown districts of the largest cities, seated thousands, and commanded top ticket prices. Second-run houses were typically located in neighborhood business districts and charged lower ticket prices. Later-run houses, going down the scale to fifth, sixth, seventh, and more, were located in outlying communities and charged still less. As A. D. Murphy said, "Feature films in former times would move down through this market structure like clockwork. In fact . . . it was a clock, with intervals separated by fixed clearance of 14 days, 28 days, 42 days and so on, between successive play-off periods."[8] The merchandising pattern of a movie was similar to that of other consumer goods—first, the exclusive shops; next, the general department store; and finally the close-out sales.

The big picture transformed this pattern from a three-tier to a two-tiered playoff. Typically, a blockbuster was released in each market first to select houses for extended runs and subsequently to large numbers of theaters to capture the leavings. Another way of characterizing this distribution pattern is slow and fast. The blockbuster changed; release schedules changed as well. Instead of releasing pictures throughout the year at regular intervals, companies tried to bring out their important pictures during the Christmas and Easter holidays and at the beginning of summer.

The grandest and most prestigious form of release was known as roadshowing. This distribution strategy existed since the earliest days of the industry and resembled the presentational format of legitimate theater. Located in the major markets, roadshow houses contained luxury appointments and technical equipment for all projection and sound systems, including such new widescreen processes as Ultra Panvision, Super Technirama 70, and the single-lens Cinerama system. A roadshow picture played exclusively in one theater in each market. Performances were typically scheduled two a day, with admission based on a hard-ticket policy—meaning reserved seats, differential pricing, and advance ticket purchase. Since roadshow pictures sometimes lasted three hours or more, they played with an intermission. For general release, the pictures were typically shortened so that exhibitors could present two performances in an evening.

Hollywood marketed around six roadshows a year during the sixties. The potency of this form of release is seen from this analysis by *Variety:* "Of twenty-five pictures that had earned at least $15 million in rentals by 1968, seventeen, at one time or another, had a hardticket premiere. More strikingly, whereas less than one percent of films released since January, 1960, have garnered $10 million or better in rentals, fully one-third of the forty-five roadshows that opened in Gotham from 1960 through 1967 topped that whopping sum."[9] *Fiddler*'s roadshow release grossed $16.9 million, the "highest total gross of any roadshow film in history," proclaimed a UA publicity brochure. The picture grossed this amount in 5 percent of the total potential bookings.

Apart from the inherent appeal of these pictures, the rental terms helped set the records. Standard terms for roadshows called for a 90-10 division of the boxoffice with 90 percent going to the distributor and 10 percent to the exhibitor. Although the terms seem excessive, this division did not occur until after the theater deducted the "house nut"—a negotiated amount that covered overhead expenses plus a built-in profit. Once reserved for first-run theaters in New York and Los Angeles, 90-10 deals eventually were used nationally as distributors attempted to recoup the big production loans as quickly as possible. Since a roadshow release involved relatively few theaters, UA reduced its distribution fee to as low as 15 percent during this phase of the release. A successful roadshow gave status to a picture and it also created invaluable word-of-mouth to build up "must see" excitement. In the process, the run buttressed UA's bargaining power with exhibitors over rental terms for the general release.

A roadshow run progressed in stages and at each stage UA evaluated the picture's performance before extending the run to other markets. The number of engagements for UA's most popular roadshows

Mat ad promoting the roadshow of *The Greatest Story Ever Told* (1965)

ranged from thirty-eight for *Hawaii* to eighty-nine for *Fiddler*. The release pattern for *Fiddler* started with a New York world premiere on November 3, 1971, followed by a Los Angeles premiere on November 5. Later that month, it opened in seven more dates (e.g., Chicago, Boston, Washington); a month later, in twenty-two more (e.g., Cleveland, Buffalo, Seattle); and then, beginning in February, the picture opened in fifty additional engagements. Meanwhile, during December, *Fiddler* premiered in England, Germany, Holland, France, Israel, Hong Kong, Australia, and South Africa, among other countries, in time for the holidays.

The exclusive engagement, a second form of slow release, was the favored form of release for a prestige picture that had commercial potential but lacked the presold strength of a roadshow attraction. Unlike a roadshow attraction, an exclusive engagement did not necessarily play downtown, but in the more affluent residential areas of major markets. In such engagements, the picture ran continuously with no reserved seats. Chris Munson has described the economics of the exclusive run as follows: "One theater overhead, one print from the distributor, advertising and promotion for one theater outlet only, and savings in later advertising-promotion efforts because the nature of the exclusive run will pre-sell the subsequent general and multiple run movie-goers."[10] A prestige picture might open only in New York and perhaps Los Angeles. In any event, making the picture difficult to see kept admission levels high, added prestige to the film, and generated favorable word-of-mouth publicity. (Obviously, this strategy depended on strong reviews.) As interest peaked, the strategy next was to release the picture wide. Since the exclusive engagement typically was used to launch a foreign picture that had great commercial potential, examples of this form of release are provided in the following chapters describing UA's international operations. See particularly the discussions of *Tom Jones* in chapter 7 and *Last Tango in Paris* in chapter 9.

If roadshows and exclusive runs are slow methods of release, the various forms of multiple runs—general release, showcasing, and saturation booking—are the fast methods. After a picture opened first-run either on a roadshow or exclusive basis, it was then placed in general release, which meant that it would play several theaters in a single market simultaneously. In these circumstances, general run was synonymous with second run. General release, of course, made the film available to more filmgoers at normal prices and often in more convenient locations.

UA innovated a multiple-run pattern in the early sixties called Premiere Showcase. This distribution pattern was originally designed to bypass the traditional and costly practice of opening every picture exclusively on Broadway. Loew's and RKO controlled exhibition in this market and had insisted on protecting their Broadway houses, which meant that new releases had to line up for one of their theaters before either circuit would play it wide. In distributing *Never on Sunday* in 1962, UA decided to premiere the picture simultaneously in ten to twelve theaters in greater New York. UA had to make do with many second-best independent theaters to prove the viability of its strategy, but when the company publicized the grosses for *Never on Sunday* and other releases, such as *Follow That Dream*, starring Elvis Presley, and *Road to Hong Kong*, starring Bing Crosby, Bob Hope, and Dorothy Lamour, other distributors fell into line.[11]

In adopting this plan, UA merely followed older practices in the merchandizing field. UA pointed out that, twenty years earlier, Macy's, after much soul-searching, opened a suburban store and found that business at its hub store had not been hurt; in fact, total sales actually grew. In 1962, Macy's had five stores throughout the New York area and was preparing to open three more.[12]

This form of multiple-run distribution took advantage of changing demographics. As central cities decayed and as the old key presentation houses lost their economic importance, shopping-center theaters, with their proximity to an expanding teen market, high traffic volume, and free parking became the new exhibition meccas. In 1963 alone, 320 movie houses were opened, announced, or under construction, at a total cost of $96.4 million, reported the *New York Times*. Most of these were small or medium-sized houses in shopping centers.[13]

Saturation booking, the fastest form of playoff, was designed to take full advantage of advertising. As Chris Munson points out, "The advertising cost per ticket sold by an advertisement in a metropolitan newspaper is considerably less if the picture is being screened in all areas covered by the newspaper."[14] The same applies to television advertising, of course. Saturation booking upgraded drive-ins to create as many first-run outlets as possible. By using large numbers of prints, saturation booking was designed for a quick kill. As a result, the strategy could be used for a picture of poor quality to skim off the curious before bad reviews or negative word-of-mouth took effect.

But saturation booking was particularly effective for action pictures which had a ready-made audience. UA claimed to have used the saturation technique the first time for a big-budget picture when it released *The Magnificent Seven* in 1960. The novel part of the plan entailed distributing the picture region by region beginning in the South, then proceeding to the Southwest, West, Midwest, and New England. In each region the picture played around 250 theaters simultaneously, linked to a heavy television and radio campaign.

Perhaps the quintessential use of saturation booking was for the Bond pictures. UA did not know quite what to do with the first Bond picture, *Dr. No.* Fleming's books had yet to become best-sellers and Sean Connery was practically unknown. After *Dr. No* broke boxoffice records, UA realized it had the makings of a successful series. UA released the subsequent Bond entries in instant mass distribution so that thousands of theaters throughout the world were showing them simultaneously, taking advantage of the built-up demand.

THE PRERELEASE AND RELEASE PHASE

After the completion of principal photography, UA's Department of Advertising, Publicity, and Exploitation took over. Before setting the main campaign in motion, however, UA waited to evaluate the commercial potential of the finished picture. Launching an important picture progressed in three steps: (1) prerelease; (2) premieres; and (3) release and playoff. UA farmed out the actual creation of the promotional materials, such as ads, TV and radio spots, teaser trailers, and TV featurettes, to publicists, ad agencies, and consultants. UA's staff publicists and photographers oversaw quality control.

Most of the material distributed earlier in the production phase was revised and reissued as part of press-release kits and pressbooks. The pressbook was to the advertising campaign what the press kit was to the publicity campaign. Designed for the exhibitor, the pressbook was the official catalog of approved advertising materials for use in newspapers, radio, and television. The contents included camera-ready ads in various sizes that could be simply clipped out and sent to a newspaper; promotional materials such as posters, publicity stills, streamers, television and radio commercials, and trailers; and feature stories on the picture and its stars and even prewritten reviews that could be planted in the local newspaper; and instructions regarding the official billing of the producer, director, star, and others on the marquee, in the lobby, or in other promotions. Pressbooks were distributed free to exhibitors by National Screen Service, which also manufactured and sold other promotional materials for use by exhibitors.

Prerelease promotion attempted to sustain interest in the picture during the lull period of editing and scoring. The objective was to stoke the publicity machine to a peak just preceding and accompanying the release. Publicity during this phase focused on the importance of the picture, reaction to previews, plans for the premiere, advance ticket sales, and anything impressive about the picture and the personalities involved.

One way to increase the amount of publicity on a picture was to create newsworthy or attention-getting events. Similarly, a good way to enlarge the advertising budget was to get someone else to share in its expense. Such strategies fall into the category of exploitation. For the big picture, exploitation might have begun with the acquisition of the movie rights to the novel. The goal was to presell the picture. UA acquired the rights to Leon Uris' *Exodus* in manuscript. The price was $250,000 plus 5 percent of the profits. In an attempt to help Doubleday get the book on the best-seller list, UA agreed to underwrite part of the promotion and to use its contacts with influential people (e.g., Ben-Gurion and Bernard Baruch) to solicit quotable opinions on the book. In exchange, the publisher agreed to play up the movie. *Exodus* remained on the best-seller list for 79 weeks, selling 400,000 in hardcover. The Bantam paperback edition sold 3,000,000 copies in ten languages. The Bantam campaign utilized 6,500 window-contest kits, 78,000 rack cards, 28,000 acetate window streamers, 11,000 truck banners, 30,000 counter-display pieces, 29,000 posters, and 9,000 dump displays costing more than $50,000 in what was acknowledged by Bantam as "the best book promotion ever seen in our industry." [15]

Another exploitation tie-in linked a picture with commercial products. During the fifties and sixties, tie-ins were used primarily to promote the picture; in the seventies, tie-ins were frequently used as sources of profit. Merchandisers looked to stars for endorsements, but big names didn't need the money or considered product promotion demeaning. However, the star on the rise might be glad for the opportunity. Since *The Pride and the Passion* was Sophia Loren's first American picture, UA developed a list of more than a dozen tie-in products to offer her, including fabrics, cosmetics, a nurse's uniform, cuff links, a carbonated beverage, and a Glenby hair design. *Fiddler* had no female star, but the three daughters interested *Good Housekeeping,* which shot a fashion layout on location in Zagreb and explored the possibility of a Simplicity pattern tie-in.

As the release date approached, promotion activities went into high gear. To generate favorable word-of-mouth, endorsements, recommendations, and reviews, UA scheduled V.I.P. and press screenings. Press screenings provided representatives of the media with lead time to prepare their stories. In accepting such an invitation, critics agreed to run their reviews concurrent with the premiere. VIP screenings enabled UA to secure endorsements from "prime movers"—educational, political, and religious leaders—to promote group sales. UA used the endorsements for *Fiddler* to convince non-Jews that the picture had appeal for people of all faiths. A news release from a public relations firm hired by UA to reach religious organizations quoted Dr. Norman Vincent Peale, pastor of New York's famed Marble Collegiate Church, as saying, "*Fiddler on the Roof* is a universal human drama which should be seen by Americans of all ages, races, and creeds." Terence Cardinal Cooke was quoted as saying, "In a time when so many productions misrepresent or denigrate religion, it is a pleasure to discover a motion picture that delivers a sound and happy message regarding the real accomplishments of religion in the lives of men." UA's efforts along this line culminated in a combined worship service and special screening for church leaders at the Rivoli Theater in New York. A Broadway first, the service was held on a Sunday morning in April well into the run and conducted by the Rev. Richard Kallaway, pastor of the Universalist-Unitarian Church in New York, and Rabbi Samuel M. Silver, pastor of Temple Sinai, Stamford, Connecticut.

Group sales were an efficient way to sell large numbers of tickets because the organization handled the marketing. Organizations typically purchased blocks of tickets at a discount and resold them to raise funds for itself or for a charity. *Exodus* demonstrated that a well-promoted, high-quality roadshow could generate a considerable advance sale. Advance sales for the first nine roadshow engagements topped $1 million, which set a record. In the New York area, UA drummed up business in a direct-mail campaign by sending letters and reprints of an important *New York Times* break to 11,000 organizations. UA also sent mailers to the New York Convention Bureau, to out-of-town groups planning to visit the city, and to restaurants and travel agencies doing business with this trade.

UA staged premieres to create the illusion of legitimate news events. For example, UA first presented Preminger's *Saint Joan* in Paris, on Sunday, May 12, 1957, which was Saint Joan Day in France. Held in the Opera under the sponsorship of the President of the French Republic, the proceeds went to the poliomyelitis fund. Stanley Kramer held the world premiere of *Judgment at Nuremberg* in Berlin. To guarantee adequate media coverage, Kramer invited more than 100 print and media journalists and industry representatives from the U.S. and Latin America to participate in the festivities. Kramer wanted the press to record the German reaction to his picture, which depicted the trial of Nazi judges after World War II for crimes against humanity. He also wanted the press to evaluate the junket itself. As *Film Bulletin* reported, the press would judge "international reaction to an American motion picture company-sponsored junket celebrating the event of the premiere."[16]

Kramer started off the proceedings by telling the more than 450 guests assembled in the Grand Ballroom of the Hilton Hotel that Berlin was "selected as the premiere city because it was the 'fitting place' both from the historical and present-day standpoints." The second day was devoted to interviews with Kramer and the film's stars—Spencer Tracy, Judy Garland, and Montgomery Clift, among others. Marlene Dietrich could not attend, but her popularity "was attested to by the fact that for two days running Berlin headlines proclaimed 'DIETRICH NOT COMING'."[17]

Judgment at Nuremberg premiered the following day at the Kongress Hall. More than 1,500 persons attended, including General Lucius Clay, President Kennedy's Special Ambassador to Berlin, and New York Senator Kenneth B. Keating. Lord Mayor Willy Brandt of Berlin told the audience, "I hope world-wide discussion will be aroused by both this film and this city and that this will contribute to the strengthening of right and justice."[18]

Kramer and UA received high marks for their efforts. In *Film Bulletin*'s opinion, "Hollywood is capable of intelligent films. American motion picture personnel are capable of intelligent films. American motion picture personnel are capable of proving themselves outstanding international hosts. Let the entire industry take note of what happened in Berlin, December 12–15. Courtesy, co-ordination and smooth execution of an all-inclusive premiere plan still equal showmanship at its best."[19]

Fiddler's premiere provides a good example of a New York send-off. As the media and communications capital of the country, with world-wide communication links, as well as an important motion picture market in its own right, New York functioned as the Cape Canaveral of the industry. Festivities for *Fiddler* started with cocktails at Arthur Krim's in honor of Norman Jewison, the director, and Topol, the star. Afterward, the guests, who included Carol Channing, Arlene Dahl, Helen Hayes, and Joel Grey, were deposited at the Rivoli Theater in limousines at two-minute intervals to be ogled by fans who jammed the sidewalk, all in time-honored tradition. Following the show, about a thousand made their way to the Americana hotel for a supper dance. The package cost $150 a head, the proceeds going to the Will Rogers Hospital in Saranac, N.Y. (This charity was the first of eleven charities that had reserved the theater in as many nights.) The *New York Times* and other newspapers covered the event. The "David Frost Show" on WNEW-TV devoted an entire ninety minutes to *Fiddler* and WOR-TV devoted thirty minutes to it.

As a blockbuster opened in each new city, the occasion was often marked by a gala celebration. For example, the Washington premiere of *The Greatest Story Ever Told* was presented "Under the Patronage of the President of the United States and Mrs. Johnson," Mrs. Hubert H. Humphrey, chair, hosts committee, as a benefit for International Cooperation Year. By surrounding these premieres with benefits, UA hoped to ennoble the picture and perhaps to neutralize any unfavorable critical opinion. *Fiddler* received negative reviews from *Time, Newsweek,* and the *New York Times.* Jewison was concerned that Bosley Crowther's review in the *Times* might influence the reception of the picture in Europe. As a counterattack, he suggested sending a positive review from United Press "to every major English speaking paper in the world with a circulation of over 100,000 daily."[20] Gabe Sumner, UA vice president in charge of advertising, promotion, and exploitation, responded that the negative reviews "didn't hurt business or word-of-mouth in New York where those reviews enjoy by far the greatest readership and, one would think, influence." He also pointed out that the reviews did not influence out-of-town critics. Sumner concluded:

> So what do we have here? I think we have a film of such unique audience appeal that it doesn't seem to be affected by any minority (or a combination) of negative reviews. The staggering local "bread-and-butter" newspaper space, the Frost Show, the 8-minute CBS featurette, the New York/Los Angeles premiere TV shows, Life magazine—and most important of all by far, the picture itself—have raised the picture above critical reproach. The people love it, and that, in the final analysis, will see us through.[21]

For some pictures, critical reviews were important. Of *Saint Joan,* for example, Max Youngstein said, "This picture will essentially be made by the reviews or broken by them."[22] In such cases, Youngstein advocated spending money on ads only when the notices were good.

After launching a picture, UA assessed the situation to determine the level of advertising support during the run. The outlay was usually commensurate with boxoffice performance. In other words, UA did not throw good money after bad. During the run, UA spent the bulk of the advertising budget for each market the opening week. During the second week, UA discontinued the TV ads and reduced the size of the print ads. Thereafter, the picture essentially had to make it on word-of-

Poster for the *Fiddler on the Roof* (1971) reissue

mouth. As Arthur Krim said, "advertising brings people out the first couple of weeks; advertising doesn't create success. It starts the ball rolling. Word of mouth takes over when there is something the audience wants to see. You can't bludgeon a large group into seeing a bad picture by an advertising campaign."[23]

A picture that received Oscar nominations and had completed its run was rereleased to provide filmgoers another chance to catch it. Ads were revised to highlight the nominations and actual awards. Since the Oscar ceremony on TV was a news event as well as a national ritual, Academy Award campaigns took on enormous importance.

ADJUSTMENTS FOR THE FOREIGN MARKET

Plans for marketing a picture abroad were formulated by UA's Foreign Department in New York as part of the worldwide distribution strategy. Rising production costs and interest rates forced pictures into wide release to recoup the investment quickly. However, this impetus had to be weighed against other considerations, such as the season of the year, censorship restrictions, local customs, and import quotas.

The first step in distributing a picture in a foreign market was to secure a censorship permit. In most countries, government agencies operated censorship boards. Each had its peculiar taboos; in Italy, cleavage and flesh; in France, touchy political issues; in Africa and the Orient, extended kissing scenes and love-play. Boards could reject a picture outright, classify it for a particular age group, and/or require cuts. In addition to governmental censorship, pictures sometimes had to be submitted to local authorities and church boards, especially in Roman Catholic countries. As mentioned in the discussion of *The Moon Is Blue*, UA retained the contractual right to require producers to edit their pictures should censorship problems arise.

UA knew its markets, of course, so the pictures it earmarked for a specific country were seldom if ever denied a censorship permit. As a result, the job of selling could begin well before the actual arrival of the prints. Distributors sold their pictures blind to exhibitors overseas just as in the United States. And in foreign markets, the same strategies concerning release patterns and promotion applied.

However, certain alterations had to be made to suit audience tastes in each country. The title, for example, might not mean anything to a foreign audience: "*Conspiracy*—what the hell does that mean?" said Leon Kamern, UA's head of distribution in Italy. "That came out *Seeds of Hatred*. That's up our alley."[24] Obviously, if a picture made it big in the United States or in its country of origin, UA would not change the title.

Following industry practice, UA dubbed its pictures for release in Italy, France, Germany, and Spain. Pictures for Spain were dubbed in Castilian and were not intelligible to Latin American audiences who spoke quite different Spanish dialects; outside these four markets, pictures were subtitled. An art unto itself, dubbing attempted to make a picture German for a German audience or French for a French audience. For popular stars—a Burt Lancaster, a Sophia Loren, or a Cary Grant—the same voices were used in each country so that in Germany, for example, the audience did not know the real voice of Sophia Loren, only the voice of the German actress who dubbed Sophia Loren.[25]

In the realm of promotion, other adjustments had to be made. Publicity material was often rewritten when the American campaign contained too much verbiage—translating into Italian, for example, three words can become a whole sentence. Sometimes the American star meant little to a foreign audience, so another cast member might be played up. And in certain markets, one element of the campaign, such as a sports angle or violence, might be stressed over others.

Lest there be any misunderstanding of the goal of UA overseas, I will quote the head of UA's operation in Germany, who said, "It is clear to the mind of distributors who the audience is for their pictures. They do not have any intellectual pretentions about film as art. They are selling film as entertainment to a mass audience. They hype the action, the sensational elements, the elements of the pictures that will grab an audience from the ages of from around 16 to around 30."[26]

CHANGES IN PUBLICITY PRACTICES

As a result of the recession that hit the motion picture industry in 1969, the banks forced companies to streamline operations, share studio facilities with competitors, distribute jointly abroad, and, most important, stop making blockbusters. Hollywood cut back on production and, for awhile at least, curtailed budgets. Publicity practices changed in the process. Companies basically shifted spending away from prerelease and opening to the run. Daniel Yankelovich, Inc., prepared a study of industry marketing practices for MPAA in 1967 which noted that "prerelease publicity can be effective only when there is a tie-in with a very familiar play or book . . . The findings indicate that unless there is a readily available hook on which to hang publicity, the public is not prepared to absorb or to remember information about movies that occur far in advance of their opportunity to see them at practical levels of publicity expenditure." The study also found that virtually half of the public learned about a picture only a few days before seeing it.[27]

It is impossible to evaluate the influence of this study, but a survey conducted by the Publicists Guild in 1972 pointed out the following:

> Among other things that have changed in this ever-changing business is the down grading of publicity as a selling instrument of motion pictures. Time was when publicity—and most of it free—was the life-blood of the industry . . . Today, along with the denigration of publicity values has gone the care and feeding of entertainment editors, film columnists, and critics. Where they used to be inundated with material about pictures, pre and post production, these important selling arms of the press are now relegated to the ash heap.[28]

Distributors relied more and more on massive media advertising to sell their films. As David Daly pointed out, "Package-goods advertisers learned long ago that it made sense to let the coverage of a station's signal determine the size of the market."[29]

Roadshows went by the boards after the recession as the industry targeted its pictures at the frequent filmgoer, the audience under thirty. As cases in this chapter reveal, UA tailor-made its campaign to create both a universal and specific appeal. But in the seventies, UA and the industry concentrated on the youth market.

Since foreign films appealed primarily to an adult audience, the majors cut back on the imports (see chapter 8). Rising advertising costs played a role in the demise of the art film since this type of picture often could not support even a minimal campaign. Fewer foreign films meant that the exclusive run was used only rarely. But as my analysis of *Last Tango in Paris* (chapter 9) demonstrates, this distribution pattern could still be effective for a specialized product.

American films that did not display commercial potential received only token publicity support. Going into the seventies, the industry cut back on production again and placed the accent on youth. "The standard promotion and exploitation for most films today," said Daly, "consists mostly of t-shirts, posters, frizbees, iron-on-transfers, contests, give-aways, buttons, or some other similar item."[30]

As Hollywood entered the era of conglomerates, the new moguls wanted to take the guessing out of the motion picture business by using market research. The goal was not only to evaluate the effectiveness of advertising, but also to predict consumer demand prior to production. Fortunately, the moguls never discovered what motivates an audience to see a movie or determined in advance all the ingredients of a hit picture. The unpredictability of audiences is what has made motion pictures such a viable art form.

JEANNE MOREAU
"THE BRIDE
WORE BLACK"

C H A P T E R S E V E N

International Operations, Part 1

Of Art Films and Great Britain

The decline of the domestic theatrical market after World War II forced UA and the other American motion picture companies to rely on overseas markets more and more. At one time, American films could at least break even at home, but no more. Foreign sales, which by 1960 accounted for about 40 percent of Hollywood's total income, spelled the difference between profit and loss. UA was the most aggressive company in this phase of the business and by 1972 had captured more than a 25 percent share of the foreign theatrical market.[1]

In the largest overseas markets—Great Britain, Italy, Germany, France, and Japan—UA operated through wholly owned subsidiaries. In others, such as Spain, Greece, Egypt, Pakistan, and Mexico, through licensed agencies. In the smaller markets, such as Korea, Turkey, and Iraq, UA sold its picture to local distributors on commission. At first, the only overseas territories in which UA did not operate were the Soviet bloc countries and Communist China. However, through the auspices of the Motion Picture Export Association, UA in 1958 successfully initiated arrangements for the sale of its pictures in Poland, East Germany, Czechoslovakia, and Hungary.

In addition to marketing American films abroad, international distribution involved marketing foreign films in the United States and investing in production overseas. The two went hand in hand and had the goal of discovering and absorbing filmmaking talent wherever it could be found. The strategy manifested itself by bidding aggressively on imports, by hiring foreign stars to give pictures some international appeal, and by absorbing directors with production deals.

THE ART FILM MARKET

Foreign films in the U.S. consisted of three types—foreign-language films that catered to ethnic groups exclusively; exploitation pictures aimed at the ordinary film goer; and art films that catered to what the *Economist* called the "egg-head" market. The first type does not concern us, since these pictures were handled outside mainstream Hollywood.

The exploitation market consisted of commercial product that was not particularly foreign in its appeal. Nothing epitomized this product as much as *Hercules,* a pseudohistorical spectacle from Italy starring American strongman Steve Reeves. Joseph E. Levine, a state's rights distributor from Boston, acquired the domestic rights to the picture in 1959 for $120,000. He arranged national distribution through Warner Brothers by putting up $1 million for a publicity campaign that combined a media blitz with saturation booking to rack up a gross of $5 million. Levine's showmanship led to the formation of Embassy Pictures Corporation, which during the sixties handled a range of highly successful foreign products represented by *Sodom and Gomorrah* (1961) at one extreme and art products like Carlo Ponti's *Two Women* (1962) and Fellini's *8½* (1963) at the other.[2]

UA participated marginally in the spear-and-sandal fad by releasing *The Last Days of Pompeii* (1960), *The Minotaur* (1961), and *The Mighty Ursus* (1962). *Pompeii* was another Steve Reeves vehicle; *Minotaur* featured Olympic decathlon winner Bob Mathias.

The art-film market was nurtured by successive waves of imports from different national cinemas. Italian Neorealism attracted interest in the immediate postwar period. Of this group, Roberto Rossellini's

Open City (1945), became the first great foreign language success since the coming of sound by grossing $1 million.

Next came a series of British imports—Michael Powell and Emeric Pressburger's *The Red Shoes* (1948) and Laurence Olivier's *Hamlet* (1948) from J. Arthur Rank and a series of Alec Guinness comedies, among them *The Lavender Hill Mob* (1951) and *The Lady Killers* (1955) from Ealing Studios. *Hamlet* had the distinction of winning the Academy Award for best picture in 1948. During the fifties, the French gave us Max Ophüls' *La Ronde* (1950) and *Le Plaisir* (1951), Henri-Georges Cluzot's *Diabolique* (1955), and Jacques Tati's *Mr. Hulot's Holiday* (1953). Other film classics imported during the decade were Bergman's *Smiles of a Summer Night* (1955) and *The Seventh Seal* (1956) from Sweden; Fellini's *I Vitelloni* (1953) and *La Strada* (1954), from Italy; Kurosawa's *Rashomon* (1950) and Mizoguchi's *Ugetsu* (1952) from Japan; and Buñuel's *Los Olvidados* (1950) from Mexico.

The art-house circuit consisted of only 83 theaters in 1950, but by 1966 the number had grown to 664.[3] The art theater is a fairly hazy entity, but as often as not it was a smallish theater (seating well under 1,000) located in a metropolitan area or university community, which specialized in foreign films and American pictures with artistic pretensions. The expansion of the circuit did not result from an infatuation with foreign films as much as the cutback of feature film production in Hollywood. As one art-house owner said, "There was always at least four theaters competing for product, which was in short supply and everybody wanted these films first-run in their area."[4] As a last resort, many theaters prolonged their lives by converting to art. Others decided to play art product occasionally to supplement their regular exhibition program.

Although the number of foreign imports rose dramatically during the fifties, their impact in economic terms was modest. Foreign films, including the British product, grossed only around $10 million in 1956, an amount representing a scant 5 percent of the approximately $190 million which Hollywood remitted in dollars from its export market that year.[5] In the postwar period only one picture—and an English one at that—broke the $5 million barrier; that production was *The Red Shoes*. In 1958 alone, according to *Variety*, Hollywood produced thirteen pictures that grossed over $5 million. Ironically, six of these pictures were produced abroad by American companies and included *The Bridge on the River Kwai, Sayanora, The Vikings,* and *The Young Lions*.[6] Commenting on the situation, art-film distributor Thomas Brandon said, "The bulk of the foreign films which reach the United States are shown only in art theaters. A few, through the enterprise of some interested distributors, get larger distribution, but not many. The foreign films which come out of cultures profoundly different from ours, because of their vastly different content and frequently different form, have had acceptance only by a minority market in the United States, much in the same way as other aspects of foreign cultures have had a limited acceptance in the United States."[7]

Foreign film distribution was originally handled by dozens of small independent outfits. The more important ones, such as Joseph Burstyn, Kingsley-International, Brandon Films, and Lopert Films, were linked together in a trade association called the Independent Film Importers & Distributors of America. The typical distributor operated out of New York with a handful of employees who sold films over the phone to key accounts. Afterward, the films would be taken over by subdistributors to milk whatever additional revenue remained outside the top markets. This type of sales campaign, coupled with inadequate capital for promotion, meant that foreign pictures were essentially unpublicized and went to "the U.S. wickets on gumshoes," said *Variety*.[8] As a result, the number of foreign-language imports that hit over the $100,000 mark was small in relation to the overall total of films released. Pictures like Fellini's *La Strada*, Cluzot's *Diabolique*, and Jules Dassin's *Rififi*, which grossed over $500,000, were rare and more than offset by the entries that earned little more than print costs.

Independent distributors experimented in different ways to build audience interest. One strategy involved leasing a showcase theater in Manhattan. New York represented 50 percent or more of an import's potential total income and it was there that a picture had to receive favorable critical notice before it could be booked in the art-theater circuit. But rising theater rentals and overhead costs priced many foreign imports out of the market.

When Brigitte Bardot hit the market in 1956, competition for foreign pictures with commercial ingredients heated up. Directed by Roger Vadim, who formulated the Bardot image, *And God Created Woman* hit the boxoffice jackpot by grossing over $3 million in the United States to become the biggest foreign [i.e., non-English] moneymaker in this country up to that time.[9] Despite a "condemned" rating from the Legion of Decency, the picture was spot booked by every major circuit in the country. For the time being, the Bardot picture became the benchmark against which all other contenders were measured. As *Variety* said, "Her golden pout was much discussed in trade and general conversation and it was sort of expected that she was a turning point, or a breakthrough, or something symbolic, in the unfolding saga of cinema."[10]

Where foreign producers were once happy to get a guarantee of

$100,000 from distributors, they now received $200,000 and more. Yet there was no accounting for audience tastes. Foreign films sometimes clicked; they sometimes clicked in New York and failed elsewhere; and, as often as not, they failed everywhere. Few independent distributors had the resources to withstand more than the occasional bomb. By the end of the fifties, distribution ended up controlled by a few large concerns and affiliates of the Hollywood majors.

LOPERT PICTURES

To tap the art-film market, UA acquired Lopert Films, an independent art-film distributor, and created a foreign film distribution subsidiary in 1958 called Lopert Pictures Corporation with Ilya Lopert as its head. Ilya Lopert had been in the film importing business since the thirties, working at Paramount's dubbing studio outside Paris, importing the occasional foreign film, which included Anatole Litvak's *Mayerling* (1936), and heading MGM's film distribution department. After organizing Lopert Films in 1947, he distributed such acclaimed films as Vittorio DeSica's *Shoeshine* (1946), Laurence Olivier's *Richard III* (1956), and Federico Fellini's *Nights of Cabiria* (1957). Lopert also produced films, one of which, David Lean's *Summertime* (1955), starring Katharine Hepburn and Rossano Brazzi, was released through UA. Also involved in exhibition, like many importers of the day, Lopert owned interests in the DuPont and Playhouse art theaters in Washington and the Plaza, a major New York showcase on 58th Street.

Lopert's releases won awards and received the plaudits of critics, and, like the market in general, had not generated much interest at the boxoffice. In 1957, Lopert invested heavily in René Clair's *Gates of Paris,* Fellini's *Nights of Cabiria,* and Lattuada's *Guendalina,* all three of which turned out to be disappointments in this country. Heavily in debt, Lopert sold his two Washington theaters and abandoned all production plans. However, he held an option on a property that had potential—an unreleased Brigitte Bardot picture entitled *La Parisienne.*

Around this option UA structured a deal to acquire the company. Putting up more money than anyone had previously paid to acquire a foreign film, UA offered $550,000 and a share of the profits for the picture.[11] To buy out the company, UA paid $360,000 in cash and assumed $480,000 in debt. UA expected to recoup most of its investment from the profits of the picture, which they estimated at $1 million. But why would UA want to acquire Lopert? This art-film distributor had few assets and serviced a soft market. A partial explanation is found by examining Columbia's relationship with its art-film subsidiary, Kingsley-International. Columbia earlier acquired this company as a means of distributing the Bardot picture, *And God Created Woman.* Knowing that the picture would have been denied a Production Code seal, Columbia, in abiding by MPAA regulations, could not have accepted it for distribution. However, nothing in the agreement with the MPAA prevented a subsidiary from handling such a picture. Another reason for the alignment was that Columbia wanted the services of Edward Kingsley, the head of the company, as an advisor on foreign acquisitions. The fomenting cultural scene in Europe spawned a host of promising young filmmakers. Kingsley-International could be used as a convenient means to distribute their pictures to the art market, but if any of their films showed commercial potential, Columbia would take over. This rationale probably also played a part in UA's thinking.

UA released *La Parisienne* under its own banner rather than Lopert's since the picture had received a respectable "B" rating from the Legion of Decency. UA, moreover, wanted to introduce Bardot to the regular commercial market. Previously, Bardot had been seen mainly in art houses and special situations. For *La Parisienne,* UA booked key downtown houses and regular neighborhood theaters with the intent of capturing the mass market. Rather than using only subtitled prints, UA released two versions—subtitled prints for art houses and dubbed versions for regular situations. *La Parisienne* did moderately well, but the market was soon flooded by more than twenty older Bardot films.

Lopert Pictures' first release was Marcel Camus's *Black Orpheus,* which captured the Grand Prix at the Cannes Film Festival in 1959 and, along with two other prizewinners—François Truffaut's *The 400 Blows* and Alain Resnais's *Hiroshima, Mon Amour*—focused international attention on the French New Wave. In this country, *Black Orpheus* won an Oscar for best foreign film in 1959. Unfortunately, the UA corporate records at the Wisconsin Center for Film and Theater Research do not contain information on the reception and distribution of this picture.

Lopert released *Never on Sunday* next. Produced and directed by American Jules Dassin at a reputed cost of $150,000, the picture grossed about $4 million to become the queen of foreign-language moneymakers in 1961. *Never on Sunday* made the *New York Times* list of the ten best foreign films of 1960. Melina Mercouri, who played the jolly Greek prostitute, won the best actress award at Cannes and became an international star. Dassin, an expatriate, had formerly developed a reputation in the United States for *film noir* pictures, particu-

Melina Mercouri in *Never on Sunday* (1960), produced and directed by Jules Dassin

larly *Brute Force* (1947) and *Naked City* (1948). Blacklisted after being named a Communist during the 1951 HUAC hearings, Dassin moved to Paris, where he began the European phase of his career. Prior to *Never on Sunday* he directed *Rififi* (1954), a thriller that won several international awards.

Lopert released *Never on Sunday* in the U.S. without the Production Code seal and with a "condemned" rating from the Legion of Decency. Thus, Lopert served the same function for UA as Kingsley-International had for Columbia. UA's attitude toward the Production Code in relationship to *Never on Sunday* is best expressed by Max Youngstein, who said to the MPAA, "The Association has provided no yardstick for an ethical, moral base for the judgment of the in toto effect of motion pictures, and until you do, you are going to find yourself on both sides of every argument, accomplishing nothing for our business." *Butterfield 8* prompted Youngstein to make the assessment: "As you point out, the producers of *Butterfield 8* submitted the picture.

What I am saying to you is that regardless of what cuts or deletions were made in this picture, it is in my opinion, obscene, and does not in any way conform with the Code, in spite of the hackneyed retribution at the end. The picture, as far as I'm concerned, is a striptease of a nymphomaniac, with some of the dirtiest scenes and dirtiest dialogue I have ever witnessed on a motion picture screen from an American producer. The Laurence Harvey character, who is the adulterer, is in no way punished, whatsoever. I don't know what cuts were made because I never saw anything but the version offered to the public, but I can tell you that this is what I meant about possible technical conformity to the Code, but a complete breach of its spirit."

"You state that *Never on Sunday* was not submitted, and that can very well be true, but you forget that the producer of this film could easily have come to the conclusion that there was no point in submitting the film on the basis of his own previous experience and the experience of many people he knows. Why go through a lot of wasted motion when you know as well as I do that there wasn't a single chance of getting *Never on Sunday* okayed in spite of the fact that most people I know think it is a much cleaner picture (even though it deals with a prostitute), than *Butterfield 8*," concluded Youngstein.[12]

In distributing *Never on Sunday,* UA conducted an experiment. Typically, a picture with an offbeat theme premiered in a class art theater in New York. If reviewed favorably, the picture might play a couple more houses, say in Chicago and San Francisco. After extended runs to allow word-of-mouth and critical praise to build up interest, the picture would then play the art-theater circuit. But major markets contained only relatively few art theaters, so the problem became how to get the picture into "non-art" theaters. As I pointed out earlier, UA modified its saturation booking techniques for *Never on Sunday* by introducing a plan called Premiere Showcase to take advantage of new population patterns.

UA financed and Lopert released two other Greek pictures—Jules Dassin's *Phaedra* (1962), a vehicle for Melina Mercouri, and Michael Cacoyannis' *Electra* (1962), starring Irene Pappas. Other than these pictures, UA and the other majors formed their alliances with filmmakers in the major European markets—that is, in Great Britain, France, and Italy. Independent distributors, as a result, turned to so-called peripheral markets—Scandinavian and Eastern European countries—for their product, but as new filmmakers were discovered, the majors seduced them as well with a host of benefits such as financial remuneration and the promise of production continuance if they clicked.[13]

Lopert released an average of five pictures a year during the sixties.

Almost without exception, they failed to attract an audience. In Great Britain, UA's principal supplier of art product was Woodfall Films, the production company of Tony Richardson and John Osborne. Woodfall's relationship with UA had started with the huge commercial success of *Tom Jones* (1963). The picture won four Academy Awards—for best picture, director, screenplay, and musical score. A foreign film had captured the Best Picture award once before, but no foreign film had come close to *Tom Jones*'s gross: $16 million in the United States and $4 million foreign. But afterward, Woodfall's output did little business here or in Europe.

As interest in "swinging Britain" waned, UA turned to France for an alternative supply of art product. Prior to the New Wave, the appeal of French films in the domestic market ranked well behind the British. French films as a group grossed a mere $2 to $5 million a year, with the exception of 1958 when *And God Created Woman* broke records. Although the French New Wave revolutionized the world of film criticism, its impact as a commercial phenomenon barely caused a ripple. When Camus, Truffaut, and Resnais swept top honors at the Cannes Film Festival in 1959, distributors bid on their films as well as the works of such directors as Louis Malle, Claude Chabrol, Philippe De Broca, and Jean-Luc Godard. But in a year or so, first films of avant-garde directors glutted the market—the result in part of France's liberal film-aid laws—and distributors became shy of the New Wave label.

In any event, UA's involvement in French production did not begin, for all practical purposes, until 1964. UA's policy had been to avoid competing with the many local distributors by sticking to strictly American product in the French market. But after the institution of coproduction agreements among Common Market members, all this changed.

Unlike UA's production ventures in Great Britain, which consisted of a diversified range of product suitable for all markets, the French ventures were confined almost exclusively to the art-theater circuit. Although UA linked up with the most commercial of the New Wave directors, such as Philippe De Broca, Claude Lelouch, and François Truffaut, and used various strategies to broaden the appeal of their pictures, the results ranged from a low of $8,000 to a high of only $325,000. In foreign situations, however, several pictures grossed in the $1 to $3 million range.

Italy experienced a second film renaissance during the sixties, created primarily by Federico Fellini and Michelangelo Antonioni. Fellini's *La Dolce Vita* became the new foreign-language champ in the U.S.

market, outstripping *And God Created Woman* and *Never on Sunday* in 1960.[14] Of added significance to the art-film trade was that *La Dolce Vita* played all its dates subtitled and captured a Production Code seal as well as a favorable Legion of Decency classification. Lopert participated in this renaissance only marginally by releasing Antonioni's *La Notte* in 1962. UA formed its alliances in Italy with Goffredo Lombardo's Titanus Films, Dino DeLaurentiis, and Alberto Grimaldi, producers who specialized in spear-and-sandal epics, James Bond imitations, and spaghetti Westerns, among other varieties of exploitation pictures.

The remaining releases of note on Lopert's roster consisted of three Ingmar Bergman pictures—*Persona* (1967), *Hour of the Wolf* (1968), and *Shame* (1968), Bergman's twenty-seventh, twenty-eighth, and twenty-ninth films, respectively. These pictures each grossed around $250,000 domestic. Earlier Bergman pictures had grossed from around $350,000 (for the controversial *The Silence* in 1964) to a high of $700,000 (for *The Virgin Spring*, which won an Oscar for best foreign language film of 1960).[15] Significant demand existed for foreign films during the sixties, but their share of the total market remained remarkably stable. Every year, one or two foreign pictures achieved the status of art-house blockbusters whose grosses compared favorably with domestic product. In addition, several others each year did moderate business, enough to turn a small profit. However, it was a volatile market. As Stuart Byron said, "Successes have followed failures; surprise hits have emerged and anticipated bonanzas have turned into financial disasters."[16]

Unlike regular commercial fare, art films could not be successfully imitated in the form of sequels or follow-ups. We can take, as an example, Claude Lelouch's *A Man and a Woman* (1966). Starring Jean-Louis Trintignant and Anouk Aimee, the picture was the first big commercial success to come out of the French New Wave. In addition to capturing the Grand Prix at Cannes, it won Academy Awards for best foreign language film and for best original screenplay. UA lost out to Allied Artists for the domestic distribution rights, but picked up the foreign rights. UA would have preferred worldwide rights; nonetheless, it got the better deal; the foreign gross amounted to $4 million, whereas the domestic did just over $3 million. Lelouch followed this picture with *Live for Life* (1967), a virtual remake of *A Man and a Woman*, but with Yves Montand and Candice Bergen. Although loved by the French, the picture grossed only $400,000 here. American audiences apparently had had enough with the first version.

Moreover, foreign stars, with the exception of Sophia Loren and

Marcello Mastroianni, had little staying power. When a popular American actor made a big splash—a Jack Lemmon or a Lee Marvin—it was almost automatic that his next few releases would attract audiences, but not so with foreign stars. As Byron said, "When a foreign-language film makes really big money in the U.S., it's purely because of a search for novelty—a novelty value that wears off after the first success of its type. The director or the stars involved mean next to nothing when they're promoted in a subsequent film."[17]

The art-film market collapsed after 1970, leading UA to close the doors on the Lopert subsidiary. *Variety* reported in 1972 that for the first time in six years, not one foreign-language picture grossed over $1 million in the domestic market.[18] As a further indication of the depressed conditions, only twelve subtitled features made it to *Variety's* list of the top 350 films in the domestic market and half of these placed in the bottom 150.

THE NEW AMERICAN CINEMA

The domestic market had undergone a radical transformation. As *Time* magazine put it in 1967, "Hollywood has at long last become part of what the French film journal *Cahiers du Cinema* calls, 'the furious springtime of world cinema,' and is producing a new kind of movie." The New American Cinema, as it was called, enjoyed "a heady new freedom from formula, convention and censorship. And they are all from Hollywood." The movies spotlighted by *Time* were *Two for the Road,* which contained a "back-and-forth juggling of chronology à la Alain Resnais's *Hiroshima Mon Amour; In the Heat of the Night,* which treated racial bigotry; *Chappaqua,* which depicted the life of drug addicts; and *The Graduate,* which presented an "alternately comic and graphic closeup of a 19-year-old boy whose sexual fantasies come terrifyingly true."[19]

But the most important film of the year and of the decade, said *Time,* was Arthur Penn's *Bonnie and Clyde* (1967), "A watershed picture, the kind that signals a new style, a new trend," like *Birth of a Nation, Scarface,* and *Citizen Kane* before it. *Bonnie and Clyde* was the American equivalent of Michelangelo Antonioni's *Blow-Up,* parodying the "modish artsiness of fashion photography to help create the swinging London mood," of Gillo Pontecorvo's *The Battle of Algiers,* reproducing "the grainy style of newsreel footage" to present "a pictorially harrowing exposition of war as an extension of politics," and of Jiri Menzel's

Closely Watched Trains that "leaped from tears to laughter in quick sequence to create the moody turmoil." The reception of these pictures in the United States meant that "innovation is no longer the private preserve of the art houses but a characteristic of the main-line American movie." *Bonnie and Clyde* may have shocked audiences, but it brought them to the boxoffice in record numbers. It also stirred up "a battle among movie critics that seemed to be almost as violent as the film itself." But the most important effect of the picture was convincing studio heads that "a segment of the public wants the intellectually demanding, emotionally fulfilling kind of film exemplified by *Bonnie and Clyde*." Consisting mostly of the young, who had embraced the cinema as its favorite art form, this segment constituted the largest share of the market and had been hitherto ignored by the majors.[20]

The new freedom of expression in Hollywood films resulted in part from Supreme Court rulings on censorship and in part from the scrapping of the Production Code. Together, they ushered in a period of imprecedented frankness in the American cinema. The rapid acceptance of all these more explicit pictures led *Variety* to conclude: "No longer does the elitist end of the American audience look solely to foreign films as the source of intellectual stimulation in the 'wasteland' of U.S. commercial 'trash.' Domestic product, even from the major companies, has passed cinematic puberty in record time, offering films with themes and treatment so adult as to knock the bottom out of what once was an art house market. Foreign films must now compete for bookings and playing time with domestic features and can no longer depend on that audience who once supported their local art house just because it was a local art house."[21]

UNITED ARTISTS' BRITISH PRODUCTIONS

From the start, UA made its pictures where they had to be made. Since UA had no studio to support, it had complete freedom and mobility to deal with independent producers all over the globe. An independent producer, in turn, could arrange for the production of his films anywhere in the world to suit the needs of the story or the economics of the venture.

Shooting on location was in line with the production policy of creating pictures with an international appeal that would take advantage of the new widescreen processes. Labor costs were lower overseas, although it was a moot point whether foreign craftsmen were as efficient

Poster for *Tom Jones* (1963)

as Hollywood's.[22] However, for productions requiring large numbers of extras, Spain, for example, was a bargain. Nonunion extras could be hired for fifty pesetas ($1.25) a day and the Spanish cavalry was available for the asking.

Tax avoidance also contributed to runaway production. Stars and producers sometimes incorporated in Switzerland and Lichtenstein, which charged no capital-gains taxes on corporations and where U.S. corporate income taxes could be avoided. Another way to avoid U.S. taxes was to arrange for salary to be paid in frozen funds. So long as this money remained unconverted into dollars, it was not taxed by the IRS.

But oddly enough, import barriers established by foreign governments to restrict the flow of American films to their borders provided the main stimulus. After World War II, when international trade was in a state of chaos, European nations attempted to stem the dollar outflow that would be caused by the unfettered distribution of American films. One such measure was frozen funds. Governments allowed American films free entry on the condition that only a portion of the earnings could be taken out. Great Britain was the first nation to adopt such a scheme and in 1948 stipulated that for two years, American film companies as a group could withdraw only $17 million from the country. The remainder of the earnings were frozen, i.e., blocked. France, Italy, and Germany instituted similar measures, with the result that the major film companies, through procedures negotiated by the Motion Picture Export Association, began investing in production abroad by investing in studios, purchasing story rights, and financing pictures.

Currency restrictions gradually relaxed with the resumption of more normal international trade. Foreign governments turned to other measures to nurture their domestic film industries, including such forms of financial assistance as prizes, production loans and credits, and subsidies. The subsidy was found to be the most effective measure and was adopted by most European countries. Although subsidy plans differed in size and operation from country to country, their general purpose was the same—to provide producers with moneys in addition to revenues collected from normal distribution. These moneys were usually generated by increasing ticket prices or entertainment taxes and were allocated to producers by a governmental or public agency. Because American companies through their wholly owned foreign subsidiaries qualified for this financial assistance, they began shifting their production activities to the main European markets—specifically to Great Britain, France, and Italy.

During the 1950s, Great Britain was the most important market for American films and it was here that UA first concentrated its overseas production efforts. Production considerations were determined mainly by the Cinematograph Films Act of 1948 and the British Film Production Fund, popularly known as the Eady Pool after Sir Wilfred Eady, the originator of the plan.[23] The Films Act perpetuated a government policy instituted twenty years earlier stipulating a quota for exhibitors and distributors; the former were required to devote a certain percentage of their playing time to British pictures, while the latter were required to release a certain percentage of British pictures. To stimulate production, Parliament in 1950 created the Eady Pool. Under this plan, a levy was placed on the price of admission and the proceeds rebated to producers of quota pictures. The amount divvied out depended on the distribution gross of the picture and the size of the pool in the given year. Anyone who made a film in the U.K. could qualify for this rebate, provided the quota laws were observed and the film made by a British company, including a foreign subsidiary of an American company. As Penelope Houston remarked, "It's one of the finer ironies of the situation rich in improbable paradoxes that this scheme, so elaborately devised to help British filmmakers, now acts as an extra incentive for the Americans."[24]

The amount of this assistance was of no small consequence. The Eady plan was designed to put a premium on commercial success and when a film clicked in a big way, it received a big reward. In essence, the plan made the rich richer. On the average, the Eady Pool remitted to a quota picture about 35 percent of the distribution gross in the U.K.[25]

The British government had devised a scheme to channel British investment to British filmmakers through the creation of the National Film Finance Corporation (NFFC) in 1949. Operating as a public corporation, the NFFC functioned as a specialized bank for film production. An initial appropriation from the Treasury went into a revolving fund to supply producers with "end money"—the riskiest 30 percent of a budget to recoup. Since British distributors, through commercial sources, guaranteed at a maximum 70 percent of a budget, NFFC money, which was recoverable after the bank loan, was mainly supposed to benefit independent producers.[26] But the most promising talent and the most commercial projects were siphoned off by American firms who offered total financing and the prospect of distribution in the lucrative American market.

UA's new management took advantage of the Eady Pool from the start. Rather than arranging pickup deals to meet quota requirements, UA annually financed a program of British-made productions. Initiating financing regularized supply and had the advantage of allowing UA to tailor the product for the American market. So the Eady Pool not only encouraged runaway production, it also aided UA in its financing efforts.

The Eady Pool was given a permanent statutory base by Parliament with the passage of the Cinematograph Films Act of 1957. The availability of this easy money played an integral role in the production plans of UA's producers, particularly those with multiple-picture contracts. The trek to London would be made by independents aligned with other American companies as well until, by the sixties, American subsidiaries in Great Britain received as much as 80 percent of the Eady Pool in every year. In addition to the UA product, Carl Foreman's *The Guns of Navarone* (1961), Sam Spiegel's *Lawrence of Arabia* (1962), Stanley Kubrick's *Dr. Strangelove* (1967) and Martin Ritt's *The Spy Who Came in from the Cold* (1965) were among the many successful independent American-interest ventures qualifying as British quota pictures.

UA did not merely confine itself to importing basically American productions using Eady Pool money; the company also invested in British talent. In 1958, for example, UA financed a package of Alec Guinness pictures that included *The Horse's Mouth,* which was the British film industry's official entry for the Venice Film Festival and the choice for the annual Royal Command Film gala. In 1958, UA also signed a three-picture deal with Hammer Films, the horror-film specialist that produced *Hound of the Baskervilles,* among others.

UA became more deeply involved in British production in 1962 when the company made two deals—one with Albert R. Broccoli and Harry Saltzman for the first James Bond film and the other with Tony Richardson for the production of an offbeat picture based on Henry Fielding's eighteenth-century novel, *Tom Jones.* The James Bond films were enormous commercial successes; they also illustrated how UA sustained a series.

Woodfall Films

At age thirty-four, Tony Richardson had established himself as a dynamic and talented director, whose innovative work in the theater and motion pictures had won him an international reputation. Richardson was the cofounder of the English Stage Company, an enterprise, said Alexander Walker, "founded to retrieve the native drama from its year-in, year-out spate of classical revivals, 'well-made' matinée plays, and West End farces, by encouraging new dramatists or established writers-turned-playwrights—anyone in fact whose view of life was contemporary and closest to truth."[27] Between 1956 and 1959, the English Stage Company staged at the Royal Court Theatre the works of such dramatists as John Osborne, Shelagh Delaney, Arnold Wesker, and John Arden, collectively dubbed "the Angry Young Men" by the media.

Richardson's production of John Osborne's *Look Back in Anger,* which opened in 1956, marked a breakthrough for social realism. Osborne's play, said Raymond Durgnat "reached and revealed a new audience whose existence had been unsuspected, not only by the film industry, but by almost all the cultural 'establishments'."[28] Richardson directed a Broadway production of *Anger* the following year. The acclaim and financial reward from these productions enabled Richardson and Osborne to form Woodfall Film Productions, Ltd., to carry the revolution to the screen in what became known as British New Cinema. The "angel" behind the venture was the Quebec-born entrepreneur, Harry Saltzman.

Influenced by Italian Neorealism and the French New Wave, British New Cinema wanted to stir the masses. As Durgant explains, "the English cinema has notoriously looked out onto the world through the rose-tinted spectacles of middle-class respectability," ignoring 70 percent of the population—the working class. Pressures toward conformism through censorship and through the industry's own idea of what people wanted partially explains it. By the late fifties, however, "the new affluence founded as the Welfare State had built up sufficiently for the screen to affirm just those aspects of working class-culture which the middle-classes—themselves losing confidence in their old standards—had hitherto found vulgar or obnoxious."[29]

Tony Richardson's adaptation of *Look Back in Anger* in 1958 marked Woodfall's first production venture. Largely on the strength of the play's reputation and the casting of Richard Burton as Jimmy Porter, Woodfall, through Saltzman's efforts, secured financing from Warner's British distribution subsidiary, Associated British-Pathé. The picture was a disaster. "It didn't do much business anywhere in the world," said Saltzman, adding ruefully, "I never made a film that got such good reviews and was seen by so few people."[30]

The second Woodfall picture, Jack Clayton's *Room at the Top* (1958), became the first social-realist picture to win commercial success. Based on the novel of John Braine and produced by James and John Woolfe's Romulus Films, *Room at the Top* won two Academy Awards in 1959 (for Simone Signoret's performance and Neil Paterson's screenplay). The picture also made a star out of Laurence Harvey.

Woodfall's third picture, *The Entertainer* (1960), which starred Laurence Olivier and featured Albert Finney, was both a commercial and artistic failure. However, Woodfall's fourth venture proved a charm. *Saturday Night and Sunday Morning,* produced by Richardson in 1960 and directed by Karel Reisz, became a "stupendous success," said Saltzman; it earned over half a million pounds profit. Adapted for the screen by Alan Sillitoe from his novel and financed in the main through Bryanston, *Saturday Night and Sunday Morning* created an international star out of Albert Finney.

Harry Saltzman resigned from Woodfall's board soon after *Saturday Night* opened. "Differences of temperament were one of the reasons. The company hadn't room for two impresarios," according to Alexander Walker.[31] Woodfall next embarked on filming Shelagh Delaney's play, *A Taste of Honey* (1962). Richardson decided to direct the play on Broadway first, however, since a hit in New York would increase the film's acceptance in the United States. The strategy worked and Woodfall had another hit. *A Taste of Honey* created a new screen personality, Rita Tushingham, whom Richardson had picked for the role of Jo from a Liverpool repertory company. Richardson's *The Loneliness of the Long Distance Runner* in 1962 marked the conclusion of Woodfall's working-class pictures. By this time, social realism was fast becoming weary, stale, and unprofitable as a commercial subject.

Richardson submitted *Tom Jones* to Bud Ornstein, UA's head of European production headquartered in London, after British financial sources found the budget rather too rich. Ornstein rather liked Osborne's witty treatment of Fielding's eighteenth-century novel and cabled New York for approval. David Picker, who was being groomed for a top executive position in the company, replied: "Consensus of opinion not to proceed Tom Jones on basis of material and cost."[32] In an attempt to shepherd the project through the executive committee at the home office, Picker advised members how to read the script: "This is Albert Finney starring, Tony Richardson directing the John Osborne screenplay. Please be careful to read the notes along with the script. This is ribald, bawdy, Hogarthian; it jumps from bed to bed, from adventure to misadventure—it could be great fun. It does have, of course, its serious overtones, but essentially it is a wild caricature of times in England in the seventeen hundreds . . . Made by these picturemakers, I see this as a potentially important worldwide grosser."[33] Picker apparently prevailed because UA did an about-face and offered Richardson a contract on May 21, 1962.

UA approved a budget of $1,250,000. Whatever doubts UA may have had about *Tom Jones* were offset by the presence of Albert Finney in the title role. So important was he to the project that UA agreed to

Academy Award for Best Picture / 1963

Tom Jones

Albert Finney

A Woodfall presentation
Starring Albert Finney, Susannah York, and Hugh Griffith
Directed and produced by Tony Richardson

Other Academy Awards* and nominations
Actor: Albert Finney
Supporting actor: Hugh Griffith
Supporting actress: Diane Cilento, Edith Evans, Joyce Redman
*Direction: Tony Richardson
*Writing *screenplay*: John Osborne
Art direction–Set decoration *color*: Ralph Brinton, Ted Marshall and
    Jocelyn Herbert, Josie MacAvin
*Music *score*: John Addison

Hugh Griffith and Dame Edith Evans

Susannah York and Albert Finney

Albert Finney and Joyce Redman

Albert Finney

give him a profit participation in the picture. Richardson was paid a modest producer's salary up front. Profits were to be divided fifty-fifty until UA's share equaled the cost of production; thereafter, profits went 75 percent to Woodfall and 25 percent to UA.

Tom Jones premiered at the London Pavilion in June 1963. Critical reception in the so-called respectable press was mixed and concentrated on Richardson's adaptation of Fielding's novel. The *London Times* said, "The only complaint . . . is that popular though it may be, it just is not a very good film." The *Sunday Telegraph* said, "It must have been as difficult to introduce cuteness into Henry Fielding's ironic tale as smuggling a nude into Westminster Abbey." Referring to the influence of the French New Wave on the picture, the review went on to say, "Richardson is a director who assimilates other men's styles as easily as a schoolboy catches measles." The *Observer* was kinder: "John Osborne and Tony Richardson's Woodfall company clearly knew what they were after with Fielding's *Tom Jones*—to provide two hours of robust entertainment, and this they have achieved." Having less intellectual pretensions, the working-class press, represented by the *Citizen*, was more to the point: "The most bawdy, rumbusticating picture ever made—that is *Tom Jones*."[34] Audiences must have agreed because the picture broke proverbial records.

UA had something special, but the cast was unknown to American audiences and, more important, American audiences had previously shown an aversion to British costume pictures. To soften up the American market, UA staged special previews in New York, Los Angeles, San Francisco, and Chicago. "Only the very top press and opinion makers as well as the exhibitors for bidding purposes" were invited. Bob Thomas's review that went out on AP wires following the L.A. preview typified the buildup: "Superlatives were being tossed over the cocktails and Chasen's chili that were served following the preview. 'The best picture in ten years' . . . 'The most imaginative film since *Citizen Kane*' . . . 'Magnificent' . . . These were a few of the comments overheard in the crowd" that contained such luminaries as Edward G. Robinson, Tony Curtis, Stanley Kramer, and Barbara Rush.[35]

UA decided to go slow with the picture. *Tom Jones* premiered in New York on October 7, 1963, at the Cinema I, an art theater located on the upper East Side, on an exclusive basis. The reviews contained everything the company could have wanted. Bosley Crowther of the *New York Times* wrote that Richardson and Osborne "have whipped up a roaring entertainment that develops its own energy as much from its cinematic gusto as from the racy material it represents." *Tom Jones* was "played with a wonderfully open, guileless and raffish attitude by the brilliant new star, Albert Finney."[36] Judith Crist of the *New York Herald Tribune* said, "They've done it—they've done it—by George, they've really done it! They've brought *Tom Jones* to the screen in all its lusty brawling sprawling human comedy and given us one of the most delightful movies of recent years."[37] In short, the critical reception, with nary a quibble, was ecstatic. Albert Finney, who earned well over $1 million in profits from the picture, had the satisfaction of a double triumph; at the time of the premiere, Finney was playing the title role of *Luther,* written by John Osborne and directed by Richardson, which had settled into a long run at the St. James Theatre on Broadway.

Rather than capitalizing on all this publicity by going wide with the picture, UA took the opposite tack; it adopted a hard-to-get policy. *Tom Jones* ran at the Cinema I on an exclusive basis until October, when the picture opened in another art theater in Los Angeles. Sensational reviews in the New York papers, and also in national magazines such as *Time, The New Yorker,* and *Saturday Review* generated a tremendous interest in the picture. UA had the sophisticated audience in its pocket; the tactic was to build word-of-mouth to attract general audiences in the hinterlands. It was not until Christmas that the picture played other metropolitan areas—a total of eighteen theaters in twelve cities.

It was not until spring, when *Tom Jones* won Academy Awards for best picture, director, screenplay, and musical score, that UA opened the picture wide. UA was still not taking chances. For metropolitan engagements, the company sometimes used the more subdued ad campaign designed by Peter Rea for the Great Britain release. Rea's poster was modern, austere, and had the picture title tucked into the sheets of a four-poster bed. However, as the picture moved into smaller, less cosmopolitan situations—particularly in the South and Midwest—UA used a more provocative poster which had the selling line "The whole world loves Tom Jones" and displayed Albert Finney in a beefcake pose with his shirt open to the navel. Round his legs are four amply endowed women who are pawing his waist and thighs. The payoff for UA amounted to $8 million in domestic rentals by May 1964. *Tom Jones* ultimately grossed twice that in the United States and $4 million foreign, making the picture one of the top non-roadshow releases up to that time.[38]

The significance of *Tom Jones,* however, extends well beyond the boxoffice. As Alexander Walker put it, "For the first time the screen was decked out with a prophetic sense of the tone that would play a dynamic part, whether actually justified by fact or not, in shaping the foreigners' impressions of Britain in the mid-1960s. That's to say, its 'swinging' mood."[39]

Walker was referring to a *Time* magazine cover story on London in 1966 which described the city as "steeped in tradition, seized by change, liberated by affluence, graced by daffodils and anemones, so green with parks and squares that, as the saying goes, you can walk across it on the grass. In a decade dominated by youth, London has burst into bloom. It swings; it is the scene."[40] London had been exporting "its plays, its films, its fads, its styles, its people." Concerning the film scene in particular, *Time* quotes Italian novelist Alberto Moravia as saying that British cinema is "undergoing a renaissance." Charlie Chaplin was filming *The Countess from Hong Kong* with Marlon Brando and Sophia Loren; François Truffaut had just finished *Fahrenheit 451* with Julie Christie and Oskar Werner; Robert Aldrich was starting a war film called *The Dirty Dozen;* and Michelangelo Antonioni was scouting locations for *Blow-Up.* The article failed to mention a significant point—British production was almost totally dependent on American investment.

As one might expect, the profits and acclaim of *Tom Jones* placed Richardson in a strong bargaining position. UA and Woodfall signed an eight-picture contract shortly after the 1963 Academy Award ceremony. Like all UA multiple-picture contracts, Richardson's was non-exclusive. As a result, he directed his next picture for MGM when UA declined the opportunity to finance *The Loved One,* based on Evelyn Waugh's novel. This satire of California burial customs released in 1965 was a failure.

Woodfall, meanwhile, produced three low-budget pictures under the supervision of Oscar Lewenstein: *The Girl with the Green Eyes* (1964), *One Way Pendulum* (1965), and *The Knack* (1965). The two latter pictures were based on plays by N. F. Simpson and Ann Jellicoe that had been produced at the Royal Court Theatre. Only *The Knack* was successful. Directed by Richard Lester on a budget of $364,000, the picture won the Golden Palm at Cannes in 1965. The gist of the plot was that there was "quite a knack in the art of making it successfully with girls"; Lester's witty direction captured a spirit of youthful hedonism. *The Knack* did substantial business in Britain, where it easily earned back the negative cost. During the New York run the picture set a house record at the Fine Arts and UA thought it might have another *Tom Jones* on its hands. However, outside art-house situations, interest dropped off. The picture was profitable, nonetheless, grossing close to $2.5 million.

The pictures Richardson directed consisted of *Mademoiselle* (1966), *Sailor from Gibraltar* (1967), *The Charge of the Light Brigade* (1968), and *Laughter in the Dark* (1969). All were commercial failures. Other than *Light Brigade,* the pictures were produced under the British-

French coproduction agreement implemented in 1966 and designed for the art-theater situation. Jeanne Moreau starred in *Mademoiselle* and *Sailor from Gibraltar;* the former picture was based on a story by Jean Genet, who wrote the screenplay, and the latter on a novel by Marguerite Duras, famed for her *Hiroshima, Mon Amour. Laughter in the Dark* attempted to transpose a Nabokov novel to the screen following, perhaps, in the wake of Kubrick's *Lolita.* The three pictures barely did any business in the United States and only a modicum in Europe, grossing a total of $575,000, $215,000, and $780,000, respectively. Richardson's antiwar film was his most ambitious undertaking. Shot on location in Turkey at a cost of close to $6 million, the hoped-for blockbuster never materialized; *The Charge of the Light Brigade* grossed only $3.2 million.[41] *Variety* provided one explanation: "Those who go along merely expecting a lavish, spectacular *Charge* may feel shortchanged . . . Richardson's treatment is almost disdainfully indifferent to the actual physical charge. He is more concerned with analyzing the reasons behind one of the most notorious blunders in military history. He's also intent on attacking by ridicule the class war and bigotry of the British mid-19th century regime, the futility of the Crimean War as a whole."[42]

Larry Kramer's Women in Love

Woodfall's art films after *Tom Jones* clearly did not make it in the American market. Of UA's British imports, only one other picture in the art class succeeded and that was *Women in Love,* produced and adapted for the screen by Larry Kramer, a thirty-three-year-old Yale graduate. After breaking into production as a story editor, Kramer coscripted the screenplay of Clive Donner's *Here We Go Round the Mulberry Bush,* a witty piece, released by UA in 1968, about "young sexual ambitions and their difficult achievement." Kramer's deft touch in the collaboration won him a hearing from UA. On the basis of a first-draft screenplay, UA decided to back the production, with Ken Russell directing. Budgeted at a lean $1.6 million, the above-the-line costs came to a modest $370,000. Alan Bates and Oliver Reed each agreed to defer most of their salaries. Kramer put up his producer's fee of $75,000 as a completion bond, if needed. UA split the profits fifty-fifty, but all profit participations, including Bates's and Reed's, had to come out of the producer's share.

Ken Russell had previously worked on Harry Saltzman's *The Billion Dollar Brain.* Apparently, Russell could not be kept in line, which caused problems and perhaps even a cost overrun. For *Women in Love,*

Glenda Jackson and Jennie Linden in *Women In Love* (1970), produced by Larry Kramer and directed by Ken Russell. Jackson won an Oscar for best actress

Kramer had to surround Russell with a staff who appreciated the problems of working with a "nervous type like Ken Russell." As a result, they hired "exactly the personnel that made up the crew on his many BBC projects." For the BBC's prestige arts program, "Monitor," Russell directed about thirty documentaries, a number of them biographies of musicians, in a style described by Alexander Walker as an "assault-and-battery approach."[43]

Conditions on this production must have been ideal, because *Women in Love* is generally regarded as Russell's finest achievement. Reviews of the London premiere ran toward hyperbole. The *Observer* review should suffice: "Larry Kramer . . . has written a script which is a distillation of Lawrence . . . He has taken the novel extremely seriously and his adaptation has been done with enormous application, love, and considerable courage. Ken Russell has taken this good work of Kramer's and turned it into a masterpiece of filming. The brilliance of the photography matches, but does not overwhelm, the intensely emotional climate of the story . . . The wrestling scene between Birkin and Gerald, their bodies sweating and writhing in the firelight, is a pas de deux of extraordinary power."[44]

Perhaps because D. H. Lawrence had no particular following among the youth audience—or at least this may have been UA's perception of his reputation—UA geared its campaign in the U.S. to adults. Vincent Canby caught the flavor of the ad campaign in the title of his *New York Times* review: "*Women in Love* Done as a Torrid Romance." To Canby, "Lawrence's rhapsodic polemic on behalf of a new form of consciousness, which would allow man to fulfill his sexual nature . . . is now, in this reduced form, an intensely romantic love story about four people and their curiously desperate struggles for sexual power."[45] Judith Crist, however, writing for *New York* magazine, praised the picture because of its fidelity to the novel. To Crist, *Women in Love* was the most successful of the films derived from Lawrence's works, "perhaps because we have reached the point where Lawrence can, after some 60 years of bowdlerization, pussyfooting and exploitation, be met on his own terms—and in them—by a filmmaker."[46]

Whatever UA's attitude in its ad campaign, the company respected the integrity of the theme. Larry Kramer hoped the picture would receive an "X" from the MPAA Code and Rating Administration, perhaps believing the rating would generate another controversy similar to *Midnight Cowboy's* (see chapter 9) and heat up the boxoffice. UA thought otherwise; speaking for David Picker, a UA executive told Kramer "that we are delighted that *Women in Love* has an R; that we worked very hard to see to it that it got an R, and that we would have been very unhappy if we had finally been forced to put an X on it. We are attempting to make the code much more intelligent, rational and meaningful, and consequently, the X rating will be reserved for pictures of purely prurient intent. At least that is our hope. Certainly none of us think that the application of an R to *Women in Love* is going to reduce its commercial potential, but rather the opposite."[47]

But as it happened, *Women in Love* did not draw the youth audiences, which UA found hard to understand. Kramer blamed the campaign. Nonetheless, the picture generated a respectable world gross of $4.5 million.

The Beatles

In attempting to mine the British pop culture scene, UA had better luck with the music from Merseyland—that is, Liverpool. As guitar groups from the British hit parade made the American charts, film

The Beatles in *A Hard Day's Night* (1964), a Walter Shenson production directed by Richard Lester

companies moved quickly to capture some of the profits. UA scored first by signing the Beatles to a three-picture contract. Call it a fluke, but UA's timing couldn't have been better.

The first Beatles' picture, *A Hard Day's Night,* was actually commissioned by UA as a favor for the company's record division, which wanted a soundtrack LP of the Beatles to exploit in the American market. To execute the idea, UA approached Walter Shenson, the producer of *The Mouse that Roared* (1959), a satire of power politics starring Peter Sellers that became a runaway moneymaker in this country. Fired by Harry Cohn from Columbia Pictures' publicity department for supposedly writing the script on company time, Shenson moved to England where he found the financing to make his picture. For a sequel, *The Mouse on the Moon* (1963), he turned to UA for assistance. Although Peter Sellers was unwilling to repeat his role, the picture is significant in that Shenson established a relationship with the director, Richard Lester. A Philadelphia native, Lester had developed a zany improvisatory comedy style directing the ad-lib program, "The Goon Show" for British commercial television, which he perfected directing 500 TV commercials and introduced into his first feature, *It's Trad, Dad* (1962), a rock music quickie for Columbia.

How Shenson signed the Beatles to a three-picture contract is a bit confusing. Alexander Walker said that UA's Bud Ornstein negotiated the initial deal with Brian Epstein, the Beatles' manager.[48] But Walker also said that Shenson had to persuade the Beatles to go along. This much is certain: Shenson formed a corporation called Proscenium Films Ltd. for the services of the group, the stock of which was owned two-thirds by Shenson and one-third by the Beatles.

The Beatles did not receive much as compensation—a fee for each of the three pictures that escalated to £70,000 plus around 30 percent of the profits. Shenson, for his services as producer, received a fee of £12,000 and 30 percent of the profits. UA's profit share amounted to around 40 percent.

That UA was able to negotiate such a favorable deal owed much to luck. At the time of the negotiations, the Beatles were not known outside Britain. Their recordings had climbed to the number-one position on the British charts, but whether the Beatles could excite interest elsewhere remained to be seen. For this reason, UA insisted on a modest budget of around $500,000 for the picture.

Beatlemania broke out in October 1963 when the group played the London Palladium and was seen over television by 15 million viewers. Fans outside the theater set up "a continuous screaming sound like the moment of mass extermination in a pig factory—the tribal sound of the early 1960s," in the words of Alexander Walker.[49] As the teenage hysteria grew, the move to merchandise the Beatles began, leading to an American tour in early 1964, which included a concert at Carnegie Hall and television appearances on "The Ed Sullivan Show."

A Hard Day's Night captured the Beatles at the height of their first enormous wave of popularity. Covering two days in the life of the Beatles, the picture portrayed the pressure and difficulties under which they worked and played. The Beatles performed eleven of their compositions informally, in practice, and on the stage. Packed into eighty-three minutes of action were excursions into other Beatles' actualities: a skirmish with the police, mob street scenes with teenagers, relations with their agents, hotel life, press conferences, and encounters with the mod world. Filmed in black and white by cinematographer Gilbert Taylor, who gave the picture a look of cinema verité, and directed by

Richard Lester, who imparted to the action the breezy vitality of a fast commercial, *A Hard Day's Night,* in the words of *Variety,* "will satisfy the legion of Beatles' followers and should make the group a lot of new friends who have sensed that there must be more behind them than the vocal twanging which has brought them such swift fame (notoriety?) and fortune."[50]

A Hard Day's Night premiered in London in July 1964 to smash business. Anticipating the same results for the U.S. release in August, UA released the soundtrack LP before the picture opened. In the first two weeks, the album sold more than 1,500,000 copies. Capitol Records released three singles from the picture as well as a separate LP, "Something New." Vee-Jay, Tollie, MGM, Atlantic, and other labels rushed to put out sides recorded years earlier by the group. As *Variety* reported, the Beatles have "cracked all previous records for selling enormous quantities of platters within a relatively short period."[51]

UA held special screenings for deejays, newspaper people, vendors of Beatles merchandise, and exhibitors—for everyone who could bang the drum for the picture. To capitalize on the extraordinary demand, UA staged special "premieres" around the country before the picture opened. Simulating a live-concert situation, UA upped admission prices and sold tickets on a reserved-seat basis. Then for the general release, UA ordered 1,000 prints to saturate the market. This strategy generated an incredible gross of $5.8 million within six weeks. *A Hard Day's Night* grossed $10 million in a year.

Walter Shenson teamed up with Richard Lester again to produce the second Beatles picture, *Help!,* in 1965. The budget, at $1.3 million, was more than twice that of *A Hard Day's Night* and involved color photography, foreign locations, and a more ambitious story line. But it was a safe investment since, by then, Beatlemania had become a worldwide phenomenon. *Help!* grossed $10 million, equally divided between foreign and domestic. Critically, *Help!* did not measure up to expectations. As *Variety* said, "The simple good spirits that pervaded *A Hard Day's Night* are now often smothered as if everybody, from director, writers, and artists to the technicians are all desperately trying to outsmart themselves and be ultra-clever-clever."[52] *Help!* was the last picture the Beatles made as a group, although in 1968, Apple Films, a Beatle enterprise, coproduced a color-animated feature, *Yellow Submarine,* in which the Beatles appeared in caricature.

Interest in "swinging Britain" had run its course by the mid-sixties, yet British producers were fixated on the subject, as if that type of picture were the only kind suitable for export. As Alexander Walker describes it, "The British cinema, encouraged by the much more merchandise-conscious reach of Hollywood grasped the dominant life-styles of these years as they succeeded each other in bewildering acceleration." At its worst, "it seemed the cinema was a continuous commercial whose dimensions were those of 'sheer fantasy'—the uninhibited sex, the progressive nudity, the frivolous dress, the rhythm of pop music, the visual intensity, the affluent hedonism of all descriptions. Everything was marketable, being sold back to the public who inspired it, or remade in an even newer trend when they had sickened of it."[53]

After 1970, UA and American film companies in general drastically cut back on production in Great Britain. The boom had come to an end. The number of pictures produced in Great Britain did not diminish. The quantity remained around seventy a year, about what it was at the peak. It was the volume of finance that declined; by 1972, it had dropped to 65 percent of what it had been in 1968, the peak year of the era.[54] UA continued to back an annual Bond picture, to be sure, and to finance the occasional "runaway" picture, but for the most part, the company ceased investing in indigenous production.

C H A P T E R   E I G H T

"007"

A License to Print Money

As the most successful series in motion picture history, the James Bond films are quintessential examples of products tailored for the international market. Financed by an American major partly with British film subsidy funds, produced by two expatriates who had incorporated in Switzerland, and based on a popular series of British espionage novels that played off Cold War tensions, the James Bond films were shot in exotic locales featuring a cast of mixed nationalities that was headed by a star of universal appeal. Equally important, the pictures contained a lot of sex and action. The purpose of this chapter is to analyze the relationship between UA and the Broccoli-Saltzman production team to demonstrate how UA sustained a successful series.

Of all the ways to rationalize the acquisition of product, a series has the greatest potential of generating profits without much attendant risk. Once launched, a series creates loyal and eager fans who form the core of its audience. By keeping production costs in line with this ready-made demand, series pictures are almost guaranteed a profit. The problem, of course, is to hit upon a theme or subject that will sustain attention beyond the sequel. After the success of the first James Bond feature, *Dr. No,* UA did not merely pull down successive titles from the Ian Fleming bookshelf and order up new pictures. Producers Cubby Broccoli and Harry Saltzman devised a formula of their own inspired by the novels that really accounted for the enduring popularity of the series. To keep the series going, UA developed a special relationship with the producers, heaped added inducements on them to keep them happy, and fought off the competition. In the process, UA perfected its marketing skills to capture the lion's share of the box office.

SECURING THE OPTION

Broccoli and Saltzman had been at loose ends when they contemplated the James Bond series. After eight years of successful producing, Broccoli's partnership with Irving Allen had disintegrated. Broccoli, a New York City native and former Hollywood agent, had moved to London where he cofounded Warwick Films with Allen in 1952. Warwick received financing from Columbia Pictures and was responsible for producing the company's British quota requirements. Specializing mostly in action pictures, Warwick turned out a string of moneymakers that included *The Red Beret, Hell Below Zero, Cockleshell Heroes, Zarak,* and *Adongo,* to name only a few. Key personnel in the James Bond series worked with Broccoli at Warwick, among them director Terence Young, writer Richard Maibaum, cinematographer Ted Moore, and art director Ken Adam.

Quebec-born, Saltzman had worked in the circus, vaudeville, theater, and television in many capacities before joining up with John Osborne and Tony Richardson in 1956. When Saltzman resigned from Woodfall Films in 1960, Woodfall had produced *Look Back in Anger, The Entertainer,* and *Saturday Night and Sunday Morning.*

Of Saltzman, Alexander Walker said, "He could make money work and things happen: not always to his advantage, though generally so. He could open and close deals, two talents by no means always found lurking together in the same person."[1] Saltzman's motivation for contacting Ian Fleming may have been a story in *Life* magazine on March 17, 1961, which named *From Russia with Love* as one of President Kennedy's ten favorite books. Regardless, Saltzman caught Fleming at "a propitious moment," said Walker; recovering from his first heart attack, Fleming was in the process of setting up a trust fund for his family. Saltzman took an option on the Bond books, but the deal was not clinched until after he met Cubby Broccoli. Broccoli had likewise become interested in the novels and was introduced to Saltzman by writer Wolf Mankowitz, a mutual friend of the two men. According to Walker, Broccoli "wrote out an agreement guaranteeing an advance of at least £1,000, and the two producers started hunting for financial backing."[2]

Fleming granted Saltzman exclusive motion picture rights to all the published James Bond novels, save his first, *Casino Royale*, in return for $100,000 per book and 2½ percent of the net profits from each film. From the start, the deal clearly contemplated a series. Saltzman was required to option a new book for a motion picture every eighteen months; otherwise the rights to the novels would revert to Fleming. Should the series succeed and consume all the published novels, Saltzman was also granted the motion picture rights to the character of James Bond, thereby enabling him to produce "original" Bond movies.

At the time of the deal, Fleming had written nine Bonds beginning with *Casino Royale* in 1953 and ending with *Thunderball*. As Alexander Walker said, "Looking back on the Bond phenomenon, it is almost unbelievable to realize how slow and hesitant a start it had. Even after writing four Bond books, one a year between 1953 and 1955, Ian Fleming still hadn't achieved a really profitable breakthrough; he had failed both to make the best-seller lists in England and America and to clinch a Hollywood deal."[3] Out of desperation, Fleming had sold the film rights to *Casino Royale* to Russian-born actor-director Gregory Ratoff in 1955 for a mere $6,000. CBS had earlier purchased the rights to televise *Casino Royale* and had broadcast a live one-hour version on its "Climax Mystery Theatre" on October 1, 1954. Starring Barry Nelson, the program generated little interest, which may account for the small price Fleming placed on the property. Ratoff could find no financial backers for *Casino Royale* and held on to the property until his death, after which his widow sold the rights to producer Charles K. Feldman in 1960.

LAUNCHING THE SERIES

Option in hand, Saltzman and Broccoli approached Bud Ornstein, UA's production head in Great Britain. Ornstein directed them to UA

Sean Connery as "007"

headquarters in New York. Broccoli has described the meeting as follows: "It was a mixture of optimism and apprehension that I carried into the meeting with Krim, Benjamin and David Picker. David said, 'I'm familiar with James Bond.' Krim said, 'If David likes the idea, we'll talk.' Frankly, they were reluctant to make the series using an unknown actor; but eventually, after some talk, we did get an understanding that the picture would be done, if it could be done cheaply. In short, a million dollar budget—tops."[4] Broccoli failed to mention that his partner Saltzman accompanied him and that the team first approached Warwick's distributor, Columbia Pictures, whose New York offices were in the same building as UA's. After getting nowhere with Columbia, they went upstairs to Krim's office and struck a deal. This was in June 1961, but it was not until April 2, 1962, that all the details were finalized.

UA agreed in principle to the financing, but the project as it then stood was nebulous, to say the least. All the principal ingredients had yet to be determined—the choice of novel for the first picture, screenplay, director, and star. UA therefore decreed that the first Bond picture had to be a low-budget item. The above-the-line costs, accounting for about half the budget, were bare bones—$140,000 for the property and screenplay, $40,000 for the director, $80,000 for the producer's fee, and $140,000 for the cast, including the star. To reduce further the risks of production financing, the picture had to qualify for an Eady Plan subsidy, which meant, among other things, that it had to have an all-British cast and be shot on "British" locations, namely within the Commonwealth.

Everyone involved wanted *Thunderball*, Fleming's most recent novel, to lead off the series, thinking that this novel had the most commercial possibilities. However, the property was tied up in litigation. In 1959, Kevin McClory, a little-known Irish writer and director, had suggested to Fleming that the time was right for a James Bond film and together with screenwriter Jack Whittingham they collaborated on a film treatment. Like Ratoff before them, they found no backers. Fleming, however, novelized the treatment, crediting no one but himself. McClory instituted a plagiarism suit, tying up the novel in court for three years.

Although Broccoli and Saltzman's solicitor considered McClory's action as being of "a purely blackmailing nature," they decided to postpone the picture and lead off with *Dr. No*. As Alexander Walker said, "If not the most exotic Bond book at that time, it was the most topical. Cape Canaveral was having an embarrassingly bad international press as its missiles either misfired or went dangerously astray. *Dr. No* provided an appealing rationalization for this in the activities of the Jamaican-based villain who was beaming confusing 'instructions' at the missiles."[5]

Richard Maibaum, who worked with Broccoli at Warwick on *Hell Below Zero* in 1954, was hired to develop a screenplay. As Maibaum labored on a second draft, Ornstein told David Picker, "I must tell you that personally, I have not been impressed to date with Maibaum's work and only hope that he will come up with something much better this time; as we have had many story conferences with him."[6]

In their search for an unknown actor to play the role of James Bond, Broccoli and Saltzman came up with Sean Connery. Said Ornstein, "He is the best we have come up with to date, and I do believe that he could be James Bond." Born in Edinburgh in 1930, Connery had played character parts in a string of unmemorable films, including Walt Disney's comedy, *Darby O'Gill and the Little People*. "He was dreadful in most of them, we thought," Saltzman said later. "He had suffered a small but fatal miscasting all the way down the line."[7] Before committing themselves, Broccoli and Saltzman tested the front-runners for the role by asking the readers of the *London Express* to choose the ideal actor to play Bond. Connery was their choice.

Finding a director was equally difficult. Ornstein said, "As based on the treatment, the directors so far have shied away from the project. I feel that it is all-important to get the director assigned as soon as possible so that he can adapt the script to his own thinking. Right now, Broccoli and Saltzman seem to favour Terence Young. They feel that they could control him in spite of his tendency to go over schedule and budget." Terence Young, like Maibaum, had worked under Broccoli at Warwick, directing *Red Beret* and *Zarak*. Broccoli and Saltzman originally leaned to Phil Karlson, a former "B" film director at Monogram, who graduated to directing nervous "A"s for Columbia and for independent producers. Karlson's agent wanted $75,000, which was well over the cap on this item.

The formal documentation on the Broccoli-Saltzman deal was not signed until April 2, 1962, well after the completion of the principal photography on *Dr. No*. At this stage in the relationship, the terms were not substantially different from any regular development deal. UA agreed to put up complete financing for the picture and pay Broccoli and Saltzman a producer's fee of $80,000, plus an overhead allowance of $24,000, plus a personal expense allowance of $700 per week during preproduction and principal photography. The pictures were cross-collateralized in groups of two. After Fleming received his 2½ percent profits off the top, UA and the producer divided the profits fifty-

fifty. The standard distribution fees prevailed. Originally, UA secured exclusive distribution rights to each picture for a period of ten years, but as the relationship progressed, UA acquired the rights in perpetuity.

UA retained the rights of approval over the principal creative ingredients of each picture, as would be expected. In addition, UA built in for itself parallel rights to those Broccoli and Saltzman had to the novels. The producers were required to option a new novel every eighteen months to keep the series alive. UA, in a sense, subsumed this responsibility. At UA's discretion, it could trigger the acquisition of the next novel and require Broccoli and Saltzman to commence principal photography within a specified period of time. If the team defaulted, UA could assign the project to another producer. UA, moreover, retained the right to pick the first four novels, after which the selection was left to the producers. However, if UA disagreed with the selection, the company could refrain from financing the picture. In such a case, the producers could acquire the option on the book and produce it through another distributor.

Broccoli and Saltzman found it to their tax advantage to incorporate in Switzerland to conduct the partnership. They formed a company called Danjaq, S.A., the name of which was derived from the first names of each of their wives—Dana (Broccoli) and Jacqueline (Saltzman). Danjaq was owned by the two couples and shared the profits equally, although the wives held nonvoting minority shares. Eon Productions, Ltd., the actual producer of the Bond pictures, was a Danjaq subsidiary.

Dr. No had its world premiere at the Pavilion Theatre in London in October 1962. The picture was released day-and-date—that is, simultaneously—in 198 theaters throughout the British Isles, grossing a herculean $840,000 in two weeks and quickly becoming one of UA's all-time boxoffice champions in that market. The film also did outstanding business in Italy, Germany, and other countries on the Continent.

The U.S. campaign began fifteen months earlier with the aim of making James Bond a familiar name in America. To launch the campaign, UA sent newspaper and media reps boxed sets of the James Bond novels; the press also received the James Bond Handbook, which listed the super-sleuth's preferences—i.e., his woman, his liquor, his arsenal, his clothes, and so on; and "an exciting prizeworthy photo of beautiful bikini-clad" Ursula Andress, who played the leading feminine role in *Dr. No.* The photo was accompanied with an appropriate "teaser" noting that "her friend James Bond was headed their way."

UA did not go all out on its campaign until after the picture proved itself in Europe. The main goal was to build up Sean Connery as a star and, to do this, they scheduled him for a cross-country tour in March 1963. Accompanied by Terence Young, the director, Connery visited New York, Chicago, Los Angeles, San Francisco, and Kansas City. In Kansas City, UA introduced Connery to a national convention of exhibitors. In the other cities, UA presented the star to important members of the press who were invited in from the surrounding markets. Every detail of the project was designed "to underscore the lady-killing, man murdering, chic, science-fiction image of James Bond." Accompanied by three models, "counterparts of the lovely companions with whom James Bond is traditionally involved in print and on the screen," Connery hosted at each city, a special preview of *Dr. No* and a gala postscreening gourmet party, "sumptuously prepared and served on a Lucullan scale." The following day at each stop he gave himself to newspaper, radio, and TV interviews.[8]

To create even more media attention, UA scheduled the Western Hemisphere premiere in Kingston, Jamaica, the principal setting for the picture, and invited 100 journalists to participate in the event. By the time of the New York premiere in May 1963, UA had the audiences primed.

UA handled the release of *Dr. No* as an action picture. Although British by origin, the Bond pictures were tailor-made for the international market. Unlike more sophisticated fare that required special nurturing, UA released *Dr. No* in New York as a Premiere Showcase attraction in major theaters. Following this run, UA saturated the metropolitan area by booking the picture in eighty theaters. This pattern was presumably duplicated in other major markets.

Dr. No grossed $2 million domestic and $4 million foreign—a hit, but nothing exceptional. Nonetheless, the performance triggered the production of James Bond number two—*From Russia with Love*. UA chose this title next not only because it was one of Fleming's best novels, but also because it was a familiar title to the public. Making the list of JFK's ten favorite books helped presell the picture and spurred sales of the books as well.

UA approved a production budget of $2 million, twice that of *Dr. No*'s. Connery received a $100,000 bonus on top of his $54,000 salary. The producers received a more generous fee, overhead allowance, and personal expenses budget. As an extra, UA agreed that if *Dr. No* and *From Russia with Love* fully recouped their costs on a cross-collateralized basis, Danjaq's share of the profits from the subsequent pictures would be increased from 50 percent to 60 percent.

From Russia with Love premiered in the United States in April

1964, about a year after *Dr. No.* The picture grossed twice as much as *Dr. No*, both domestic and foreign—$12.5 million worldwide. Unlike the first Bond entry, *Russia* stuck close to Fleming's original story and is thus a departure from the rest of the series. "Missing are Ken Adam's futuristic, expressionistic sets, as well as the science fiction aspects that would dominate most of the Bond films," said Raymond Benson.[9]

With *Goldfinger*, the third Bond picture, the series really took off. Produced on a budget of around $3 million, *Goldfinger* grossed a phenomenal $46 million worldwide the first time around. The picture had its world premiere at the Odeon Leicester Square Theatre in London in late September 1964. The picture grossed over $400,000 in two weeks; by the New Year, *Goldfinger* had recouped its negative cost from its British run alone and, in addition, qualified for about $1.4 million in Eady money. Until budgets skyrocketed in the late seventies, the Bond pictures would regularly break even in their home market.

Banking on the "instant recognition" of the Bonds, UA saturated the market even more with *Goldfinger*. *Goldfinger* opened in New York and 40 other U.S. and Canadian cities for a total of 150 engagements. Within fourteen weeks, the picture grossed over $10 million in rentals. Said *Variety*: "No other film in memory of film historians has ever performed with such speed for such a volume."[10] Saturation booking was used overseas as well, requiring a total of 1,100 prints to distribute the picture worldwide. In Germany alone, UA flooded the country with 100 prints, when normally the market required a mere 20.

Until *Goldfinger*, the Bond films earned about twice as much in the foreign market as they did domestic. But as a result of UA's distribution strategy, the ratio leveled off. Increasing popularity of the pictures was certainly a factor, but UA also set out to capture most of the boxoffice dollar. As *Variety* said of *Goldfinger*'s performance, "What is impressive is the percentage of the take corralled by United Artists." UA sold the picture first run on a 90-10 basis. For this type of rental, the distributor and exhibitor split the box-office gross, with 90 percent going to the distributor and 10 percent to the exhibitor. Out of its share, UA paid the advertising and publicity expenses and the "house nut"—a negotiated figure covering the overhead expenses of the theater. *Variety* estimated that UA captured about 80 percent of what *Goldfinger* grossed in the domestic market during its first run.[11] After opening the picture, UA renegotiated deals with the 60-40 engagements to get a 70-30 split instead. In many instances, the theaters "volunteered" to increase the distributor's share.

Goldfinger was the first Bond film released during the Christmas season in this country. *Thunderball*, the fourth entry, repeated the pattern; thereafter UA released the pictures at eighteen-month intervals, alternating between summer and Christmas—the two peak seasons of the year for moviegoing.

The success of *Goldfinger* triggered the reissue of the first two Bond pictures as a double feature. Released during the 1965 Easter season, the pair grossed $8 million. Dividing the rental among the two brought *Dr. No*'s take from $2 million to $6 million and *Russia*'s from $4 million to $8 million. UA asked for 50 percent terms for the reissue and later regretted it when the pictures as a group grossed substantially more than their original separate release. The second reissue linked *Dr. No* with *Goldfinger* and this time the terms were set at 60 percent of the boxoffice take. Reissuing the latter combo served the dual purpose of capitalizing on the popularity of the series and of filling a hole in the release schedule. *Thunderball* was released during Christmas 1965. *You Only Live Twice,* the next in line, was not scheduled for release until summer 1967. Since UA did not want a year to go by without a Bond, the company reissued *Dr. No* and *Goldfinger* during the fall of 1966.

"Bondmania," the merchandising of James Bond, created instant recognition of the pictures. Ian Fleming, who died in August 1964, never saw the full extent of Bondmania. The phenomenon erupted beginning with *From Russia with Love*. Paperback sales had tripled, generating interest in the pictures and vice versa. By the time *From Russia with Love* was released, UA proclaimed that the novels had sold in excess of 30 million copies and had been translated into almost every major language. *Playboy* began serializing the novels early in the sixties and regularly featured spreads of Bond and his women. By the time of *Thunderball*, an avalanche of "007" products had hit the market. Colgate-Palmolive manufactured toiletries, Milton Bradley produced games, Endicott-Johnson made shoes, Weldon created a complete line of "007" sleepware, and Multiple Toy Makers manufactured James Bond attaché cases. The merchandising campaign, which UA called the most comprehensive ever, covered "anything that can be made with a label or a trademark" and provided the pictures with free advertising evaluated at $30 million by 1965.

THE BOND FORMULA

Many explanations have tried to account for the enduring success of the Bond pictures. Alexander Walker stated that "Bond was the first film series at that time to work *with an audience*. In a way, it *was* a return to those Saturday afternoon serials. People who went to see the Bond films henceforth knew the game and anticipated playing it and even working at it as the film-makers fed them the clues. Once Broccoli and Saltzman had tumbled to this factor, which they soon did, then the formula was theirs and Connery-Bond gave them a world patent." [12]

Broccoli and Saltzman had perfected this formula with *Goldfinger*. Unlike the novels, the pictures were laced with humor, ranging from subtle tongue-in-cheek in the early efforts to broad farce in the later ones. The films, in addition, differ in plot details, ranging from only slight changes as in *From Russia with Love* to the total departure from the Fleming story as in *You Only Live Twice*. What Broccoli and Saltzman produced and served to the public was the Bond formula, which, although based on the novels, had its own peculiar structure. Containing a series of "Bondian effects," the structure was the handiwork not only of Broccoli and Saltzman, but also of their production staff, many of whom worked on the series from its inception. This list included screenwriter Richard Maibaum, directors Terence Young and Guy Hamilton, production designer Ken Adam, music composer John Barry, and main title designer Maurice Binder.

The formula is well known and need not be analyzed here. In summary, though, the formula consists of the famous gun-barrel logo, which begins every picture, followed by the distinctive "James Bond theme," the precredits sequence, and then the main titles, the latter typically accompanied by a title tune. The plot consisted of a series of what Broccoli called "bumps"—that is, a series of self-contained action sequences strung together as set pieces. Most of the plots, said Penelope Houston, "are just variations on Jack the Giant Killer, with appropriately extreme trimmings. Dispatched by M, the Prospero of the Secret Service, Bond stages a one-man assault on a fairytale stronghold furnished out of *House and Garden* and the travel supplements. The ogre (Dr. No, Mr. Big, Ernst Stavro Blofeld) captures him; there is a great smash-up; and Bond swims, skis or shoots his way out." [13] For each picture, the producers introduced a new exotic locale, a new James Bond woman, and fantastic gadgets to enliven the formula.

The formula proved to be durable because it continued with minor modification to captivate the mass audience. The formula even withstood changes of the star. In the sixties, Sean Connery had been the number-one boxoffice draw in the world. His compensation had grown to about $1.25 million per picture plus 5 percent of the profits. Connery, nonetheless, had grown weary of playing James Bond even though

the production pace of the series allowed him time to pursue other acting interests. After *You Only Live Twice* (1967), Connery made it absolutely clear that this was his final Bond picture.

IN SEARCH OF A NEW JAMES BOND

Broccoli and Saltzman held a massive talent hunt and came up with
an unusual choice—Australian model George Lazenby. Lazenby had
worked in TV commercials but had no previous acting experience. *On
Her Majesty's Secret Service* (1969), the picture in which he debuted,
departed from the formula by sticking close to the Fleming original. As
Raymond Benson put it, "This meant the script had to concentrate
more on character and plot than on art direction and gadgetry. Commercially, the gambit didn't pay off. Critics blamed George Lazenby.
The producers blamed the departure from the established formula *and*
George Lazenby."[14] *On Her Majesty's Secret Service* broke even and
then some, probably. Produced at $10 million, it grossed $23 million
worldwide.

For the next Bond picture, *Diamonds Are Forever* (1971), UA wanted
Connery back. Broccoli and Saltzman were reluctant to go along at
first because Connery had become a little heavier, a little balder, and a
little less energetic with each picture. However, if they were to use
Lazenby again or to cast about for another replacement and find out
that he too was unacceptable to the public, the series would come to a
premature end. So Broccoli and Saltzman decided to approach Connery. Connery agreed to return for one more picture; to persuade him
UA and Eon offered to pay him 12½ percent of the gross. In addition,
UA gave Connery a two-picture deal in which he could produce and/or
star. For *Diamonds Are Forever*, the producers reverted to the standard
Bond formula, but added more humor to attract a younger audience.
This did the trick once again; the picture grossed $42 million, almost
twice as much as the Lazenby picture. Connery's total compensation
came to more than $5 million, $1.25 million of which he donated to the
Scottish International Education Trust.

Diamonds Are Forever merely postponed the inevitable. UA wanted
a superstar for the new James Bond, suggesting perhaps Paul Newman, Robert Redford, or Burt Reynolds. To the last suggestion Broccoli
responded, "Over my dead body." Choosing the replacement was made
more difficult because the producers had been at odds with one another for years (more about this later). UA, in fact, contemplated tak-

Publicity poster for *Live and Let Die* (1973), introducing Roger Moore as the new James Bond

ing over the next Bond production should there be an impasse over the candidate. The choice of Roger Moore, though, was a master stroke. Moore had sophistication, experience, and good looks. Moreover, he had achieved international fame playing Simon Templar in the British TV series, "The Saint."

Eon agreed to pay Moore a straight salary of $180,000 for his first Bond picture, *Live and Let Die* (1973). Moore's contract also gave Eon options on his services for two additional pictures that raised his salary in $60,000 increments and gave him a percentage of the profits, 2½ percent to start, rising to 3¾ percent. "Moore arrived on the scene just as the direction in the Bond films began veering towards comedy," said Benson. "Since Moore's forte *is* light comedy, he fit right in. From *Live and Let Die* on, the scriptwriters tailored the screenplays to fit Roger Moore's personality. As a result, James Bond lost much of the *machismo* image which was so prominent in the sixties."[15] The gross of *Live and Let Die* more than matched *Diamonds Are Forever*, but the added significance of Moore's picture was its popularity overseas. With *Goldfinger*, the Bonds grossed about the same foreign and domestic. After *Live and Let Die*, the foreign market once again outperformed the domestic market by at least $10 million. Moore had clearly given the Bond series a new lease on life.

RIVAL BONDS

Kevin McClory's plagiarism suit against Fleming over the rights to *Thunderball* had an effect on UA's Bond series. Fleming, in ill health, agreed to an out-of-court settlement with McClory in 1963. (Fleming died of a heart attack in 1964.) The settlement permitted Fleming to continue harvesting royalties from the novel with the stipulation that republications had to credit the origins of the novel. Coming as a shock, though, the court adjudicators bestowed the motion picture rights on McClory. McClory had been anxious to produce the picture afterward but could find no one suitable to play the role of James Bond. In the mind of the public, Sean Connery was James Bond. Nonetheless, Broccoli and Saltzman, who had been interested in *Thunderball* from the start, wanted to protect their series from a rival Bond picture and were willing to deal. They offered to produce *Thunderball* as the fourth Bond picture and give McClory full production credit. As compensation, they offered him $250,000 cash plus 20 percent of the profits. In return, McClory had to agree not to produce a remake of the picture for a period of ten years. *Thunderball* grossed $50 million world-wide, making it the most profitable picture in the series. (*Moonraker* in 1979 grossed a little more money, but cost $33 million to produce compared to *Thunderball's* budget of $6.5 million.)

In producing *Casino Royale*, Charles Feldman encountered the problem that also faced Kevin McClory—who should play James Bond? While he pondered this, UA suddenly had two Bond pictures under its belt and a series in the making. UA realized that Feldman was sitting on a potential gold mine and could easily "make a deal with five other companies," said Krim. The best course for UA to follow was to persuade Feldman to make a deal with Broccoli and Saltzman. If this attempt failed, UA should make a separate deal with Feldman rather than letting him make the picture with another company. In investigating the matter, UA determined that *Casino Royale* was excluded from all relationships between Fleming and Danjaq, and Danjaq and UA. Further, should UA strike a deal with Feldman, it was not obligated to share any of the benefits with Danjaq.

Broccoli and Saltzman objected to a deal with Feldman because they wanted at least three pictures of their own in distribution to solidify the series and also because they did not want to see any picture made without Connery. (They were not about to assign Connery to the picture). Personality differences between all three producers also contributed to a breakdown in communications. UA, as a result, backed off.

A frustrated Feldman threatened to sue, claiming that he owned the exclusive rights to the James Bond character and that Broccoli and Saltzman in *Goldfinger* plagiarized a key situation from *Casino Royale*. Threats ebbed and flowed; meanwhile, UA released *Goldfinger* and then *Thunderball* and in the process, boxed Feldman out of the market.

To salvage whatever value remained in *Casino Royale*, Feldman changed tactics. Rather than making a regular Bond starring Sean Connery, he would produce a satire of the Bond phenomenon. Woody Allen, a star in the picture, told *Look* that Feldman intended to "eliminate the Bond films forever." *Look* went on to say that "Such writers as the late Ben Hecht, Joseph Heller, Terry Southern, Billy Wilder, Wolf Mankowitz, Michael Sayers, even Peter Sellers, worked with Feldman over the years trying to brew a screenplay so outrageous that it would leave other Bond movies and pseudo-Bonds far behind."[16]

The success of the third Bond picture, *Goldfinger*, had sent the majors to the drawing boards in search of successful imitations. In 1965, Universal introduced the antiromantic Harry Palmer in *The Ipcress File*, produced by none other than Harry Saltzman. Later that year,

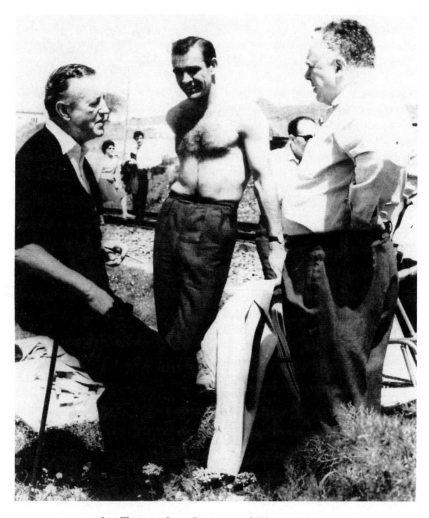

Ian Fleming, Sean Connery, and Harry Saltzman

Paramount released *The Spy Who Came in from the Cold*. The deluge of Bond imitations began in 1966. Twentieth Century–Fox released the first of its Flint series—*Our Man Flint*—and Columbia released *The Silencers*, the first of three Matt Helm entries starring Dean Martin. MGM rewove several episodes from its popular TV series, "The Man from U.N.C.L.E.," into two programmers, *To Trap a Spy* and *The Spy with My Face*. In addition, a horde of low-budget efforts, some of which were released by UA, capitalized on the sudden interest in espionage. As *Variety* stated, "The cycle soon separated into two factions—the spoofy offspring of Ian Fleming, with elaborate gadgets and buxom dames competing for a viewer's attention, and the glumly nonheroic disciples of Len Deighton and John Le Carré."[17] Neither faction, as it turned out, did much business at the boxoffice.

An example of the former type, *Casino Royale,* was released in this country by Columbia Pictures in the spring of 1967 to compete head on with *You Only Live Twice,* the fifth Bond entry. Both companies spent big bucks on their ad campaigns. UA's ad blurb stated that "Sean Connery *Is* James Bond," while Columbia's countered with "*Casino Royale Is* Too Much for One James Bond." Feldman patterned the picture after *What's New, Pussycat?,* a successful "mod comedy" which he had just produced starring Woody Allen and Peter Sellers. The two stars were brought into the *Casino Royale* project, but this time the result was less than successful. An overlong shooting schedule utilizing the efforts of five directors and five screenwriters, plus cameo appearances of an international cast of stars, jacked the production costs to almost $8 million, compared to the $10 million budget of *You Only Live Twice.* Although *Casino Royale* was a commercial failure, it did damage *You Only Live Twice,* which grossed $19 million domestic, compared to $28.5 million for *Thunderball* and $22.8 million for *Goldfinger.* However, no permanent damage was done to the series.

Subsequently, UA bought out Feldman's production company. In addition to acquiring Feldman's rights to *Casino Royale,* UA picked up *What's New, Pussycat?* and several other pictures. As a result, the *Casino Royale* remake rights are owned jointly by UA and Columbia if they mutually decide that the market could ever absorb another version of the picture or another picture based on Fleming's original novel.

Feldman had originally represented to Columbia that his rights to *Casino Royale* also included TV series rights. UA and Danjaq disputed his claim and were prepared to go to court to protect their interests. Fleming had given Broccoli and Saltzman an option on the television rights as part of the original deal. The terms stipulated that the option could not be exercised until after Eon produced three Bond pictures nor could it be exercised later than three years after the release of the last Bond feature. Upon the exercise of the option, Fleming was to receive $15,000 plus 2½ percent of the profits from any television series. American and British television had spawned a number of successful spy series, among them "The Man from U.N.C.L.E.," "The Avengers" (1961), "I Spy" (1965), and "Mission Impossible" (1966). According to

Herb Schottenfeld, UA considered producing a James Bond television series more than once, but the theatrical demand never diminished sufficiently to warrant such a move.[18] UA would use television only as a secondary market for the Bond pictures, but it was not until 1972—ten years after the inception of the series—that UA exploited this market. Until then, the company believed that it could generate additional revenue from the pictures simply by rerunning them in theaters. In 1972, UA signed a deal with ABC giving the network the right to broadcast the first seven Bonds for a price of $2.5 million each.

The Bond series had already become the worldwide record holder, grossing an aggregate rental, both theatrical and television, of $350 million by 1974. UA collected in distribution fees approximately $112 million, while Broccoli and Saltzman for their efforts received over $70 million in profits. Broccoli estimated that over 700,000,000 people worldwide had seen at least one Bond picture—that's one in five people on earth. As *Variety* quipped, "Perhaps Bond is as ubiquitous as Coca-Cola, perhaps more so."

TWO SCORPIONS IN A BOTTLE

As would be expected, the success of the series won for Broccoli and Saltzman improvements, as they say, in their compensation from UA. The improvements were in two areas: production fees and profit participation. The original deal called for a producer fee of $80,000 per picture, but for the second picture, UA increased the amount to $120,000, and on subsequent pictures UA continued bumping the fee until it hit $420,000 in 1967. The rationale for a producer fee was to provide a reward for putting together an attractive package. A producer normally had to wait for the real reward, namely the profits, if there were any. But Broccoli and Saltzman did more than package the ingredients; they devised the Bond formula and continually came up with ways of keeping it alive. They really performed a service different from or greater than most producers. In adjusting the producer fees, UA recognized this special contribution.

UA originally divided the profits with Danjaq fifty-fifty, but by 1967, UA had sweetened the deal by giving the producers 75 percent. The rationale for this is obvious. Although UA put up total financing for the Bond pictures, the company incurred no financial risk to speak of and hence did not require profits to offset losses. Demand for the product sustained itself at a high level. Ten years into the series, UA could see no reason why Bondmania could not go on forever. Moreover, UA, through its distribution strategy, met this demand in a way that allowed the company to recoup its investment early into the run—whereas normally it took a year or two for most pictures to go into profits. This could only happen, of course, if production costs remained at a reasonable level, which they did. Despite the phenomenal success of *Goldfinger,* UA and Danjaq kept production costs around $7 million. This money went a long way; Broccoli's philosophy was "All I ask is if they see every dollar on the screen." When it became apparent that the Bond ingredients would yield enormous grosses, there was no sense spending money needlessly. Keeping costs at a reasonable level meant that the producers maximized their profits. Production costs did not rise until the tenth Bond, *The Spy Who Loved Me* in 1977, which cost $13.5 million. Budgets thereafter began to spyrocket in a successful attempt to capture the adolescent audience.

Be that as it may, the total amount of improvements UA gave Broccoli and Saltzman came to a tidy $30 million. This figure was based on the performance of the first nine pictures, which were produced by 1974, and included adjustments on the TV distribution fees and foreign tax credits as well.

The problems surrounding the production of *The Spy Who Loved Me* were symptomatic of the deterioration of the Broccoli-Saltzman partnership and precipitated a basic change in the relationship between UA and the Bond series. To say that the "dual titans of Bondism" never got along would be an understatement. By 1966, Broccoli and Saltzman felt they could no longer work together. Thereafter they decided informally to take turns being the real producer of the subsequent pictures. "Saltzman would do one and Broccoli would stand in the wings, then it was Broccoli's turn and Saltzman would stand in the wings," said Herb Schottenfeld. This did not mean that only one of them was involved in a production, only that one had the final say.[19]

Provisions of their partnership in Danjaq exacerbated tensions. For one thing, all corporate actions required the approval of all stockholders. In addition, Swiss law stated that to dissolve a corporation all stockholders had to agree. Although Danjaq had accumulated a tremendous fortune from the Bond series, Broccoli and Saltzman were in different financial shape. Not content with his lot of merely producing the most successful series in motion picture history, Saltzman branched out into other film-related ventures. He invested heavily in Technicolor and in a French camera company; Saltzman also produced other pictures. Saltzman had hoped to launch another spy series by producing adaptations of Len Deighton novels, starring Michael Caine as Harry

Palmer. *The Ipcress File* (1965) and *Funeral in Berlin* (1967) were financed and released outside UA, but after UA gave Saltzman a multiple-picture contract to keep him happy, Saltzman released the third Harry Palmer picture, *Billion Dollar Brain* (1968), through the company. Saltzman made several other pictures for UA, including *Battle of Britain* (1969), a $14 million blockbuster containing a host of prominent British thespians, including Laurence Olivier, Ralph Richardson, Suzannah York, and others who lent "their presence to scenes, almost as if it were a patriotic duty," said Vincent Canby.[20] All the UA pictures lost money—to the tune of $15 million. Broccoli made only one non-Bond picture for UA, *Chitty, Chitty, Bang, Bang* (1968). Based on a children's book by Ian Fleming, this picture lost $8 million.

Without going into the details of Saltzman's financial condition, which are not germane here, suffice it to say that he had overextended himself and needed cash. Broccoli, on the other hand, had not dissipated his assets and was in fine financial shape. Because of this, Broccoli would not agree to a declaration of dividends. In retaliation, Saltzman refused to permit Eon to proceed with the production of the next Bond film, *The Spy Who Loved Me*. Broccoli and Saltzman's relationship at that time might be likened to two scorpions in a bottle.

Ten years had passed since the release of *Thunderball*. Kevin McClory was free to do a remake. He claimed that he also had equal rights in the James Bond character and that he could produce a James Bond series of his own based on his screenplay. UA and Danjaq took him to court, asserting that the success of the Bond series was not so much the result of the underlying properties but of the formula devised by the producers. In pressing the case, UA and Danjaq believed that their common-law copyright protected the formula. Acknowledging that McClory could produce a picture based on the *Thunderball* story, UA and Danjaq contended that he could not infringe on the Bond character and formula in the process. Tied up by this litigation, McClory failed in his attempt to produce a remake and eventually sold off his rights to Hollywood producer Jack Schwartzman. Schwartzman commissioned a script and interested a foreign distributor and Warner Brothers in the project. Schwartzman then convinced the British courts that the film would be essentially a remake of the original. In producing the picture, Schwartzman not only overcame tremendous legal obstacles, he even persuaded Sean Connery to come out of retirement to play James Bond. Released in 1983, *Never Say Never Again* differed in several significant respects from the novel, and kept to a more realistic framework than its predecessor. The picture was well received, but did not affect the results of the Bond picture before it or the one that followed.

Meanwhile, *The Spy Who Loved Me* just wasn't being made. Broccoli and Saltzman were not on speaking terms; they weren't even doing business with one another. Finally, to break the impasse, Saltzman, through an intermediary, offered to sell his interest in Danjaq to UA. According to Herb Schottenfeld, UA said to Broccoli, "Gee, isn't this great; but Broccoli didn't think it was so great." Broccoli had been sitting tight expecting that Saltzman would ultimately approach him for a buyout. At Broccoli's behest, UA backed off the deal. But after Saltzman started talking to Columbia Pictures about a buyout, UA "made some noises" and forced the issues. Said Schottenfeld, "We completed the transaction—no longer over the objections of Broccoli—but certainly not with his blessing. We wound up being Broccoli's partner."[21] UA announced the acquisition of Saltzman's 50 percent interest in Danjaq on December 17, 1975. UA had technically become the coproducer of the Bond series, but it took nearly a year to work out the logistics. In essence, UA agreed to continue functioning solely as financier with its usual rights of approval as distributor.

UA paid $36 million for Saltzman's share of Danjaq, but the actual cash outlay was only $26 million; to cover the difference, UA released Saltzman from an outstanding obligation to Danjaq in the amount of $10 million. Saltzman presumably used the $26 million to pay off loans on personal ventures. UA spread the payments over a period of five years so that the buyout qualified as a tax-free transaction under Swiss law. In determining the price for Saltzman's share, UA calculated the value of Danjaq's liquidable assets—such as cash, securities, and investments—the residuals due on the first nine Bonds, and the anticipated income on the future Bonds. By taking a conservative approach in evaluating the latter two items, UA once again "paid for the cow with its own milk." As a UA memo explained, "The advantages to UA are considerable. The actual residuals of the nine Bonds already made, in fact, substantially exceed those which are used in the computation, since we left out all reissue values and estimated our remaining network and TV syndication residuals at a low figure. We therefore expect that we will have a substantial additional profit on the existing Bonds." But, as the memo went on to say, the main value resided in the future Bonds. Danjaq received 75 percent of the profits. Through this deal, UA acquired a 50 percent interest in Danjaq's share—that is, 37½ percent of 100 percent of the total profits—which would be added to the company's existing 25 percent profit share plus the distribution fee.

This extra profit share for *The Man with the Golden Gun* would have been worth $5 million, the company estimated.

One final note on the Bond series. The original deal with Danjaq gave UA distribution rights to the Bond pictures for ten years. The term was later extended by five years. Now that UA and Danjaq were partners, UA effectively had perpetual distribution rights to the series.

NO ONE UNDER
17 ADMITTED

United
Artists

C H A P T E R   N I N E

International Operations, Part 2

France and Italy

If the James Bond series epitomized the commercial exploitation of the "swinging London" scene, *Last Tango in Paris* represented the quintessential manipulation of the European art cinema. A coproduction of Alberto Grimaldi's PEA Produzioni Europee Associate S.A.S.-Rome and UA's French subsidiary Les Production Artistes Associes S.A.-Paris, *Last Tango in Paris* was directed by Bernardo Bertolucci and starred Marlon Brando. After the presentation of the picture at the New York Film Festival on October 14, 1972, Pauline Kael said "that date should become a landmark in movie history compared to May 29, 1913—the night *Le Sacre du Printemps* was first performed—in music history. [*Tango* has] altered the face of an art form. This is a movie people will be arguing about for as long as there are movies." [1]

Last Tango was spawned after American film companies switched their investments overseas from Great Britain to France and Italy. By

1970, the latter two countries generated nearly 30 percent of the revenues in Europe for the majors, compared to Great Britain's 8 percent. Despite the inroads made by television, moviegoing had remained strong, particularly in Italy. Both markets were capable of showing a substantial return on American-financed "national" pictures.

UNITED ARTISTS' FRENCH PRODUCTIONS

UA's involvement in French production did not begin, for all practical purposes, until 1964. UA's policy until then was to avoid handling French films in France so as not to compete with the local distributors. UA distributed French films abroad, but, with a few exceptions, stuck to American product in the French market.

The reception of French films in the U.S. had ranked well behind the British. From 1956 to 1960, before the New Wave, French films as a group grossed from $2 to $5 million a year, with the exception of 1958, when *And God Created Woman* grossed $4 million and sent the total to the $8 million mark. Earnings from British pictures in this period rose from $2 million to $20 million.[2]

To stimulate the expansion of French film business in foreign markets, the French government in 1959 liberalized its protective policies by lifting all remaining restrictions on American earnings, including import quotas. Earlier, in 1953, the government had modified its state aid laws to encourage production. State aid was channeled through the Centre National de la Cinématographe (CNC), an administrative agency regulating all production, distribution, exhibition, importation, and exportation activities. The CNC granted production licenses, handled censorship, negotiated foreign agreements, and kept the industry balanced by allocating film aid to producers. In essence, the French film industry was partially nationalized. Aid to French films consisted of rebates amounting to 13 percent of the French home box-office for a period of five years. This was roughly equivalent to 50 percent of the gross rental. Funds for the aid program came from a tax on theater tickets, and, like British Eady money, encouraged commercially viable pictures.

Changes in the law in 1954 made short films also eligible for aid. Taking the form of a jury prize, this aid was designed to encourage production, since it was a direct grant as opposed to an advance on receipts for a film already in circulation. New Wave filmmakers—Truffaut, Godard, Resnais, Malle, Franju, Varda, Demy, and others—

learned their craft making short films. Their features, in other words, did not materialize out of nowhere, but resulted from positive government encouragement.

The aid law was further modified in 1959 to encourage quality feature film production. In addition to rebates, features now became eligible for prizes, but unlike the evaluation procedure for shorts, a filmmaker could submit his screenplay to a jury in advance of production. The basis of evaluation was not commercial potential, but, rather, aesthetic quality. As Steven Lipkin said, "In the first few years after the 1959 aid law, the possibilities for the newcomer were tremendous. For the first time, any new filmmaker could, in effect, become his own producer, either through receiving aid advanced on his script, or by working with a producer who would allow the freedom desired for a particular project."[3] From 1958 to 1961, there were over 100 feature films made in France by new directors.

French New Wave filmmakers attracted attention when they swept top honors at the Cannes Film Festival in 1959: François Truffaut's *The 400 Blows* won for best director; Alain Resnais's *Hiroshima, Mon Amour* took the International Critics Prize; and Marcel Camus's *Black Orpheus* captured the Grand Prix. Bidding on these films and the works of such directors as Louis Malle, Claude Chabrol, Philippe De Broca, and Jean-Luc Godard became hectic as distributors, exhibitors, and the public welcomed the revolution. The New Wave phenomenon became international in scope as filmmaking in Great Britain, Italy, the United States and elsewhere felt its impact.

More opportunities for financing and more channels for production resulted in the inevitable glut of unsuccessful New Wave productions as early as 1961. *Variety* described the situation as follows: "The authentic talents of the 'New Wave' have been absorbed but the dregs of the vintage are running thick. In short, the French film market is glutted with first films which were last films and avant garde gestures which cannot get a playdate."[4] After 1962, producers and distributors became shy of the New Wave label, making it extremely difficult for a new director to get his first film into production.

Various explanations have been offered for the decline of the New Wave—the overliterary quality of some films, the flaunting of conventional values, and the preoccupation with questions of sex, philosophy of love, and the existence of God. Also, too many ordinary pictures were made as lesser talents slavishly imitated the hits. Favorites on the French screen in 1954 were *Cleopatra*, Jerry Lewis in *The Nutty Professor,* and a Fernandel comedy, *Cooking with Butter.*[5]

France's film-aid laws were originally intended for development; the assumption was that state aid would diminish to nothing by the end of the sixties. However, declining attendance, the result of the spread of television and more leisure-time options, kept the French cinema dependent on aid for sustenance. Only the rare film amortized itself in the French market. The pressure to export grew stronger, yet of all the major national film industries, France's was both structurally and tempermentally ill-equipped to plan production for international distribution. The multiplicity of producers—around 300 in 1962—and their relative smallness, coupled with the rarity or perhaps the inability of big-scale daring meant that France did not recoup over 10 percent of its production costs from foreign markets.[6]

Thus, the national subsidy system had to be supplemented increasingly by the benefits of coproduction. After the founding of the Common Market, coproduction became a regular aspect of film production in Europe. As Thomas Guback described it, coproduction "brings together financial, artistic, and technical contributions from two or more countries under criteria established by formal bilateral governmental agreements."[7] The economic benefit of the scheme eased the financial strain for producers in different countries by enabling them to collect film aid twice and, if a venture were tripartite, three times. France, Italy, Spain, and West Germany, the chief Continental producers, became the most heavily involved; during the sixties, approximately 67 percent of French films, 52 percent of Italian, 40 percent of Spanish, and 36 percent of German were coproduced.[8]

The extent of France's dependence on this form of aid is seen in the production statistics for 1965. In that year, of the 142 films made, only 34 were completely French; the remainder consisted of 56 majority-French coproductions and 52 minority French coproductions. French investment in the all-French pictures amounted to $17 million; for the majority coproductions, it came to $15 million, and for the minority coproductions, $7 million. Of France's coproduction partners, Italy was the most popular, with 28 French-Italian majority coproductions and 22 minority investments. The roster also included coproductions with Sweden, Russia, Japan, Portugal, Belgium, Greece, Spain, Germany, and Israel. Of the twelve top-grossing French pictures in 1965, eight were coproduced.[9]

Coproduction led to cross-fertilization of talent. Some French stars became more popular in other markets and, for example, played in majority productions in Italy and/or Germany. Similarly, Italian stars such as Marcello Mastroianni, Claudia Cardinale, Sophia Loren, Gina Lollobrigida, and others acted in French-majority pictures. The effect of all this led to a developing European cinema, with the inevitable U.S. participation.

Les Films Ariane

The first production group UA became linked to was Les Films Ariane, headed by Alexandre Mnouchkine and Georges Dancigers. The first entry, *The Train*, was actually initiated in the United States, but later supervised by Ariane. Starring Burt Lancaster and directed by John Frankenheimer, *The Train* was shot in France with a French and German cast and told the story of an elaborate railroad resistance plot to keep a train filled with French art treasures from being shipped to Germany at the end of the war. The picture featured Paul Scofield as the fanatic German colonel; Jeanne Moreau had a small cameo part. Produced at a cost of $6.7 million, *The Train* earned $6 million foreign, but only $3 million in the United States.

Ariane's subsequent ventures utilized New Wave talent, particularly Philippe De Broca and Claude Lelouch. Unusual among New Wave directors, De Broca specialized in comedy. In fact, he has been referred to as the Mack Sennett of the New Wave. After directing a few short documentaries, De Broca broke into features at the age of twenty-six when Claude Chabrol offered to produce *The Love Game* for him. François Truffaut and Jean-Luc Godard assisted De Broca in bringing off a perfect little farce. De Broca's second film, *The Joker* (1961), was picked up by Lopert Films for distribution in the U.S. His third film, *The Five-Day Lover*, clearly established his reputation. All three films featured the brilliant young actor, Jean-Pierre Cassel. With Ariane, De Broca exploited the comic talents of Jean-Paul Belmondo, first in *That Man from Rio* (1964), which teamed Belmondo with Ursula Andress and won the New York Film Critics award for best foreign film, and *Up to His Ears* (1966). Both pictures were French/Italian coproductions. Afterward, De Broca formed his own production company, called Fildebroc, and, with UA's financing, directed *King of Hearts* (1967) starring Alan Bates and Genevieve Bujold, *The Devil by the Tail* (1969) starring Yves Montand and Maria Schell, and *Give Her the Moon* (1970), starring Marthe Keller and Bert Convoy. Although *King of Hearts* is De Broca's most enduring feature, it was his least successful effort financially, grossing initially a mere $580,000 worldwide.

After De Broca turned independent, Ariane linked up with Claude Lelouch. Lelouch's sixth film, *A Man and a Woman* (1966), starring Jean-Louis Trintignant and Anouk Aimee, had scored the first big commercial success among New Wave entries. In addition to capturing the Grand Prix at Cannes, it won two Academy Awards, for best foreign language film and for best original screenplay. UA lost out to Allied Artists for the domestic distribution rights, but picked up the foreign rights. UA would have preferred worldwide rights, but, as it

Brigitte Bardot and Jeanne Moreau in *Viva Maria!* (1965), directed by Louis Malle

turned out, UA got the better deal; the foreign gross amounted to $4 million and the domestic did just over $3 million. Lelouch followed up on a good thing by producing *Live for Life*, a virtual remake of *A Man and a Woman*, but the picture flopped outside France.

Lelouch formed his own production company, Films 13, but remained associated with Ariane and UA for several ventures. Lelouch said he made his commercial pictures to enable him to make weighty ones. Perhaps this explains why he turned independent. In any event, for his debut, *Life, Love, Death* (1969), he treated the theme of capital punishment. A low-budget French-Italian coproduction, the picture grossed only $800,000 foreign and $10,000 in the United States. In the tradition of established New Wave directors, Lelouch supported the first-time efforts of aspiring filmmakers by producing *Les Gauloises Bleues* (1969), written and directed by the noted Parisian critic for *Le Nouvel Observateur*, Michel Cournot. These ventures all proved to be failures and could not even recover their modest negative costs.

The type of commercial product of interest to UA is found in *Viva Maria!* (1966) directed by Louis Malle, which teamed the French screen's two *grande demoiselles*—Brigitte Bardot and Jeanne Moreau. As *Variety* reviewed it, "Big Bertha pic looks geared for big business internationally . . . Here is a film that measures up to its advance publicity. It has the wit, scope and color for both arty and playoff or regular first run chances." Moreau, who became firmly established as a motion picture actress playing the soft-spoken heroine in such art films as Louis Malle's *The Lovers*, Truffaut's *Jules and Jim*, and Antonioni's *La Notte*, became elevated to a boxoffice star. Bardot's character was "an epitome of her sex-kitten shenanigans." Shot on location in Mexico in Panavision, *Viva Maria!* struck "the right note of larger-than-life adventure, uses sex in a delicious, rather than luring or over-exploited manner and deftly pays homage to the Yank films of this kind in its stable, good natured succession of gags, leavened with some frisky but never blue French humor."[10] Produced on a budget of $2.2 million, *Viva Maria!* grossed over $4 million foreign, but only $875,000 domestic.

François Truffaut

François Truffaut was the final New Wave filmmaker financed by UA. The relationship began in 1968 and involved four pictures—*The Bride Wore Black* (1968), *Stolen Kisses* (1969), *Mississippi Mermaid* (1970), and *The Wild Child* (1970). Truffaut, who published his book-length interview with Alfred Hitchcock in 1967, was much influenced by Hitchcock. Two of these films—*The Bride Wore Black* and *Mississippi Mermaid*—are Truffaut's homages to the master and are adapted from William Irish suspense novels. Playing an unusual role of a widow who methodically wipes out a group of men responsible for the death of her husband, Jeanne Moreau was the main promotional angle of *The Bride Wore Black* and accounted for its success, however modest.

Coproduced by Truffaut's Les Films du Carrosse and Dino DeLaurentiis's Cinematografica at a cost of $747,000, *The Bride Wore Black* grossed around $2 million worldwide, $1.75 million of which came from foreign receipts. *Mississippi Mermaid*, which starred Jean-Paul Belmondo and Catherine Deneuve, was produced by Truffaut alone at a cost of $1.6 million. This effort, however, failed, generating a worldwide gross of only $1.3 million.

With *Stolen Kisses* and *The Wild Child*, Truffaut returned to a more personal vision. *Stolen Kisses,* the second of his Antoine Dionel pictures, won the Cannes Grand Prix, the Prix Méliès, and an Oscar nomination for best foreign film of 1968. Although Truffaut improvised much of the shooting, he kept costs to $350,000. Grossing $1.5 million worldwide, *Stolen Kisses* generated a nice profit. *The Wild Child,* which ranks among Truffaut's finest films, was also among his least commercial. The picture describes a young doctor's attempt to civilize a "retarded" boy found living in the woods in southern France in the eighteenth century. Because Truffaut had kept costs low, the worldwide gross of $800,000 turned a modest profit. *Variety* said, "United Artists deserves a bow for backing this unusual, offbeat film made in black and white."

UNITED ARTISTS' ITALIAN PRODUCTIONS

Italy was the least affected in the European market by the advent of television. With the return of prosperity, new, modern, and comfortable theaters were constructed all over the country. Eitel Monaco, the president of ANICA, estimated that the loss of spectators to television did not reach 15 percent. Italian theaters sold 640 million tickets a year during the sixties—more than double the number of movie spectators of Great Britain, Germany, or France. In terms of boxoffice, the Italian market yielded $265 million in 1966, 50 percent higher than the English market and 70 percent higher than those of France and Germany.[11]

Rome became the principal production center in Europe. Film-aid legislation was just one factor. Recognizing that the motion picture business was one of Italy's most vital export industries, the Italian government had instituted a subsidy scheme similar to the French and financed the construction and modernization of production and technical facilities. In 1962, for example, Dino DeLaurentiis opened a huge $11 million facility containing four immense sound stages on a

Clint Eastwood in *For a Few Dollars More* (1965), produced by Alberto Grimaldi and directed by Sergio Leone

750-acre site outside Rome. Here DeLaurentiis produced his $30 million, twelve-hour adaptation of *The Bible,* as well as *The Taming of the Shrew, Barabbas,* and other epics. Rome was within easy reach of the most disparate and colorful backdrops—just like Hollywood—and had a mild climate that allowed a long season of location shooting. It also had trained extras and horses for all those biblical epics.

Although Italy was the biggest market outside the U.S. and although Italian films captured over 60 percent of the boxoffice gross, this was not sufficient to cover spiraling costs and guarantee a margin of profit. The Italians, like the British and French, developed an international policy. But the Italians were more aggressive and vigorously sought out coproductions, coparticipations, and international financing arrangements. By 1966, Italian-other joint ventures outdistanced the purely "national" product; over 50 percent of Italian production was given over to coproduction. Concerning American participation in particular, Monaco said that in the fifteen years after the first MPEA-ANICA agreements in the early fifties, American film companies spent around $320 million in Italy for (a) shooting American films in Rome studios, (b) for the financing of films in Italo-American coparticipation, and (c) for purchase of distribution or television rights to Italian pictures for Italy and abroad.[12]

UA's involvement in Italian production goes back to the fifties. The original impetus was to convert the frozen lire; later on, UA participated marginally in the spear-and-sandal fad. As the Italian market opened up, UA signed coproduction pacts with top-ranked producers starting with Goffredo Lombardo's Titanus Films, and then with Dino DeLaurentiis and Alberto Grimaldi.

Dino DeLaurentiis

Dino DeLaurentiis began his career as a producer in the Neorealist period. Teaming up with Carlo Ponti to form Ponti-DeLaurentiis Productions in 1950, they produced some of the finest Italian films of the decade, including Fellini's *La Strada* (1954) and *Nights of Cabiria* (1957), as well as the epic U.S./Italian coproduction, *War and Peace* (1956). The partnership was dissolved in 1957, when Ponti married Sophia Loren and produced her pictures on his own. DeLaurentiis went on to produce Antonioni's *La Notte* (1960), which Lopert distributed in the United States and such epics as *Barabbas* (1962) and *The Bible* (1966). DeLaurentiis's program for UA consisted of two James Bond imitations and two spaghetti Westerns. The Bond imitations, one of which starred Sean Connery's brother, Neil Connery, flopped. The low-budget pictures did well in Italy, but barely generated any business in the U.S.

Alberto Grimaldi

Alberto Grimaldi's association with UA grew out of the phenomenal success of the Sergio Leone–Clint Eastwood spaghetti Westerns. Leone had imported Eastwood, the lanky raw-boned drover of TV's "Rawhide," to play the Man with No Name in *A Fistful of Dollars.* This picture did not begin the Italian version of the Hollywood genre. Indeed, some twenty-five Westerns had earlier been produced at Rome's Cinecitta studios.[13] It would be more accurate to say that *Fistful* revived a dying fad. The picture took Europe by storm in the fall of 1964, outgrossing such blockbusters as *Mary Poppins, My Fair Lady,* and even *Goldfinger.*[14] *Fistful* was a tripartite production of Harry Columbo's and George Papi's Jolly Films and Spanish and German interests, made at a cost of $400,000. To produce the sequel, *For a Few Dollars More,* Leone turned to Grimaldi for financing.

It was at this point that UA became involved. UA purchased the U.S. distribution rights to *Fistful* and bankrolled *A Few Dollars More* plus a third picture in the series, *The Good, the Bad, and the Ugly.* Production costs ranged from $400,000 for *Fistful* to $972,000 for *The Good, the Bad, and the Ugly.* Designed for a quick kill, the distribution timetable released these "Italo-oaters" as *Variety* called them at four-month intervals, beginning in January 1967. From the beginning, the campaign plugged the series. *Fistful* is the "first motion picture of its kind, it won't be the last," read the ad copy. In introducing Eastwood as "This Is the Man with No Name, he's going to trigger a whole new style of adventure," UA attempted to establish "a James Bond of the West." By May of 1968, *Variety* reported in its international issue that the three pictures ranked "among the half-dozen biggest grossers of the past sixteen months."[15] The first two pictures grossed between $3.5 and $4 million domestic and probably close to three times that much foreign. *The Good, the Bad, and the Ugly* grossed $5.2 million domestic and $5 million foreign. The series by no means matched the Bonds but, by any other measurement, the pictures did spectacularly well given their relatively modest production costs.

On the strength of the "Dollar" series, UA signed Grimaldi to a multiple-picture deal in 1968. Unlike DeLaurentiis and Ponti, Grimaldi was a relative newcomer to the business. After studying law, he formed

Produzioni Europee Associate (PEA) in 1961, which churned out low-budget exploitation and action films, including forty spaghetti Westerns. The UA deal specified "more complex, larger scale pictures," according to a UA press release. To accomplish this, Grimaldi had signed up Federico Fellini, Francesco Rossi, Gillo Pontecorvo, and Elio Petri. Fellini, of course, needs no introduction, but the type of film he made after his Neorealism phase, characterized by *La Dolce Vita,* was what UA and Grimaldi had envisioned. *La Dolce Vita* (1960) had become the all-time foreign language champ in the U.S. market, outstripping *And God Created Woman* (1957). Rossi had directed two semidocumentaries, *Hands over the City* (1963) and *Moment of Truth* (1965). Pontecorvo's most significant work was *The Battle of Algiers* (1965), a documentary reconstruction of the events leading up to the liberation of Algeria. Petri, a Marxist, directed social satires such as *The Assassin* (1961) and the *Tenth Victim* (1965).

Grimaldi's escalation of standards prompted industry observers to speculate that he had "suddenly gone high brow to purge his conscience for a three-year streak of very successful westerns and other action fare . . . and seemed destined to squander his millions on unpredictable film authors." Grimaldi asserted that he did not want to make art, but to make money with art. These directors had broken from the elitist, "art-cinema" market to appeal to a broader, that is, commercial sector, he said. Yet at the same time, they had good festival records. With these talents, his job as producer was "to influence his directorial . . . stable to bridge screen art and spectacle."[16]

To produce Grimaldi's program, UA put up 80 percent of the financing, leaving Grimaldi to come up with the remainder and to furnish the completion bonds. UA also agreed to pay Grimaldi a producer's fee of $100,000 per picture, to supply an overhead allowance, and to split profits fifty-fifty. UA's rationale for putting up only partial financing might have been a result of a concession allowing Grimaldi to retain the Italian distribution rights and the subsidy benefits that went along with them. Dealing with most other American companies, said *Variety,* Grimaldi would have found himself "in a take-it-or-leave-it position," as Italy was one of the strongest markets outside the United States. With UA, the understanding was friendly and comprehensive before and after they signed the deal.[17]

Grimaldi delivered two variants of the Italian Western—*The Mercenary* (1970), directed by Sergio Corbucci and starring Franco Nero, Tony Musante, and Jack Palance, and *Burn!* (1970), directed by Gillo Pontecorvo and starring Marlon Brando. Neither picture improved on the genre nor generated much interest at the boxoffice. The production that redeemed the deal and added lustre to Grimaldi's reputation was *Fellini Satyricon.* Premiering at the Venice Film Festival in September 1969, the picture reaffirmed Fellini's stature as an artistic talent. Fellini had not made a full-length picture since *Juliet of the Spirits,* four years earlier. The festival recognition ameliorated the controversy surrounding Alfredo Bini's version of the *Satyricon,* which was confiscated in Italy on charges of obscenity and corruption of minors, and helped Fellini's picture to pass censorship boards in Italy and the United States. To make certain that Bini's film would not stir up additional trouble, UA simply bought out the picture.

Fellini described his picture as a "science-fiction trip into the past instead of the future." In presenting "Rome. Before Christ. After Fellini." (from an ad line), Fellini debunked the long Hollywood tradition (that had its roots in early Italian cinema) of depicting ancient Rome "in all its marble-pillared splendor and all its battlefield invincibility." [18] Aimed at the youth market, the picture had two youthful protagonists, one of whom, Hiram Keller, who played Ascyltus, was recruited from the Broadway production of *Hair.* Produced at a negative cost of $3 million, *Fellini Satyricon* grossed $8 million outside of Italy.

UA renegotiated its contract with Grimaldi in 1970. For a three-year period, UA had exclusive call on all Grimaldi productions (the previous deal was nonexclusive). Significantly, UA acquired all worldwide distribution rights. Profits were again split fifty-fifty and all projects cross-collateralized. To begin the second phase of the UA-Grimaldi relationship, Grimaldi launched two series—the Sabata Westerns and Pier Paolo Pasolini's Trilogy of Life. *Sabata* (1970), *Adios Sabata* (1971), and *Return of Sabata* (1972) were all directed by Gianfranco Parolini, who referred to himself as Frank Kramer in the credits (à la Sergio Leone's Bob Robertson) and featured as the title character a soldier of fortune dressed in black and brandishing a triple-barrel Derringer. Lee Van Cleef, Clint Eastwood's costar in *For a Few Dollars More* and *The Good, the Bad, and the Ugly,* starred in the first picture. Produced in the $700,000–$900,000 range, the pictures each grossed around $3 million worldwide.

Pasolini's trilogy consisted of *The Decameron* (1970), *The Canterbury Tales* (1970), and *The Arabian Nights* (1974). As Italy's most controversial filmmaker, Pasolini had been decidedly anticommercial in almost everything he created. But with these three films, which were based upon medieval narratives, "Pasolini rejected his small, elite following and its intellectual preoccupations in order to broaden his appeal and to tell for the simple pleasure involved stories that nonetheless retained an ideological dimension that could not be ignored," according to Peter Bondanella.[19] Of the three, only *The Decameron* was released in the United States, it had a limited run that generated a mere $160,000. In Europe, however, the triology did well, grossing $6.5 million, $2 million, and $4.5 million, respectively.

THE *LAST TANGO* MEDIA ORGY

When Grimaldi completed his next picture, *Last Tango in Paris*, UA realized it had something special. The picture had all the ingredients of a commercial art film—an American star, a highly esteemed European director, and an erotic story. UA had approved the project in November 1971 and set a budget of $1.25 million.

Brando's reputation was at a low ebb. He had finished *The Godfather*, but the picture had yet to be released. After his stunning Broadway performance in *A Streetcar Named Desire* in 1947, Brando went

Maria Schneider and Marlon Brando in *Last Tango in Paris* (1973), produced by Alberto Grimaldi and directed by Bernardo Bertolucci

to Hollywood and made six hit pictures in five years, including *The Wild One, On the Waterfront,* and *Julius Caesar.* During the sixties, his career went into decline. Some of his movies were indifferent (*Countess from Hong Kong*) and some disasters (*Mutiny on the Bounty*). To find employment, Brando had joined the migration of has-been American stars to Europe. But by the time *Last Tango* was in the can, Brando had become a megastar once again. By Labor Day 1972— six weeks before the New York Film Festival presentation of *Tango*— *The Godfather* had grossed $75 million domestic and was on its way to becoming the first picture to gross $100 million in this market.[20] For his performance of Don Vito Corleone, Brando was being touted as an Academy Award contender.

To test the waters before release, UA arranged a screening of *Last Tango* on the closing night of the New York Film Festival on October 14, 1972. A single print was flown over (reportedly under security guard) and after the screening was immediately returned to Italy. UA described the distribution strategy as making the picture "tough to see."

As a French/Italian coproduction, *Last Tango* premiered both in Paris and in Rome during the Christmas holiday season. The picture met with no interference from French authorities and played uncut in eight theaters around the city, grossing nearly $100,000 in five days at the boxoffice. In Rome, however, the picture ran into trouble, even though it had been issued a seal by the Italian censor board. The public prosecutor charged the film with "obscene content offensive to public decency, characterized by an exasperating pansexualism for its own end, presented with obsessive self-indulgence, catering to the lowest instincts of the libido, dominated by the idea of stirring unchecked appetites for sexual pleasure, permeated by scurrilous language—with crude, repulsive, naturalistic and even unnatural representation of carnal union, with continued and complacent scenes, descriptions, and exhibitions of masturbation, libidinous acts and lewd nudity—accompanied offscreen by sounds, sighs and shrieks of climax pleasures."[21] The action was initiated on December 21, 1972. A month later, the court indicted Grimaldi, Bertolucci, UA executive Ubaldo Matteuci, and Maria Schneider, the costar, on obscenity charges.

Meanwhile, UA prepared for the New York premiere on February 1, 1973. Instead of submiting *Last Tango* to the Code and Rating Administration, UA took the self-imposed "X" rating. Concerning the "X," UA's president David Picker said, "It's the rating we should get; no one under seventeen should see this film."[22] The Legion of Decency gave it a "C" for "condemned" because the picture presented "a value system contrary to a Christian value system."[23]

UA's strategy in distributing *Tango* must be understood in context. Beginning in 1968 and lasting for five years, sex in motion pictures had been exploited as never before. The MPAA's rating system, which supplanted the outmoded Production Code was one cause; the Warren Court's attitude toward both prior restraint and obscenity prosecutions was another. The industry's rating system, adopted in 1968, provided for the systematic classification of motion pictures. The "X" rating which prohibited young people under age seventeen from attending a movie, gave producers license to treat with a greater range of expression themes and subjects designed specifically for an adult audience. In matters relating to the depiction of sex, the law of obscenity was in "a hopeless mess," according to the MPAA.[24] As Richard Randall explains it, the Supreme Court in the famous *Roth* case held that obscene material is not protected by the First Amendment: "But it added, pointedly, that 'sex and obscenity are not synonymous,' and that the portrayal of sex in art, literature, and scientific works was entitled to the constitutional protection of speech and press. The test to be used in determining whether a particular book, magazine, or film was obscene was 'whether to the average person, applying contemporary community standards, the dominant theme of the material taken as a whole appeals to the prurient interest'." Following the 1957 *Roth* decision, "the Court appeared to add still another measure to be met before obscenity could be legally established—that of 'patent offensiveness.' Thus, in addition to the *Roth* test and the fact that a film, book, or magazine in question must be 'utterly without redeeming social importance,' it must also be 'so offensive as to affront current community standards of decency.' With these tests, much of what was formerly thought to be obscene became constitutionally protected speech. Thus, speculation grew that the only proscribable obscenity left was so-called hard-core pornography." And as Randall concludes, "Exactly what constitutes hard-core pornography has never been established with much precision in the law or even in popular discussion."[25]

A lucrative sex-film industry flourished, as a result, and culminated with the release of *Deep Throat* in 1972, a feature-length hard-core film in 35mm starring Linda Lovelace, which grossed over $3 million in six months playing in seventy theaters across the country. In New York, playing at the New Mature World Theater on West 49th Street, the picture attracted an average of 5,000 people a week, "including celebrities, diplomats, critics, businessmen, women alone and dating couples, few of whom, it might be presumed, would previously have gone to see a film of sexual intercourse, fellatio and cunnilingus."[26]

Variety described this booming theatrical sex business as rivaling "the fare that once made Havana a hot stopover for tourist voyeurs."[27] Although the major film companies regularly released X-rated pictures—sometimes under the aegis of distribution subsidiaries to avoid notoriety—the market was taken over by small independents who had much less to protect in the way of reputation and who were willing to bear vice-squad harassment and expensive legal costs as the price of the considerable hard-core profits. The majors and class independents opted out of sex competition in part because many local newspapers and theater chains refused to advertise or play even the conventional X-rated product, much less their unrated hard-core relatives. By the seventies, the United States had a glut of pornographic filmmakers and performers, a growing number of conventional and 16mm houses devoted exclusively to the sexploitation output, and an ample number of distributors to fill their product needs.

Before continuing with *Last Tango,* it might be instructive to discuss first UA's handling of another X-rated picture, *Midnight Cowboy.* *Midnight Cowboy* was one of the films of 1969 that appealed to the "youth" audience through its journey into American culture and psyche, its depiction of the disintegrating American city, and its attitude toward sex and drugs. A Jerome Hellman–John Schlesinger production, *Midnight Cowboy* was directed by Schlesinger from a novel by James Leo Herlihy and starred Dustin Hoffman in his first role since *The Graduate.* Jon Voight made his screen debut in the title role.

Although *Midnight Cowboy* was released with an "X," this was not the rating given by the Code and Rating Administration. The picture had originally received an "R," but Krim, after consulting with Dr. Aaron Stern, a Columbia University psychiatrist, opted to take the self-applied "X." Stern feared the adverse effect of the "homosexual frame of reference" on youngsters.[28] The producers concurred in the decision. Jerome Hellman said that the project "had been conceived long before the MPAA began its system of film classification . . . and both he and the director would have taken steps to limit the audience for the film to adults had no such system been inaugurated by the time *Cowboy* was released."[29]

Although the "X" originally did not connote "pornography, or obscenity, or violence," in the words of MPAA president Jack Valenti, but merely "unsuitable for viewing by children," the public's perception of the rating was otherwise. Part of the confusion was due to Valenti himself who, for example, told members of the Hollywood Radio and Television Society that X-rated pictures were "trash and garbage, made by people out to exploit."[30]

To counteract these feelings, UA adopted a risky marketing plan. Instead of going wide to capitalize on the so-called sordid elements of the picture, UA did just the opposite. UA booked the picture initially in one theater, the 598-seat Coronet on New York's East Side. And then it scheduled a special screening for critics weeks before the premiere on May 6, 1969. If the critics had panned the picture, UA's campaign would have proven disastrous. But *Cowboy* received rave reviews and, on opening day, a new attendance record was set at the Coronet. While continuing with this "hard to see" policy, UA sent review ads to key exhibitors and the press. The goal, in Gabe Sumner's words, was "to overcome whatever negative gut reactions some people have to the 'X' rating. The most recent and consequently best-remembered publicity is *not* the quality of the film and the acclaim it has gotten, but rather stories in the papers—all of which are justifications for those people who need the excuse to 'punish' the 'X' picture."[31] A second goal of the campaign was to convince the public that *Midnight Cowboy* was not just another youth picture—like *The Graduate* or *Easy Rider*—but stood by itself as a serious work. UA, it seemed, worked at cross purposes, because the company used the following line as a lead to all trade ads and news releases: "Whatever You Hear About Midnight Cowboy Is True."

In July, the picture opened out of town in single theaters in ten major cities and proved that it had "legs" in areas not familiar with New York's 42nd Street and all it implied. Moreover, the picture did not face significant local harassment; the voices of "moral outrage" had been weakened.

Overseas, UA adopted a different approach. Said Gabe Sumner, "Make certain those reviews which call attention to the fact that the film shows the underbelly of American life are heavily underscored and circulated among the press abroad. It's right in here, I feel, that our enormous grosses lie in foreign."[32]

By the time the picture was placed in general release, it had been nominated for seven Academy Awards. And at the awards ceremony, *Midnight Cowboy* became the only X-rated picture to win the best picture Oscar. John Schlesinger, in addition, won for best director as did Waldo Salt for best screenplay. Produced at a cost of $3.2 million, *Midnight Cowboy* grossed $18 million in the U.S. and $8 million foreign.

Cowboy's acclaim was partially responsible for the Code and Rating Administration's decision in early 1970 to broaden the "R" category, raising the age limit from sixteen to seventeen in order to allow more quality films into that category. Earlier, producers reedited many highly respected pictures to secure the less restrictive "R" rating. Some of these pictures were *Bob & Carol & Ted & Alice, Last Summer,* and

If. . . . As *Film Bulletin* said, "the evidence indicates . . . that the MPAA is awarding X ratings solely on the basis of the objectionable nature of individual elements rather than on overall considerations." The magazine pointed out as an example that "when two brief nudity shots were deleted from *If* . . . , the film qualified for the less restrictive 'R'—meaning apparently, that these shots alone, totaling slightly more than 30 seconds of a 111-minute film, were what earned the picture its original 'X,' and not its theme or treatment, which were such as to win it a number of awards and world-wide praise." *Film Bulletin* did not want the "X" equated with prurience only, but the MPAA chose to broaden the "R" rather than wage a campaign to erase the confusion over the "X."[33] In any event, the MPAA rereviewed *Midnight Cowboy* in January 1971 and gave the picture an "R" without requesting a single cut.

In keeping with its "tough to see" policy, UA scheduled *Last Tango* to open in only one theater, the 561-seat Trans-Lux East. Tickets were to be sold on a reserved-seat basis, at the price of $5.00 (which, coincidentally, was the going price for pornographic films). Showings would be limited to two a day and, on weekends, three a day. One week into the run, advance ticket sales topped $100,000.

To get started, UA took out a two-page ad reprinting Kael's 6,000-word rave review in the Sunday *New York Times* on December 24. UA explained that Kael's prestige as a critic "would help pave the way of artistic acceptance of *Tango* despite its much-vaunted sex scenes."[34] The spread in the *Times* cost $32,000, but UA would not have to spend much additional money to promote the picture.

Interest in the picture picked up as a result of UA's preopening screening policy which limited screenings to a select group of critics. It was later charged that UA passed out invitations in exchange for media coverage—an allegation UA denied.[35] Rex Reed, appearing on the "Barry Gray Show" on WMCA radio in New York, panned UA for "declaring war on the critics." UA had barred Rex Reed from all such screenings because of his "negative and offensive" review of *Man of La Mancha,* a review that appeared in Reed's syndicated column in more than 100 newspapers across the country. Reed, however, attended a screening as a guest of an invitee. According to Reed, a man (who turned out to be Gabe Sumner, UA's advertising/publicity vice president) barred the door and shouted "Get out of here. We hate you. You're vicious, petulant, hostile, and an enemy of the film industry."[36] On the Gray show, Reed stated flatly that UA was "trying to deny the public's right to know." UA's version of the incident differed, but Rex's behavior created a cause célèbre, especially because other critics, no-

Academy Award for Best Picture / 1969

Midnight Cowboy

Jon Voight and Sylvia Miles

A Jerome Hellman–John Schlesinger presentation
Starring Dustin Hoffman and Jon Voight
Directed by John Schlesinger
Produced by Jerome Hellman

Other Academy Awards* and nominations
Actor: Jon Voight
Supporting actress: Sylvia Miles
*Direction: John Schlesinger
*Writing *screenplay*: Waldo Salt
Film editing: Hugh A. Robertson

Dustin Hoffman and Jon Voight

tably Gail Rock of *Ms.* magazine, Liz Smith of *Cosmopolitan*, and Gene Shalit of NBC-TV, were also barred from screenings or reportedly had some difficulty obtaining admission.[37]

Thus began what David Denby of the *Atlantic* called a "Media Orgy."[38] A week before the opening, *Time* magazine ran a cover story on the picture featuring a portrait of Brando on the cover, with the banner "Sex and Death in Paris" brandished across the top. Entitled "Self-

Portrait of an Angel and Monster," the story was illustrated with photos of Brando and Schneider making love in the nude, Schneider in the bathtub, and other such scenes. Like a piece out of Irving Wallace, this steamy description introduced the article:

> The man is middle-aged, leonine, ravaged. The girl is young, foxlike, insouciant. Total strangers to each other, they are inspecting an unfurnished Paris apartment that is for rent. Suddenly, the man scoops the girl up in his arms, carries her to the side of the room, then embraces and kisses her hungrily. He tears off her panties and has sex with her while still dressed and standing. The camera rests steadily on them as he thrusts her against the wall and she hitches herself up on him, clinging to his body with her knees. Finally, gasping and groaning, they tumble to the floor, roll apart and lie still.[39]

If that wasn't enough to capture the reader, the article continued: "any moviegoers who are not shocked, titillated, disgusted, fascinated, delighted or angered by this early scene . . . should be patient. There is more to come." Summarizing the plot, the article concluded, "a story of sex as a be-all and end-all. For boldness and brutality, the intimate scenes are unprecedented in feature films. Frontal nudity, four-letter words, masturbation, even sodomy—Bertolucci dwells uncompromisingly on them all with a voyeur's eye, a moralist's savagery, an artist's finesse."[40]

Time asks, "Is the movie basically pornography with an overlay of philosophic angst—and pornography of a peculiarly vulgar type since it features one of the world's most famous actors capering up there on the screen?" Although critics, intellectuals, theologians, and editorial writers would debate the meaning and merits of the picture, *Time* definitely linked *Tango* to the pornography scene:

> There is no escaping the fact that *Tango* bears some kinship to the kinds of movies that play down the street and around the corner from it in the more permissive West European and U.S. cities: the *Bad Barbaras*, the *Highway Hustlers*, the *Deep Throats*. The audacity of *Tango* might not have been possible, either in terms of the law or of audience acceptance, without the example of out-and-out porno flicks.[41]

Another point the *Time* piece pounded home was that Brando and the character of Paul he portrayed were one and the same. Quoting Christian Marquand, the French actor and friend of Brando, *Time* reported, "It is Brando talking about himself, being himself. His relations with his mother, father, children, lovers, friends—all come out in his

performance as Paul." And, finally, concerning the relationship between Brando and Maria Schneider: "Inevitably, there were whispers
that he [Brando] was more than a daddy, that the intense sexual encounters in the film were not all simulated."[42]

Reflecting on the media coverage, Vincent Canby of the *New York
Times* called *Last Tango in Paris* a "Now" film: "It's a movie for the
breathless weekly news magazines that discover, analyze and embalm
trends when the trends are still in nascent states."[43] Not only for news
magazines, but for the *New York Times,* as well, he should have noted
because the paper carried major stories for a month following the
Trans-Lux opening. In an interview appearing in a Sunday edition,
Maria Schneider revealed that she left home at fifteen, had her first
affair at sixteen, earned $4,000 in Bertolucci's film, and had twenty fe-
male lovers and fifty male.[44]

Art vs. pornography dominated the reviews. Charles Champlin of
the *Los Angeles Times* attempted to dispel the notion that *Tango* was
simply legitimated pornography by contrasting *Tango* to *Deep Throat:*
"If *Deep Throat* is a cost of the new freedom, *Last Tango* is a reward,
an examination in recognizable individual terms of some of the most
guarded but universal fears, fantasies, desires and pains in human nature."[45] Robert Hatch of the *Nation* said, "I would not call it pornography at all . . . Bertolucci's concern for his characters is manifestly
much warmer and much more humane than mere preoccupation with
their physical exploits."[46] Stanley Kauffmann of *The New Republic* said
that *Tango* was physically fake "where porno is not." He added that
although "the publicity has carefully suggested that you can actually
see Brando "'do it,' you can't. You never see him fully nude, though
Schneider frisks about in her pelt. (When I told a lecture audience that
they wouldn't see Brando's organ, the ladies groaned.)" "Nonetheless
the *atmosphere* of hard sex is there."[47]

Like a forest fire feeding on itself, the "media orgy" became an event
to be dissected and analyzed. In a cover story of its own appearing one
week after the premiere, *Newsweek* exposed *Tango* as a *succès de scan-
dale.* Entitled "*Tango:* The Hottest Movie," the article described the
Playboy spread "showing Brando and his baby-faced co-star, French
actress Maria Schneider, cavorting in the nude," mentioned talk-show
celebrities who had attended a screening enlivening their "late-night
blather with a titter or two about *Tango*'s torrid sex scenes," and reported that William F. Buckley and Harry Reasoner had denounced
the picture on TV without having seen it. *Newsweek*'s was a more responsible piece of reporting than *Time*'s. The description of the picture
begins with the opening sequence rather than one of the erotic scenes.
Actually, the piece played down the sex angle. "To many viewers,

[Bertolucci's] filming of the sex acts may seem joltingly 'real,' but it has neither the explicit, clinical emotionalessness of blue movies nor the murky prurience of *Portnoy's Complaint*." *Newsweek* also points out that Brando and Paul are similar, but the article focuses most of its attention on Bertolucci—his childhood, his apprenticeship to Pier Pasolini, and his films—*Before the Revolution, The Spider's Stratagem*, and *The Conformist*.[48]

David Denby in his article for the *Atlantic* offered an explanation for *Time*'s treatment of the subject. Apparently, a rumor got out that *Newsweek* had approached Brando for an exclusive interview and planned a cover story around it. *Time* decided to beat them to the draw, since *Newsweek* had won the previous race on *The Godfather*. "But Brando, who loathes interviews to begin with, refused to cooperate because of his distaste for *Time*'s foreign-policy positions." With the star missing, how do you make the story a winner? Denby said that in its eagerness to stir up interest, *Time* offended many of its readers. "Within two weeks the magazine had received over three thousand letters, almost all of them negative and many of them furious, as well as hundreds of subscription cancellations. It was the largest outburst of reader antagonism since the "Is God Dead?" issue a few years ago."[49]

In the midst of the "media orgy," Krim received a call from John Beckett, chairman of UA's parent company, Transamerica Corporation (see chapter 10). Beckett said that as a result of the *Last Tango* publicity, which implied that UA was distributing a pornographic film, Transamerica's insurance agents complained that they would never be able to sell to the family trade again. Krim couldn't believe what he was hearing, he told me, and replied to Beckett, "If we don't distribute the picture, do you have any objection to Bob Benjamin and I and others buying the picture from Transamerica?" Beckett then said, "Do you mind showing *Last Tango* to our directors?" Krim felt certain that this "septuagenarian group" would find the picture offensive, but to his pleasant surprise, as he put it, the board considered *Last Tango* innocuous and persuaded Beckett to let UA release it.[50]

By strictly controlling preopening fanfare and screenings, UA managed to pave the way for a highly disputatious film and at the same time made it "difficult to see." The two effusive cover stories, accompanied by color photos from the film, provided the kind of publicity that quite literally cannot be bought because its greatest value lay in its appearance as "objective" news reporting. Advertising costs had been kept to a minimum; UA would not say how much actually was spent, but David Picker stated that *Tango* had the "lowest ratio of costs to rentals in our history." So extraordinary was *Tango*'s holding power that during its eight-week run at the Trans-Lux East, the picture took in over $350,000 at the boxoffice. More amazing, only two performances during that period failed to sell out (one was during the broadcast of the Academy Awards). The total number of seats left unsold was eighteen.[51]

Overseas, *Tango* broke boxoffice records, playing in roughly forty-five situations located anywhere from Finland to Australia. In Italy, where the picture wended its way through a series of much-publicized obscenity trials, *Tango* racked up a boxoffice gross of close to $10 million by July, setting the record for a six-month period.[52] After an Italian federal court cleared *Tango* of all obscenity charges on February 2, 1973, it opened the way for exhibition of the picture in its original uncut version throughout Italy.[53] In Great Britain, which required only a ten-second cut, *Tango* was a smash hit, breaking records at the Prince Charles Theatre engagement.[54]

New York's Trans-Lux East remained the sole exhibition outlet for *Tango* in the U.S. for nearly eight weeks. Afterward, UA opened *Tango* in a single theater in Los Angeles, the 602-seat Fine Arts. A month later, UA opened the picture in thirty-three key cities nationwide. For this run, UA used a special strategy called "fourwalling," whereby the company in effect rented the theaters and instituted a hard-ticket policy. UA adopted this strategy because it could ill afford to allow the exhibitors to handle such a controversial film alone.

In contrast to the media coverage, UA's campaign muted the eroticism. Posters and marquee displays featured a photo of Brando in profile, reclining in a chair and bathed in the amber tones of Vittorio Storaro's cinematography. The prewritten stories in the pressbook foregrounded the production ("Real Locations, Not Sets Used for Last Tango") and described Grimaldi's production background, Bertolucci's reputation (winning prizes for *The Conformist* and other films), Brando's character ("Most Emotionally Charged Role"), and Schneider's casting ("A Typical Cinderella Story.") The plot synopsis was straightforward, devoid of sensationalism.

Last Tango did not open wide until July, six months after the premiere. UA made 450 prints available for the summer push, which *Variety* saw as possibly "the first major test of whether the X-rated Italo import [would] be found offensive in the nabes."[55] In anticipation, UA instituted a policy whereby local law authorities could request a screening of the film prior to its opening to determine if charges would be pressed. UA wanted to avert legal confrontations and possible seizure of prints. In its limited-run situations, *Tango* had given every indication of setting a new record for UA. The goal was to keep *Tango* on the screens to take advantage of the publicity buildup. Officials in six cities took advantage of the opportunity and passed the picture for exhibition. Some authorities, however, actually declined UA's offer. The sheriff in Essex County, New Jersey, for example, wanted to wait to view the film opening night to determine whether the film could be confiscated under a state antiobscenity law.

When the political complexion of the Supreme Court changed, matters became more complicated. To replace two retiring liberals, Hugo Black and John Marshall Harlan, President Nixon appointed Davis F. Powell, Jr., and William Rehnquist and thus established under Chief Justice Warren Burger one of the most conservative courts since before the New Deal. Pending before the Court was an obscenity case, *Miller v. California*. The decision, handed down in June 1973, established guidelines to determine whether pornography was protected under the First and Fourteenth Amendments. The Court revised the test for obscenity in two important ways, according to Richard Randall:

> First, it modified the requirement that proscribable obscenity must be "utterly without redeeming social importance," saying instead, that "at a minimum, prurient, patently offensive depiction or description of sexual conduct must have serious literary, artistic, political, or scientific value to merit First Amendment protection."
>
> Second, in a declaration that shook the entire film industry, the Court returned to an element in the original *Roth* test that had never been satisfactorily defined, "contemporary community standards," and held that "community" referred not to the national community, as many had supposed and as many civil libertarians had urged, but to the state or local community.[56]

Of particular significance to *Last Tango* was the corollary of establishing the state or locality as the "community" whose standards would prevail—meaning that "the local trial judge or jury would be the agent for making that determination rather than the higher courts." *Last Tango*'s high visibility made it the ideal and perhaps obvious choice for testing the *Miller* decision. To arm itself in this eventuality and to finesse costly and time-consuming legal wrangles, UA kept Louis Nizer on retainer (Nizer had successfully argued the *Carnal Knowledge* case before the Supreme Court).

But as it happened, *Miller* was not used against *Tango*. Although DAs, justices of the peace, and sheriffs took legal action to halt the exhibition of the picture, they cited violation of state obscenity laws. However, most of the actions never reached litigation and for those that did, UA won every case. As *Variety* said, *Tango* "defied prognostications that it would encounter rough sledding in the stix."[57]

Moreover, the expected attack from conservatives proved largely base-less. *Tango* grossed at the boxoffice close to $40 million in the United States and $60 million overseas. UA's take in the form of rentals came to $16 million domestic and $21 million foreign for a grand total of $37 million. Marlon Brando received $250,000 for his acting services plus 10 percent of the distribution gross worldwide in excess of $3 million. Profits were divided as follows: 17 percent to Bertolucci, 42 percent to Grimaldi, and 41 percent to UA.

A confluence of unusual circumstances had made *Last Tango in Paris* a huge commercial success. But this foreign film was a quirk and did not rekindle demand for the art film. The major American film companies stuck to their policy of releasing mostly homegrown product aimed at the youth market. UA occasionally financed a French or Italian picture after 1973, but these pictures were distributed mostly in European markets. Not until 1979 did UA release another foreign picture of consequence in the United States—*La Cage aux Folles*, with Michel Serrault and Ugo Tognazzi, directed by Edouard Molinaro. This immensely popular French hit outgrossed *Last Tango*, inspired a Broadway musical, and spawned a sequel.

Italy remained the largest market for American films during the seventies, but the Hollywood majors as well as Italian producers cut back on quality film production when the oil embargo of 1973 ravaged Italy's economy. Increased production costs, the result of skyrocketing interest rates, inflation, and plummeting boxoffice made it nearly impossible for indigenous pictures to recoup in the national market. Moreover, the standard of Italian film quality dropped sharply in one eighteen-month period as Italy mourned the deaths of Vittorio De Sica, Pietro Germi, Pier Paolo Pasolini, and Luchino Visconti. The Italian film industry was in a perpetual state of crisis during this period. Dominated almost exclusively by Hollywood, the market, in the opinion of ANICA chairman Carmine Cianfarani had lost much of its former vitality—and audiences.[58]

United Artists
A Transamerica Company

C H A P T E R   T E N

Life with a Conglomerate

On Friday the thirteenth, January 1978, UA chairman Arthur B. Krim, UA finance committee chairman Robert S. Benjamin, and UA president and chief executive Eric Pleskow announced their intention to resign. The following Monday, two additional UA executives—William Bernstein, senior vice president in charge of business affairs, and Mike Medavoy, senior vice president in charge of West Coast production—tendered their resignations as well. Virtually the entire top management of UA had quit. The dismantling of what had been the industry's most stable management team "stunned the film trade at every level" and climaxed years of friction between the company and its conglomerate parent, Transamerica Corporation (TA). Krim described UA's merger with TA in 1967 as the "biggest mistake we ever made. But you have to reconstruct the climate of the time. Conglomerates were selling at very high multiples, and when Transamerica approached us, we succumbed to the seduction. And for a while we thought we had made a very wise decision because the value of the Transamerica stock to our stockholders was something like $175 million at the time of the merger and within two years, the value jumped to over $500 million.

And it was caused by United Artists, or it had the appearance of being caused by a glamorous company putting a spotlight on a less glamorous conglomerate. So it worked beautifully until everything changed after 1969."[1]

The American film industry entered the age of conglomerates during the sixties as motion picture companies were either taken over by huge multifaceted corporations, absorbed into burgeoning entertainment conglomerates, or became conglomerates through diversification.[2] The transformation reflected changes in the economy as well as the vagaries of the motion picture market. After World War II, American business underwent a period of consolidation as large numbers of firms merged and as corporate control and decision making became centralized among a relatively few companies. Mergers had been common to business before this time, but growth had proceeded along rational lines. A book publisher, for example, might have merged with another publisher, or a steel company might have acquired an appliance manufacturer. After World War II, however, a new type of corporate entity came into being—the conglomerate, which can be defined as a diversified company with major interests in several unrelated fields.

Gulf & Western Industries, Inc., was an example of the new breed of sixties conglomerate whose growth had been achieved through mergers and acquisitions rather than through internal growth. Merger was its usual business activity.[3] The creation of Charles Bluhdorn in 1958, Gulf & Western started out as a producer of automobile bumpers and then entered such diverse fields as sugar, cigars, zinc, real estate, fertilizer, investment, and, with the acquisition of Paramount in 1966, motion pictures. Gulf & Western expanded at the rate of about one company every six weeks. In 1960, its total assets amounted to $12 million; by 1968, the total approximated $3 billion. One of the hottest stocks on the New York Stock Exchange, Gulf & Western's stock at one point more than doubled in price within three months.

Conglomerates from outside the motion picture industry were attracted to motion picture companies for several reasons: (1) film stocks were undervalued during the sixties as a result of erratic earnings records; (2) studios owned strategically located real estate and other valuable assets such as music publishing houses and theaters in foreign countries; and (3) film libraries had the potential of being exploited for cable and pay television as well as for entirely new forms of exhibition by electronic means.[4]

The Gulf & Western takeover of Paramount in 1966 marked the first such entry of a conglomerate into the motion picture industry. This move was followed by the merger of UA with TA in 1967 and by the

acquisition of Warner Brothers by Kinney Services in 1969. The conglomerization of the film industry from within is discussed later in this
chapter as part of the 1968–72 recession.

Charles Bluhdorn, the Gulf & Western chief, gave the following explanation for the Paramount takeover: "There is a tremendous future
in the leisure field . . . Movies on cassettes for home viewing will open
a tremendous market. Satellites someday will relay first-run movies
into millions of homes. It's a great challenge."[5] Paramount had been a
setup for outside raiders. Its assets included a library of recent movies
that had an ancillary value of more than $200 million. Yet the company
was nearly moribund. Barney Balaban, its president, was in his seventies and the average age of the board of directors was not far behind.
The studio experienced continued production losses, shied away from
telefilm production, and was anything but aggressive in its dealings
with the networks. To remedy the situation, Bluhdorn installed himself
as president, pumped $20 million into the company to open the doors
to independent producers, to move seriously into television production, and to embark on an ambitous acquisitions program. By the time
Paramount released *The Godfather* in 1972, the company was once
again a going concern.

THE MERGER WITH TRANSAMERICA

Unlike Paramount, UA was in excellent shape at the time of its merger
with TA. After dropping into the red for the first time in 1963, UA re-
gained its momentum. In 1964, theatrical rentals reached $150 mil-
lion—up from $90 million the year before—and represented a market
share of nearly 25 percent. Net earnings for 1964 hit $9.2 million,
equal to $4.72 a share, compared to a net loss of $831,000 or $4.20 a
share for 1963. UA's stock by midyear had topped 34, up from the low
of 18 in 1963. Nonetheless, UA stock continued to sell at a low price/
earnings multiple and had failed to achieve the glamour status Krim
felt it deserved.

Although the motion picture business stabilized during the sixties,
Wall Street still classified the industry as high risk. As *Financial World*
said, "Inasmuch as motion picture and television earnings depend so
much on fickle public taste, equities in this field must always be regarded as speculative."[6] Thus, in this era of rapid economic expansion,
motion picture stocks as a group performed sluggishly. And because

these stocks were undervalued, those who had a stake in these companies—executives holding stock as well as public stockholders—saw themselves being shortchanged.

In a move to impress Wall Street in 1966, UA declared a stock split, "which, it was felt, would focus the moneymen's eyes on the company's achievement thereby boosting UA's multiple and, consequently, its price." Because the stubborn financiers wouldn't budge, UA shopped around for acquisitions and mergers that would enhance its growth potential. And in July 1966, UA announced that it would be acquired by Consolidated Foods. The merger was called off, however, as suddenly and silently as it began. "It was as simple as this," said Benjamin, "the reaction from a great many of our stockholders was bad; they wanted us to go on by ourselves, the way we were going. They thought our idea of diversification was a good one, but they didn't like this marriage at this price."[7]

After breaking off the discussion with Consolidated, UA immediately sat down with TA. Formed in 1928 as a corporate umbrella for the expanding financial enterprises of the Bank of America, TA had metamorphosed into a diversified financial service organization. With assets of $2.4 billion, TA owned the Occidental Life Insurance Company of California, the nation's ninth-largest life insurance firm, Pacific Financial Corporation, the consumer loan giant, and over twenty-five other related firms. The architect of TA's expansion was John R. Beckett, a former securities analyst, who became president in 1960 at age forty-two.

Beckett's strategy had originally been to acquire only those companies that could work in harmony with one another. Now he wanted to transform TA into a "multi-service" organization. Beckett based the rationale "on a few simple things": "One, the population is getting richer; two, as a man becomes more affluent he spends a greater amount of his money on services rather than goods. Three, most everyone has more leisure time and can look forward to still more of it in the next few years. And, four, the population is showing a greater number of young people while at the other end the older person is retiring earlier and living longer."[8]

UA and TA reached an agreement in principle in November 1966 and UA's stock jumped 1½ points in anticipation of the merger. The deal was consummated on April 11, 1967. The tender offer to UA stockholders contained the option of either a swap of common stock one-for-one or a swap of one UA common for a combination of fractional shares of TA common and preferred. The merger was a "pooling of interest"

John R. Beckett

transaction that qualified as a tax-free exchange for UA stockholders. On the day of the merger, UA's stock hit 36¾, up 8½ points, while TA stock rose a similar amount to 38.

Although UA became a wholly owned subsidiary of TA, it continued to operate with complete autonomy. TA considered UA's policy of creative freedom for independent producers "the most important contribution" in bringing about a renaissance in the motion picture business and UA's management "the best in the industry."[9] To effect the merger, Benjamin and Krim and ten other officers of the company agreed to remain with UA a minimum of five years. To link parent and subsidiary, Krim and Benjamin joined TA's board and Beckett and another TA officer joined UA's board. After the merger, Krim and Benjamin received the same annual salary of $52,000.

UA's senior management now consisted of Arnold M. Picker, former vice president in charge of foreign distribution, who had moved up to chairman of the executive committee in 1961, and his nephew, David Picker, head of UA's music operations, who was being groomed for the top post in the company. Max E. Youngstein, a vice president and an original partner in the group, retired from the company in 1961.

Krim and Benjamin as joint tenants of the management syndicate had owned close to 800,000 shares or 18 percent of UA. After the merger, members of the syndicate could vote their stock individually. The exchange of stock made Krim and Benjamin the largest TA shareholders, owning 101,674 and 84,267 shares of TA common, respectively, in addition to 25,827 and 22,331 shares of TA preferred, respectively. Krim and Benjamin and other key UA executives had thus been able to liquidate their large holdings in UA without depressing the market value of the stock.

Transamerica—A Multi-Market Corporation

After acquiring UA, TA expanded further into leisure time by picking up Liberty Records, one of the largest independent producers and distributors of records in the business; Trans International Airlines, the second largest supplemental air carrier in the nation; and Budget Rent-A-Car, ranked number four. By the end of the sixties, TA's leisure-time subsidiaries accounted for about 30 percent of total profits.[10]

By any yardstick, TA had become one of the biggest companies on the Big Board, ranking in size between Shell Oil and Eastman Kodak, yet it suffered an identity crisis. The public simply did not know Transamerica, and the few people who had heard of it thought it was a bank holding company or an airline. To increase visibility, TA launched an extensive institutional advertising campaign. Double-page spreads in *Time,* illustrated with candid shots of Beckett, stressed "the new breed of business" TA represented. It was in *Time* that TA introduced its new corporate logo—a branching tree meant to look like a stylized "T." TA claimed the campaign transformed Transamerica from a company nobody ever heard of to one that could be identified by the single letter "T."

TA received unwanted publicity when it unveiled plans in 1968 for a new world headquarters in San Francisco. An ultramodern pyramidal building designed by William L. Pereira, it departed radically in style from the old headquarters, a three-story, turn-of-the-century structure, replete with false columns and friezes. The plans were greeted by outrage from ecologists, citizen groups, and critics all across the country. Wolf von Eckardt of the *Washington Post* called it "an abomination, an irresponsible piece of advertising that rapes the San Francisco skyline." [11] After the completion of the building in late 1972, the criticism had yet to die down. One civic leader said the building belonged in Los Angeles, "perhaps the most insulting put-down a San Franciscan can make." [12] Although Beckett insisted the Pyramid was not built to establish an identity for the company, the building was featured in a new series of advertisements which read, "We're the people in the Pyramid."

As chief architect of TA's growth, Beckett had to justify the ways of his company to the financial world. Perhaps the fullest statement of his business philosophy was spelled out in a lecture he presented to a seminar for financial analysts. Entitled "The Case for the Multi-Market Company," the lecture contained the tune that Beckett sang throughout the seventies. [13] Beckett argued that the multi-market company was the most appropriate structure for an era of rapid technological and social change. However, he was quick to differentiate TA from the archetypical conglomerate, such as Gulf & Western. Beckett also emphasized that TA had grown out of its holding company stage. A holding company, he said, implied a passive structure "often contrived mainly for legal or investment reasons, with the subsidiaries creating the character of the parent company." Transamerica was a multi-market company containing "*diversified but interrelated interests* operating under a plan of logical development," similar to the way General Electric or Union Carbide operated in the industrial world.

Beckett then described TA's structure and operations. Headquartered in San Francisco, TA consisted of a corporate staff of fifty. TA did not control the subsidiaries per se: "Transamerica believed in a strong centralization of policy and staff functions and equally in a decentrali-

Transamerica's new world headquarters designed by William L. Pereira

zation of day-to-day operations." A company joining TA operated in much the same way as before. "We want all our subsidiary managers to feel like they are entrepreneurs and act accordingly," said Beckett.[14]

The function of the corporate staff, according to Beckett, was to assimilate new information. The subsidiaries "provided information inputs as a by-product of their ongoing business," which the corporate staff, free from day-to-day operating responsibility, could relate to the corporate plan. Thus, the multi-market company could be considered "listening posts"—a constantly scanning "radar screen" across a broad spectrum of areas "with a central group to lend direction to the search and interrelate this knowledge as it is received." [15]

This interrelationship was synergistic, according to Beckett. The term "synergy" was bandied about by the new breed of corporate manager to describe the beneficial side effects of conglomerization. Beckett defined synergy as "the art of making two and two equal five." "We believe in the synergistic effects of running more than one business. By that I mean the sales effect, the cost control effect, the cost spreading effect. And as a result, we can run these businesses and make more money from them than can be done running them individually. What we're trying to do is get more utilization out of the same set of executives and the same computers and very much the same overhead and payroll. We think this is the way modern business is going." [16]

Whether all this was more than rhetoric remained to be seen. But so far, the beneficent business climate of the sixties had yet to prove otherwise. TA's stock continued to climb, hitting a high of 87½ in 1968, after which it split two for one. [17]

A CONVULSION IN THE FILM INDUSTRY

Once the merger between UA and TA had been completed, Krim and Benjamin decided to retire from UA's day-to-day management and pursue personal interests. Taking up the reins was David V. Picker, age thirty-eight, who was named president of UA in June 1969. Krim and Benjamin's semiretirement fit into TA's policy of putting the accent on youth. John Beckett, who had moved up to TA chairman in late 1968 and had appointed Edward L. Scarff, a thirty-nine-year-old former mutual-fund executive, as his replacement in the president and chief executive officer slots, articulated the policy. "Young men, or at least men young in outlook," Beckett told TA's top executives, "create change and are willing to try new things. Young men see more clearly than most the major changes that are taking place in the existing social structure and can sense opportunities in such changes." Beckett contrasted his view to board chairmen and presidents who have become the "senior statesmen" of their businesses: "These 'senior statesmen' attend conventions, they become important people in town and are on all the 'do-gooder' lists. The government asks them to act as consul-

United Artists' management team in 1969: (l. to r.) Arthur B. Krim, Arnold M. Picker, Robert S. Benjamin, and David V. Picker

tants and they are often asked to speak at gatherings of various kinds. I hope this is something we can avoid. As far as I know, few ideas about new or better ways to make money are discussed at conventions."[18]

Beckett no doubt considered Krim and Benjamin to be "do gooders." Krim was a long-time board member of the Weizmann Institute, finance director of the Democratic party, and a trusted counselor to both Presidents John F. Kennedy and Lyndon B. Johnson. After going on leave from UA, Krim went to Washington to serve as special consultant to Johnson. In his book on the Johnson era, Jack Valenti, a former presidential aide, wrote that "no man in the country had the total confidence of the president to the degree of intimacy and respect as did Arthur Krim. The president offered him various cabinet posts, as well as ambassador to the United Nations. Krim turned them all down. He preferred to serve the president without an official position and Johnson turned to him for advice across the board—foreign policy and political strategy."[19] No ordinary movie mogul he; Krim later served as chairman of the board of trustees of Columbia University, chairman of the Policy Committee of the Democratic party, and member of President Jimmy Carter's General Advisory Committee, which advised the president on matters of arms control. In recognition of such service, the Academy of Motion Picture Arts and Sciences conferred on Krim the Jean Hersholt Humanitarian Award in 1974.

Benjamin had worked doggedly to forge the prestigious United Nations Association and had been its chairman since 1964. He had been appointed by President Johnson as delegate and ambassador to the Twenty-Second General Assembly of the United Nations in 1967 to serve under Ambassador Arthur J. Goldberg. Benjamin was a trustee of Brandeis University. After Benjamin went on leave from UA, President Johnson appointed him a director of the Corporation for Public Broadcasting (CPB). Benjamin later served as chairman of the board of CPB and the Brandeis trustees. This is only a partial list of Benjamin's outside political and philanthropic interests. In recognition of his service, the Academy posthumously conferred on Benjamin the Jean Hersholt Humanitarian Award in 1980.

David Picker, UA's new president, represented the third generation of a family prominent in the motion picture business. Named after his grandfather, a vice president of Loew's, Inc., Picker was the son of Eugene Picker, former president of Loew's Theatres and currently president of Trans-Lux Entertainment. Dartmouth-educated, David Picker joined UA in 1956. Moving up the corporate ladder, he served as executive assistant to Max E. Youngstein, vice president of UA Records, and then first vice president in charge of production. His appointment as president in June 1969 was the latest of a series of moves by the industry to fill top positions with young executives who supposedly were more in tune with the times. At Paramount, Charles Bluhdorn had appointed thirty-six-year-old Robert Evans head of production. At Twentieth Century–Fox, Darryl Zanuck had put his son, Richard Zanuck, at age twenty-seven, in charge of the studio operation.

It wasn't until late in 1969 that things began to sour. In December 1969, Krim discovered that UA's motion picture inventory had ballooned enormously, with pictures in development that were alarmingly out of sync with public taste. Appalled both by the discovery itself and also by TA's failure to question the extent of UA's commitments, Krim dropped the bombshell on Beckett and said, "'I want your blessing to return to the company and take control.' Beckett said, 'of course, of course'."[20] (Beckett, meanwhile, was back at the helm at TA. As *Busi-*

ness Week put it, Scarff was "apparently a bit too dynamic to suit either Beckett or the subsidiaries" and resigned after a year in office.)[21]

Evaluating the inventory, Krim determined that thirty-five films placed in production in late 1968 or 1969, costing a total of $80 million, would lose in the neighborhood of $50 million. "The simplest and the most accurate way of explaining what happened," said Krim, "was that the policy of product selection completely changed from emphasis on the risk of loss to emphasis on the prospect of profit. In other words, instead of playing red or black on the roulette table, playing a number in the hopes of hitting the jackpot."[22] Krim had to satisfy UA's auditors and the Securities Exchange Commission (SEC) that the write-off on the unreleased pictures was not an accounting ploy to create future profits. A sample of his evaluations provides the specifics:

Leo the Last—This director [John Boorman] had a very special reputation with campus film groups and youth oriented filmmakers in the United States and the United Kingdom. He was considered one of the voices of the new wave of picture making—daring, innovative, imaginative. This is the type of director motion picture companies were gravitating to in 1969 when it appeared that all traditional picture making was outmoded and audiences—mainly youthful—were ready to support only the off beat. By the time the picture was made, this premise had been proven erroneous. The actual audience for this type of film could justify a cost of only a few hundred thousand dollars, if that much—not the substantial budget allocated here, which in turn was exceeded by hundreds of thousands of dollars through the director's excessive preoccupation with his own ideas of "perfection." The picture came out much too long and slow but this director—as part of his unrealistic approach to picture making—refused to make necessary cuts. By contract he could not be overruled.

Ned Kelly—When we programmed this picture we thought Mick Jagger would be a big personality with the younger audience. Unfortunately, his other film, *Performance*, came out just before *Ned Kelly* and failed. We have every belief that *Ned Kelly* will not do well either. In addition, Tony Richardson, the filmmaker, handled the material in a very slow-paced manner and we have not been able to persuade him to make the cuts necessary to improve the film. This is again a case of programming a film in a time of much greater optimism about the size of the so-called youth oriented audience—particularly starring one of the new folk heroes.

The Landlord—What was expected to be provocative material to the new modern film audience of 1968–1969 in depicting black and white relationships in an urban setting, emerged as a film which we felt would be of limited interest to the audience of 1970—an audience more and more sated with films of this genre. This is still a type of film we intend to continue to make but at one-quarter the cost. Unfortunately, at the time this film was programmed, unrealistic optimism about the potential audience for this type film prevailed.

Cannon for Cordoba—In 1970 there was a marked change in global acceptance of western and adventure film. The results of films of other companies—for instance *McKenna's Gold, Murphy's War, Last Valley*—as well as our own—*Play Dirty, Bridge at Remagen*—indicated a need for substantial downward revision in assessing proper budget costs for pictures in this category—even with the so-called big name action stars. This picture falls in that category. If programmed today, it would be considered acceptable only if it could be made at half its cost.

Cold Turkey—An old commitment to Dick Van Dyke, and what seemed to be a good idea for the American market, became an overpriced film with a has-been personality by the time of its release. Albeit funny, the picture is way overpriced for its value, which is strictly for the American market—mainly for mid America. The producer and director went over a million dollars over budget on the film to deliver a minor American comedy with no overseas value. This film would be programmed today only if it could be made at one-half the cost.[23]

A revolution in movie audiences had occurred. As Charles Champlin described it, "The movies entered the sixties as a mass family entertainment medium in trouble and they leave them as a mass but minority art-form, important and newly influential, wildly divergent and addressed to many divergent audiences."[24] According to Krim, "an evaluation of this change could not occur until 1970." And even in 1970, he said, "the accumulation of evidence first began to be ominous, and, in management's opinion, incontrovertible, only as the year went on and approached its close." By then, films slated for release in late 1970 and 1971 were either too far along in production to be abandoned or had been completed—"at costs unrelated to the new reduced expectations in the marketplace."[25]

UA's backlog created this dilemma: prudence dictated an orderly playoff of the pictures to maximize boxoffice return, but such a strategy would create a cash-flow problem—there would be a long time lag until money became available for future production. Compounding the problem, UA suffered a pretax operating loss of $35 million—in addition to the film inventory write-down—as a result of a 20 percent drop in gross revenues from $269 million in 1969 to $212 million in 1970. UA had no choice but to take the operating loss, but the inventory write-down could have been handled by spreading the amount over several years as the problem pictures were released. This would have spared UA the indignity of taking a combined pretax loss of $85 million, which set a new industry record. But the company took this stiff, albeit one-time, medicine with the approval of its auditor based on the evaluations prepared by the SEC and with the knowledge that other motion picture companies had endured similar misfortunes. MGM, for example took a pretax loss in 1969 of $72 million, setting the former industry record. That same year, Fox was close behind with a pretax loss of $65 million.[26] However, the clincher for the decision was the discovery that TA qualified for a special credit on its tax return resulting from a change in insurance accounting procedures. This credit offset UA's write-down, for all practical purposes, so that the effect of UA's "unusual" charge on TA's balance sheet was nil. Nonetheless, Krim said of the write-down that "Beckett never let us live it down."[27]

The industry had undergone a convulsion. A. H. Howe, a Bank of America executive in charge of production financing, asserted that conditions could be matched "in seriousness, dislocation and change by only two events in film history, the sound revolution of 1930 and the television upheaval of the 1950s."[28] Howe's analysis revealed that as of 1969, the seven majors had already lost $200 million. This state of affairs had its roots in the boom years of the sixties. As audiences returned to the theaters, lured by the James Bond pictures, *The Sound of Music*, and other blockbusters, prices at the boxoffice rose and the movie business entered a healthy period. According to industry analyst David Londoner, "Three developments arising from that profitability and the complacency it brought were to have dire consequences by the end of the decade."[29]

First was the acceptance of the big-budget philosophy. At Twentieth Century–Fox, the production policy under Darryl Zanuck had been to produce one key picture each season to keep the company in the black.

It started with *The Longest Day*, a smash hit that reversed the company's fortunes after the *Cleopatra* fiasco. Zanuck thereupon launched three pictures in 1965–67: *The Sound of Music, The Agony and the Ecstasy,* and *The Bible. The Sound of Music* set the pace. Although it cost a hefty $10 million, the picture grossed over $100 million within two years. "Other studios quickly embraced the larger risks of high cost films," said Londoner, "and by 1968 six of the eight majors were contentedly producing blockbuster movies."[30]

Second was the entry of several new film companies into the market, which altered the supply/demand relationships in the industry. Three instant majors sprang forth in the late sixties—CBS, ABC, and National General—boosting the number of principal suppliers to eleven. Each produced around ten films per year. With these new entries came increased bidding for talent and a decline in returns per film as output increased.

"Third was the appetite that television was developing for feature films and the rose-colored glasses through which the film industry viewed this market," said Londoner.[31] Television had become a regular secondary market for theatrical films. Conventional theatrical exhibition had once been considered the primary source of revenues, with anything from TV just gravy. But as relations between the two industries normalized, television income became expected and planned for. Few new film projects were put into production without assessing their potential on TV, and a TV sale was used as collateral in obtaining financing.

Everything seemed to come apart by the end of 1968. Confronted with seven movie nights a week during the 1968–69 season, audiences became selective and ratings dropped. Some movies audiences considered too racy and too violent. Another blow to the industry was that by then, the networks had sufficient product to get them through 1972 and stopped bidding on theatrical films. On the theatrical side, the new entrants had created a glut in the market. There was more than enough product to meet the needs of exhibitors, which meant that the big-budget inventories worked their way through the distribution system at staggering losses. Hollywood nearly collapsed. ABC, CBS, and National General ultimately lost collectively over $80 million and dropped out of the motion picture business. Fox and Columbia became potential candidates for receivership.

Under pressure from the banks, Hollywood entered a period of retrenchment that lasted until 1972. MGM, for example, disposed of all assets that were economically unproductive. Kirk Kerkorian, the new owner of the company, hired James Aubrey, Jr., the controversial former president of CBS-TV, to use draconian methods to revive the ailing lion. Kerkorian apparently wanted to create a low-overhead company like UA. After selling Trans International Airlines to TA in 1968, Kerkorian joined the TA board. According to Irwin Ross, who wrote an in-depth profile on Kerkorian for *Fortune,* Kerkorian observed the operations of studioless UA and wondered why Metro could not do as well.[32] Aubrey auctioned off the studio's old props, sets, and wardrobe, sold the backlot, put the Borehamwood studio in England on the block, and moved the company's world headquarters from the old Loew's building in New York to the Irving Thalberg building on the MGM lot in Culver City. In addition, Aubrey canceled $44 million worth of dubious production deals and consolidated the MGM distribution network. As a result, Aubrey turned a $35 million deficit into a $9 million profit in 1971.

Columbia and Warner Brothers merged their land and other physical assets and jointly operated the old Warner studio, now renamed the Burbank Studios. To reduce operating costs, personnel reductions were made in the executive, production, technical, and clerical departments. Columbia and Warner would not only share studio space, but also rent the facilities to third-party motion picture and television production companies—a practice also followed by Paramount, MGM, and Fox. To reduce distribution overhead, Hollywood closed the doors on its exchanges and consolidated activity overseas. For example, MCA and Paramount formed Cinema International Corporation in 1970 to distribute theatrical films of both companies outside the domestic market. The most radical change from the old ways involved production policy. Companies both cut back on production and placed ceilings on budgets, ranging from $1.5 million to $3 million. For the time being, anyway, the era of the blockbuster had ended.

Of the majors, only Disney and MCA escaped unscathed. Walt Disney Productions in 1969 had become a broad-based entertainment-recreation company.[33] Films accounted for only about one-third of Disney's business. About half of the company's revenues and a whopping 60 percent of profits came from Disneyland. The balance came from other entertainment activities, such as television, music and records, publications, and character merchandising—e.g., Mickey Mouse watches. From 1966, the year Walt Disney died, to 1969, revenues jumped from $117 million to over $148 million. In the same period, net income rose from $12 million to $16 million. By October 1969, Disney's stock had broken 100, an all-time high for the company. Disney had demonstrated that diversification could stabilize the traditionally precarious motion picture business.

MCA's net income plummeted from $13.5 million in 1968 to $2.5 million in 1969, the result of its moviemaking arm, Universal Pictures. But MCA kept its head above water by combining the historically volatile movie business with its own remarkably stable TV operations. Television production and distribution accounted for over 40 percent of MCA's revenue; motion pictures accounted for only around 30 percent. The remainder of MCA's revenues came from music, records, and other sources, such as Columbia Savings and Loan in Colorado and Spencer Gifts, a novelty outlet and mail-order operation. The acquisition of these latter two firms marked MCA's diversification efforts outside the entertainment field, in a further attempt to stabilize operations.

TRANSAMERICA CLAMPS DOWN

The recession had a catastrophic effect on motion pictures stocks and the hardest hit were the conglomerates. Prompted in part by tight money and a U.S. Senate investigation of conglomerate merger practices, *Variety*'s group of amusement conglomerates declined by 55 percent in 1969, compared to a 12.5 percent rise in 1968: "With their primary acquisition tool blunted (high PE ratio), conglomerates have been forced out of the acquisition business and now must prove that they can grow internally." [34]

TA's earnings had grown for eight successive years during the sixties. Beginning in 1969, however, the conglomerate saw the price of its stock drop $32—from $44 to $12—by the end of 1970. Wall Street's reevaluation of conglomerates started the decline in 1969 and UA's loss in 1970 shoved it over the brink. TA's consolidated profits dropped from $87 million in 1969 to $43 million in 1970; UA's losses in 1970 accounted for nearly 80 percent of the differential.

Other companies in the TA family also experienced serious financial trouble. Liberty Records lost $5.1 million in 1970 and $3.8 million in 1971. And Transamerica Computer, facing stiff competition from IBM in the form of price cuts, lost $5 million in 1971 and $4.3 million in 1972. With the red ink running, Beckett took drastic action. After easing out several executives at TA headquarters, Beckett restructed the company by organizing the subsidiaries into four operating groups, each under a group vice president. "Now that times are tough," Beckett said, "there is greater need than ever for *organization* within a company structure . . . *Cooperation* is mandatory . . . No subsidiary is an island unto itself, particularly those companies in distress, financial or otherwise." [35]

In addition to instituting a strict chain of command in each group, leading to the group vice president, Beckett issued a 150-page "Management Guide" containing an organizational chart "so that people know whom they report to and who reports to them"; written job descriptions "so that employees know what they are to do and what is expected of them"; a policy manual "so that major policy decisions are known to everyone;" and written office routines, so that, among other things, a time could be set aside each week "for discussion of progress in respective departments."[36]

To keep the conglomerate on course, Beckett organized an annual ritual called "Opportunity Planning." At the end of each year, the subsidiaries were supposed to come up with a list of potential new ventures. Beckett wanted nothing of gut feelings and hunches; he wanted hard data. "It is only by quantifying decisions that we can weigh the arguments for and against the decision," he said.[37]

In the new scheme, UA had to report to James R. Harvey, age thirty-eight, group vice president for leisure services. There was a quirk in this arrangement. Krim and Benjamin owned substantial blocks of TA stock and were members of the board of directors, yet in the new chain of command, they were outranked by a man who had hardly any equity interest in the company and who did not sit on the board.

TA's hands-off policy had abruptly changed. As part of TA's belt tightening, UA fired 300 employees, closed overseas offices, and placed a cap of $2 million on production budgets. Beckett also insisted on regular meetings with UA to review financing commitments, the status of current pictures, revenue forecasts, and so on.

Moreover, Beckett installed a policeman to keep tabs on the company. Ostensibly part of a move by TA to computerize UA's accounting operations, Beckett appointed Joseph L. Bos vice president for finance at UA in March 1972. Bos had previously worked for another TA subsidiary, DeLaval, a turbine manufacturer. At UA, Bos outranked the company's three financial vice presidents. According to Krim, Bos "knew as little about United Artists when he left as when he came in . . . Bos was absolutely unaware of what was going on right in front of him. Finally, he decided to play golf most of the time. That was the way the policeman operated. He would rubber stamp everything that was done, but then would try to avoid taking responsibility if something was criticized."[38]

TA never questioned UA's picture choices, but it did try to get the company to adopt a more scientific process. Beckett suggested that an in-house analyst or statistician examine UA's successful pictures and "try to determine the key features of each and then develop a system of assigning weights to these different features. New pictures could then be screened against these values to help assure their success or mini-mize the likelihood of failure." [39] In addition, Beckett thought UA should hire a sociologist, psychologist, or an anthropologist to appraise trends in society that shape the tastes of the moviegoing public.

THE MARRIAGE GOES SOUR

UA's turnaround took until 1974. Going into 1970, the inventory of pic-tures stood at $300 million. By the end of 1973, the investment had been sharply reduced to around $125 million, "a level somewhat higher than current average industry numbers, but well out of deep water," said *Variety*.[40] In the interim, UA produced about 100 features at an average cost of around $1.4 million. The results of these pictures offset the losses incurred in 1970 and even earned a profit of $31 million after taxes. As Krim told TA's board, "I put this achievement on a par with the job in 1951 of taking a bankrupt company and building it to the point where Transamerica paid some ten million shares of stock to acquire it."

By now the Transamerica–United Artists marriage had gone sour. UA had had enough of TA and wanted out. Krim spelled out the rea-sons in a detailed report to the TA board of directors in December 1973. Contrary to TA flack, the turnaround resulted exclusively from two factors "managed under my personal direction," said Krim: (1) "A return to picture selection under principles established by us in 1951 and temporarily by-passed in 1968 and 1969; and (2) the management of a sophisticated and careful program of network and TV syndication packages, here and abroad, calculated to reduce inventories to a point of unquestionable viability." [41]

In public statements and at meetings with security analysts, TA claimed the turnaround resulted from "new management techniques." As Krim put it, "This left us baffled" when UA was asked to explain what these techniques were. "The reference to a model computer which predicts results and gives management an important decision making tool has caused us nothing but further embarrassment when asked what is meant. Substantial sums have been spent on a computer model: this belief that any meaningful picture decision can be based on use of the computer model or of demographics is unacceptable to the nth degree. I don't quarrel with the applicability to any other busi-ness of TA. I just don't know. But, when an analyst asks us what is this TA device that has turned UA around, we really have egg on our face.

Either we would have to say TA doesn't know what it is talking about—which we do not do—or we have to double talk our way out of the question."[42]

Beckett never backed off from his opinion that by installing computers, TA "put in one of the finest management systems in the movie business." Krim didn't need it, Beckett said later, because "he had all the figures in his head. But it helped us—and his staff as well." "That I kept everything in my head is ridiculous," responded Krim. "This is no candy store. I devised systems for tracking pictures, costs, receipts, residuals, and distribution rates, and put them into charts. And the computer models were never really used. They are a joke around here. Transamerica confused getting information which they could understand with a change in the basic method of doing business."[43]

Krim asserted that UA's financial health was attained "first and foremost by assessing each project from the point of view of avoiding unacceptable risks of loss—which in turn, meant assessing potential audiences for each type of picture, whether in this country or abroad." Although projects were generated by production executives under David Picker and then under Eric Pleskow, "I exercised the right of final veto at all times . . . No project was allowed to go forward until I had personally approved it, based on my reading of most of the scripts, an analysis in each case of the creative elements, budgets, and talent terms."[44]

In going back to basic principles, Krim had stemmed the losses; the profits came by luck of the draw. UA was not a free agent. It could only select from the projects which gelled, either through the company's initiative or that of independent producers. "We cannot decree that we want projects of such and such a nature and press a button to have them made," said Krim. UA chose the best of the alternatives presented to it. "If the proof is in the pudding, our choices were sound—and, in fact, outstanding. I can say with some satisfaction that I do not know of a single picture in this period which Bob and I vetoed that became a hit for any other company. The converse is not the case. Many pictures rejected by us failed when made elsewhere."[45]

Concerning the sales to network television, Krim said that he personally negotiated the deals. His efforts, plus that of UA's TV department in the syndication market, resulted in combined sales of $125 million over three years. "Because of the nature of the inventory program," said Krim, "the UA share of practically all of these TV revenues—approximately $75 million—was applied to inventory reduction."[46]

TA, for its part, created an obstacle course. By putting a group vice president over UA, UA lost its visibility. Said Krim, "In public statements, brochures, annual reports and the like, care is taken to avoid ever to mention the name of any UA executive—only that of TA executives, who are known in the trade to be inexperienced in this field. We are constantly constrained to reiterate our autonomy to the creative talents that are our stock in trade, to insure them that we, and not some remote non-picture executive, are in charge of picture selection, to assure them that we are not stressing only 'family films' as is at times suggested, that we are not abandoning *Tango,* that we are still the company that lives by broad variety, that those of us who understand them and they us are still making the decisions."[47]

Other obstacles concerned trivial matters such as salaries, stock options, location of offices, retirement benefits, and so forth. These matters involved "relatively small amounts and should have been left exclusively to management on the spot. But because of Transamerica's management guidelines, we are always invariably overruled on what we consider to be an arbitrary basis from afar." Amplifying this point, Krim later told me, "We could invest $10 million to $15 million in a picture, but a $10,000 increase to an executive would have to go through a computer. Salary levels in the motion picture business are normally much higher than in any other business and bonus compensation is usually far in excess of anything that is done in most other businesses. I don't know of any business where there is such a direct relationship between what an individual management does in choice of film and the profits that are realized, and therefore there is a real pressure to adequately compensate these people in good times. The business between those who make picture choices and creative talent is frequently conducted on a very personal basis. When a picture grosses many millions, those responsible for the relationship feel entitled to some piece of the pie because they're making multi-millionaires out of others at the same time they themselves are just earning a salary. So this is the pressure point at which the conglomerate is usually in on a confrontation course with the management of a picture unit within the conglomerate."[48]

As major stockholders in TA, Krim and Benjamin suffered huge losses on paper. Yet, as TA was structured, they were powerless to reverse the situation. TA consisted of over twenty-five companies. Since 50 percent of TA's earnings came from insurance, UA, which accounted for 15 percent of TA's earnings, had little, if any, impact on the parent company's stock. In other words, UA's impressive performance during the three years after the 1970 debacle did nothing to offset the debilitating effects of inflation and high interest rates that kept TA's stock as of June 1974 at 80 percent of its all-time high in 1968.[49] Thus, stock options were ineffective. Krim later told *Fortune*, "All my executives are . . . bait for other companies."[50]

Resting his case, Krim asserted that the movie business was different from the other TA operations and would always conflict with TA's prognostications. "The uncertainties of the future are great, and there simply is no way of forecasting them intelligently," he said. As an example, Krim alluded to a director's meeting early in 1972, when a TA analyst "displayed a chart which showed that over a five year period, TA would have to provide United Artists with an additional $60 million over and above the $40 million still owing from UA. This was based on some mechanically drawn projections which had no relation to reality. I pointed out at the meeting that from my knowledge of the business, not only would the $60 million not be needed but UA would shortly repay to TA the amount then owing. As one other director remarked in surprise, this was a saving of $100 million, as indeed it was."[51]

Krim suggested a spin-off to change UA's status from a subsidiary to a holding. As *Fortune* explained it, "a separate United Artists with its own class of stock would presumably command a much higher multiple in the market than TA's . . . Under such an arrangement Transamerica would retain a controlling interest in UA stock as well as have a majority position on its board."[52] TA staff analysts had earlier stated that "all a spinoff would accomplish would be to relieve UA of a discipline of financial controls and systems necessary to its long term success and survival." Krim responded, "Here in this one sentence, is the heart of the problem. For Transamerica to draw this kind of conclusion in light of the facts speaks for itself. United Artists has a long history of doing pretty well without disciplines other than those it has imposed on itself specially suited to its own business."[53] The TA board of directors apparently agreed with the analysts and voted down Krim's proposal.

THE REVIVAL

Repudiating TA's claim that UA could not survive without the discipline of TA's financial controls and systems, UA resumed sending dividends upstream, amounting, in 1974, to $7 million, based on total sales of $289 million and profits of $10 million. In 1975, UA sent up $7 million more in dividends, based on total sales of $320 million and profits of $11.5 million.

This renewal was the result in part of a management reorganization. After David Picker resigned as president in October 1973 to go into in-

United Artists' management team in 1973: (l. to r.) Eric Pleskow, Mike Medavoy, Arthur B. Krim, Robert S. Benjamin, and William Bernstein

dependent production, Krim became chairman of the board and Benjamin became chairman of the finance committee. To replace Picker, they named Eric Pleskow president and chief executive officer. Vienna-born, Pleskow, age forty-five, had been with UA for twenty-two years, mainly in foreign sales. Reorganizing film production, Pleskow appointed Mike Medavoy, age thirty-two, vice president in charge of West Coast productions. A Universal mailroom alumnus, Medavoy became one of Hollywood's hottest agents, working for CMA and International Famous Agency (IFA). At IFA, he headed the entire motion picture department. In his new position at UA, Medavoy functioned as a talent buyer instead of a seller. Pleskow, Medavoy, and Bernstein formed the nucleus of the team that Krim said was responsible for the most successful period in UA's history.

The revival also received an unexpected boost from MGM. The recession had convinced Kirk Kerkorian that the motion picture business was still too risky for his blood, even after streamlining the studio by selling off the unproductive assets. In 1973, he shocked the industry by divesting MGM of its distribution arm. This move freed the company from the necessity of producing a full roster of pictures on a regular basis. Kerkorian wanted to exploit more profitable ventures in the leisure-time field, particularly two massive resort hotels, MGM Grand—

Las Vegas and MGM Grand–Reno.

Reducing itself to the role of a passive financier of independent productions, Kerkorian approached Krim to secure distribution for MGM's pictures—that is, the pictures in its vault and future product. Observing UA close up while serving on TA's board had convinced Kerkorian that UA could get top dollar for MGM's product. Originally, Kerkorian offered some of MGM's foreign assets, which included theaters, in addition to world distribution rights. But Krim opted only for the domestic rights. However, since Kerkorian needed cash to continue his Las Vegas hotel ventures, Krim agreed to purchase MGM's remaining music interests—the Robbins-Feist-Miller music publishing companies and a Canadian record company—for $15 million. (In a separate deal, MGM sold off the foreign distribution rights to its film library to the Paramount-Universal overseas partnership, Cinema International Corporation.)

UA acquired the distribution rights to all of MGM's pictures from day one to the domestic theatrical market and to syndicated television for ten years. Since UA would not incur any additional overhead expense in handling the MGM product, the deal called for a lower-than-normal distribution fee of 22 percent. UA now controlled three major film libraries in addition to its own—Warner Brothers, RKO, and MGM. Together, they made the largest vault in the industry.

The MGM deal proved to be a smart move from the beginning. UA immediately sold off the Canadian record company, which reduced the investment by $3 million. MGM had the potential of becoming UA's principal supplier of product—another Mirisch, perhaps. The first season, MGM delivered *That's Entertainment!*, a compilation of the great MGM musicals. Produced by Jack Haley, Jr., the picture became a runaway hit in 1974. By 1975, UA had recovered nearly half of its investment. By 1976, such pictures as *The Sunshine Boys* (1975), *Logan's Run* (1976), and *Network* (1976) had completely recouped UA's investment. Rentals from the library thereafter constituted pure profit.

Building on the cushion provided by the MGM deal, UA reestablished ties with the creative community. After Norman Jewison completed his commitments to the Mirisches with *Fiddler on the Roof*, UA gave him a separate multiple-picture contract. UA also signed new contracts with Woody Allen, Blake Edwards, Elliott Kastner, and the production team of Robert Chartoff and Irwin Winkler, among others.

Woody Allen had delivered four pictures to UA—*Bananas* (1971), *Everything You Always Wanted to Know about Sex* (1972), *Sleeper* (1973), and *Love and Death* (1975). With the exception of *Bananas*, which broke even after a long playoff, the others made substantial profits of around $5 million each. Allen attracted a faithful audience.

Academy Award for Best Picture / 1975

One Flew over the Cuckoo's Nest

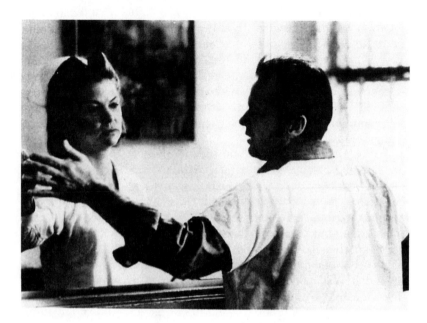

Louise Fletcher and Jack Nicholson

A Fantasy Films presentation
Starring Jack Nicholson, Louise Fletcher, and William Redfield
Directed by Milos Forman
Produced by Saul Zaentz and Michael Douglas

Other Academy Awards* and nominations
*Actor: Jack Nicholson
*Actress: Louise Fletcher
Supporting actor: Brad Dourif
*Direction: Milos Forman
*Writing *adaptation screenplay*: Lawrence Hauben and Bo Goldman
Cinematography: Haskell Wexler and Bill Butler
Film editing: Richard Chew, Lynzee Klingman, and Sheldon Kahn
Music *score*: Jack Nitzsche

Jack Nicholson giving a baseball commentary in front of a blank TV

Jack Nicholson

The Academy Awards sweep for *One Flew over the Cuckoo's Nest*: (l. to r.) Michael Douglas, Milos Foreman, Louise Fletcher, Jack Nicholson, and Saul Zaentz

Demand for his pictures remained relatively constant, each grossing around $11 million worldwide. Allen's pictures were produced by Jack Rollins and Charles Joffe, both big-time theatrical agents who helped shape Allen's career. Allen had unusual control over his pictures. So long as Allen kept production costs under $2 million, Allen, in his roles as director, star, and writer, had rights of approval over the script, cast, and final cut. However, Allen had to submit at least five separate concepts for each picture and UA had to approve one before the go-ahead could be given. In any event, the relationship was an enduring one.

Under the new management team beginning in 1974, UA released a string of hits that included the James Bond film, *The Man with the Golden Gun*, Marvin Worth's *Lenny*, Blake Edwards' *The Return of the Pink Panther*, Norman Jewison's *Rollerball*, and the Saul Zaentz–Michael Douglas production of *One Flew over the Cuckoo's Nest*. Eleven years had elapsed since the last Pink Panther picture, *A Shot in the Dark*. UA acquired the sequel fully financed by Sir Lew Grade. To the surprise of the industry, *The Return of the Pink Panther*, a G-rated picture, hit it big, grossing $31 million worldwide. On the strength of this performance, UA gave Edwards a separate contract and, during the next few years, he delivered two more sequel-blockbusters, *The Pink Panther Strikes Again* (1976) and *Revenge of the Pink Panther* (1978).

Cuckoo's Nest was another pickup deal. Directed by Milos Foreman and starring Jack Nicholson, *Cuckoo's Nest* grossed $90 million—more than any former UA release. Moreover, it achieved what no other picture in over forty years had done—a sweep at the Academy Awards (*It Happened One Night* was the first, in 1934). Nominated for nine Oscars, *Cuckoo's Nest* won the top five—best picture, best director, best actor, best actress, and best screenplay adaptation.

Produced by Fantasy Films, a production company formed by Saul Zaentz and Michael Douglas, *Cuckoo's Nest* was based on Ken Kesey's celebrated cult novel, which had been a steady best-seller ever since 1962. The stage version, written by Dale Wasserman, ran for nearly nine years on Broadway. Kirk Douglas, who originally played R. P. McMurphy on stage, acquired the motion picture rights after he left the run. Litigation and other delays had persuaded him to turn over the project to his son, Michael. Michael soon connected with Zaentz, chairman of Fantasy Records, who bought the film rights and put up the financing. Afterward, Zaentz and Douglas approached UA.

In 1976, UA released another string of hits, which included the James Bond film, *The Spy Who Loved Me*, Blake Edwards' *The Pink Panther Strikes Again*, Paddy Chayefsky's *Network*, and Chartoff-Winkler's *Rocky*. *Rocky* won the Oscar for best picture, the second time in a row for a UA picture, and grossed nearly $100 million worldwide the first year. *Rocky* also won Oscars for best director and best film editing; *Network*, an MGM/UA production, picked up Academy Awards for best actor (Peter Finch), best actress (Faye Dunaway), best supporting actress (Beatrice Straight), and best screenplay (Paddy Chayefsky).

Rocky was the fourth picture produced for UA by Robert Chartoff and Irwin Winkler. Before UA, the team produced *Point Blank* (1967), directed by John Boorman for MGM, and *They Shoot Horses, Don't They?* (1969), directed by Sydney Pollack for Cinerama Releasing Corporation. Signed up during the David Picker era, UA stuck with the team despite the disastrous results of their UA debut, *Leo the Last* (1970), directed by John Boorman. *The Mechanic* (1972) produced in association with Lewis John Carlino, directed by Michael Winner, and starring Charles Bronson, fared fairly well in the action market. But

Academy Award for Best Picture / 1976

Rocky

Sylvester Stallone and Carl Weathers

A Robert Chartoff–Irwin Winkler presentation
Starring Sylvester Stallone and Talia Shire
Directed by John G. Avildsen
Produced by Irwin Winkler and Robert Chartoff

Other Academy Awards* and nominations
Actor: Sylvester Stallone
Actress: Talia Shire
Supporting actor: Burgess Meredith, Burt Young
*Direction: John G. Avildsen
Writing *original screenplay*: Sylvester Stallone
Sound: Harry Warren Tetrick, William McCaughey, Lyle Burbridge,
  and Bud Alper
*Editing: Richard Halsey and Scott Conrad
*Music *song*: "Gonna Fly Now," Bill Conti (music), Carol Connors
  and Ayn Robbins (lyrics)

Sylvester Stallone and Talia Shire

the next entry, *Busting* (1974), written and directed by Peter Hyams and starring Elliott Gould, was a "confused, inane and vulgar police meller," a "total shambles," in the opinion of *Variety*.[54] *Rocky*, of course, redeemed matters. Produced on a comparatively low budget of around $1 million and starring an unknown actor with the unlikely name of Sylvester Stallone, who also wrote the original script, *Rocky* and its sequels would join the James Bond and Pink Panther pictures as another veritable money machine.

With four blockbusters in release in 1977—*Rocky, The Pink Panther Strikes Again, Network,* and a new hit, *Carrie,* produced by Paul Monash, UA set the all-time film industry record for theatrical film rentals—$318 million. This figure was 10 percent higher than the previous record of $289 million posted by MCA-Universal in 1975, the year it released *Jaws.*[55]

For some studios, boxoffice hits had sent the price of their stock soaring, as happened with *Jaws* for MCA and with *Star Wars* for Twentieth Century–Fox in 1977. But, as *Variety* noted, "Wall Street doesn't get nearly as excited when a film company is part of a conglomerate." TA had rebounded somewhat by 1971, but as of 1973, earnings had grown only an average of 1 percent a year. This was far below Beckett's goal of 10 to 15 percent growth on earnings, which he had established in the sixties. TA experienced continued difficulty in 1974 due to inflation and high interest rates before stabilizing in 1975. However, TA's stock continued to hang listlessly in the $13–$16 range, a long way from the high of $44 in 1968 after the two-for-one split. The irony was that TA's stock probably would have performed like that even without UA's big hits. As *Variety* explained, "To be sure, there are plausible reasons why the stock boom doesn't reflect in conglomerate shares—a far greater number of shares outstanding being the arithmetic explanation. Still, the UA people don't get the dual thrill of a hit at the b.o. and a hot stock on Wall Street."[56]

The catalyst for the walkout, said *Variety,* was an article in the latest issue of *Fortune* titled "United Artists' Script Calls For Divorce." What had been UA's internal executive-suite restlessness over relations with TA had been made visible to the film and financial community by author Peter J. Schuyten. Trading cross-country barbs, Beckett called Krim's demand for a spin-off as "the grousing of an entrepreneur." He continued, "sure, in successful times every company we've got wants to be off by themselves. That's life." Beckett didn't see how such a move could benefit stockholders over the long run. Then, as Schuyten described it, "setting aside his casual, almost folksy veneer, Beckett, fifty-nine, delivers what in effect are his final thoughts on the subject of a UA spin-off: 'And if the people at United Artists don't like it, they can quit and go off on their own'."[57]

Michael Cimino's

HEAVEN'S GATE

C H A P T E R E L E V E N

To MGM and Beyond

THE WALKOUT

The Krim-Benjamin walkout received national press coverage, which was piqued in part by the Begelman affair. A story by David McClintick in the *Wall Street Journal*, followed by a *Washington Post* exposé by Jack Egan and John Berry, had revealed that Columbia Pictures President David Begelman had forged checks, overbilled the company, and padded his expense account—a misappropriation amounting to $80,000. The UA story broke just around the time mounting public and media pressure forced Begelman's resignation on February 5, 1978. As the *Los Angeles Times* said, "Having populated its preceding Hollywood stories with nothing but villains, the press seized upon Krim and his colleagues as the heroes of the moment. After all, in an age of ever-growing media conglomerates, hadn't the UA Five turned their backs on their corporate rulers at Transamerica? And, at a time when most studio executives were being pictured as unscrupulous wheeler-dealers, the men from UA appeared to have earned the trust of the creative community." [1]

Testimony to this trust came the following week when sixty-three producers and directors from Hollywood's creative community, including Francis Ford Coppola, Blake Edwards, William Friedkin, Norman Jewison, François Truffaut, Saul Zaentz, and Fred Zinnemann, published an open letter to John Beckett in the Hollywood trades bemoaning the loss of "their creative and financial leadership." Pointing out that "the success of United Artists . . . has been based upon the personal relationships of these executive officers of United Artists with us, the film makers," the letter seriously questioned "the wisdom of the Transamerica Corporation in losing the talents of these men." [2]

Beckett may have been stunned by the walkout, but he did not capitulate. Rather, he announced there would be no change in UA's philosophy or method of operation and appointed James R. Harvey, TA's group vice president for leisure-time services, the new UA chairman and Andy Albeck, UA senior vice president of operations, the new president.

Just three weeks after the defection, the former UA management quintet founded Orion Pictures Company. Named after the great hunter constellation of stars at the equator, Orion was a joint venture with Warner Communications. With a $100 million line of revolving credit, which Krim arranged through a consortium of banks headed by the First National Bank of Boston, Orion planned to function as a financier and distributor using the facilities of Warner Brothers. [3]

James Harvey characterized the walkout as follows: "I think in the overall scheme, their complaints were so minor that they weren't really relevant . . . they left basically to form their own company. It's just that simple—to make pictures and to make money. And evidently they thought they could make more money. Maybe they can." [4] Money obviously played a large role in the decision, but leaving the matter at that would be to trivialize UA's grievances with its conglomerate parent, TA.

UA never complained about any interference from TA over the selection of motion pictures. As Krim explained, "In all the years that we were at United Artists as a part of Transamerica, the issue never came up in respect to what should or should not be made. We always made film decisions on our own. And only once did the issue come up as to whether we should release a picture which we had already made, and that was *Last Tango*." [5] UA's performance, in other words, continued to depend exclusively on decisions made by its management and not on advice from TA or synergy from the association with a conglomerate.

Grievances arose mainly out of TA's attempt to force UA into a mold that was incompatible with the motion picture business. In the beginning, TA appreciated UA for what it was and permitted this subsidiary to function pretty much on its own. However, the 1970 debacle altered the relationship. As Herb Schottenfeld explained, "the debacle came as a shock to Transamerica, not only because of its magnitude, but also because it was years in the making. Although UA had been reporting to Transamerica on a regular basis, TA probably either realized that it was not really smart enough to ask the right questions or assumed that UA's management had not levelled with them. Even though Krim returned to rescue the company, TA decided this is a business that needs watching. And while TA never understood the business, they tried to fit a motion picture company into a mold with which they were familiar. And of course, it didn't work. Rather than appreciating the nuances of running a motion picture business, rather than using TA's resources to help UA solidify its position in the industry, TA did just the opposite. Said Schottenfeld, "TA decided instead to control UA by putting up financial limitations, reporting requirements, and projections that really made no sense in the business. And once Beckett took this adversarial approach, he set Transamerica and its subsidiary on a collision course."[6]

The money issue referred to by Harvey involved executive compensation and stock options. In the previous chapter, I discussed the compensation issue. Concerning stock options, Krim discovered that the stock of a conglomerate which owns a motion picture company is not price sensitive to the boxoffice performance of the subsidiary's motion pictures. Said Krim, "we had the largest grosses in the industry after 1973 and won Academy Awards for best picture three years running and nothing happened to TA's stock. This had a tremendous psychological impact on top management who were given stock options in the conglomerate. But there was no way to give them stock options in the subsidiary."[7] Krim had no stock option in TA. He had held on to his TA stock, though, and saw its dismal performance wipe out most of the gains from the merger. This obviously had a "tremendous psychological impact" on him as well.

Because TA did not understand the motion picture business, it saw no necessity to seek a rapprochement with the Krim-Benjamin team. Instead, TA elevated Andy Albeck and made sure he conducted UA's business by the book. Albeck, age fifty-six, had come to UA from Eagle-Lion after the buyout in 1951. At Eagle-Lion, Albeck was the assistant foreign sales manager. He was not involved in sales, however, but operations. At UA, Albeck continued in operations and for a while

Annie Hall

Diane Keaton and Woody Allen

A Jack Rollins–Charles H. Joffe presentation
Starring Woody Allen and Diane Keaton
Directed by Woody Allen
Produced by Charles H. Joffe

Other Academy Awards* and nominations
Actor: Woody Allen
*Actress: Diane Keaton
*Direction: Woody Allen
*Writing *original screenplay*: Woody Allen and Marshall Brickman

Woody Allen and Diane Keaton

Tony Roberts, Woody Allen, and Diane Keaton

served as Eric Pleskow's assistant until Pleskow became president. Because Albeck wanted a title, UA named him assistant treasurer, but, according to Herb Schottenfeld, the title had no meaning. Albeck held the title of vice president for a short time when Krim assigned him to liquidate UA's unprofitable broadcasting operations, which consisted of one FM station and two UHF-TV stations. Afterward, he resumed overseeing operations in UA's international department.

Although Albeck had no experience in the production end, Steven Bach, who became senior vice president and head of worldwide production for UA and who has chronicled the post–Krim-Benjamin era in his book, *Final Cut: Dreams and Disaster in the Making of "Heaven's Gate,"* considered Albeck's promotion to president and chief executive officer as a "classical corporate gesture." Promotion from within, said Bach, displayed "monolithic (or pyramidal) calm, evolutionary progression, an executive-come, executive-go sangfroid. To the attentive it implied Transamerica didn't want (or need) a star to decorate the top of its corporate tree; to the *very* attentive it removed the Krim-Benjamin layer of insulation between United Artists and Transamerica."[8]

Bach offered two additional reasons for the choice of Albeck. First, TA wanted someone to run the company in a way TA could understand. After the 1970 fiasco, Beckett installed a system that could provide an early warning in case of trouble. Said Bach, "What Albeck lacked in style, he more than made up for in numbers, Transamerica numbers: systems of budget control, cost estimates, profit projections, returns on investments, all the minutiae . . . which were the standard reporting systems Transamerica now required of all its subsidiaries."[9] Second, TA wanted to bolster company morale. This was the humane consideration. Bach said that "before confidence could sink without a trace, an internal appointment might serve to buoy drowning spirits . . . [Albeck] would bring no new arbitrary broom to sweep clean paths that he had, even if only by association, help pave."[10] Bach's last point is particularly apt. "Of all the companies," said *Variety*, "UA is the most familial . . . It's like a tribe, not a company, and Krim is the father figure."[11] UA's success and Krim and Benjamin's stature as executives had engendered loyalty in the ranks from management to clerical. Now that the company had made a magnificent comeback, the future of a few thousand employees suddenly became clouded.

The Krim-Benjamin regime "left behind in excess of a billion dollars in revenues over the next three years," said Eric Pleskow. The legacy included an Academy Award for Woody Allen's *Annie Hall* in 1977, which marked the third time in a row a UA picture won the Oscar for best picture, the first time in the fifty-year history of the Academy of Motion Picture Arts and Sciences that a motion picture company achieved this feat. Winning the best picture Oscar for *Annie Hall* brought UA's total for such awards to ten, another all-time industry record. In addition to *Annie Hall*, UA inherited from the Krim-Benjamin era a group of hits consisting of Francis Ford Coppola's *Apocalypse Now* and *The Black Stallion*, the James Bond *Moonraker*, *Rocky II*, Woody Allen's *Manhattan*, and *La Cage aux Folles*.

THE *HEAVEN'S GATE* FIASCO

Albeck's regime is best remembered for the *Heaven's Gate* fiasco. Proposed at $7.5 million, budgeted at $11.5 million, and written off finally at $44 million, Michael Cimino's *Heaven's Gate* led to at least temporary unemployment for almost everyone associated with the picture and ultimately to the demise of UA itself. Appalled not only by the incompetence of its subsidiary, but also by the horrendous publicity that the film generated, TA sold UA to MGM in 1981.

Earlier, UA had passed on the project, as had executives at other studios. Cimino's agent submitted the script to UA a second time just as "the advance word on [Cimino's] *The Deer Hunter* was . . . buzzing quickly through Hollywood," said Bach.[12] Jeered at in the press by their predecessors and overeager to prove themselves, UA's new management happily signed Cimino. Steven Bach, who was promoted to senior vice president and head of worldwide production for UA during the filming of *Heaven's Gate*, blamed Cimino, in part, for the fiasco, stating that "independent production on a laissez-faire basis—that is, without authentic producers—was breaking down as a reliable method of production. Even those studios still exercising strong production control were plagued by runaway budgets . . . and UA did not have the structure or staff to enforce its own contractual protections without extreme disruption of routine, as *Heaven's Gate* had shown."[13]

But *Heaven's Gate* was just as much the result of a vacuum of leadership that existed from the start of the Albeck regime. Bach himself had complained that authority to select projects had slipped from the production department to distribution. Instead of the production department having the final say, story ideas, treatments, screenplays, casting, and directing selections "all were routinely submitted to the distribution staff for review and comment," said Bach. He went on to say that "the production staff was in effect placed in a position of having to sell to the distribution staff any idea they wanted to develop, any talent they wanted to hire, no matter how minor, with Albeck serving as the final arbiter." Albeck's reasoning for giving distribution approval rights, said Bach, "was simply that the salesmen ought to have a say regarding their merchandise . . . As a management theory it seemed simple enough and even made a certain kind of sense, but in practice it became the tail wagging the dog up, down, right, left, and in violent circles." [14]

Albeck's reorganization of the production department further complicated decision making. The new management started out with one head of production, Danton Rissner. But after ill health forced Rissner to resign at the end of 1979, Albeck instituted a tandem system. The production committee now had cochairmen—David Field, located in Hollywood, and Steven Bach, located in New York. Bach was expected to spend one week a month on the West Coast to stay close to the action. Pictures could not be made without their joint approval. In any disagreement, Albeck functioned as the final court of appeal. Such a system was almost unheard of in the business.

But *Heaven's Gate* was booby-trapped from the start. Just one month after UA approved *Heaven's Gate,* Cimino's *The Deer Hunter* opened in New York and Los Angeles to smash business and won the New York Critics Award for best film. In March 1979, Cimino won the directing award from the Directors' Guild. In April, *The Deer Hunter* won five Oscars for best picture, director, supporting actor, editing, and sound. This situation, obviously, was analogous to that of the one-and-only fiasco of the Krim-Benjamin regime, *The Greatest Story Ever Told.*

Cimino began shooting *Heaven's Gate* within days of the Awards ceremony. Two weeks into production, Cimino fell two weeks behind schedule. Sixteen weeks into production, costs had escalated to $21 million. Four weeks later, Cimino held a champagne party to celebrate the shooting of the millionth foot of film. Although UA took the drastic step of assuming fiscal control of the picture, the action came too late. A UA executive admitted that UA seemed to have lost control of the film early on. "There was no one strong enough to do anything about what was happening. No one went to Andy . . . and said something had to be done. Or, if they did, he didn't listen until it was too late . . . Even if UA had wanted to fire Cimino from the production—and it was legally feasible—it would have been psychologically impossible," said a production executive at another company. "It would have created a crisis of confidence in a company which had built its reputation on giving directors the right to work without intervention. Had they taken the film away from Cimino, they would have lost regardless of whether the picture failed or succeeded. (a) If it had failed, the director would have contended he could have made it work. (b) If it succeeded, he could say 'it was me'." [15]

After a disastrous November 18, 1980, press screening in New York and a November 19 theatrical screening in New York and Toronto, UA pulled *Heaven's Gate* on November 20 at Cimino's request to permit him to edit the film down from over three and a half hours to some reasonable length. The Los Angeles opening, scheduled for November 21, was canceled at the last minute. Reviewers did more than just advise people not to see *Heaven's Gate;* "they used their columns as platforms from which to roast Cimino publicly, turning him into a scapegoat/representative for everything that is supposedly wrong with contemporary American filmmaking," said Michael Bliss. [16] Vincent Canby of the *New York Times* led the attack. "*Heaven's Gate* fails so completely," he began, "you might suspect Mr. Cimino sold his soul to the Devil to obtain the success of *The Deer Hunter,* and the Devil has just come around to collect." Canby concluded, "*Heaven's Gate* is something quite rare in movies these days—an unqualified disaster." [17] In its first theatrical run, the $44 million (including promotion costs) superbomb grossed at the boxoffice exactly $12,032.61.

Regardless of the motives critics may have had, they correctly discerned that UA was partly responsible for the fiasco. Pauline Kael said that "if the company had thought that the critics were wrong, they would have put millions in advertising and they might have recouped on the picture. A lot of terrible movies get by if the companies believe in them. But [UA] didn't believe in [*Heaven's Gate*] and that is why they listened to the press." [18] UA further undermined the picture by telling *Variety* a scant five days after the premiere that an unspecified part of the cost of *Heaven's Gate* was being written off by UA's parent, TA, "which admitted . . . that it considered the film to be a loser . . . A spokesman for TA . . . conceded TA now takes the position that the film has no chance of turning a profit." [19]

The reedited version of *Heaven's Gate* did disastrously at the box office, "killed by word of mouth (unchecked by the film's distributor), fostered by vengeful and most regrettably, far from perspicacious reviewers," said Michael Bliss. [20] TA had always enjoyed basking in UA's limelight; now it had to endure the humiliation of being associated with one of the most public motion picture failures of all time. TA, therefore, was receptive to a preemptive offer from Kirk Kerkorian to take UA off its hands. TA sold UA to MGM Film Company in May 1981. TA got out of the motion picture business with a nice profit. The conglomerate paid $185 million for UA in 1967; Kerkorian offered and TA accepted $320 million for the company in 1981.

THE MERGER WITH MGM

"We have recovered our distribution," said MGM chairman and chief executive officer, Frank Rosenfelt. MGM had a ten-year domestic distribution agreement with UA, which was to have expired in 1983. At the time of the walkout, Rosenfelt commented, "All we can do is wait and see what happens, and we are anxiously awaiting developments."[21] The developments undermined MGM's confidence in UA. Now that MGM had a string of big pictures in the works, the studio wanted to control distribution. So MGM figured how much it might have to pay UA in distribution fees and used that amount to make a preemptive bid to buy the company.

In acquiring UA, MGM merged the company into a new corporate entity, MGM/UA Entertainment Company. United Artists, the company founded by Mary Pickford, Charlie Chaplin, Douglas Fairbanks, and D. W. Griffith, disappeared. Kerkorian discovered, to his chagrin, that he had to turn over UA's product to CIC for foreign distribution. When MGM disbanded its distribution in 1973, it contracted with CIC to handle its product abroad. In negotiating the purchase of UA, no one at MGM thought to shield UA's product from the agreement with CIC. This was a costly mistake that deprived MGM of an enormous amount of distribution fees. Since CIC would not let MGM off the hook, UA's entire foreign distribution arm, built over the years by Arnold Picker, Charles Smadja, and Eric Pleskow and long considered the jewel of UA's operation, was made redundant. Ultimately, MGM fired this half of UA's tribe. In deference to the Department of Justice, Kerkorian guaranteed that the acquisition of UA would not lessen competition in the motion picture industry. Through the UA-MGM merger, one operation would distribute the product of both companies, just as before. And just as before, said Kerkorian, both companies would operate in tandem and compete for product. But, in essence, there was one company, controlled by Kerkorian.

In one of the finer ironies of UA's denouement, Kerkorian installed David Begelman as the new chairman and chief operating officer of UA just months after the takeover. Deemed rehabilitated by the court after his check-forgery conviction, Begelman was hired by Kerkorian to head MGM's film division in January 1980. Begelman's aggressive program of production, which led to an expensive slate of pictures, had triggered MGM's purchase of UA. The rationale for the dramatic game of executive musical chairs, said Frank Rosenfelt, was this: "We are looking to David to duplicate at UA the production miracle he wrought at MGM."[22] Begelman resigned shortly afterward, though, when every one of his MGM pictures failed. These pictures were *Buddy, Buddy, All the Marbles, Whose Life Is It Anyway?, Yes, Giorgio, Cannery Row,* and *Pennies from Heaven. Pennies* alone cost $22 million and returned perhaps $3 million, said Bach, who concluded, "It is likely that the aggregate losses to MGM equalled or surpassed those sustained by UA with *Heaven's Gate.*"[23]

To recoup his losses, Kerkorian sold MGM/UA to Atlanta television entrepreneur Ted Turner in 1986 for $1.5 billion. As part of the deal, Kerkorian then repurchased UA for $480 million, which he financed in part by selling UA stock to the public. "The company retained by Kerkorian, called United Artists Pictures, is neither the original company nor a successor company in the technical sense of an orderly legal succession," said Schottenfeld. "It's a separate new company that owns some of the assets that belonged to the old United Artists."[24] When Kerkorian again decided to get out of motion picture distribution, this half of UA's tribe lost their jobs.

THE KRIM-BENJAMIN LEGACY

TA made out well on UA and presumably so did Kerkorian. The assets they traded consisted of more than 1,000 pictures, including the James Bond series, the Pink Panther series, the Stanley Kramer, Woody Allen, Hecht-Lancaster, and Mirisch pictures, in addition to a long list of blockbusters. These pictures had grossed in excess of $10 billion at the boxoffice and had won 108 Academy Awards, including ten Oscars for best picture. UA's film vault also included the pre–1948 Warner Brothers and RKO film libraries. The combined residual value of the vault is limited only by the technologies that may be developed to exploit the films.

When Krim and Benjamin took over UA in 1951, the company owned practically nothing. By putting their money on talent and by introducing a new formula for independent production, UA revolutionized the industry. Spanning nearly three decades, the Krim-Benjamin management provided a stable and receptive home to talent. Management knew what the company stood for and where it wanted to go. Production decisions were made by Krim or by a few trusted associates who shared the same philosophy and not by an anonymous committee.

Although other studios opened their doors to independents, UA lost none of its momentum. UA did not compete with talent because the

Robert S. Benjamin (1909–79)

company did not produce motion pictures. As solely a distributor, UA needed talent to stay in business. For the competition, however, the transition to independent production was difficult to make since these companies continued to produce under their own name.

The "psychological climate" at UA, as Krim called it, was therefore different.[25] Since UA's top executives had never lived in the studio sys-

Arthur B. Krim

tem, it was natural for the company to treat an independent producer as a partner. This partnership arrangement functioned at every level of UA's relationship with a producer. Since UA owned no studio, UA charged no overhead and allowed producers to make their pictures wherever necessary. Once UA approved a project, the producer could work in an atmosphere of autonomy and creative freedom. Despite all the legal safeguards built into the financing-distribution contracts, the company bet on the person, the integrity of the producer to make the picture as mutually agreed. UA's producers, with few exceptions, had the right to the final cut, whereas only the biggest names had this right elsewhere. UA knew it could die by the sword as well as live by it with the policy, but Krim and Benjamin made the decision to adopt it at the start.

The partnership extended even to the area of distribution. UA offered producers the opportunity of hiring producers' representatives to work alongside UA's sales staff at the home office. A representative reviewed every exhibition contract on a picture and had the right to improve the terms of any deal UA was willing to accept. UA's sales department accepted this as a given, whereas other companies resisted the arrangement. As a partner with UA, as a result, a producer stood a better chance of seeing a profit than anywhere else.

In retrospect, Steven Bach may have been half right when he blamed the *Heaven's Gate* fiasco on the breakdown of "independent production on a laissez-faire basis." Clearly, Michael Cimino set out to make a picture different from the one that had been approved. It is idle to speculate what Krim might have done either to discipline the director or to salvage the picture. We can note, however, that although Krim and Benjamin did not "discipline" George Stevens during the production of *The Greatest Story*, the company devised a marketing plan to recoup a significant portion of the costs. And because UA had such an impressive lineup of pictures at the time, any loss on *The Greatest Story* could not destabilize the company. TA's guidelines were ineffective in handling *Heaven's Gate*, it turned out, and when the conglomerate finally realized this, it sold the company. The decision resulted in the disbanding of a once-proud motion picture company. It also resulted in less competition in the motion picture business. Less competition means fewer options for independent producers and also for the people who ultimately have to foot the bills—the moviegoers.

APPENDICES

NOTES

INDEX

Appendix 1: United Artists' Domestic Releases, 1951–1978 (Including Lopert Releases)

Title	Producer
The African Queen	Romulus-Horizon (Sam Spiegel– John Huston)
Badman's Gold	Jack Schwarz
The Big Night	Philip A. Waxman
The Blue Lamp (British)	J. Arthur Rank
A Christmas Carol (British)	Brian Desmond Hurst
Circle of Danger (British)	Joan Harrison
Cyrano de Bergerac	Stanley Kramer
Fabiola (Italian)	Jules Levey
The First Legion	Douglas Sirk
Fort Defiance	Frank Melford
Four in a Jeep (Swiss)	Lazar Wechsler
Gold Raiders	Jack Schwarz
He Ran All the Way	Bob Roberts
The Hoodlum	Jack Schwarz
Hotel Sahara (British)	J. Arthur Rank
Korea Patrol	Jack Schwarz
The Long Dark Hall (British)	Peter Cusick–Five Oceans
The Man from Planet X	Aubrey Wisberg–Jack Pollexfen

Title	Producer
Man with My Face	Edward F. Gardner
Mister Drake's Duck (British)	Daniel M. Angel–Douglas Fairbanks, Jr.
Mr. Peek-A-Boo (French, orig.: *Garou-Garou, Le Passe-Muraille*)	Jacques Bar
Mr. Universe	Laurel Films–Joseph Lerner
My Brother, the Outlaw	Benedict Bogeaus
Naughty Arlette (British)	J. Arthur Rank
New Mexico	Joseph Justman
Obsessed (British)	Ernest Gartside
Odette (British)	Herbert Wilcox–Anna Neagle
Oliver Twist (British)	J. Arthur Rank
Pardon My French (French/American)	Peter Cusick–Andre Sarrut
The Prowler	Sam Spiegel
Queen for a Day	Robert Stillman
St. Benny the Dip	Danziger Bros.
The Scarf	I. G. Goldsmith
The Second Woman	Harry M. Popkin
Skipalong Rosenbloom	Wally Kline
So Long at the Fair (British)	J. Arthur Rank
The Sound of Fury	Robert Stillman
Sun Sets at Dawn	Helen H. Rathvon–Paul H. Sloane
They Were Not Divided (British)	J. Arthur Rank
Three Steps North	W. Lee Wilder
Tom Brown's Schooldays (British)	George Minter

Title	Producer
Two Gals and a Guy	Weisner Bros.
The Well	Harry M. Popkin
When I Grow Up	Sam Spiegel
Wicked City (French, orig.: *Hans Le Marin*)	Sacha Kamenka

1952

Actors and Sin	Ben Hecht
Another Man's Poison (British)	Daniel M. Angel–Douglas Fairbanks, Jr.
Babes in Bagdad	Danziger Bros.
Buffalo Bill in Tomahawk Territory	Jack Schwarz
The Captive City	Theron Warth
Chicago Calling	Joseph Justman
Cloudburst (British)	Alexander Paal
Confidence Girl	Andrew Stone
Cry, the Beloved Country (British)	London Films
The Fighter	Alex Gottlieb
The Green Glove	George Maurer
High Noon	Stanley Kramer
Island of Desire	David Rose
The Lady Says No	Frank Ross–John Stillman, Jr.
Limelight	Charles Chaplin
Monsoon	Film Group–Forrest Judd
Mutiny	King Bros.
One Big Affair	Benedict Bogeaus
Outcast of the Islands (British)	London Films
Outpost in Malaya	John Stafford
Park Row	Samuel Fuller

Title	Producer
Red Planet Mars	Donald Hyde–Anthony Veiller
The Ring	King Bros.
The River	Kenneth McEldowney–Jean Renoir
Sound Barrier (British)	London Films
Strange World	Al O'Camp–A. O. Bayer–Franz Eichorn
A Tale of Five Women (British)	Alexander Paal
Tales of Hoffmann (British)	London Films
The Thief	Harry M. Popkin
Untamed Women	Richard Kay
Without Warning	Jules V. Levy–Arthur Gardner–Arnold Laven

1953

Act of Love	Anatole Litvak
The Assassin (British)	J. Arthur Rank
The Bandits of Corsica	Edward Small
Bwana Devil	Arch Oboler
Captain John Smith and Pocahontas	Edward Small
Captain Scarlett (British)	Howard Dimsdale
The Captain's Paradise (British)	London Films
Donovan's Brain	Tom Gries
Dragon's Gold	Edward Small
The Fake (British)	Steven Pallos
Fort Algiers	Joseph N. Ermolieff

Title	Producer
The Gay Adventure (British)	Anatole De Grunwald
Genghis Khan	Manuel Conde
Guerrilla Girl	John Christian
Gun Belt	Edward Small
I, the Jury	Victor Saville
The Joe Louis Story	Walter P. Chrysler, Jr.–Stirling Silliphant
Kansas City, Confidential	Edward Small
Luxury Girls (Italian, orig.: *Fanciulle Di Lusso*)	Carlo Civallero
The Magnetic Monster	Ivan Tors
Man in Hiding (British)	Alexander Paal
The Marshal's Daughter	Ken Murray
Melba (British)	Sam Spiegel
The Moon Is Blue	Otto Preminger–F. Hugh Herbert
Moulin Rouge	Romulus–John Huston Productions
My Heart Goes Crazy (British)	Wesley Ruggles
The Neanderthal Man	Edward Small
99 River Street	Edward Small
No Escape	Aubrey Schenck–Howard W. Koch
Phantom from Space	W. Lee Wilder
Raiders of the Seven Seas	Edward Small
Return to Paradise	Theron Warth
Sabre Jet	Edward Small
Shark River	John Rawlins
Shoot First (British)	Raymond Stross
Son of the Renegade	Jack Schwarz

Title	Producer
The Steel Lady	Edward Small
Stranger on the Prowl (Italian/American)	Noel Calef
That Man from Tangier	Robert Elwyn
The Twonky	Arch Oboler
Vice Squad	Jules V. Levy–Arthur Gardner– Arnold Laven
The Village (Swiss)	Lazar Wechsler
Volcano (Italian/American, orig.: *Vulcano*)	Panarla Films
War Paint	Aubrey Schenck–Howard W. Koch
Wicked Woman	Edward Small

1954

Adventures of Robinson Crusoe	Oscar Dancigers–Henry F. Ehrlich
Apache	Hecht-Lancaster
The Barefoot Contessa	Figaro Productions (Joseph L. Mankiewicz) and Angelo Rizzoli and Roberto Haggiag
Beachhead	Aubrey Schenck–Howard W. Koch
Beat the Devil	Romulus-Santana (John Huston– Humphrey Bogart)
Black Tuesday	Robert Goldstein
Captain Kidd and the Slave Girl	Edward Small
Crossed Swords	J. Barrett Mahon–Vittorio Vassarotti
The Diamond Wizard (British)	Steven Pallos
Down Three Dark Streets	Edward Small
Gog	Ivan Tors
The Golden Mask	Aubry Baring–Maxwell Setton
The Golden Mistress	Richard Kay–Harry Rhynick

Title	Producer
Go, Man, Go	Anton M. Leader
The Great Gilbert and Sullivan (British)	London Films
Heidi (Swiss)	Lazar Wechsler
Hobson's Choice (British)	London Films
Jesse James' Women	Lloyd Royal–T. V. Garraway
Khyber Patrol	Edward Small
The Lawless Rider	Alex Gordon–Yakima Canutt
The Little Kidnappers (British)	J. Arthur Rank
The Lone Gun	Edward Small
The Long Wait	Victor Saville
Malta Story (British)	J. Arthur Rank
The Man Between (British)	London Films
Man with a Million (British)	J. Arthur Rank
Operation Manhunt	Fred Feldkamp
Overland Pacific	Edward Small
Personal Affair (British)	J. Arthur Rank
Return to Treasure Island	Edward Small
Riders to the Stars	Ivan Tors
Romeo and Juliet (British)	Sandro Ghenzi–Joseph Janni
The Scarlet Spear	Charles Reynolds
Shield for Murder	Aubrey Schenck–Howard W. Koch
Sitting Bull	W. R. Frank
Snow Creature	W. Lee Wilder
Southwest Passage	Edward Small

Title	Producer
The Steel Cage	Walter Doniger–Berman Swartz
Suddenly	Robert Bassler
Top Banana	Albert Zugsmith–Ben Peskay
Twist of Fate	Maxwell Setton–John R. Sloan
Vera Cruz	Hecht-Lancaster
The White Orchid	Aubrey Schenck–Howard W. Koch
Witness to Murder	Chester Erskine
The Yellow Tomahawk	Aubrey Schenck–Howard W. Koch
You Know What Sailors Are (British)	J. Arthur Rank

1955

Battle Taxi	Ivan Tors–Art Arthur
The Beachcomber (British)	J. Arthur Rank
The Big Bluff	M. Lee Wilder
Big House, U.S.A.	Aubrey Schenck–Howard W. Koch
The Big Knife	Associates & Aldrich
Break to Freedom (British)	Daniel M. Angel
A Bullet for Joey	Sam Bischoff–David Diamond
Canyon Crossroads	William F. Joyce
Desert Sands	Aubrey Schenck–Howard W. Koch
Fort Yuma	Aubrey Schenck–Howard W. Koch
Gentlemen Marry Brunettes	Jane Russell–Robert Waterfield
The Good Die Young (British)	Romulus
Heidi and Peter (Swiss)	Lazar Wechsler
The Indian Fighter	Kirk Douglas
The Kentuckian	Hecht-Lancaster

Title	Producer
Killer's Kiss	Morris Bousel–Stanley Kubrick
Kiss Me Deadly	Associates & Aldrich
The Man Who Loved Redheads (British)	London Films
Man with the Gun	Samuel Goldwyn, Jr.
Marty	Hecht-Lancaster
The Naked Street	Edward Small
The Night of the Hunter	Paul Gregory
Not as a Stranger	Stanley Kramer
Othello	Orson Welles
The Purple Plain (British)	J. Arthur Rank
Robber's Roost	Robert Goldstein
Sabaka	Frank Ferrin
Savage Princess	Mehboob
Stranger on Horseback	Robert Goldstein
Summertime	Ilya Lopert–David Lean
The Tiger and the Flame (Indian)	Sohrab M. Modi
Top Gun	Edward Small
Top of the World	Michael Baird–Lewis R. Foster

1956

Title	Producer
Alexander the Great	Robert Rossen
The Ambassador's Daughter	Norman Krasna
Around the World in 80 Days	Michael Todd
Attack!	Associates & Aldrich
Bandido	Robert Goldstein
The Beast of Hollow Mountain	Nassour Bros.
The Black Sheep	Aubrey Schenck–Howard W. Koch

Title	Producer
The Boss	Frank N. Seltzer
The Brass Legend	Robert Goldstein
The Broken Star	Aubrey Schenck–Howard W. Koch
Comanche	Edward Small
The Creeping Unknown	Hammer Films
Crime against Joe	Aubrey Schenck–Howard W. Koch
Dance with Me, Henry!	Robert Goldstein
Emergency Hospital	Aubrey Schenck–Howard W. Koch
Flight to Hong Kong	Joseph M. Newman
Foreign Intrigue	Sheldon Reynolds
Ghost Town	Aubrey Schenck–Howard W. Koch
Gun Brothers	Edward Small
Gun the Man Down	Robert Morrison
Hot Cars	Aubrey Schenck–Howard W. Koch
Huk!	Collier Young
Johnny Concho	Frank Sinatra
The Killer Is Loose	Robert Goldstein
The Killing	James B. Harris–Stanley Kubrick
The King and Four Queens	Jane Russell–Robert Waterfield–Clark Cable
A Kiss before Dying	Robert Goldstein
Let's Make Up (British)	Herbert Wilcox
Man from Del Rio	Robert Goldstein
The Man with the Golden Arm	Otto Preminger
Manfish	W. Lee Wilder
Nightmare	William H. Pine–William C. Thomas
Patterns	Michael Myerberg
The Peacemaker	Hal Makelim
Quincannon, Frontier Scout	Aubrey Schenck–Howard W. Koch

Title	Producer
Rebel in Town	Aubrey Schenck–Howard W. Koch
Run for the Sun	Jane Russell–Robert Waterfield
Running Target	Jack C. Couffer
The Sea Shall Not Have Them (British)	Daniel M. Angel
Shadow of Fear	Charles A. Leeds
Shadow of the Eagle (British)	J. Arthur Rank
The Sharkfighters	Samuel Goldwyn, Jr.
Star of India	Raymond Stross
Storm Fear	Cornel Wilde
Three Bad Sisters	Aubrey Schenck–Howard W. Koch
Timetable	Mark Stevens
Trapeze	Hecht-Lancaster
UFO	Edward Small
The Wild Party	Security Pictures

1957

Baby Face Nelson	Al Zimbalist
The Bachelor Party	Hecht-Hill-Lancaster
Bailout at 43,000	William H. Pine–William C. Thomas
Bayou	Edward I. Fessler–M. A. Ripps
The Big Boodle	Lewis F. Blumberg
The Big Caper	William H. Pine–William C. Thomas
Bop Girl Goes Calypso	Aubrey Schenck–Howard W. Koch
Buckskin Lady	Carl K. Hittleman
The Careless Years	Kirk Douglas
Chicago Confidential	Edward Small
Crime of Passion	Robert Goldstein

Title	Producer
The Dalton Girls	Aubrey Schenck–Howard W. Koch
The Delinquents	Elmer Rhoden, Jr.
Drango	Jeff Chandler–Meyer Mishkin
Enemy from Space	Hammer Films
Five Steps to Danger	Edward Small
Four Boys and Gun	Security Pictures
Fury at Showdown	Robert Goldstein
The Fuzzy Pink Nightgown	Jane Russell–Robert Waterfield
The Girl in Black Stockings	Aubrey Schenck–Howard W. Koch
Gun Duel in Durango	Edward Small
Gunsight Ridge	Robert Bresler
The Halliday Brand	Collier Young
Hell Bound	Aubrey Schenck–Howard W. Koch
Hidden Fear	Robert St. Aubrey–Howard E. Kohn II
Hit and Run	Hugo Haas
The Iron Sheriff	Edward Small
Jungle Heat	Aubrey Schenck–Howard W. Koch
Lady of Vengeance	Burt Balaban
Legend of the Lost	John Wayne–Roberto Haggiag
Man on the Prowl	Sol Lesser
Men in War	Security Pictures
Monkey on My Back	Edward Small
The Monster that Challenged the World	Jules V. Levy–Arthur Gardner–Arnold Laven
The Monte Carlo Story	Titanus
My Gun Is Quick	Victor Saville
Outlaw's Son	Aubrey Schenck–Howard W. Koch
Pharaoh's Curse	Aubrey Schenck–Howard W. Koch
The Pride and the Passion	Stanley Kramer
Revolt at Fort Laramie	Aubrey Schenck–Howard W. Koch

Title	Producer
The Ride Back	Associates & Aldrich
Ride Out for Revenge	Kirk Douglas
Saint Joan	Otto Preminger
Spring Reunion	Kirk Douglas
Street of Sinners	Security Pictures
Sweet Smell of Success	Hecht-Hill-Lancaster
Time Limit	Richard Widmark–William Reynolds
Tomahawk Trail	Aubrey Schenck–Howard W. Koch
Trooper Hook	Sol Baer
Twelve Angry Men	Henry Fonda–Reginald Rose
Valerie	Hal R. Makelim
The Vampire	Jules V. Levy–Arthur Gardner–Arnold Laven
Voodoo Island	Aubrey Schenck–Howard W. Koch
War Drums	Aubrey Schenck–Howard W. Koch

1958

Title	Producer
The Big Country	Gregory Peck–William Wyler
China Doll	Romina Productions–Frank Borzage
Cop Hater	Morris Helprin–Alfred Crown
Crossup	Robert Baker–Monty Berman
Curse of the Faceless Man	Edward Small
The Defiant Ones	Stanley Kramer
Edge of Fury	Robert Gurney, Jr.
The Fearmakers	Martin H. Lancer
The Flame Barrier	Jules V. Levy–Arthur Gardner–Arnold Laven
Fort Bowie	Aubrey Schenck–Howard W. Koch
Fort Massacre	Mirisch

Title	Producer
God's Little Acre	Security Pictures
Gun Fever	Harry Jackson–Sam Weston
The Gun Runners	Seven Arts
Hong Kong Confidential	Edward Small
I Bury the Living!	Louis Garfinkle–Albert Band
I Want to Live!	Figaro Productions (Joseph L. Mankiewicz)
Island Women	Security Pictures
It! The Terror from beyond Space	Edward Small
Kings Go Forth	Frank Sinatra
The Last Paradise	Golfiero Colonna
The Lone Ranger and the Lost City of Gold	Jack Wrather
Lost Lagoon	John Rawlins
The Lost Missile	Morris Helprin–Alfred Crown
Machete	J. Harold Odell
Man of the West	Mirisch
Menace in the Night (British)	Charles A. Leeds
The Mugger	Morris Helprin–Alfred Crown
Paris Holiday	Bob Hope
La Parisienne (French/Italian, orig.: *Une Parisiene*)	Films Ariane–Filmsonor-Cinetel-Rizzoli
Paths of Glory	James B. Harris–Stanley Kubrick
The Quiet American	Figaro Productions (Joseph L. Mankiewicz)
The Return of Dracula	Jules V. Levy–Arthur Gardner–Arnold Laven
Run Silent, Run Deep	Hecht-Hill-Lancaster
Separate Tables	Hecht-Hill-Lancaster
Steel Bayonet	Hammer Films

Title	Producer
Ten Days to Tulare	George Sherman–Clarence Eurist
Terror in a Texas Town	Frank N. Seltzer
Thunder Road	Robert Mitchum
Toughest Gun in Tombstone	Edward Small
The Vikings	Kirk Douglas
Wink of an Eye	Fernando Carrere
Witness for the Prosecution	Edward Small–Arthur Hornblow, Jr.

1959

Title	Producer
Alias Jesse James	Bob Hope
Anna Lucasta	Security Pictures
Cast a Long Shadow	Mirisch
Counterplot	J. Harold Odell
Cry Tough	Hecht-Hill-Lancaster
Day of the Outlaw	Security Pictures
The Devil's Disciple (British)	Hecht-Hill-Lancaster and Kirk Douglas
Escort West	Robert E. Morrison–Nate H. Edwards
The Four Skulls of Jonathan Drake	Edward Small
The Great St. Louis Bank Robbery	Charles Guggenheim
The Gunfight at Dodge City	Mirisch
Guns, Girls and Gangsters	Edward Small
Happy Anniversary	Joseph Fields
A Hole in the Head	Frank Sinatra–Frank Capra
The Horse Soldiers	Mirisch
The Horse's Mouth (British)	John Bryan–Ronald Neame
The Hound of the Baskervilles (British)	Seven Arts–Hammer Films

Title	Producer
Inside the Mafia	Edward Small
Invisible Invaders	Edward Small
The Last Mile	Max J. Rosenberg–Milton Subotsky
Lonelyhearts	Dore Schary
The Man in the Net	Mirisch
Mustang	Robert Arnell
The Naked Maja	Titanus
Odds against Tomorrow	Harry Belafonte
On the Beach	Stanley Kramer
Pier 5, Havana	Edward Small
Pork Chop Hill	Gregory Peck
The Rabbit Trap	Hecht-Hill-Lancaster
Riot in Juvenile Prison	Edward Small
Shake Hands with the Devil (British)	George Glass–Walter Seltzer
Solomon and Sheba	Edward Small
Some Like It Hot	Mirisch
Subway in the Sky (British)	Seven Arts
Take a Giant Step	Hecht-Hill-Lancaster
Ten Seconds to Hell	Seven Arts–Hammer Films
Timbuktu	Edward Small
Vice Raid	Edward Small
The Wonderful Country	Robert Mitchum–Chester Erskine

LOPERT RELEASES

Black Orpheus (French/Italian/Brazilian, orig.: *Orfeu Negro*	Dispatfilm-Gemma-Tupan

Title	Producer

1960

The Alamo	John Wayne
And Quiet Flows the Don (Russian)	Gorky Film Studio
The Apartment	Mirisch
The Boy and the Pirates	Bert I. Gordon
Cage of Evil	Edward Small
Dog's Best Friend	Edward Small
Elmer Gantry	Richard Brooks
Exodus	Otto Preminger
The Facts of Life	Norman Panama–Melvin Frank
The Fugitive Kind	Martin Jurow–Richard A. Shepherd–Marlon Brando
The Gallant Hours	James Cagney–Robert Montgomery
Gunfighters of Abilene	Edward Small
Inherit the Wind	Stanley Kramer
The Last Days of Pompeii (Italian/Spanish, orig.: *Gli Ultimi Giorni Di Pompeii*)	Ambrosiana
Macumba Love	M. A. Ripps–Steve Barclay
The Magnificent Seven	Mirisch
The Music Box Kid	Edward Small
The Night Fighters	Robert Mitchum–Raymond Stross
Noose for a Gunman	Edward Small
Oklahoma Territory	Edward Small
The Pusher	Gene Milford–Sidney Katz
Studs Lonigan	Security Pictures
The Summer of the Seventeenth Doll (British)	Hecht-Hill-Lancaster
A Terrible Beauty (British)	Robert Mitchum–Raymond Stross

Title	Producer
Three Came to Kill	Edward Small
The Unforgiven	Hecht-Hill-Lancaster
The Walking Target	Edward Small
A Woman Like Satan (French/Italian, orig.: *La Femme et le Patin*)	Pathé–Gray–D.E.A.R. Films

LOPERT RELEASES

Never on Sunday (Greek)	Jules Dassin
Tunes of Glory (British)	Colin Lesslie

1961

The Boy Who Caught a Crook	Edward Small
By Love Possessed	Mirisch–Seven Arts
The Cat Burglar	Edward Small
Dr. Blood's Coffin (British)	Edward Small
The Explosive Generation	Stanley Colbert
Five Guns to Tombstone	Edward Small
The Flight that Disappeared	Edward Small
Frontier Uprising	Edward Small
The Gambler Wore a Gun	Edward Small
Goodbye Again	Anatole Litvak
Gun Fight	Edward Small
The Hoodlum Priest	Don Murray–Walter Wood
Judgment at Nuremberg	Stanley Kramer
The Last Time I Saw Archie	Jack Webb
Mary Had a Little (British)	Edward Small
A Matter of Morals	Steve Hopkins–John Hess

Title	Producer
The Minotaur (Italian, orig.: *Teseo Contro Il Minotauro*)	Iliria
The Misfits	Seven Arts
The Naked Edge (British)	George Glass–Walter Seltzer
One, Two, Three	Mirisch
Operation Bottleneck	Edward Small
Paris Blues (British)	George Glass–Walter Seltzer
Pocketful of Miracles	Frank Capra
Police Dog Story	Edward Small
Revolt of the Slaves (Italian/Spanish/German, orig.: *La Rivolta Degli Sciavi*)	Ambrosiana-C.B.-Ultra
Secret of Deep Harbor	Edward Small
The Snake Woman (British)	Edward Small
Something Wild	George Justin
Teenage Millionaire	Howard B. Kreitsek
Three on a Spree (British)	Edward Small
Town Without Pity	Mirisch
West Side Story	Mirisch–Seven Arts
When the Clock Strikes	Edward Small
X-15	Frank Sinatra
You Have to Run Fast	Edward Small
The Young Doctors	Stuart Millar–Lawrence Turman
The Young Savages	Harold Hecht

LOPERT RELEASES

The Joker (French, orig.: *Le Farceur*)	AJYM

Title	Producer

1962

Beauty and the Beast	Edward Small
Birdman of Alcatraz	Hecht-Hill-Lancaster
The Children's Hour	Mirisch
The Clown and the Kid	Edward Small
Dead to the World	National Film Studios
Deadly Duo	Edward Small
Dr. No (British)	Harry Saltzman–Albert R. Broccoli
Follow That Dream	Mirisch
Geronimo	Jules V. Levy–Arthur Gardner– Arnold Laven
Gun Street	Edward Small
The Happy Thieves	James Hill
Hero's Island	Leslie Stevens–James Mason
Incident in an Alley	Edward Small
Jack the Giant Killer	Edward Small
Jessica	Jean Negulesco
Kid Galahad	Mirisch
The Magic Sword	Bert I. Gordon
The Manchurian Candidate	George Axelrod–John Franken- heimer–Howard W. Koch
The Mighty Ursus (Italian/Spanish, orig.: *Ursus*)	Ciné Italia
The Miracle Worker	Fred Coe
The Nun and the Sergeant	Eugene Frenke
Pressure Point	Stanley Kramer
The Road to Hong Kong (British)	Norman Panama–Melvin Frank
Saintly Sinners	Edward Small
Sergeants 3	Frank Sinatra

Title	Producer
Sword of the Conqueror (Italian, orig.: *Rosmuna E Alboino*)	Titanus
Taras Bulba	Harold Hecht
Third of a Man	Robert Lewin–William Redlin
Tower of London	Edward Small
Two for the Seesaw	Mirisch–Seven Arts
The Valiant (British)	Jon Penington
War Hunt	Terry Sanders–Denis Sanders

LOPERT RELEASES

Electra (Greek)	Michael Cacoyannis
La Notte (Italian/French)	Dino DeLaurentiis
Phaedra (Greek)	Jules Dassin
Stowaway in the Sky (French, orig.: *Le Voyage en Ballon*)	Filmsonor-Montsouris

1963

Call Me Bwana (British)	Harry Saltzman–Albert R. Broccoli
The Caretakers	Hal Bartlett
The Ceremony	Laurence Harvey
A Child Is Waiting	Stanley Kramer
The Diary of a Madman	Edward Small
Five Miles to Midnight (French/Italian)	Filmsonor–D.E.A.R. Films
The Great Escape	Mirisch
I Could Go on Singing	Stuart Millar–Lawrence Turman

Title	Producer
Irma La Douce	Mirisch
It's a Mad, Mad, Mad, Mad World	Stanley Kramer
Johnny Cool	Peter Lawford
Kings of the Sun	Mirisch
Ladybug, Ladybug	Frank Perry
Lilies of the Field	Ralph Nelson
Love Is a Ball	Martin A. Poll
McLintock!	John Wayne
Stolen Hours	Mirisch
Tom Jones (British)	Woodfall Films
Toys in the Attic	Mirisch
Twice Told Tales	Edward Small

LOPERT RELEASES

Mouse on the Moon (British)	Walter Shenson

1964

The Best Man	Stuart Millar–Lawrence Turman
Flight from Ashiya	Harold Hecht–Daiei Films
For Those Who Think Young	Aubrey Schenck–Howard W. Koch
Goldfinger (British)	Harry Saltzman–Albert R. Broccoli
A Hard Day's Night (British)	Walter Shenson
Invitation to a Gunfighter	Stanley Kramer
Kiss Me, Stupid	Mirisch
One Man's Way	Frank Ross
The Pink Panther	Mirisch
From Russia, with Love (British)	Harry Saltzman–Albert R. Broccoli
The Secret Invasion	Roger Corman–Gene Corman

Title	Producer
The Seventh Dawn	Charles K. Feldman–Karl Tunberg
A Shot in the Dark	Mirisch
633 Squadron	Mirisch
Topkapi	Filmways–Jules Dassin
Woman of Straw (British)	Michael Relph–Basil Dearden
The World of Henry Orient	Jerome Hellman

LOPERT RELEASES

The Girl with the Green Eyes (British)	Woodfall Films
That Man from Rio (French/Italian, orig.: *L'Homme De Rio*)	Films Ariane–D.E.A.R. Films– Vides

1965

Billie	Peter Lawford–Patty Duke
Ferry Cross the Mersey (British)	Brian Epstein
The Glory Guys	Jules V. Levy–Arthur Gardner– Arnold Laven
The Greatest Story Ever Told	George Stevens
The Hallelujah Trail	Mirisch
Help! (British)	Walter Shenson
How to Murder Your Wife	George Axelrod
I'll Take Sweden	Edward Small
Masquerade (British)	Michael Relph–Basil Dearden
Mister Moses	Frank Ross
One Way Pendulum	Woodfall Films
A Rage to Live	Mirisch
Return from the Ashes	Mirisch
The Satan Bug	Mirisch

Title	Producer
Thunderball (British)	Harry Saltzman–Albert R. Broccoli
The Train (French/Italian)	Films Ariane–D.E.A.R. Films
What's New, Pussycat?	Charles K. Feldman

LOPERT RELEASES

The Knack (British)	Woodfall Films
My Wife's Husband (French/Italian, orig.: *La Cuisine au Beurre*)	Corona–D.E.A.R. Films

1966

After the Fox (British/Italian)	Delgate–Nancy Enterprises–Compagnia Cinematografico Montoro
Ambush Bay	Aubrey Schenck–Hal Klein
Boy, Did I Get a Wrong Number	Edward Small
Cast a Giant Shadow	Mirisch
Duel at Diablo	Ralph Nelson–Fred Engel
The Fortune Cookie	Mirisch
Frankie and Johnny	Edward Small
A Funny Thing Happened on the Way to the Forum	Melvin Frank
The Group	Charles K. Feldman
Hawaii	Mirisch
It Happened Here (British)	Kevin Brownlaw–Andre Mollo
Khartoum (British)	Julian Blaustein
Lord Love a Duck	George Axelrod
Namu, the Killer Whale	Ivan Tors

Title	Producer
Return of the Seven (Spanish/American)	Mirisch
The Russians Are Coming, the Russians Are Coming	Mirisch
A Thousand Clowns	Fred Coe
Viva Maria! (French/Italian)	N.E.F.–Oscar Dancigers–Vides
What Did You Do in the War, Daddy?	Mirisch

LOPERT RELEASES

Title	Producer
Fantomas (French/Italian, orig.: *Fantomas Contre Scotland Yard*)	P.A.C.-Gaumont
Mademoiselle (British/French)	Woodfall Films–Procinex
Muriel (French/Italian, orig.: *Muriel, ou Le Temp D'Un Retour*)	D.E.A.R. Films–Argos-Alpha–Films De La Pleiade
1o:3o *P.M. Summer* (Spanish)	Jules Dassin–Anatole Litvak
Up to His Ears (French/Italian, orig.: *Les Tribulations D'Un Chinois en Chine*)	Films Ariane–Vides

1967

Title	Producer
Beach Red	Cornel Wilde
Clambake	Jules V. Levy–Arthur Gardner–Arnold Laven
Eight on the Lam	Bob Hope
Finders Keepers (British)	George H. Brown
A Fistfull of Dollars (Italian/German/Spanish, orig.: *Un Pugno di Dollari*)	Jolly Film–Constantin-Ocean
Fitzwilly	Mirisch

Title	Producer
For a Few Dollars More (Italian/German/Spanish, orig.: *Per Qualche Dollaro in Più*)	Alberto Grimaldi-Arturo Gonzales– Constantin
The Good, the Bad, and the Ugly (Italian, orig.: *Il Buono, il Brutto, il Cattivo*)	Alberto Grimaldi
The Hills Run Red (Italian, orig.: *Un Fiume Di Dollari*)	Dino DeLaurentiis
The Honey Pot	Charles K. Feldman
Hour of the Gun	Mirisch
How I Won the War (British)	Richard Lester
How to Succeed in Business Without Really Trying	Mirisch
In the Heat of the Night	Mirisch
Kill a Dragon	Aubrey Schenck–Hal Klein
Matchless (Italian)	Dino DeLaurentiis
Marat/Sade (British)	Michael Birkett
Navajo Joe (Italian/Spanish)	Dino DeLaurentiis
Operation Kid Brother (Italian)	Dario Sabatello
The Way West	Harold Hecht
You Only Live Twice (British)	Harry Saltzman–Albert R. Broccoli

LOPERT RELEASES

King of Hearts (French/Italian, orig.: *Le Roi De Coeur*)	Fildebroc
Naked among the Wolves (East German, orig.: *Nackt Unter Wölfen*)	D.E.F.A.

Title	Producer
Persona (Swedish)	Svensk Filmindustri
Sailor from Gibraltar (British/French)	Woodfall Films
Thief of Paris (French/Italian, orig.: *Le Voleur*)	Nouvelles Editions Du Films– Compagnia Cinematografica Montoro
The Whisperers (British)	Michael S. Laughlin–Ronald Shedlo

1968

Attack on the Iron Coast (British)	Mirisch
Billion Dollar Brain (British)	Harry Saltzman
The Charge of the Light Brigade (British)	Woodfall Films
Chitty, Chitty, Bang, Bang (British)	Albert R. Broccoli
Danger Route (British)	Max Rosenberg–Milton Subotsky
The Devil's Brigade	David L. Wolper
Hang 'Em High	Clint Eastwood
Inspector Clouseau (British)	Mirisch
Live for Life (French/Italian, orig.: *Vivre Pour Vivre*)	Films Ariane–Vides
Massacre Harbor	Mirisch
Paper Lion	Stuart Millar
The Party	Mirisch
The Private Navy of Sergeant O'Farrell	Bob Hope–NBC
Salt and Pepper (British)	Peter Lawford–Sammy Davis, Jr.
The Scalphunters	Jules V. Levy–Arthur Gardner– Arnold Laven

Title	Producer
Shock Troops (French/Italian, orig.: *Un Homme De Trop*)	Harry Saltzman–Terra
The Thomas Crown Affair	Mirisch
Thunderbirds Are Go (British)	Gerry Anderson
A Twist of Sand (British)	Fred Engel
The Ugly Ones (Italian/Spanish)	Jose Maesso
The Wicked Dreams of Paula Schultz	Edward Small
Yellow Submarine (British)	Apple Films–King Features
Yours, Mine and Ours	Lucille Ball–Robert F. Blumofe

LOPERT RELEASES

The Bride Wore Black (French/Italian, orig.: *La Mariée Etait en Noir*)	François Truffaut–Dino DeLaurentiis
The Climax (Italian/French, orig.: *L'Immorale*)	D.E.A.R. Films–Delphos
Here We Go Round the Mulberry Bush (British)	Clive Donner
Hour of the Wolf (Swedish, orig.: *Vargtimmen*)	Svensk Filmindustri
We Still Kill the Old Way (Italian, orig.: *A Ciascuno Il Suo*)	Cemo Films

1969

Alice's Restaurant	Arthur Penn
Battle of Britain (British)	Harry Saltzman
The Bridge at Remagen	David L. Wolper

United Artists' Domestic Releases

Title	Producer
Buona Sera, Mrs. Campbell	Melvin Frank
Death Rides a Horse (Italian, orig.: *Da Uomo A Uomo*)	Alfonso Sansone–Enrico Chroscicki
The File of the Golden Goose (British)	Edward Small
The First Time	Mirisch
Gaily, Gaily	Mirisch
Halls of Anger	Mirisch
Hannibal Brooks (British)	Michael Winner
If It's Tuesday, This Must Be Belgium	David L. Wolper
Impasse	Aubrey Schenck–Hal Klein
Midnight Cowboy	Jerome Hellman–John Schlesinger
More Dead than Alive	Aubrey Schenck–Hal Klein
The Night They Raided Minsky's	Norman Lear–Bud Yorkin
Number One	Walter Seltzer
On Her Majesty's Secret Service (British)	Harry Saltzman–Albert R. Broccoli
Out of It	Edward Pressman–Paul Williams
Play Dirty (British)	Harry Saltzman
Popi	Herbert B. Leonard
Sam Whiskey	Jules V. Levy–Arthur Gardner–Arnold Laven
The Secret of Santa Vittoria	Stanley Kramer
Sinful Davey (British)	Mirisch
Some Kind of Nut	Mirisch
Submarine X-1 (British)	Mirisch
Support Your Local Sheriff	James Garner
The Thousand Plane Raid (British)	Mirisch

Title	Producer
Where It's At	Frank Ross
Young Billie Young	Talbot-Youngstein

LOPERT RELEASES

Title	Producer
The Bed Sitting Room (British)	Richard Lester–Oscar Lewenstein
La Chamade (French/Italian)	Films Ariane–Artistes Associes
The Devil by the Tail (French/Italian, orig.: *Le Diable par Le Queue*)	Fildebroc-Delphos–Artistes Associes
Les Gauloises Bleues (French)	Films 13–Films Ariane–Artistes Associes
Laughter in the Dark (British/French)	Woodfall Films–Gershwin Kastner–Films Marceau
Life, Love, Death (French/Italian, orig.: *La Vie, L'Amour, La Mort*)	Films 13–Films Ariane–P.E.A.–Artistes Associes
Listen, Let's Make Love (Italian, orig.: *Scuse, Facciamo L'Amoure*)	Alberto Grimaldi
The Sex of Angels (Italian/German, orig.: *Il Sesso Degli Angeli*)	Filmes Cinematografica–Franz Seitz
Shame (Swedish, orig.: *Skammen*)	Svensk Filmindustri
Stolen Kisses (French, orig.: *Baisers Voles*)	François Truffaut
The Voyage of Silence (French, orig.: *O Salto*)	Fildebroc
The Witches (French/Italian, orig.: *Le Streghe*)	Dino DeLaurentiis

1970

Title	Producer
The Angel Levine	Harry Belafonte
Barquero	Aubrey Schenck–Hal Klein

Title	Producer
Burn! (French/Italian, orig.: *Queimada*)	Alberto Grimaldi–Artistes Associes
Cannon for Cordoba	Mirisch
The Christine Jorgensen Story	Edward Small
Cotton Comes to Harlem	Samuel Goldwyn, Jr.
Fellini Satyricon (Italian)	Alberto Grimaldi–Artistes Associes
Give Her the Moon (French/Italian, orig.: *Les Caprices De Marie*)	Alberto Grimaldi–Artistes Associes
Halls of Anger	Mirisch
The Happy Ending	Richard Brooks
The Hawaiians	Mirisch
Hellboats (British)	Mirisch
Hornet's Nest	Stanley S. Canter
Kes (British)	Woodfall Films
The Landlord	Mirisch
The Last Escape (British)	Mirisch
Leo the Last (British)	Robert Chartoff–Irwin Winkler
Let It Be (British)	The Beatles
The McKenzie Break	Jules V. Levy–Arthur Gardner–Arnold Laven
The Mercenary (Italian/Spanish, orig.: *Il Mercenario*)	Alberto Grimaldi–Delphos
Mississippi Mermaid (French, orig.: *La Sirene du Mississippi*)	François Truffaut
Mosquito Squadron (British)	Mirisch

Title	Producer
Ned Kelly (British)	Woodfall Films
One More Time (British)	Peter Lawford–Sammy Davis, Jr.
The Passion of Anna (Swedish, orig.: *En Passion*)	Svensk Filmindustri
Pieces of Dreams	Robert F. Blumofe
Pound	Robert Downey
The Private Life of Sherlock Holmes (British)	Mirisch
Pussycat, Pussycat, I Love You	Jerry Bresler
The Revolutionary (British)	Edward Pressman–Paul Williams
Sabata (Italian)	Alberto Grimaldi–Delphos
They Call Me Mr. Tibbs	Mirisch
Underground (British)	Jules V. Levy–Arthur Gardner– Arnold Laven
The Way We Live Now	Barry Brown
What Do You Say to a Naked Lady?	Allen Funt
The Wild Child (French, orig.: *L'Enfant Sauvage*)	François Truffaut–Artistes Associes
Women in Love (British)	Larry Kramer–Martin Rosen

1971

Adios Sabata (Italian)	Alberto Grimaldi
Bananas	Woody Allen–Jack Rollins– Charles H. Joffe
Born to Win	Philip Langner–George Segal– Jerry Tokofsky
Cold Turkey	Norman Lear–Bud Yorkin

Title	Producer
The Decameron (Italian/French/German, orig.: *Il Decamerone*)	Alberto Grimaldi
Diamonds Are Forever (British)	Harry Saltzman–Albert R. Broccoli
Doc	Frank Perry
Fiddler on the Roof	Mirisch
The Hospital	Paddy Chayefsky–Howard Gottfried
The Hunting Party (British)	Jules V. Levy–Arthur Gardner–Arnold Laven
Jennifer on My Mind	Bernard Schwartz
Lawman	Michael Winner
Mrs. Pollifax—Spy	Frederick Brisson
The Music Lovers (British)	Ken Russell
The Organization	Mirisch
Sunday Bloody Sunday (British)	Joseph Janni
Support Your Local Gunfighter	James Garner–Bill Finnegan
That Splendid November (Italian/French, orig.: *Un Bellissimo Novembre*)	Adelphia–Artistes Associes
Two Hundred Motels (British)	Jerry Good–Herb Cohen
Valdez Is Coming	Ira Steiner
Von Richthofen and Brown	Roger Corman–Gene Corman
What's the Matter with Helen?	Martin Ransohoff
Where's Poppa?	Jerry Tokofsky–Marvin Worth

1972

Title	Producer
Across 110th Street	Fouad Said–Ralph Serpe
Avanti	Mirisch

Title	Producer
Chato's Land	Michael Winner
Daughters of Satan	Aubrey Schenck
Duck, You Sucker! (Italian)	Sergio Leone
Everything You Always Wanted to Know about Sex But Were Afraid to Ask	Woody Allen–Jack Rollins– Charles H. Joffe and Brodsky/ Gould
Fuzz	Martin Ransohoff
Hammer	Essaness Pictures
Hickey and Boggs	Fouad Said
The Honkers	Jules V. Levy–Arthur Gardner– Arnold Laven
Last Tango in Paris (Italian/French)	Alberto Grimaldi–Artistes Associes
The Magnificent Seven Ride	Mirisch
Man of La Mancha	Alberto Grimaldi
The Mechanic	Robert Chartoff–Irwin Winkler– Lewis John Carlino
Money Talks	Allen Funt
Pulp (British)	Michael Klinger
Roma (Italian/French)	Ultra-Artistes Associes
Superbeast	Aubrey Schenck
The Visitors	Chris Kazan–Nick Proferes

1973

Cops and Robbers	Elliott Kastner
Electra Glide in Blue	James William Guerico
Five on the Black Hand Side	Brock Peters–Michael Tolan
Harry in Your Pocket	Bruce Geller
I Escaped from Devil's Island	Roger Corman–Gene Corman

Title	Producer
Jeremy	Elliott Kastner
Live and Let Die (British)	Harry Saltzman–Albert R. Broccoli
The Long Goodbye	Elliott Kastner
The Offence (British)	Sean Connery
Scorpio	Mirisch
Sleeper	Woody Allen–Jack Rollins– Charles H. Joffe
The Spook Who Sat by the Door	Ivan Dixon–Sam Greenlee
Theatre of Blood (British)	John Kohn–Stanley Mann
Tom Sawyer	Reader's Digest–Arthur P. Jacobs
White Lightning	Jules V. Levy–Arthur Gardner– Arnold Laven

1974

Amazing Grace	Matt Robinson
Bank Shot	Hal Landers–Bobby Roberts
Billy Two Hats	Norman Jewison
Bring Me the Head of Alfredo Garcia	Martin Baum
Busting	Robert Chartoff–Irwin Winkler
Huckleberry Finn	Reader's Digest–Arthur P. Jacobs
Juggernaut (British)	David V. Picker
Lenny	Marvin Worth
The Man with the Golden Gun (British)	Harry Saltzman–Albert R. Broccoli
Mr. Majestyk	Mirisch
Mixed Company	Melville Shavelson
The Spikes Gang	Mirisch

Title	Producer
The Super Cops	MGM
The Taking of Pelham One, Two, Three	Gabriel Katzka–Edgar Scherick
That's Entertainment!	MGM
Thieves Like Us	Robert Altman
Thunderbolt and Lightfoot	Clint Eastwood
Visit to a Chief's Son	Robert Halmi
Where the Lilies Bloom	Robert B. Radnitz

1975

Brannigan (British)	Jules V. Levy–Arthur Gardner–John Wayne
Hearts of the West	MGM
The Killer Elite	Martin Baum–Helmut Dantine–Arthur Lewis
Love and Death	Woody Allen–Jack Rollins–Charles H. Joffe
The Manchu Eagle Murder Caper Mystery	Edward K. Dobbs
Mr. Ricco	MGM
Moonrunners	Robert B. Clark
One Flew over the Cuckoo's Nest	Saul Zaentz–Michael Douglas
The Passenger (Italian)	MGM
Rancho Deluxe	Elliott Kastner
Report to the Commissioner	M. J. Frankovitch
The Return of the Pink Panther (British)	Blake Edwards
Rollerball	Norman Jewison
Rosebud	Otto Preminger
Shark's Treasure	Cornel Wilde
Smile	David V. Picker–Michael Ritchie

Title	Producer
The Sunshine Boys	MGM
That's the Way of the World	Sig Shore
Undercovers Hero (British)	John Boulting
The Wilby Conspiracy (British)	Martin Baum–Helmut Dantine
The Wind and the Lion	MGM

1976

Bound for Glory	Robert F. Blumofe–Harold Leventhal
Breakheart Pass	Elliott Kastner–Jerry Gershwin
Buffalo Bill and the Indians	Dino DeLaurentiis–Robert Altman
Burnt Offering	Dan Curtis
Carrie	Paul Monash
Dandy, the All-American Girl	MGM
Drum	Dino DeLaurentiis–Ralph Serpe
From Noon till Three	M. J. Frankovitch–William Self
Gator	Jules V. Levy–Arthur Gardner
Inserts	Davina Belling–Clive Parson
Logan's Run	MGM
It's Showtime	Fred Weintraub–Paul Heller
The Missouri Breaks	Elliott Kastner–Robert M. Sherman
Network	MGM
92 in the Shade	Elliott Kastner
Norman . . . Is that You?	MGM
The Pink Panther Strikes Again (British)	Blake Edwards
The Return of a Man Called Horse	Sandy Howard–Richard Harris
Rocky	Robert Chartoff–Irwin Winkler
Stay Hungry	Harold Schneider–Bob Rafelson

Title	Producer
That's Entertainment, Part 2	MGM
Trackdown	Bernard Schwartz
Vigilante Force	Gene Corman
Welcome to LA	Robert Altman

1977

Annie Hall	Woody Allen–Jack Rollins–Charles H. Joffe
Another Man, Another Chance (French)	Films 13–Films Ariane
Audrey Rose	Robert Wise
A Bridge Too Far (British)	Joseph E. Levine
Demon Seed	MGM
Equus	Elliott Kastner–Lester Persky
New York, New York	Robert Chartoff–Irwin Winkler
Semi-Tough	David Merrick
The Spy Who Loved Me (British)	Albert R. Broccoli
Telefon	MGM
Valentino (British)	Robert Chartoff–Irwin Winkler
The White Buffalo	Dino DeLaurentiis–Pancho Kohner

1978

The Big Sleep (British)	Lew Grade–Elliott Kastner–Michael Winner
Brass Target	MGM
Coma	MGM
Comes a Horseman	Robert Chartoff–Irwin Winkler

Title	Producer
Coming Home	Jerome Hellman
Convoy	Robert M. Sherman
Corvette Summer	MGM
The End	Lawrence Gordon
F.I.S.T.	Norman Jewison
Interiors	Woody Allen–Jack Rollins– Charles H. Joffe
International Velvet (British)	MGM
Invasion of the Body Snatchers	Robert H. Solo
The Last Waltz	Martin Scorcese–Robbie Robertson
Lord of the Rings	Saul Zaentz
Message from Space (Japanese)	Toli Co.–Tohokushinsa Co.
Revenge of the Pink Panther	Blake Edwards
Slow Dance in the Big City	Michael Level–John Avildsen
Uncle Joe Shannon	Robert Chartoff–Irwin Winkler
Who'll Stop the Rain	Herb Jaffe–Gabriel Katzka

Appendix 2: United Artists' Principal Producers, 1951–1978

Robert Aldrich
  The Big Knife / 1955
  Kiss Me Deadly / 1955
  Attack! / 1956
  The Ride Back / 1957
Woody Allen
  see Jack Rollins–Charles H. Joffee
Robert Altman
  The Delinquents / 1957
    (Elmer Rhoden, Jr.)
  Thieves Like Us / 1974
  *Buffalo Bill and
    the Indians* / 1976
    (with Dino DeLaurentiis)
  Welcome to LA / 1976
Daniel M. Angel
  Mister Drake's Duck / 1951
    (with Douglas Fairbanks, Jr.)
  Another's Man's Poison / 1952
    (with Douglas Fairbanks, Jr.)
  Break to Freedom / 1955
  *The Sea Shall Not Have
    Them* / 1956
George Axelrod
  The Manchurian Candidate / 1962
    (with John Frankenheimer)
  How to Murder Your Wife / 1965
  Lord Love a Duck / 1966
Lucille Ball
  see Robert F. Blumofe
Martin Baum
  *Bring Me the Head of Alfredo
    Garcia* / 1974
  The Killer Elite / 1975
    (with Helmut Dantine and
    Arthur Lewis)
  The Wilby Conspiracy / 1975
    (with Helmut Dantine)
The Beatles
  Yellow Submarine / 1968
  Let It Be / 1970

Harry Belafonte
  Odds Against Tomorrow / 1959
  The Angel Levine / 1970
Julian Blaustein
  Khartoum / 1966
  How I Won the War / 1967
Robert F. Blumofe
  Yours, Mine and Ours / 1968
    (with Lucille Ball)
  Pieces of Dreams / 1970
  Bound for Glory / 1976
    (with Harold Leventhal)
Humphrey Bogart
  See John Huston
Albert R. Broccoli
  see Harry Saltzman–
    Albert R. Broccoli
Richard Brooks
  Elmer Gantry / 1960
  The Happy Ending / 1969
Frank Capra
  A Hole in the Head / 1959
    (with Frank Sinatra)
  Pocketful of Miracles / 1961
Charles Chaplin
  Limelight / 1953
Robert Chartoff–Irwin Winkler
  Leo the Last / 1970
  The Mechanic / 1972
    (with Lewis John Carlino)
  Busting / 1974
  Rocky / 1976
  New York, New York / 1977
  Valentino / 1977
  Comes a Horseman / 1978
  Uncle Joe Shannon / 1978
Paddy Chayefsky–Howard Gottfried
  The Hospital / 1971
Fred Coe
  The Miracle Worker / 1962
  A Thousand Clowns / 1965

Roger Corman–Gene Corman
  The Secret Invasion / 1964
  Von Richtofen and Brown / 1971
  I Escaped from Devil's
    Island / 1973
  Vigilante Force / 1976
Georges Dancigers
  see Films Ariane
Oscar Dancigers
  Adventures of Robinson
    Crusoe / 1954
    (with Henry F. Ehrlich)
  Viva Maria! / 1966
Jules Dassin
  Never on Sunday / 1960
  Phaedra / 1962
  Topkapi / 1964
    (with Filmways)
  10:30 p.m. Summer / 1966
    (with Anatole Litvak)
Sammy Davis, Jr.
  see Peter Lawford
Philippe De Broca
  King of Hearts / 1967
  The Devil by the Tail / 1969
  The Voyage of Silence / 1969
Kirk Douglas
  The Indian Fighter / 1955
  The Careless Years / 1957
  Ride Out for Revenge / 1957
  Spring Reunion / 1957
  Paths of Glory / 1958
    (with Kubrick-Harris)
  The Vikings / 1958
  The Devil's Disciple / 1959
    (with Hecht-Hill-Lancaster)
Michael Douglas
  see Saul Zaentz–Michael Douglas
Clint Eastwood
  Hang 'Em High / 1968
  Thunderbolt and Lightfoot / 1974
Blake Edwards
  The Return of the Pink Panther /
    1975
  The Pink Panther Strikes Again /
    1976

  Revenge of the Pink Panther /
    1978
Douglas Fairbanks, Jr.
  see Daniel M. Angel
Charles K. Feldman
  The Seventh Dawn / 1964
    (with Karl Tunberg)
  What's New, Pussycat? / 1965
  The Group / 1966
  The Honey Pot / 1967
Films Ariane
(Georges Dancigers–
  Alexandre Mnouchkine)
  That Man from Rio / 1964
  The Train / 1965
  Up to His Ears / 1966
  Live for Life / 1968
  La Chamade / 1969
  Les Gauloises Bleues / 1969
    (with Films 13)
  Life, Love, Death / 1969
    (with Films 13)
  Another Man, Another
    Chance / 1977
    (with Films 13)
Henry Fonda–Reginald Rose
  Twelve Angry Men / 1957
Melvin Frank
  A Funny Thing Happened on the
    Way to the Forum / 1966
  Buona Sera, Mrs. Campbell / 1969
John Frankenheimer
  see George Axelrod
M. J. Frankovitch
  Report to the
    Commissioner / 1975
  From Noon till Three / 1976
    (with William Self)
Allen Funt
  What Do You Say to a Naked
    Lady? / 1970
  Money Talks / 1972
George Glass–Walter Seltzer
  Shake Hands with the
    Devil / 1959
  The Naked Edge / 1961
  Paris Blues / 1961

Robert Goldstein
  Black Tuesday / 1954
  Robber's Roost / 1955
  Stranger on Horseback / 1955
  A Kiss Before Dying / 1956
  Bandido / 1956
  The Brass Legend / 1956
  Dance With Me, Henry! / 1956
  The Killer Is Loose / 1956
  Man from Del Rio / 1956
  Crime of Passion / 1957
  Fury at Showdown / 1957
Samuel Goldwyn, Jr.
  Man with the Gun / 1955
  The Sharkfighters / 1956
  Cotton Comes to Harlem / 1970
Bert I. Gordon
  The Boy and the Pirates / 1960
  The Magic Sword / 1962
Paul Gregory
  The Night of the Hunter / 1955
Alberto Grimaldi
  For a Few Dollars More / 1967
  The Good, the Bad, and the Ugly / 1968
  Listen, Let's Make Love / 1969
  Burn! / 1970
  Fellini Satyricon / 1970
  The Mercenary / 1970
  Sabata / 1970
  Adios Sabata / 1971
  The Decameron / 1971
  Last Tango in Paris / 1972
  Man of La Mancha / 1972
Hammer Films
  The Creeping Unknown / 1956
  Enemy from Space / 1957
  Steel Bayonet / 1958
  The Hound of the Baskervilles / 1959
    (with Seven Arts)
  Ten Seconds to Hell / 1959
    (with Seven Arts)
Harold Hecht
  The Young Savages / 1961
  Taras Bulba / 1962

  Flight from Ashiya / 1964
  The Way West / 1967
Hecht-Lancaster
  Apache / 1954
  Vera Cruz / 1954
  The Kentuckian / 1955
  Marty / 1955
  Trapeze / 1956
Hecht-Hill-Lancaster
  The Bachelor Party / 1957
  Sweet Smell of Success / 1957
  Run Silent, Run Deep / 1958
  Separate Tables / 1958
  Cry Tough! / 1959
  The Devil's Disciple / 1959
    (with Kirk Douglas)
  The Rabbit Trap / 1959
  Take a Giant Step / 1959
  The Unforgiven / 1960
  Summer of the Seventeenth Doll / 1960
  Birdman of Alcatraz / 1962
Jerome Hellman
  The World of Henry Orient / 1964
  Midnight Cowboy / 1969
    (with John Schlesinger)
  Coming Home / 1978
Morris Helperin–Alfred Crown
  Cop Hater / 1958
  The Lost Missile / 1958
  The Mugger / 1958
James Hill
  The Happy Thieves / 1962
Bob Hope
  Paris Holiday / 1958
  Alias Jesse James / 1959
  Eight on the Lam / 1967
  The Private Navy of Sergeant O'Farrell / 1968
John Huston
  Moulin Rouge / 1953
  Beat the Devil / 1954
    (with Humphrey Bogart)
Joseph Janni
  Romeo and Juliet / 1954
    (with Sandro Ghenzi)
  Sunday Bloody Sunday / 1971

Norman Jewison
  Billy Two Hats / 1974
  Rollerball / 1975
  F.I.S.T. / 1978
Elliott Kastner
  Cops and Robbers / 1973
  Jeremy / 1973
  The Long Goodbye / 1973
  Rancho Deluxe / 1975
  Breakheart Pass / 1976
    (with Jerry Gershwin)
  The Missouri Breaks / 1976
    (with Robert M. Sherman)
  92 in the Shade / 1976
  Equus / 1977
    (with Lester Persky)
  The Big Sleep / 1978
    (with Lew Grade and Michael
    Winner)
Larry Kramer–Martin Rosen
  Women in Love / 1970
Stanley Kramer
  Cyrano de Bergerac / 1951
  High Noon / 1952
  Not as a Stranger / 1955
  The Pride and the Passion / 1957
  The Defiant Ones / 1958
  On the Beach / 1959
  Inherit the Wind / 1960
  Judgment at Nuremberg / 1961
  Pressure Point / 1962
  A Child Is Waiting / 1963
  It's a Mad, Mad, Mad, Mad World
    / 1963
  Invitation to a Gunfighter / 1964
  The Secret of Santa Vittoria /
    1969
Stanley Kubrick–James B. Harris
  Killer's Kiss / 1955
    (Morris Bousel)
  The Killing / 1956
  Paths of Glory / 1958
    (with Kirk Douglas)
Dino DeLaurentiis
  La Notte / 1962
  The Hills Run Red / 1967

Matchless / 1967
Navajo Joe / 1967
The Bride Wore Black / 1968
  (with François Truffaut)
The Witches / 1969
Buffalo Bill and the Indians /
  1976
  (with Robert Altman)
Drum / 1976
The White Buffalo / 1977
Peter Lawford
  Johnny Cool / 1965
  Billie / 1965
    (with Patty Duke)
  Salt and Pepper / 1968
    (with Sammy Davis, Jr.)
  One More Time / 1970
    (with Sammy Davis, Jr.)
Norman Lear–Bud Yorkin
  The Night They Raided Minsky's /
    1969
  Cold Turkey / 1971
Claude Lelouch
  Les Gauloises Bleues / 1969
    (with Films Ariane)
  Life, Love, Death / 1969
    (with Films Ariane)
  Another Man, Another Chance /
    1977
    (with Films Ariane)
Joseph E. Levine
  A Bridge Too Far / 1977
Jules V. Levy–Arthur Gardner–
  Arnold Laven
  Without Warning / 1952
  Vice Squad / 1953
  *The Monster that Challenged the
    World* / 1957
  The Vampire / 1957
  The Flame Barrier / 1958
  The Return of Dracula / 1958
  Geronimo / 1962
  The Glory Guys / 1965
  Clambake / 1967
  The Scalphunters / 1968
  Sam Whiskey / 1968

Underground / 1970
The McKenzie Break / 1970
The Hunting Party / 1971
The Honkers / 1972
White Lightning / 1973
Brannigan / 1975
    (with John Wayne)
Gator / 1976
Anatole Litvak
    Act of Love / 1953
    Goodbye Again / 1961
    10:30 P.M. *Summer* / 1966
        (with Jules Dassin)
London Films
    Sound Barrier / 1952
    Cry, the Beloved Country / 1952
    Outcast of the Islands / 1952
    Tales of Hoffman / 1952
    The Captain's Paradise / 1953
    Hobson's Choice / 1954
    The Great Gilbert and Sullivan /
        1954
    The Man Between / 1954
    The Man Who Loved Redheads /
        1955
Ilya Lopert–David Lean
    Summertime / 1955
MGM
    The Super Cops / 1974
    That's Entertainment! / 1974
    Hearts of the West / 1975
    The Passenger / 1975
    Mr. Ricco / 1975
    The Sunshine Boys / 1975
    The Wind and the Lion / 1975
    Dandy, the All-American Girl / 1976
    Logan's Run / 1976
    Network / 1976
    Norman . . . Is that You? / 1976
    That's Entertainment, Part 2 /
        1976
    Demon Seed / 1977
    Telefon / 1977
    Brass Target / 1978
    Coma / 1978

Corvette Summer / 1978
International Velvet / 1978
Joseph L. Mankiewicz
    The Barefoot Contessa / 1954
    I Want to Live! / 1958
    The Quiet American / 1958
Stuart Millar–Lawrence Turman
    The Young Doctors / 1961
    I Could Go on Singing / 1963
    The Best Man / 1964
    Paper Lion / 1968
        (Stuart Millar)
Mirisch Corporation
    Fort Massacre / 1958
    Man of the West / 1958
    Cast a Long Shadow / 1959
    The Gunfight at Dodge City / 1959
    The Horse Soldiers / 1959
    The Man in the Net / 1959
    Some Like It Hot / 1959
    The Apartment / 1960
    The Magnificent Seven / 1960
    By Love Possessed / 1961
        (with Seven Arts)
    One, Two, Three / 1961
    Town Without Pity / 1961
    West Side Story / 1961
        (with Seven Arts)
    The Children's Hour / 1962
    Follow That Dream / 1962
    Kid Galahad / 1962
    Two for the Seesaw / 1962
        (with Seven Arts)
    The Great Escape / 1963
    Irma La Douce / 1963
    Kings of the Sun / 1963
    Stolen Hours / 1963
    Toys in the Attic / 1963
    Kiss Me, Stupid / 1964
    The Pink Panther / 1964
    A Shot in the Dark / 1964
    633 Squadron / 1964
    The Hallelujah Trail / 1965
    A Rage to Live / 1965
    Return from the Ashes / 1965

The Satan Bug / 1965
Cast a Giant Shadow / 1966
The Fortune Cookie / 1966
Hawaii / 1966
Return of the Seven / 1966
*The Russians Are Coming, the
    Russians Are Coming* / 1966
*What Did You Do in the War,
    Daddy?* / 1966
Fitzwilly / 1967
Hour of the Gun / 1967
*How to Succeed in Business
    Without Really Trying* / 1967
In the Heat of the Night / 1967
Attack on the Iron Coast / 1968
Inspector Clouseau / 1968
Massacre Harbor / 1968
The Party / 1968
The Thomas Crown Affair / 1968
The First Time / 1969
Gaily, Gaily / 1969
Guns of the Magnificent Seven /
    1969
Sinful Davey / 1969
Some Kind of Nut / 1969
Submarine X-1 / 1969
The Thousand Plane Raid / 1969
Cannon for Cordoba / 1970
The Hawaiians / 1970
Halls of Anger / 1970
Hellboats / 1970
The Landlord / 1970
The Last Escape / 1970
Mosquito Squadron / 1970
They Call Me Mr. Tibbs / 1970
*The Private Life of Sherlock
    Holmes* / 1970
Fiddler on the Roof / 1971
The Organization / 1971
Avanti / 1972
The Magnificent Seven Ride / 1972
Scorpio / 1973
Mr. Majestyk / 1974
The Spikes Gang / 1974

Robert Mitchum
    Thunder Road / 1958
    (with Arthur Ripley)
    The Wonderful Country / 1959
    (with Chester Erskine)
    The Night Fighters / 1960
    (with Raymond Stross)
    A Terrible Beauty / 1960
    (with Raymond Stross)
Alexandre Mnouchkine
    see Films Ariane
Paul Monash
    Carrie / 1976
Ralph Nelson
    Lilies of the Field / 1963
    Duel at Diablo / 1966
    (with Fred Engel)
Arch Oboler
    Bwana Devil / 1953
    The Twonky / 1953
Norman Panama–Melvin Frank
    Facts of Life / 1960
    The Road to Hong Kong / 1962
Gregory Peck
    The Big Country / 1958
    (with William Wyler)
    Pork Chop Hill / 1959
Arthur Penn
    Alice's Restaurant / 1969
Brock Peters–Michael Tolan
    Five on the Black Hand Side / 1973
David V. Picker
    Juggernaut / 1974
    Smile / 1975
    (with Michael Ritchie)
William H. Pine–William C. Thomas
    Nightmare / 1956
    Bailout at 43,000 / 1957
    The Big Caper / 1957
Harry M. Popkin
    The Second Woman / 1951
    The Well / 1951
    The Thief / 1952
Otto Preminger
    The Moon Is Blue / 1953

The Man with the Golden Arm /
 1956
Saint Joan / 1957
Exodus / 1960
Rosebud / 1975
J. Arthur Rank
 Blue Lamp / 1951
 Hotel Sahara / 1951
 Naughty Arlette / 1951
 Oliver Twist / 1951
 So Long at the Fair / 1951
 They Were Not Divided / 1951
 The Assassin / 1953
 The Little Kidnappers / 1954
 Malta Story / 1954
 Man with a Million / 1954
 Personal Affair / 1954
 You Know What Sailors Are / 1955
 The Beachcomber / 1955
 The Purple Plain / 1955
 Shadow of the Eagle / 1956
Jack Rollins–Charles H. Joffe
 Bananas / 1971
 *Everything You Always Wanted
 to Know about Sex But Were
 Afraid to Ask* / 1972
 (with Brodsky/Gould)
 Sleeper / 1973
 Love and Death / 1975
 Annie Hall / 1977
 Interiors / 1978
Frank Ross
 The Lady Says No / 1952
 (with John Stillman, Jr.)
 One Man's Way / 1964
 Mister Moses / 1965
 Where It's At / 1969
Robert Rossen
 Alexander the Great / 1956
Jane Russell–Robert Waterfield
 Gentlemen Marry Brunettes / 1955
 The King and Four Queens / 1956
 Run for the Sun / 1956
 The Fuzzy Pink Nightgown / 1957
Ken Russell
 The Music Lovers / 1971

Harry Saltzman–Albert R. Broccoli
 Call Me Bwana / 1963
 Dr. No / 1963
 From Russia with Love / 1964
 Goldfinger / 1964
 Thunderball / 1965
 Billion Dollar Brain / 1967
 (Harry Saltzman)
 You Only Live Twice / 1967
 Chitty, Chitty, Bang, Bang / 1968
 (Albert R. Broccoli)
 Shock Troops / 1968
 (Harry Saltzman)
 Battle of Britain / 1969
 (Harry Saltzman)
 Play Dirty / 1969
 (Harry Saltzman)
 On Her Majesty's Secret Service /
 1969
 Diamonds Are Forever / 1971
 Live and Let Die / 1973
 The Man with the Golden Gun /
 1974
 The Spy Who Loved Me / 1977
 (Albert R. Broccoli)
Victor Saville
 I, the Jury / 1953
 The Long Wait / 1954
 My Gun Is Quick / 1957
Aubrey Schenck–Howard W. Koch
 No Escape / 1953
 War Paint / 1953
 Beachhead / 1954
 Shield for Murder / 1954
 The White Orchid / 1954
 The Yellow Tomahawk / 1954
 Desert Sands / 1955
 Big House, U.S.A. / 1955
 Fort Yuma / 1955
 The Black Sheep / 1956
 The Broken Star / 1956
 Crime Against Joe / 1956
 Emergency Hospital / 1956
 Ghost Town / 1956
 Hot Cars / 1956
 Quincannon, Frontier Scout / 1956

Rebel in Town / 1956
Three Bad Sisters / 1956
Bop Girl Goes Calypso / 1957
The Dalton Girls / 1957
The Girl in Black Stockings / 1957
Jungle Heat / 1957
Hell Bound / 1957
Outlaw's Son / 1957
Pharaoh's Curse / 1957
Revolt at Fort Laramie / 1957
Tomahawk Trail / 1957
Voodoo Island / 1957
War Drums / 1957
Fort Bowie / 1958
For Those Who Think Young / 1964
Ambush Boy / 1966
Kill a Dragon / 1967
  (Schenck–Hal Klein)
Impasse / 1969
  (Schenck–Hal Klein)
More Dead than Alive / 1969
  (Schenck–Hal Klein)
Barquero / 1970
  (Schenck–Hal Klein)
Daughters of Satan / 1972
  (Schenck)
Superbeast / 1972
  (Schenck)
Martin Scorcese–Robbie Robertson
The Last Waltz / 1978
Jack Schwarz
Badman's Gold / 1951
Gold Raiders / 1951
The Hoodlum / 1951
Korea Patrol / 1951
*Buffalo Bill in Tomahawk
  Territory* / 1952
Son of the Renegade / 1953
Security Pictures
The Wild Party / 1956
Four Boys and Gun / 1957
Men in War / 1957
Street of Sinners / 1957
God's Little Acre / 1958
Island Women / 1958
Anna Lucasta / 1959

Day of the Outlaw / 1959
Studs Lonigan / 1960
Seven Arts
The Gun Runners / 1958
The Hound of the Baskervilles /
  1959
  (with Hammer)
Subway in the Sky / 1959
Ten Seconds to Hell / 1959
  (with Hammer)
By Love Possessed / 1961
  (with Mirisch)
The Misfits / 1961
West Side Story / 1961
  (with Mirisch)
Two for the Seesaw / 1962
  (with Mirisch)
Walter Shenson
Mouse on the Moon / 1963
A Hard Day's Night / 1964
Help! / 1965
Frank Sinatra
Johnny Concho / 1956
Kings Go Forth / 1958
A Hole in the Head / 1959
  (with Frank Capra)
X-15 / 1961
Sergeants 3 / 1962
Douglas Sirk
The First Legion / 1951
Edward Small
Bandits of Corsica / 1953
*Captain John Smith and
  Pocahontas* / 1953
Dragon's Gold / 1953
Gun Belt / 1953
Kansas City, Confidential / 1953
The Neanderthal Man / 1953
99 River Street / 1953
Raiders of the Seven Seas / 1953
Sabre Jet / 1953
The Steel Lady / 1953
Wicked Woman / 1953
Captain Kidd and the Slave Girl /
  1954
Khyber Patrol / 1954

The Lone Gun / 1954
Overland Pacific / 1954
Return to Treasure Island / 1954
Southwest Passage / 1954
Down Three Dark Streets / 1954
The Naked Street / 1955
Top Gun / 1955
Comanche / 1956
Gun Brothers / 1956
UFO / 1956
Chicago Confidential / 1957
Five Steps to Danger / 1957
Gun Duel in Durango / 1957
The Iron Sheriff / 1957
Monkey on My Back / 1957
Curse of the Faceless Man / 1958
Hong Kong Confidential / 1958
It! The Terror from beyond Space / 1958
Toughest Gun in Tombstone / 1958
Witness for the Prosecution / 1958 (with Arthur Hornblow, Jr.)
The Four Skulls of Jonathan Drake / 1959
Guns, Girls and Gangsters / 1959
Inside the Mafia / 1959
Invisible Invaders / 1959
Pier 5, Havana / 1959
Riot in Juvenile Prison / 1959
Solomon and Sheba / 1959
Timbuktu / 1959
Vice Raid / 1959
Cage of Evil / 1960
Dog's Best Friend / 1960
Gunfighters of Abilene / 1960
The Music Box Kid / 1960
Noose for a Gunman / 1960
Oklahoma Territory / 1960
Three Came to Kill / 1960
The Walking Target / 1960
Boy Who Caught a Crook / 1961
The Cat Burglar / 1961
Dr. Blood's Coffin / 1961
Frontier Uprising / 1961
Five Guns to Tombstone / 1961
The Flight that Disappeared / 1961

The Gambler Wore a Gun / 1961
Gun Fight / 1961
Mary Had a Little / 1961
Operation Bottleneck / 1961
Police Dog Story / 1961
Secret of Deep Harbor / 1961
The Snake Woman / 1961
Three on a Spree / 1961
When the Clock Strikes / 1961
You Have to Run Fast / 1961
Beauty and the Beast / 1962
The Clown and the Kid / 1962
Deadly Duo / 1962
Gun Street / 1962
Incident in an Alley / 1962
Jack the Giant Killer / 1962
Saintly Sinners / 1962
Tower of London / 1962
The Diary of a Madman / 1963
Twice Told Tales / 1963
I'll Take Sweden / 1965
Boy, Did I Get a Wrong Number / 1966
Frankie and Johnny / 1966
The Wicked Dreams of Paula Schultz / 1968
The File of the Golden Goose / 1969
The Christine Jorgensen Story / 1970

Sam Spiegel
The Prowler / 1951
When I Grow Up / 1951
The African Queen / 1952
Melba / 1953

George Stevens
The Greatest Story Ever Told / 1965

Svensk Filmindustri
Persona / 1967
Hour of the Wolf / 1968
Shame / 1969
The Passion of Anna / 1970

Titanus (Goffredo Lombardo)
The Monte Carlo Story / 1957
The Naked Maja / 1959
Sword of the Conqueror / 1962

Michael Todd
 Around the World in 80 Days /
  1959
Ivan Tors
 The Magnetic Monster / 1953
 Gog / 1954
 Riders to the Stars / 1954
 Battle Taxi / 1955
 Namu, the Killer Whale / 1966
François Truffaut
 The Bride Wore Black / 1968
  (with Dino DeLaurentiis)
 Stolen Kisses / 1969
 Mississippi Mermaid / 1970
 The Wild Child / 1970
John Wayne
 Legend of the Lost / 1957
  (with Roberto Haggiag)
 The Alamo / 1960
 McLintock! / 1963
 Brannigan / 1975
  (with Levy-Gardner-Laven)
Lazar Wechsler
 Four in a Jeep / 1951
 The Village / 1953
 Heidi / 1954
 Heidi and Peter / 1955
Orson Welles
 Othello / 1955
Cornel Wilde
 Storm Fear / 1956
 Beach Red / 1967
 Shark's Treasure / 1975
W. Lee Wilder
 Three Steps North / 1951
 Phantom from Space / 1953

The Snow Creature / 1954
The Big Bluff / 1955
Manfish / 1956
Michael Winner
 Hannibal Brooks / 1969
 Lawman / 1971
 Chato's Land / 1972
 The Big Sleep / 1978
  (with Elliott Kastner and Lew
  Grade)
David L. Wolper
 The Devil's Brigade / 1968
 The Bridge at Remagen / 1969
 *If It's Tuesday, This Must Be
  Belgium* / 1969
Woodfall Film Productions
 Tom Jones / 1963
 The Girl with the Green Eyes / 1964
 One Way Pendulum / 1965
 The Knack / 1965
 Mademoiselle / 1966
 Sailor from Gibraltar / 1967
 The Charge of the Light Brigade /
  1968
 Laughter in the Dark / 1969
 Kes / 1970
 Ned Kelly / 1970
Marvin Worth
 Lenny / 1974
William Wyler
 See Gregory Peck
Saul Zaentz–Michael Douglas
 One Flew over the Cuckoo's Nest /
  1975
 Lord of the Rings / 1978
  (Saul Zaentz)

Appendix 3: United Artists
Collection Addition, 1950–1980

The United Artists Collection Addition, 1950–80, of the Wisconsin Center for Film and Theater Research is housed in the manuscripts library of the State Historical Society of Wisconsin, Madison. The original United Artists Collection was donated to the Center in 1969 and is described in my *United Artists: The Company Built by the Stars* (Madison, Wis.: Univ. of Wisconsin Press, 1975), pp. 289–91. The inventory of the UA Collection Addition that follows is my temporary arrangement of the corporate records, which I found convenient to research this book. Now that I have concluded my research, the Center will formally accession and catalog the addition. As the inventory reveals, the addition contains material documenting the corporate history of UA and its relations with independent producers. The types of documents found in the addition are similar to those in the original collection and consist of annual reports, executive correspondence, distribution agreements, accounting records, publicity and advertising materials, newspaper clippings, and the like.

BOX 1
    Folder 1 Annual Reports
            2 Annual Reports
            3 Annual Reports
            4 Minutes of Annual Meetings
            5 Krim-Benjamin Takeover Agreements, 1951
            6 Corporate History Correspondence
            7 Corporate History Correspondence
            8 Releases, 1974–77, and Grosses
            9 Financial Correspondence
         10 Transamerica—Analysis of Leisure Services Group
        11 Transamerica—Correspondence on Policies
        12 Transamerica—Financial Correspondence
        13 Release Schedules—1951–59
         14 Mary Pickford Correspondence
         15 Foreign Distribution

BOX 2
    Folder 1 Model Distribution Contracts
            2 Eagle-Lion
            3 Advertising and Publicity
            4 Advertising, Publicity, Promotion Manual
            5 Agents
            6 UA Television

7 MGM Distribution
8 Censorship and Rating
9 MPAA Classification and Rating
10 Lopert Pictures
11 Press Releases on Corporate History
12 Critics and Trades
13 Audience Analyses
14 Daniel Yankelovich, Inc., Audience Survey, 4 vols.
15 Exhibitor Relations
16 MPAA
17 MPEA
18 MPEA—Surveys
19 MPEA—Reports on Billings

BOX 3
Folder 1 Woody Allen
2 James Bond Deals
3 James Bond Deals
4 Bond Films—*Dr. No*
5 Bond Films—*Thunderball*
6 Bond Films—*From Russia with Love*
7 Bond Films—*You Only Live Twice*
8 Bond Films—*Man with the Golden Gun*
9 Bond Films—*Diamonds Are Forever*
10 Bond Films—*Live and Let Die*
11 Bond Films—*Goldfinger*
12 Beatles
13 Richard Brooks—*Elmer Gantry*
14 Bryna Corp.—Kirk Douglas
15 Bryna Corp.—*The Vikings*
16 *Casino Royale*
17 Frank Capra
18 Charles Chaplin—*Limelight*
19 Chartoff-Winkler
20 Paddy Chayefsky
21 Michael Cimino—*Heaven's Gate*

BOX 4
Folder 1 Francis Ford Coppola—*Apocalypse Now*
2 Jules Dassin
3 Hillard Elkins—*Alice's Restaurant*
4 Samuel Goldwyn, Jr.—*Cotton Comes to Harlem*
5 Alberto Grimaldi
6 Grimaldi—*Last Tango in Paris*
7 Grimaldi—*Man of La Mancha*
8 Gulu Pictures—*Bwana Devil*

8 Jewison—*Rollerball* Publicity Stories
9 Jewison—*Rollerball*—CARA
10 Jewison—*Rollerball* Reviews, England
11 Jewison—*Rollerball* Reviews, U.S.
12 Jewison—*Rollerball* Reviews, France
13 Jewison—*Rollerball*, England Distribution
14 Jewison—*Rollerball*, Photos
15 Joseph Mankiewicz—*Barefoot Contessa*
16 Otto Preminger—*The Moon Is Blue*
17 Preminger—*Man with the Golden Arm*
18 Preminger—*Exodus*
19 Preminger—*Saint Joan*

BOX 7
Folder 1 *One Flew over the Cuckoo's Nest*
2 Larry Kramer—*Women in Love*
3 Harry Saltzman
4 John Schlesinger—*Sunday, Bloody Sunday*
5 John Schlesinger—*Midnight Cowboy*
6 Seven Arts
7 Seven Arts—*The Misfits*
8 Seven Arts—*Anatomy of a Murder*
9 Edward Small
10 Edward Small—*Solomon and Sheba*
11 Edward Small—*Solomon and Sheba*
12 Sam Spiegel—*The African Queen*
13 George Stevens—*The Greatest Story Ever Told*
14 Michael Todd
15 Woodfall Films—*Tom Jones*
16 Marvin Worth—*Lenny*

NOTES

Primary documents cited in the notes are contained in the United Artists Collection Addition, 1950–80. Transcripts of the interviews are in my personal possession.

Introduction

1. Michael E. Porter, *Competitive Strategy: Techniques for Analyzing Industries and Competitors* (New York: The Free Press, 1980).
2. Porter, *Competitive Strategy*, p. 23.
3. "The Changing Economics of Entertainment," in Tino Balio, ed., *The American Film Industry* (Madison: University of Wisconsin Press, rev. ed., 1985), p. 607.

Chapter One: Prelude at Eagle-Lion

1. Interview with Arthur B. Krim, August 1, 1983. Hereafter Krim is referred to as ABK.
2. Tino Balio, *United Artists: The Company Built by the Stars* (Madison, Wis.: Univ. of Wisconsin Press, 1975).
3. Ibid., p. 241.
4. ABK interview, December 8, 1972.
5. ABK interview, August 1, 1983.
6. Robert Murphy, "Rank's Attempt on the American Market, 1944–9," in James Curran and Vincent Porter, eds., *British Cinema History* (Totowa, N.J.: Barnes & Noble Books, 1983), pp. 164–78.
7. Alan Wood, *Mr. Rank: A Study of J. Arthur Rank and British Films* (London: Hodder and Stoughton, 1952), pp. 99–116.
8. Joseph Borkin, *Robert R. Young, The Populist of Wall Street* (New York: Harper & Row, 1969). Explaining the curious spelling of "Alleghany," Borkin said: "According to what may be an apocryphal story, the adventurous but poorly educated Van Swerigans [Cleveland industrialists] had intended to name their new holding company after the Allegheny Mountains but could only approximate the spelling. After all the legalities were completed and the certificates printed, a horrified clerk in J. P. Morgan & Company discovered the misspelling—but too late." Borkin, *Young*, p. 28n.
9. George N. Fenin and William K. Everson, *The Western* (New York: Grossman Publishers, 1973), pp. 257–58.
10. Young's nonrailroading interests were segregated in a holding company called the Midamerica Corporation, which changed its name to Pathé Industries after the Pathé merger. For a history of PRC, see Don Miller, "A Brief History of Producers Releasing Corporation," in Wheeler Dixon, ed., *Producers Releasing Corporation* (Jefferson, N.C.: McFarland & Company, 1986), pp. 9–32.

11. ABK interview, August 1, 1983.
12. "Eagle-Lion to Distrib 20 Pix This Year," *Variety*, August 21, 1946, p. 11.
13. Robert S. Benjamin to Robert R. Young, May 26, 1946. Hereafter, Benjamin is referred to as RSB.
14. RSB to Robert R. Young, May 26, 1946.
15. ABK interview, August 1, 1983.
16. *Variety Film Reviews*, January 22, 1947 (New York: Garland, 1983–).
17. *Variety Film Reviews*, May 28, 1947.
18. "Wall Street Analysis of Film Grosses," *Variety*, November 16, 1949, p. 10.
19. "Movies: End of an Era?", *Fortune* 39 (April 1949): 99–102+.
20. "Eagle Lion's Krim Has His Own Ideas on Picture Star Values," *Variety*, November 3, 1948, p. 4.
21. RSB to Walter Nates, October 24, 1947.
22. ABK to Serge Semenenko, April 13, 1949.
23. Don Miller, "Eagle Lion: The Violent Years," *Focus on Film* 31 (November 1978): 26.
24. ABK to Robert W. Purcell, March 3, 1948.
25. Miller, "Eagle Lion," p. 30.
26. RSB to John Davis, May 8, 1948.
27. "Customer at 850G Keys Ingenuity on Prod. Economies," *Variety*, November 3, 1948, pp. 3, 16.
28. ABK to John Davis, October 4, 1948.
29. ABK to Joe Vogel, August 21, 1948.
30. "Eagle Lion Heirs Lose Antitruster," *Variety*, June 13, 1946, p. 5; *Eagle Lion Studios, Inc., v. Loew's Inc.*, 248 F. 2d 438 (2d Cir. 1957), aff'd by equally divided court, 358 U.S. 100 (1958).
31. ABK to Robert W. Purcell, March 18, 1949.
32. RSB to F. B. F. West, July 8, 1948.
33. "EL Embarks on New Economy Prod. Measure," *Variety*, January 19, 1949, p. 7.
34. "Stix Still Nix British Pix," *Variety*, June 18, 1947, pp. 1, 16.
35. S. L. Seidelman to RSB, May 12, 1948.
36. Robert R. Young to Robert W. Purcell, December 4, 1947.
37. RSB to ABK, June 2, 1948.
38. RSB to ABK, May 13, 1948.
39. RSB to ABK, June 2, 1948.
40. ABK to Robert R. Young, December 16, 1948.
41. ABK to Serge Semenenko, April 13, 1949.
42. ABK to Louis Nizer, June 8, 1949.
43. Louis Nizer to ABK, June 24, 1949.
44. ABK interview, August 1, 1983.
45. "The Derring-Doers of the Movie Business," *Fortune* 57 (May 1958): 137–41+.

Chapter Two: Gambling on Independent Production

1. David Pirie, *Anatomy of the Movies* (New York: Macmillan, 1981), p. 42.
2. "Trend to Semi-Indie Units," *Variety*, July 12, 1950, pp. 5, 18.
3. "'Show Me,' Says Banks to Indies," *Variety*, June 13, 1951, p. 5.
4. ABK interview, August 1, 1984.
5. Porter, *Competitive Strategy*, p. 30.
6. Ibid., p. 17.
7. Janet Wasko, *Movies and Money: Financing the American Film Industry* (Norwood, N.J.: Ablex, 1982), p. 108.
8. UA memorandum, April 17, 1951.
9. Sam Spiegel to ABK, January 12, 1950.
10. Stanley Kramer, "The Independent Producer," *Films in Review* 2 (March 1951): 3.
11. Richard Dyer MacCann, "Independence with a Vengeance," *Film Quarterly* 15 (Summer 1962): 14.
12. Frank Capra, "Breaking Hollywood's Pattern of Sameness," *New York Times Magazine*, May 5, 1946, p. 19.
13. Abel Green, "Tri-Dimension's Hectic Race," *Variety*, January 28, 1953, p. 18.
14. "No Letup in 3-D's Sock Impact," *Variety*, February 4, 1953, p. 7.
15. "3-D Crowded Out of Conversation," *Variety*, February 10, 1954, p. 11.
16. Quoted in Balio, *United Artists: The Company Built by the Stars*, p. 210.
17. Quoted in Theodore Huff, *Charlie Chaplin* (New York: Schumann, 1951), p. 285.
18. Quoted in Terry Hickey, "Accusations Against Charles Chaplin for Political and Moral Offenses," *Film Comment* 5 (Winter 1969): 53.
19. Ibid., p. 53.
20. John Cogley, *Report on Blacklisting I: The Movies* (New York: Fund for the Republic, 1956).
21. Robert A. Bunch to UA, July 31, 1952.
22. Max E. Youngstein to RSB, August 28, 1952.
23. Hickey, "Accusations," p. 44.
24. Quoted in Hickey, "Accusations," p. 56.
25. "Is 'Charlot' a Menace?" *New York Times*, September 21, 1952, IV:10.
26. RSB to L. K. Gough, October 17, 1952.
27. "Gough Defends 'Limelight' Stand in Chaplin Rap," *Variety*, February 25, 1953, p. 4.
28. William Hogan, "'Limelight' Is Failing to Pack U.S. Theaters," *San Francisco Chronicle*, December 31, 1952, p. 4.
29. William Murray, "*Limelight*: Chaplin and His Censors," *The Nation*, March 21, 1953, pp. 247–48.
30. RSB to ABK, December 18, 1952.
31. Murray, "*Limelight*," p. 248.
32. William Huie, "Mr. Chaplin and the Fifth Freedom: The Sovereign Right to Be a Fool," *American Mercury* 75 (November 1952): 123–28.

33. "'Limelight' Takings in N.Y. Key Nabes Disappointing," *Variety*, February 11, 1953, p. 5.
34. "O.K. B.O. in D.C." *Variety*, February 25, 1953, p. 20.
35. "N. O. Daily Raps Legion Nix," *Variety*, February 25, 1953, p. 20.
36. Michael Conant, *Antitrust in the Motion Picture Industry* (Berkeley and Los Angeles: Univ. of California Press, 1960); Richard S. Randall, "Censorship: From *The Miracle* to *Deep Throat*," in Tino Balio, ed., *The American Film Industry*, rev. ed. (Madison, Wis.: Univ. of Wisconsin Press, 1985): 510–36 (hereafter referred to as *AFI* rev. ed.), and Douglas Ayer, Roy E. Bates, and Peter J. Herman, "Self-Censorship in the Movie Industry: A Historical Perspective on Law and Social Change," *Wisconsin Law Review*, no. 3 (1970): 791–838.
37. Balio, *United Artists: The Company Built by the Stars*, pp. 203–5.
38. Richard Corliss, "The Legion of Decency," *Film Comment* 4 (Summer 1968): 24–61.
39. Quoted in Alan F. Westin, "The Miracle Case: The Supreme Court and the Movies," *Inter-University Case Program #64* (Indianapolis, Ind.: Bobbs-Merrill, n.d.), p. 32.
40. Corliss, "Legion of Decency," p. 43.
41. Otto Preminger, *Preminger: An Autobiography* (Garden City, N.Y.: Doubleday, 1977), pp. 99–100.
42. Ibid., p. 108.
43. Gerald Pratley, *The Cinema of Otto Preminger* (New York: A. S. Barnes, 1971), pp. 100–101; Preminger tells a variation of this story in his *Preminger: An Autobiography*, p. 108.
44. Jack Vizzard, "Why No Seal for *The Moon*," *Film Bulletin*, July 27, 1953.
45. Jack Vizzard, *See No Evil: Life Inside a Hollywood Censor* (New York: Simon and Schuster, 1970), pp. 154–55.
46. Robert Blumofe to W. J. Heineman, April 14, 1953.
47. *Film Daily*, June 3, 1953, p. 4.
48. *New York Times Film Reviews*, July 9, 1953 (New York: New York Times, 1970–).
49. *New York Journal-American*, June 16, 1953, p. 27.
50. Francis Cardinal Spellman to the pastors of the churches in the Archdiocese of New York, June 24, 1953.
51. Gene Arneel, "Church Slant on Censorship," *Variety*, October 28, 1953, pp. 7, 16.
52. B. G. Kranze to W. J. Heineman, n.d.
53. *New York Post*, October 18, 1953.
54. Arneel, "Church Slant on Censorship," p. 16.
55. Decision of the Maryland State Board of Motion Picture Censors, August 31, 1953.
56. "Baltimore Court Voids State Ban," *New York Times*, December 9, 1953, p. 11.
57. *Commercial Pictures Corp. v. Board of Regents*, 346 U.S. 587 (1954) and *Superior Films v. Dep't of Education*, 346 U.S. 387 (1954).

58. "Censors: 'We've Been Censored,'" *Variety*, January 20, 1954, pp. 5, 20.
59. *Holmby Productions v. Vaughn*, 177 Kansas 728 (1955), 350 U.S. 870 (1955).
60. E. A. Bigley to W. J. Heineman, March 4, 1954.
61. RSB to Eric Johnston, November 9, 1955.
62. "Presidents Vote No Exception for Preminger-UA 'Golden,'" *Variety*, December 7, 1955, p. 3.
63. *United Artists Corp. v. Maryland State Board of Censors*, 210 Md. 586 (1956). For a discussion of this case, see Ira H. Carmen, *Movies, Censorship, and the Law* (Ann Arbor: Univ. of Michigan Press, 1966), pp. 159–60.
64. "Shurlock's 'Interpretation' Eased," *Variety*, December 19, 1956, p. 10.
65. Douglas Ayer, "Self-Censorship in the Movie Industry," p. 808.
66. George Yousling, *Bank Financing of the Independent Motion Picture Producer* (New Brunswick, N.J.: Graduate School of Banking, Rutgers Univ., 1948), pp. 30–31.
67. ABK to Mary Pickford, December 27, 1955.
68. David G. Wittels, "Star-Spangled Octopus," *Saturday Evening Post* 218 (August 10, 17, 24, and 31, 1946), various pages; Edward T. Thompson, "There's No Business Like MCA's Business," *Fortune* 62 (July 1960): 114–19+; Bill Davidson, "MCA: The Octopus Devours the World," *Show* 2 (February and March 1962), various pages; MacCann, "Independence with a Vengeance," pp. 14–21; Peter J. Schuyten, "How MCA Rediscovered Movieland's Golden Lode," *Fortune* 94 (November 1976): 122+; Dan E. Moldea, *Dark Victory: Ronald Reagan, MCA, and the Mob* (New York: Viking, 1986).
69. Thompson, "There's No Business Like MCA's Business," p. 152.
70. Robert Windeler, *Burt Lancaster* (New York: St. Martin's Press, 1984), p. 57.
71. *Variety Film Reviews*, July 13, 1955.
72. Windeler, *Burt Lancaster*, p. 82.
73. Robert Blumofe to ABK, May 24, 1954.
74. Quoted in Murray Teigh Bloom, "What Two Lawyers Are Doing to Hollywood," *Harper's Magazine* 216 (February 1958): 43.
75. ABK interview, August 2, 1983.
76. Ibid.
77. Ibid.
78. ABK to William W. Shea, September 27, 1955.
79. ABK interview, August 2, 1983.
80. "P.S. to UA Success Story," *Variety*, February 29, 1956, p. 3.

Chapter Three: The Company in Place

1. Interview with Herbert T. Schottenfeld, March 19, 1985. Hereafter, Schottenfeld is referred to as HTS.

2. Irving Bernstein, *Hollywood at the Crossroads* (Hollywood, Calif.: A. F. of L. Film Council, 1957); Michael Conant, *Antitrust in the Motion Picture Industry* (Berkeley and Los Angeles: Univ. of California Press, 1960); Janet Staiger, "Individualism Versus Collectivism," *Screen* 24 (July–October 1983): 68–79.

3. Michael Conant, "The Impact of the *Paramount* Decrees," in Tino Balio, ed., *The American Film Industry* (Madison, Wis.: Univ. of Wisconsin Press, 1976), p. 354. Hereafter referred to as *AFI*.

4. Bernstein, *Hollywood at the Crossroads*, pp. 30–36.

5. Conant, "Impact of the *Paramount* Decrees," p. 351.

6. Conant, *Antitrust in the Motion Picture Industry*, pp. 107–53.

7. See Robert W. Crandall, "The Postwar Performance of the Motion Picture Industry," *Antitrust Bulletin* 20 (Spring 1975): 49–88; David Gordon, "Why the Movie Majors Are Major," in *AFI*, pp. 458–70; Douglas Gomery, "The Film Industry Today," *Screen* 21 (Spring 1980): 15–17; and Douglas Gomery, "The American Film Industry of the 1970's," *Wide Angle*, vol. 5, no. 4, pp. 52–59.

8. Gordon, "Why the Movie Majors Are Major," p. 460.

9. Crandall, "Postwar Performance of the Motion Picture Industry," p. 62.

10. Thomas Guback, *The International Film Industry* (Bloomington, Ind.: Indiana Univ. Press, 1969), p. 10.

11. David J. Londoner, "The Changing Economics of Entertainment," in *AFI* rev. ed., p. 607.

12. Quoted in "The Derring-Doers of the Movie Business," *Fortune* 57 (May 1958): 137–41+.

13. Ibid., p. 141.

14. Bloom, "What Two Lawyers Are Doing to Hollywood," p. 43.

15. Ibid.

16. "Studio O'Head: What to Do?" *Variety*, March 12, 1958, p. 5.

17. Steven Bach, *Final Cut: Dreams and Disaster in the Making of "Heaven's Gate"* (New York: William Morrow, 1985), p. 48.

18. ABK interview, March 20, 1985.

19. HTS interview, March 19, 1985.

20. ABK interview, August 3, 1983.

21. ABK to John R. Beckett, April 1, 1970.

22. Stanley Penn," United Artists Takes Lead in Movie Industry Backing Independents," *Wall Street Journal*, May 9, 1966, p. 15.

23. Thompson, *"There's No Business Like MCA's Business,"* 114–19.

24. "The Company of the Independents," *Variety*, June 24, 1959, p. 13.

25. "The Derring-Doers of the Movie Business," pp. 137–40. (Copyright © 1958 Time Inc. All rights reserved.)

26. HTS interview, March 19, 1985.

27. Alan Wilson interview, February 3, 1976.

28. Larry DeWaay interview, November 14, 1975.

29. William Bernstein interview, October 19, 1983.

30. I have extrapolated this apportionment from data contained in Crandall, "The Postwar Performance of the Motion Picture Industry."

31. "Smooth Going for TV at UA Meet," *Broadcasting*, June 16, 1958, p. 46.
32. "Pix-Video Wedding Closer," *Variety*, December 31, 1952, p. 19.
33. *AFI* rev. ed., p. 435.
34. ABK interview, October 20, 1983.
35. Ibid.
36. Albert Kroeger, "A Long Hard Look at the Genealogy of Network TV," *Television* 23 (April 1966), p. 39.
37. ABK interview, October 20, 1983.
38. Kroeger, "A Long Hard Look at the Genealogy of Network TV," p. 34.
39. ABK interview, October 20, 1986.
40. Kroeger, "A Long Hard Look at the Genealogy of Network TV," pp. 36–39.
41. Morris Gelman, "The Winning Ways of Movies," *Television* 22 (May 1965): 74.
42. ABK interview, October 20, 1983.
43. Crandall, "Postwar Performance of the Motion Picture Industry," p. 85.
44. Herm Schoenfeld, "Big New Sound of Music Biz Is Stereo," *Variety*, January 7, 1959, p. 210.
45. Herm Schoenfeld, "Music in Conglomerate World," *Variety*, January 8, 1969, p. 195.
46. Herm Schoenfeld, "Pop Music's Money Message'," *Variety*, January 5, 1966, p. 203.
47. Schoenfeld, "Music in Conglomerate World," p. 159.
48. Ibid.
49. Herm Schoenfeld, "Disks Head for $2-Bil Level," *Variety*, January 3, 1973, p. 135.
50. Herm Schoenfeld, "Music Business Awaits Climax to 'Payola Follies of '73'," *Variety*, January 9, 1974, p. 131.

Chapter Four: Making Them Big

1. Penn, "United Artists Takes Lead in Movie Industry Backing Independents," p. 15.
2. ABK interview, March 20, 1985.
3. David J. Londoner, "The Changing Economics of Entertainment," in *AFI* rev. ed., p. 618.
4. Gary R. Edgerton, *American Film Exhibition and an Analysis of the Motion Picture Industry's Market Structure, 1963–1980* (New York: Garland Publishing, 1983), p. 29.
5. Freeman Lincoln, "The Comeback of the Movies," *Fortune* 51 (February 1955): 155.
6. Thomas Patrick Doherty, "Teenagers and Teenpics, 1955–1960: The Juvenilization of American Movies," Ph.D. dissertation, Univ. of Iowa, 1984, p. 37.
7. "Eddie Small as '1-Man Industry,'" *Variety*, June 16, 1948, p. 4.
8. ABK memorandum, September 28, 1953.

9. "Film 'Future': GI Baby Boom," *Variety*, March 5, 1958, p. 1.
10. Doherty, "Teenagers and Teenpics, 1955–1960," pp. 171–72.
11. "Pix Static in Boom Economy," *Variety*, April 24, 1957, pp. 1, 16.
12. "C'Scope Gets Spotlight," *Variety*, September 16, 1953, pp. 1, 62.
13. Lincoln, "Comeback of the Movies," p. 127.
14. "Pix History Encore," *Variety*, September 8, 1954, p. 3.
15. "Getting Them Back to the Movies," *Business Week*, October 22, 1955, p. 58+.
16. Edgerton, *American Film Exhibition*, p. 26.
17. John McDonald, "Now the Bankers Come to Disney," *Fortune* 73 (May 1966): 239–41+.
18. Robert B. Frederick, "'Sound' Blows 'Wind' Off No. 1," *Variety*, January 4, 1967, p. 23.
19. Gene Arneel, "1962's Big Money Product," *Variety*, January 9, 1963, p. 61.
20. "Hollywood's New Leader," *Business Week*, January 7, 1967, pp. 80–84.
21. "TV Cleo Price: $5 Million," *Variety*, January 28, 1966, p. 3.
22. "Hollywood's New Leader," p. 84.
23. For a discussion of the founding of the United Artists Theatre Corporation, see Balio, *United Artists: The Company Built by the Stars*, pp. 64–66.
24. Crandall, "Postwar Performance of the Motion Picture Industry," pp. 70, 72.
25. "Cut!" *Newsweek*, September 18, 1961, p. 78.
26. "Forget the Incense," *Time*, December 28, 1962, p. 34.
27. William Trombley, "The Greatest Story Ever Told," *Saturday Evening Post*, October 19, 1963, p. 40.
28. UA memorandum, June 28, 1963.
29. *New Yorker*, February 20, 1965, p. 137.
30. *Time*, February 26, 1965, p. 96.
31. *New York Times Film Reviews*, February 16, 1965.
32. *Time*, February 26, 1965, p. 96.
33. *Life*, February 26, 1965, p. 25.
34. *Variety Film Reviews*, February 17, 1965.
35. United Artists Corporation, *1964 Annual Report*.
36. Bosley Crowther, "Hollywood's Producer of Controversy," *New York Times Magazine*, December 10, 1961, p. 76.
37. Bosley Crowther, "'A' Movies on 'B' Budgets," *New York Times Magazine*, November 12, 1950, pp. 20–25+.
38. Crowther, "Hollywood's Producer of Controversy," p. 82.
39. "Kramer's Next Likely for UA," *Variety*, March 21, 1951, pp. 5, 15.
40. Peter Cowie, "The Different One," *Films & Filming* 9 (March 1963), p. 17.
41. Quoted in Donald Spoto, *Stanley Kramer: Film Maker* (New York: G. P. Putnam's Sons, 1978), p. 178.
42. Crowther, "Hollywood's Producer of Controversy," p. 84.
43. Quoted in Spoto, *Stanley Kramer: Film Maker*, p. 179.

44. Ibid., p. 178.
45. Ibid., p. 187.
46. Peter Cowie, "Different One," p. 18.
47. *Los Angeles Herald Express*, February 10, 1960; Crowther, "Hollywood's Producer of Controversy," p. 79.
48. *Variety Film Reviews*, December 2, 1959.
49. Crowther, "Hollywood's Producer of Controversy," p. 76.
50. Quoted in Spoto, *Stanley Kramer: Film Maker*, p. 222.
51. Ibid., p. 229.
52. Ibid.
53. Crowther, "Hollywood's Producer of Controversy," p. 82.
54. Stanley Kramer to ABK, n.d.
55. Ibid.
56. ABK to Seymour Peyser, February 23, 1955.
57. ABK memorandum, February 21, 1955.
58. ABK to Robert F. Blumofe, May 5, 1954.
59. ABK memorandum, January 31, 1956.
60. ABK memorandum, February 21, 1955.
61. *Daily Variety*, June 6, 1958, p. 1.
62. Max E. Youngstein to ABK, June 13, 1958.
63. Quoted in Windeler, *Burt Lancaster*, p. 98.
64. *Variety Film Reviews*, December 3, 1958.
65. *Variety Film Reviews*, August 12, 1959.
66. *Variety Film Reviews*, July 8, 1959.
67. *Variety Film Reviews*, July 29, 1959.
68. Quoted in Windeler, *Burt Lancaster*, p. 108.
69. Quoted in Mel Schuster, "Burt Lancaster," *Films in Review* 20 (August–September 1969), p. 403.
70. *Variety Film Reviews*, April 26, 1961.
71. *New York Times Film Reviews*, December 26, 1962.
72. *New York Times Film Reviews*, April 23, 1964.
73. *Variety Film Reviews*, January 10, 1962.
74. ABK to Burt Lancaster, April 6, 1964.
75. HTS interview, March 22, 1985.
76. "Derring-Doers of the Movie Business," pp. 137–41+.
77. ABK to Kirk Douglas, April 24, 1956.
78. Max E. Youngstein to James B. Harris, October 18, 1956.
79. Kirk Douglas to ABK, May 7, 1957.
80. ABK to Kirk Douglas, June 23, 1960.
81. Kirk Douglas to ABK, June 20, 1960.
82. ABK to Kirk Douglas, June 25, 1960.
83. Robert F. Blumofe to ABK, January 17, 1959.

Chapter Five: The Studio without Walls

1. UA publicity release, n.d.
2. "Fade Out for Blockbuster Films?" *Business Week*, October 20, 1962, p. 178.
3. ABK interview, August 3, 1983.
4. HTS interview, March 22, 1985.
5. ABK interview, August 3, 1983.
6. Walter M. Mirisch interview, May 16, 1984.
7. "Casting Their Own UA Horoscope," *Variety*, December 10, 1958, p. 4.
8. "Majors Originated Outrageous Wages," *Variety*, December 10, 1958, p. 4.
9. Walter M. Mirisch interview, May 16, 1984.
10. ABK interview, March 20, 1985.
11. David V. Picker to ABK, March 9, 1962.
12. Walter M. Mirisch interview, May 16, 1984.
13. Tom Wood, *The Bright Side of Billy Wilder, Primarily* (New York: Doubleday, 1969), p. 179.
14. Patrick Palmer interview, November 4, 1975.
15. Ibid.
16. Marvin E. Mirisch to ABK, February 10, 1961.
17. ABK interview, August 3, 1983.
18. "Casting Their Own UA Horoscope," *Variety*, pp. 3, 17.
19. Bernard F. Dick, *Billy Wilder* (Boston: Twayne Publishers, 1980), p. 91.
20. *Variety Film Reviews*, December 13, 1961.
21. *Variety Film Reviews*, June 26, 1963.
22. Walter M. Mirisch to Max E. Youngstein, August 15, 1958.
23. *Variety Film Reviews*, December 18, 1963.
24. Walter M. Mirisch interview, May 16, 1984.
25. Ibid.
26. Peter Lehman and William Luhr, *Blake Edwards* (Athens, Ohio: Ohio Univ. Press, 1981), p. 19.
27. *New York Times Film Reviews*, October 19, 1961.
28. "'West Side'—The Lead 'Story,'" *Variety*, January 9, 1963, pp. 13, 61.
29. "Mirisches as Big UA Stockholders," *Variety*, January 29, 1964, p. 4.
30. "UA–Mirisch's $600,000 for Michener's 'Hawaii,'" *Variety*, August 26, 1959, p. 5.
31. Marvin E. Mirisch to ABK, August 25, 1965.
32. Walter M. Mirisch interview, May 16, 1984.
33. ABK to Marvin E. Mirisch, May 15, 1967.
34. Axel Madsen, *Billy Wilder* (London: British Film Institute, 1968), p. 138.
35. *Variety Film Reviews*, December 16, 1964.
36. *Time*, January 1, 1965, p. 69.
37. Interview with Walter M. Mirisch, February 19, 1987; Peter Sellers to David V. Picker, May 2, 1964; David V. Picker to Peter Sellers, May 4, 1964.

38. Peter Stamelman, "Blake Edwards Interview—In the Lair of the Pink Panther," *Millimeter* 5 (January 1977): 18–22+.
39. *Variety Film Reviews*, March 20, 1968.
40. Walter M. Mirisch interview, May 16, 1984.
41. Robert J. Landry, "Poitier: Negro Image-Maker," *Variety*, July 26, 1967, p. 5.
42. *Time*, July 12, 1968, p. 77.
43. HTS interview, March 22, 1985.
44. *Variety Film Reviews*, February 26, 1970.
45. *Film Daily*, December 3, 1969.
46. Harold Mirisch to ABK, n.d.
47. *Time*, November 22, 1971, p. 107.
48. *New York Times Film Reviews*, November 28, 1961.
49. *New Republic*, November 20, 1971, p. 28.
50. ABK interview, August 3, 1984.
51. Walter M. Mirisch interview, May 16, 1984.
52. Ibid.

Chapter Six: Selling Them Big

1. Max E. Youngstein, "Return to Showmanship," *Variety*, June 24, 1959, p. 15.
2. Max E. Youngstein to Stanley Kramer, February 14, 1961.
3. Max E. Youngstein to ABK, March 21, 1957.
4. Hy Hollinger, "Preminger's Private Hornet: Trumbo," *Variety*, January 27, 1960, p. 5.
5. Nat Rudich to Otto Preminger, July 7, 1958.
6. *Life*, December 10, 1975, p. 16.
7. Stanley Kramer to Max E. Youngstein, n.d.
8. A. D. Murphy, "Distribution and Exhibition: An Overview," in Jason E. Squire, ed., *The Movie Business Book* (Englewood Cliffs, N.J.: Prentice-Hall, 1983), p. 259.
9. Lee Beaupre, "What Makes for a Click Roadshow?" *Variety*, August 21, 1968, p. 3.
10. Chris Munson, *The Marketing of Motion Pictures* (Los Angeles: Chris Munson Company, 1969), p. 164.
11. Vincent Canby, "UA: Format Maker & Breaker," *Variety*, October 10, 1962, p. 5.
12. "United Artists Plot to Overthrow Old N.Y. Playoff," *Variety*, May 30, 1962, pp. 5, 16.
13. William M. Freeman, "Movie Theaters Stage Comeback," *New York Times*, July 5, 1964, Part III: 12.
14. Munson, *Marketing of Motion Pictures*, p. 173.
15. Tim Horan to Fred Goldberg, December 12, 1959.
16. *Film Bulletin*, December 25, 1961.

17. Ibid.
18. Ibid.
19. Ibid.
20. Norman Jewison to Gabe Sumner, November 27, 1971.
21. Gabe Sumner to Norman Jewison, December 7, 1971.
22. Max E. Youngstein to George Schaefer, June 7, 1957.
23. ABK interview, June 28, 1979.
24. Leon Kamern interview, December 3, 1975.
25. For a discussion of the ideological implications of dubbing, see Geoffrey Nowell Smith, "Italy Sotto Voce," *Sight and Sound* 37 (Summer 1968): 145–47.
26. Alfred Sorg interview, December 6, 1975.
27. Daniel Yankelovitch, Inc., "The Size and Character of the Movie-Going Public," prepared for the Motion Picture Association of America, January 1968.
28. "The Journal Looks at the Changing Role of Motion Picture Publicity Practices," *Journal of the Screen Producers Guild* 14 (March 1972): 1, 3–11.
29. David Anthony Daly, *A Comparison of Exhibition and Distribution Patterns in Three Recent Feature Motion Pictures* (New York: Arno Press, 1980), p. 48.
30. Ibid., p. 170.

Chapter Seven: International Operations, Part 1

1. "Yank Majors O'Seas Shares," *Variety*, August 22, 1973, p. 3.
2. Katherine Hamill, "Supercolossal, Well, Pretty Good: World of Joe Levine," *Fortune* 69 (March 1964): 130–32+.
3. Douglas Ayer, et al., "Self-Censorship in the Movie Industry," p. 800.
4. David Paletz and Michael Noonan, "The Exhibitors," *Film Quarterly* 19 (Winter 1965–66): 23–24.
5. Fred Hift, "Foreign Films 'Arrive' in U.S.," *Variety*, January 30, 1957, p. 1.
6. Fred Hift, "Time Favors Foreign Films in U.S.," *Variety*, April 15, 1959, p. 28.
7. Edouard de Laurot and Jonas Mekas, "Foreign Film Distribution in the U.S.A.," *Film Culture* 2.7 (1956): 16.
8. Robert J. Landry, "Unsold in the Land of Sell," *Variety*, April 24, 1957, p. 5.
9. "Ed Kingsley: A Respected Importer," *Variety*, February 7, 1962, p. 6.
10. Robert J. Landry, "10 Years of World Films & Festivals," *Variety*, April 26, 1967, p. 41.
11. "Lopert, UA Advances 220G for Bardot Pic," *Variety*, February 19, 1958, pp. 3, 16.
12. Max E. Youngstein to Kenneth Clark, May 8, 1961.

13. "U.S. Market for Foreigns," *Variety*, May 12, 1965, p. 30; "UA's Pair from Ingmar Bergman," *Variety*, January 11, 1967, pp. 5, 78.
14. Vincent Canby, "O'Seas Films' $69,000,000 in U.S." *Variety*, May 2, 1962, p. 18.
15. Ibid.
16. Stuart Byron, "On Imported Films, U.S. Public Fickle," *Variety*, May 8, 1968, p. 40.
17. Ibid.
18. Robert B. Frederick, "Runaway: Par's 'Love Story'," *Variety*, January 5, 1972, p. 9.
19. "The Shock of Freedom in Films," *Time*, December 8, 1967, pp. 66–76.
20. Ibid.
21. Addison Verrill, "Hard Going in U.S. for Foreign Films," *Variety*, May 3, 1972, p. 31.
22. Bernstein, *Hollywood at the Crossroads*, pp. 45–70.
23. Guback, *International Film Industry*, pp. 153–56.
24. Penelope Houston, "England Their England," *Sight and Sound* 35 (Spring 1966): 56.
25. Bernstein, *Hollywood at the Crossroads*, pp. 62–63.
26. Guback, *The International Film Industry*, pp. 147–79.
27. Alexander Walker, *Hollywood UK: The British Film Industry in the Sixties* (New York: Stein & Day, 1974), p. 41.
28. Raymond Durgnat, "The Loved One," *Films & Filming* 12 (February 1966): 20.
29. Ibid., pp. 19–20.
30. Quoted in Walker, *Hollywood UK*, p. 58.
31. Ibid., p. 90.
32. David V. Picker to Bud Ornstein, April 30, 1962.
33. David V. Picker to Arnold M. Picker, April 23, 1962.
34. Clippings, n.d.
35. Ibid.
36. *New York Times Film Reviews*, October 7, 1963.
37. *New York Herald Tribune*, October 8, 1963, p. 18.
38. "'Tom Jones,' Lad to Make a Packet," *Variety*, September 23, 1964, p. 3.
39. Walker, *Hollywood UK*, p. 145.
40. "London: The Swinging City," *Time*, April 15, 1966, pp. 30–34.
41. For an analysis of Richardson's productions after *Tom Jones*, see George Lellis, "Cashing the Bank Cheque," *Sight and Sound* 38 (Summer 1969): 130–33.
42. *Variety Film Reviews*, April 17, 1968.
43. Walker, *Hollywood UK*, p. 388.
44. Clipping, n.d.
45. *New York Times Film Reviews*, March 26, 1970.
46. *New York Magazine*, March 30, 1970, p. 54.
47. Samuel W. Gelfman to Larry Kramer, February 2, 1970.

48. Walker, *Hollywood UK*, pp. 231–33.
49. Ibid., p. 233.
50. *Variety Film Reviews*, July 15, 1964.
51. "Beatlemania's Second Wind," *Variety*, July 22, 1964, p. 73.
52. *Variety Film Reviews*, July 27, 1964.
53. Walker, *Hollywood UK*, p. 464.
54. Ibid., p. 451.

Chapter Eight: "007": A License to Print Money

1. Walker, *Hollywood UK*, p. 57.
2. Ibid., p. 184.
3. Ibid., p. 182.
4. Ibid., p. 185.
5. Ibid., p. 186.
6. Bud Ornstein to David V. Picker, October 6, 1961.
7. Quoted in Walker, *Hollywood UK*, p. 187.
8. Gabe Sumner to Harry Saltzman, February 5, 1963.
9. Raymond Benson, *The James Bond Bedside Companion* (New York: Dodd, Mead, 1984), p. 172.
10. Vincent Canby, "United Artists' Fort Knox," *Variety*, March 31, 1965, p. 3.
11. "United Artists Profit Rampage," *Variety*, January 13, 1965, p. 1.
12. Walker, *Hollywood UK*, p. 194.
13. Penelope Houston, "007," *Sight and Sound* 34 (Winter 1964–65): 15.
14. Benson, *The James Bond Bedside Companion*, p. 195.
15. Ibid., p. 206.
16. "Who Is the *Real* James Bond Anyhow?" *Look*, November 15, 1966, p. 56.
17. Lee Beaupre, "Espionage Fights Off Ennui," *Variety*, April 24, 1968, pp. 3, 22.
18. HTS interview, March 21, 1985.
19. Ibid.
20. *New York Times Film Reviews*, October 19, 1969.
21. HTS interview, March 21, 1985.

Chapter Nine: International Operations, Part 2

1. *New Yorker*, October 28, 1972, p. 133.
2. Guback, *International Film Industry*, p. 86.
3. Steven Lipkin, "The Film Criticism of François Truffaut: A Contextual Analysis," Ph.D. dissertation, Univ. of Iowa, 1977, p. 66.
4. "Requiem for France's 'New Wave,'" *Variety*, April 26, 1961, p. 26.
5. "Screen Leadership in France," *Variety*, April 29, 1964, p. 61.

6. Gene Moskowitz, "French Look Beyond France," *Variety*, May 2, 1962, p. 65; Penelope Houston, "The Rewards of Quality," *Sight and Sound* 31 (Spring 1962): 71–72.
7. Guback, *International Film Industry*, p. 181.
8. Ibid., p. 182.
9. "The Saga of Coproduction," *Variety*, May 4, 1966, p. 62.
10. *Variety Film Reviews*, December 8, 1965.
11. Eitel Monaco, "All Film Roads Lead to Rome," *Variety*, April 26, 1967, p. 41A.
12. Ibid., p. 41A.
13. Peter Bondanella, *Italian Cinema: From Neorealism to the Present* (New York: Frederick Ungar Publishing Co., 1983), p. 253.
14. "The Horse, Italian Style," *Newsweek*, June 18, 1965, pp. 87–88.
15. "Fickle U.S. Vs. O'Seas Pix," *Variety*, May 8, 1968, p. 40.
16. Hank Werba, "Italo-U.S. Coprod. Trend Continues," *Variety*, January 10, 1968, p. 26.
17. "B.O. Response to 'Fellini's Satyricon,'" *Variety*, April 23, 1969, p. 35.
18. *Variety Film Reviews*, September 17, 1970.
19. Bondanella, *Italian Cinema*, p. 287.
20. Abel Green, "Oscar in 'Godfather' Future," *Variety*, September 6, 1972, p. 1.
21. "KO 'Tango' Case in Italy," *Variety*, February 7, 1973, p. 6.
22. "UA's 'Biggest Quote' Ad Ever," *Variety*, December 27, 1972, p. 3.
23. "Catholics 'C' on 'Tango'," *Variety*, February 21, 1973, p. 5.
24. James Bouras to Gerald Phillips, April 25, 1973.
25. Randall, "Censorship: From *The Miracle* to *Deep Throat*," pp. 517–18.
26. Ralph Blumenthal, "Porno Chic," *New York Times Magazine*, January 21, 1973, p. 28.
27. "Yanks Out-Sexploit Europe," *Variety*, May 12, 1971, pp. 1, 238.
28. Stephen Farber, *The Movie Rating Game* (Washington, D.C.: Public Affairs Press, 1972), p. 85.
29. Quoted in Gene D. Phillips, *John Schlesinger* (Boston: Twayne Publishers, 1981), p. 129.
30. Farber, *Movie Rating Game*, p. 47.
31. Gabe Sumner memorandum, January 23, 1970.
32. Gabe Sumner memorandum, May 28, 1969.
33. "A Call for Modification of the [X]," *Film Bulletin* July 21, 1969, pp. 4, 8.
34. "UA's 'Biggest Quote' Ad Ever," *Variety*, December 27, 1972, p. 3.
35. Frank Segers, "Bertolucci Rues $5 Bite on 'Tango,'" *Variety*, February 7, 1973, p. 7.
36. "Sumner Bars Reed," *Variety*, January 31, 1973, p. 4.
37. Ibid., pp. 4, 26.
38. David Denby, "Media Orgy," *Atlantic* 231 (April 1973): 120–23.
39. "Self-Portrait of an Angel and Monster," *Time*, January 22, 1973, pp. 51–55.

40. Ibid.
41. Ibid.
42. Ibid.
43. *New York Times Film Reviews*, January 27, 1973.
44. Judy Klemesrud, "Maria Says Her 'Tango' Is Not Blue," *New York Times*, February 4, 1973, Part II:13.
45. Charles Champlin, "'Throat,' 'Tango,': High and Low of Sex on Screen," *Los Angeles Times Calendar*, February 4, 1973, p. 1+.
46. *Nation*, February 12, 1973, p. 222.
47. *New Republic*, March 3, 1973, p. 20.
48. "*Tango*: The Hottest Movie," *Newsweek*, February 12, 1973, pp. 54–58.
49. Denby, "Media Orgy," pp. 120–23.
50. ABK interview, October 19, 1983.
51. Frank Segers, "Picker Forecasts 'Tango' as UA's Top All-Timer," *Variety*, April 4, 1973, p. 3.
52. "Deconfiscate Prints of 'Tango' in Italy," *Variety*, July 30, 1975, p. 37.
53. "KO 'Tango' Case in Italy," *Variety*, February 7, 1973, p. 6.
54. Guy Phelps, "Censorship of the Press," *Sight and Sound* 42 (Summer 1973): 138–40.
55. "UA: 2,000 Prints for Summer Four," *Variety*, June 13, 1973, p. 4.
56. Randall, "Censorship: From *The Miracle* to *Deep Throat*," p. 519.
57. "130 Dates Yield UA $11,000,000 on 'Last Tango,'" *Variety*, August 22, 1973, p. 3.
58. "ANICA's Chairman Has Plans," *Variety*, October 20, 1976, p. 74.

Chapter Ten: Life with a Conglomerate

1. ABK interview, June 28, 1979.
2. The literature about the conglomerization of American industry is vast, but for an introduction to the subject, see: Federal Trade Commission, Staff Report, *Economic Report on Corporate Mergers* (Washington, D.C.: U.S. Government Printing Office, 1969); the Editors of *Fortune*, *The Conglomerate Commotion* (New York: Viking Press, 1970); Willard F. Mueller, "Conglomerates: A 'Nonindustry,'" in Walter Adams, ed., *The Structure of American Industry* (New York: Macmillan, 1977), pp. 442–81.
3. "Mergers: It's a Deal," *Newsweek*, July 18, 1966, pp. 77–78; "Charles Bluhdorn, Collector of Companies," *Life*, March 20, 1967, pp. 43–50; "Gulf & Western Industries," *Forbes*, November 1, 1967, pp. 48–55; William S. Rukeyser, "Gulf & Western's Rambunctious Conservatism," *Fortune* 77 (March 1968): 122–25+.
4. For an overview of the conglomerization of the American film industry, see Tino Balio, "The Industry in the Age of Conglomerates," in *AFI* rev. ed., pp. 387–406; for analyses of the effects of conglomerization on production, see Joseph D. Phillips, "Film Conglomerate 'Blockbusters,'" *Journal of Communication* 25 (Spring 1975): 171–81; James Monaco,

American Film Now (New York: Oxford Univ. Press, 1979): 29–48, 387–406; Thomas Guback, "Theatrical Film," in Benjamin M. Compaine, ed., *Who Owns the Media?* (White Plains, N.Y.: Knowledge Industry Publications, 1979), pp. 179–250; Robert Gustafson, "What's Happening to Our Pix Biz? From Warner Bros. to Warner Communications, Inc.," in *AFI*, rev. ed., pp. 574–602; Douglas Gomery, "The American Film Industry of the 1970s," *Wide Angle*, Vol. 5, no. 4, pp. 52–59; and Michael F. Mayer, *The Film Industries*, rev. ed. (New York: Hastings House, 1978).

5. "The Day the Dream Factory Woke Up," *Life*, February 27, 1970, p. 44.
6. "United Artists 'Profit Revival,'" *Financial World* 20 (May 1964): 14.
7. "United Artists Consol. Food Cancel," *Variety*, August 10, 1966, p. 3.
8. Robert A. Bedingfield, "Conglomerate Tale: Transamerica Corp.," *New York Times*, September 1, 1968, III:12.
9. Transamerica Corporation, *1967 Annual Report*.
10. Smith, Barney & Co., *Transamerica Corporation* (New York, 1968).
11. Quoted in "The Identity Crisis at Transamerica," *Dun's Review* 101 (May 1973): 67.
12. Ibid.
13. John R. Beckett, "The Case for the Multi-Market Company," a lecture presented to Financial Analysts Seminar, sponsored by the Financial Analysts Federation in association with the University of Chicago, Rockford, Ill., August 22, 1969. Transamerica published this lecture as a pamphlet, n.d.
14. Ibid.
15. Ibid.
16. Ibid.
17. "Leisure-Time Headaches at TA," *Business Week*, October 31, 1970, p. 41.
18. John R. Beckett, "Principles of Management," remarks presented to the 1969 Management Conference of Transamerica Corporation, Solvang, Calif., May 11–13, 1969. Transamerica published these remarks as a pamphlet, n.d.
19. Jack Valenti, *A Very Human President* (New York: W. W. Norton, 1975), p. 368.
20. ABK interview, August 2, 1983.
21. "Leisure-Time Headaches at TA," p. 46.
22. ABK interview, August 2, 1983.
23. ABK to John R. Beckett, February 12, 1971.
24. Charles Champlin, "The 1960s: A Revolution in Movie Audiences," *Los Angeles Times Calendar*, January 18, 1970, pp. 1, 55, 59.
25. ABK to John R. Beckett, February 12, 1971.
26. "United Artists' Preliminary-Estimated 1970 Loss," *Variety*, February 3, 1971, p. 4.
27. ABK interview, August 3, 1983.
28. A. H. Howe, "A Banker Looks at the Picture Business," *Journal of the Screen Producers Guild* 11 (March 1969): 15–22.
29. Londoner, "The Changing Economics of Entertainment," pp. 606–8.

30. Ibid.

31. Ibid.

32. Irwin Ross, "Kirk Kerkorian Doesn't Want All the Meat Off the Bone," *Fortune* 80 (November 1969): 8+.

33. Thomas Murray, "The Men Who Followed Mickey Mouse," *Dun's Review* 94 (December 1969): 35–38.

34. Richard Souyoul, " '69: Year of the Bear on Wall St.," *Variety*, January 7, 1970, p. 22.

35. John R. Beckett, Remarks presented to the Transamerica Management Conference, Fairmont Hotel, San Francisco, Calif., April 28, 1972.

36. John R. Beckett, "The Authority and Responsibilities of the Group Vice Presidents and Their Relationships with Subsidiary Chief Executive Officers," a position paper sent to Transamerica's officers and directors, May 26, 1972.

37. John R. Beckett, Remarks presented to the Transamerica Management Conference, April 28, 1972.

38. ABK interview, August 2, 1983.

39. John R. Beckett to ABK, December 31, 1970.

40. A. D. Murphy, "United Artists 'Stabilized,'" *Variety*, March 27, 1974, p. 7.

41. ABK, "United Artists 1970–1973: Background Report," December 1973.

42. Ibid.

43. Quoted in Peter J. Schuyten, "United Artists' Script Calls for Divorce," *Fortune* 97 (January 16, 1978): 137.

44. ABK, "United Artists 1970–1973."

45. Ibid.

46. Ibid.

47. Ibid.

48. ABK interview, June 18, 1979.

49. "All Together. One, Two . . . ," *Forbes*, June 1, 1974, pp. 42–43.

50. Schuyten, "United Artists' Script Calls for Divorce," p. 137.

51. ABK, "United Artists 1970–1973."

52. Schuyten, "United Artists' Script Calls for Divorce," p. 137.

53. ABK, "United Artists 1970–1973."

54. *Variety Film Reviews*, January 30, 1974.

55. A. D. Murphy, "UA Global Rentals," *Variety*, January 11, 1978, p. 3.

56. "Hits Less 'Fun' for Conglomerated UA," *Variety*, June 15, 1977, p. 3.

57. Schuyten, "United Artists' Script Calls for Divorce," pp. 130–31.

Chapter Eleven: To MGM and Beyond

1. Gregg Kilday, "Orion: A Humanistic Production," *Los Angeles Times*, January 5, 1979, IV:26; David McClintick, *Indecent Exposure* (New York: William Morrow, 1976).

2. This open letter to John Beckett appeared in the Hollywood trades during the week of January 24, 1978.

3. The Orion group terminated by mutual consent its joint-venture agreement with Warner Communications in 1982 to acquire Filmways, Inc. Subsequently, the group changed the name of Filmways to Orion Pictures Corporation, which today is a publicly held company, headed by Krim et al., engaged in the financing, production, and distribution of motion pictures.
4. Quoted in Charles Schreger, "Shootout at the UA Corral: Artists vs. Accountants," *Los Angeles Times Calendar*, August 26, 1979, p. 7.
5. ABK interview, June 28, 1979.
6. HTS interview, October 8, 1986.
7. ABK interview, June 28, 1979.
8. Steven Bach, *Final Cut: Dreams and Disaster in the Making of "Heaven's Gate"* (New York: William Morrow, 1985), p. 62.
9. Ibid., p. 64.
10. Ibid., p. 65.
11. "United Artists Shorn of Chiefs," *Variety*, January 18, 1978, p. 42.
12. Bach, *Final Cut*, p. 121.
13. Ibid., pp. 308–9.
14. Ibid., p. 85.
15. Geri Fabrikant, "UA, Directors' Paradise, Under Cloud," *Variety*, November 26, 1980, pp. 3, 19.
16. Michael Bliss, *Martin Scorcese and Michael Cimino* (Metuchen, N.J.: Scarecrow Press, 1985), p. 248.
17. *New York Times Film Reviews*, November 19, 1980.
18. *New Yorker*, December 22, 1980, p. 102.
19. "Transamerica Writes Off 'Gate,'" *Variety*, November 26, 1980, p. 3.
20. Bliss, *Martin Scorcese and Michael Cimino*, p. 249.
21. *Hollywood Reporter*, January 17, 1978, p. 1.
22. "Begelman Furnishes UA with New Chair," *Variety*, October 7, 1981, p. 5.
23. Bach, *Final Cut*, p. 418.
24. HTS interview, October 8, 1986.
25. ABK interview, October 8, 1986.

I N D E X
of Motion Picture Titles

GENERAL INDEX

Abbott and Costello, 19, 31, 76
ABC, 110, 316
Academy Awards:
—*The African Queen*, 46
—*Annie Hall*, 336–37, 338–39
—*The Apartment*, 117, 162, 170, 172–73
—*Around the World in 80 Days*, 129, 130–31
—*Black Orpheus*, 227
—*Casablanca*, 153
—Chaplin's special Oscar, 61
—*Cyrano de Bergerac*, 47
—*The Deer Hunter*, 340
—Disney's Oscars, 13
—*Elmer Gantry*, 117, 154, 170
—*The Fortune Cookie*, 184
—*From Here to Eternity*, 71, 79
—*Giant*, 135
—*Hamlet*, 224
—*High Noon*, 47
—*In the Heat of the Night*, 117, 162, 187, 188–89
—Irving G. Thalberg Memorial Award, 135, 143, 195
—Jean Hersholt Humanitarian Award, 312
—*Judgment at Nuremberg*, 117
—*Lilies of the Field*, 117, 186–87
—*A Man and a Woman*, 231, 275
—*Marty*, 80–81, 82, 147
—*Midnight Cowboy*, 117, 292, 294–95
—*Network*, 329
—*One Flew over the Cuckoo's Nest*, 326–28, 329
—*A Place in the Sun*, 135
—*Rocky*, 330–31
—*Room at the Top*, 238
—*Separate Tables*, 117
—*Some Like It Hot*, 170

—*Tom Jones*, 117, 230, 240–42
—*West Side Story*, 117, 162, 177, 178–79
Achard, Marcel, 184
Adam, Ken, 261, 263
Advertising. *See* Promotion
Agee, James, 46
Agents, 75–78, 94–95
Aimee, Anouk, 231, 279
Albeck, Andreas, 334, 335–43
Aldrich, Richard, 64
Aldrich, Robert, 79, 245
Aleichem, Shalom, 205
Alexander, Shana, 137
Algren, Nelson, 71
Allen, Irving, 254
Allen, Woody, 267, 269, 325–26, 338–39, 343
Allied Artists Pictures, 162–65, 169, 279
Alpert, Hollis, 170, 205
Alton, John, 26
American Civil Liberties Union, 69, 72
American International Pictures, 121
American Legion, 53–55, 57–58, 60–61, 143–44
American Optical Company, 129
Amvets, 59
Anastasia, Albert, 124
Andersen, Hans Christian, 34
Anderson, Michael, 154
Andress, Ursula, 259, 279
Andrews, Julie, 128, 181
Anet, Claude, 164
Antonioni, Michelangelo, 230, 231, 232, 245, 281, 284
Apple Films, 251
Arden, John, 238
Arkin, Alan, 185, 186